Computer Systems: Construction Algorithms and Analysis

Computer Systems: Construction Algorithms and Analysis

Edited by
Henry Skinner

WILLFORD PRESS

www.willfordpress.com

Published by Willford Press,
118-35 Queens Blvd., Suite 400,
Forest Hills, NY 11375, USA

ISBN: 978-1-64728-447-3

Cataloging-in-publication Data

Computer systems : construction algorithms and analysis / edited by Henry Skinner.
    p. cm.
Includes bibliographical references and index.
ISBN 978-1-64728-447-3
1. Computer systems. 2. Computer software. 3. Computer algorithms. 4. Programming by example (Computer science). I. Skinner, Henry.
QA76 .C66 2023
004--dc23

For information on all Willford Press publications
visit our website at www.willfordpress.com

Contents

Preface

A computer system is a machine which simplifies complex operations. It improves performance while lowering costs and power usage. An algorithm is a series of steps utilized for completing a particular task. It consists of three basic building blocks, which include sequencing, selection and iteration. It serves as the foundation for programming, allowing computers, websites and smartphones to function. Analysis and construction of algorithms and data structures is a fundamental and crucial element of computer science. The development of algorithms necessitates an understanding of the various options available for solving a computational problem, including networking, programming language, hardware and performance restrictions that come with a specific solution. This book unfolds the innovative aspects of computer systems. The readers would gain knowledge that would broaden their perspective about the construction algorithms and their analysis. The book will serve as a valuable source of reference for graduate and postgraduate students.

The information shared in this book is based on empirical researches made by veterans in this field of study. The elaborative information provided in this book will help the readers further their scope of knowledge leading to advancements in this field.

Finally, I would like to thank my fellow researchers who gave constructive feedback and my family members who supported me at every step of my research.

Editor

Modular and Efficient Divide-and-Conquer SAT Solver on Top of the Painless Framework

Ludovic Le Frioux[1,2]([✉]), Souheib Baarir[2,3], Julien Sopena[2,4],
and Fabrice Kordon[2]

[1] LRDE, EPITA, 94270 Le Kremlin-Bicêtre, France
`ludovic@lrde.epita.fr`
[2] Sorbonne Université, CNRS, LIP6, UMR 7606, 75005 Paris, France
{`ludovic.le-frioux,souheib.baarir,julien.sopena,fabrice.kordon`}`@lip6.fr`
[3] Université Paris Nanterre, 92000 Nanterre, France
[4] Inria, DELYS Team, 75005 Paris, France

Abstract. Over the last decade, parallel SATisfiability solving has been widely studied from both theoretical and practical aspects. There are two main approaches. First, divide-and-conquer (`D&C`) splits the search space, each solver being in charge of a particular subspace. The second one, portfolio launches multiple solvers in parallel, and the first to find a solution ends the computation. However although `D&C` based approaches seem to be the natural way to work in parallel, portfolio ones experimentally provide better performances.

An explanation resides on the difficulties to use the native formulation of the SAT problem (*i.e.,* the CNF form) to compute an *a priori* good search space partitioning (*i.e.,* all parallel solvers process their subspaces in comparable computational time). To avoid this, dynamic load balancing of the search subspaces is implemented. Unfortunately, this is difficult to compare load balancing strategies since state-of-the-art SAT solvers appropriately dealing with these aspects are hardly adaptable to various strategies than the ones they have been designed for.

This paper aims at providing a way to overcome this problem by proposing an implementation and evaluation of different types of divide-and-conquer inspired from the literature. These are relying on the `Painless` framework, which provides concurrent facilities to elaborate such parallel SAT solvers. Comparison of the various strategies are then discussed.

Keywords: Divide-and-conquer · Parallel satisfiability · SAT solver · Tool

1 Introduction

Modern SAT solvers are now able to handle complex problems involving millions of variables and billions of clauses. These tools have been used successfully to solve constraints' systems issued from many contexts, such as planning decision [16], hardware and software verification [7], cryptology [23], and computational biology [20], etc.

State-of-the-art complete SAT solvers are based on the well-known Conflict-Driven Clause Learning (CDCL) algorithm [21,28,30]. With the emergence of many-core machines, multiple parallelisation strategies have been conducted on these solvers. Mainly, two classes of parallelisation techniques have been studied: divide-and-conquer (D&C) and portfolio. Divide-and-conquer approaches, often based on the guiding path method, decompose recursively and dynamically, the original search space in subspaces that are solved separately by sequential solvers [1,2,12,14,26,29]. In the portfolio setting, many sequential SAT solvers compete for the solving of the whole problem [4,5,11]. The first to find a solution, or proving the problem to be unsatisfiable ends the computation. Although divide-and-conquer approaches seem to be the natural way to parallelise SAT solving, the outcomes of the parallel track in the annual SAT Competition show that the best state-of-the-art parallel SAT solvers are portfolio ones.

The main problem of divide-and-conquer based approaches is the search space division so that load is balanced over solvers, which is a theoretical hard problem. Since no optimal heuristics has been found, solvers compensate non optimal space division by enabling dynamic load balancing. However, state-of-the-art SAT solvers appropriately dealing with these aspects are hardly adaptable to various strategies than the ones they have been designed for [1,2,6]. Hence, it turns out to be very difficult to make fair comparisons between techniques (*i.e.*, using the same basic implementation). Thus, we believe it is difficult to conclude on the (non-) effectiveness of a technique with respect to another one and this may lead to premature abortion of potential good ideas.

This paper tries to solve these problems by proposing a simple, generic, and efficient divide-and-conquer component on top of the `Painless` [18] framework. This component eases the implementation and evaluation of various strategies, without any compromise on efficiency. Main contributions of this paper are the followings:

- an overview of state-of-the-art divide-and-conquer methods;
- a complete divide-and-conquer component that has been integrated to the `Painless` framework;
- a fair experimental evaluation of different types of divide-and-conquer inspired from the literature, and implemented using this component.

These implementations have often similar and sometimes better performances compared with state-of-the-art divide-and-conquer SAT solvers.

Let us outline several results of this work. First, our `Painless` framework is able to support implementation of multiple D&C strategies in parallel solvers. Moreover, we have identified "axes" for customization and adaptation of heuristics. Thus, we foresee it will be much easier to explore next D&C strategies. Second, our best implementation at this stage is comparable in terms of performance, with the best state-of-the-art D&C solvers, which shows our framework's efficiency.

This paper is organized as follows: Sect. 2 introduces useful background to deal with the SAT problem. Section 3 is dedicated to divide-and-conquer based parallel SAT solving. Section 4 explains the mechanism of divide-and-conquer we have implemented in `Painless`. Section 5 analyses the results of our experiments, and Sect. 6 concludes and gives some perspectives.

2   Background

A *propositional variable* can have two possible values $\top$ (True), or $\bot$ (False). A *literal l* is a propositional variable (x) or its negation ($\neg x$). A *clause ω* is a finite disjunction of literals (noted $\omega = \bigvee_{i=1}^{k} \ell_i$). A clause with a single literal is called *unit clause*. A *conjunctive normal form (CNF) formula φ* is a finite conjunction of clauses (noted $\varphi = \bigwedge_{i=1}^{k} \omega_i$). For a given formula φ, the set of its variables is noted: V_φ. An *assignment $\mathcal{A}$* of variables of φ, is a function $\mathcal{A} : V_\varphi \to \{\top, \bot\}$. $\mathcal{A}$ is total (complete) when all elements of V_φ have an image by $\mathcal{A}$, otherwise it is partial. For a given formula φ, and an assignment $\mathcal{A}$, a clause of φ is satisfied when it contains at least one literal evaluating to true, regarding $\mathcal{A}$. The formula φ is satisfied by $\mathcal{A}$ iff $\forall \omega \in \varphi, \omega$ is satisfied. φ is said to be SAT if there is at least one assignment that makes it satisfiable. It is defined as UNSAT otherwise.

Algorithm 1. CDCL algorithm

```
1  function CDCL()
2  │   dl ← 0                                    // Current decision level
3  │   while not all variables are assigned do
4  │   │   conflict ← unitPropagation()
5  │   │   if conflict then
6  │   │   │   if dl = 0 then
7  │   │   │   │   return ⊥                       // φ is UNSAT
8  │   │   │   end
9  │   │   │   ω ← conflictAnalysis()
10 │   │   │   addLearntClause(ω)
11 │   │   │   dl ← backjump(ω)
12 │   │   end
13 │   │   else
14 │   │   │   assignDecisionLiteral()
15 │   │   │   dl ← dl + 1
16 │   │   end
17 │   end
18 │   return ⊤                                  // φ is SAT
```

Conflict Driven Clause Leaning. The majority of the complete state-of-the-art sequential SAT solvers are based on the Conflict Driven Clause Learning (CDCL) algorithm [21,28,30], that is an enhancement of the DPLL algorithm [9, 10]. The main components of a CDCL are presented in Algorithm 1.

At each step of the main loop, `unitPropagation`[1] (line 4) is applied on the formula. In case of conflict (line 5), two situations can be observed: the conflict is detected at decision level 0 ($dl == 0$), thus the formula is declared UNSAT (lines 6–7); otherwise, a new asserting clause is derived by the conflict analysis and the algorithm backjumps to the assertion level [21] (lines 8–10). If there is no conflict (lines 11–13), a new decision literal is chosen (heuristically) and the algorithm continues its progression (adding a new decision level: $dl \leftarrow dl + 1$). When all variables are assigned (line 3), the formula is said to be SAT.

The Learning Mechanism. The effectiveness of the CDCL lies in the *learning mechanism* (line 10). Each time a conflict is encountered, it is analyzed (`conflictAnalysis` function in Algorithm 1) in order to compute its reasons and derive a *learnt clause*. While present in the system, this clause will avoid the same mistake to be made another time, and therefore allows faster deductions (conflicts/unit propagations).

Since the number of conflicts is very huge (in avg. 5000/s [3]), controlling the size of the database storing learnt clauses is a challenge. It can dramatically affect performance of the `unitPropagation` function. Many strategies and heuristics have been proposed to manage the cleaning of the stored clauses (*e.g.*, the Literal Block Distance (LBD) [3] measure).

3   Divide-and-Conquer Based Parallel SAT Solvers

The divide-and-conquer strategy in parallel SAT solving is based on splitting the search space into subspaces that are submitted to different workers. If a subspace is proven SAT then the initial formula is SAT. The formula is UNSAT if all the subspaces are UNSAT. The challenging points of the divide-and-conquer mechanism are: *dividing the search space, balancing jobs between workers*, and *exchanging learnt clauses*.

3.1   Dividing the Search Space

This section describes how to create multiple search subspaces for the studied problem, and the heuristics to balance their estimated computational costs.

Techniques to Divide the Search Space. To divide the search space, the most often used technique is the *guiding path* [29]. It is a conjunction of literals (called cube) that are assumed by the invoked solver (worker). Let φ be a formula, and $x \in \mathcal{V}_\varphi$ a variable. Thanks to Shannon decomposition, we can rewrite φ as $\varphi = (\varphi \wedge x) \vee (\varphi \wedge \neg x)$. The two guiding paths here are reduced to a single literal: (x) and $(\neg x)$. This principle can be applied recursively on each subspaces to create multiple guiding paths.

---

[1] The `unitPropagation` function implements the Boolean Constraint Propagation (BCP) procedure that forces (in cascade) the values of the variables in unit clauses [9].

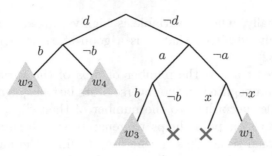

Fig. 1. Using guiding path to divide the search space

Figure 1 illustrates such an approach where six subspaces have been created from the original formula. They are issued from the following guiding paths: $(d \wedge b)$, $(d \wedge \neg b)$, $(\neg d \wedge a \wedge b)$, $(\neg d \wedge a \wedge \neg b)$, $(\neg d \wedge \neg a \wedge x)$, $(\neg d \wedge \neg a \wedge \neg x)$. The subspaces that have been proven UNSAT, are highlighted with red crosses. The rest of the subspaces are submitted to workers (noted w_i).

It is worth noting that other partitioning techniques exist that were initially developed for distributed systems rather than many-cores machines. We can cite the *scattering* [13], and the *xor partitioning* [27] approaches.

Choosing Division Variables. Choosing the best *division variable* is a hard problem, requiring the use of heuristics. A good division heuristic should decrease the overall total solving time[2]. Besides, it should create balanced subspaces w.r.t. their solving time: if some subspaces are too easy to solve this will lead to repeatedly asking for new jobs and redividing the search space (phenomenon known as *ping pong effect* [15]).

Division heuristics can be classified in two categories: *look ahead* and *look back*. Look ahead heuristics rely on the possible future behaviour of the solver. Contrariwise, look back heuristics rely on statistics gathered during the past behaviour of the solver. Let us present the most important ones.

Look Ahead. In stochastic SAT solving (chapters 5 and 6 in [8]), look ahead heuristics are used to choose the variable implying the biggest number of unit propagations as a decision variable. When using this heuristic for the division, one tries to create the smallest possible subspaces (*i.e.*, with the least unassigned variables). The main difficulty of this technique is the generated cost of applying the unit propagation for the different variables. The so-called "cube-and-conquer" solver presented in [12] relies on such an heuristic.

Look Back. Since sequential solvers are based on heuristics to select their decision variables, these can naturally be used to operate the search space division. The idea is to use the variables' VSIDS-based [25] order[3] to decompose the search

---

[2] Compared to the solving time using a sequential solver.
[3] The number of their implications in propagation conflicts.

in subspaces. Actually, when a variable is highly ranked w.r.t. to this order, then it is commonly admitted that it is a good starting point for a separate exploration [2, 13, 22].

Another explored track is the number of *flips* of the variables [1]. A flip is when a variable is propagated to the reverse of its last propagated value. Hence, ranking the variables according to the number of their flips, and choosing the highest one as a division point helps to generate search subspaces with comparable computational time. This can be used to limit the number of variables on which the look ahead propagation is applied by preselecting a predefined percentage of variables with the highest number of flips.

Another look back approach, called propagation rate (PR), tends to produce the same effect as the look ahead heuristics [26]. The PR of a variable v is the ratio between the numbers of propagations due to the branching of v divided by the number of time v has been chosen as a decision. The variable with the highest PR is chosen as division point.

3.2   Load Balancing

Despite all the effort to produce balanced subspaces, it is practically impossible to ensure the same difficulty for each of them. Hence, some workers often become quickly idle, thus requiring a dynamic load balancing mechanism.

A first solution to achieve dynamic load balancing is to rely on *work stealing*: each time a solver proves its subspace to be UNSAT[4], it asks for a new job. A target worker is chosen to divide its search space (*e.g.*, extends its guiding path). Hence, the target is assigned to one of the new generated subspaces, while the idle solver works on the other. The most common architecture to implement this strategy is based on a master/slave organization, where slaves are solvers.

When a new division is needed, choosing the best target is a challenging problem. For example, the `Dolius` solver [1] uses a FIFO order to select targets: the next one is the worker that is working for the longest time on its search space. This strategy guarantees fairness between workers. Moreover the target has a better knowledge of its search space, resulting in a better division when using a look back heuristic.

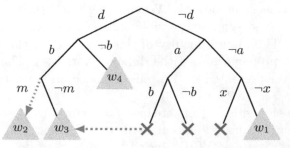

Fig. 2. Load balancing through work stealing

---

[4] If the result is SAT the global resolution ends.

Let us suppose in the example of Fig. 1 that worker w_3 proves its subspace to be UNSAT, and asks for a new one. Worker w_2 is chosen to divide and share its subspace. In Fig. 2, m is chosen as division variable and two new guiding paths are created, one for w_2 and one for w_3. Worker w_3 now works on a new subspace and its new guiding path is $(d \wedge b \wedge \neg m)$, while the guiding path of w_2 is $(d \wedge b \wedge m)$.

Another solution to perform dynamic load balancing is to create more search subspaces (jobs) than available parallel workers (cube-and-conquer [12]). These jobs are then managed via a work queue where workers pick new jobs. To increase the number of available jobs at runtime, a target job is selected to be divided. The strategy implemented in `Treengeling` [6] is to choose the job with the smallest number of variables; this favours SAT instances.

3.3   Exchanging Learnt Clauses

Dividing the search space can be subsumed to the definition of constraints on the values of some variables. Technically, there exist two manners to implement such constraints: (i) constrain the original formula; (ii) constrain the decision process initialisation of the used solver.

When the search space division is performed using (i), some learnt clauses cannot be shared between workers. This is typically the case of learnt clauses deduced from at least one clause added for space division, otherwise, correctness is not preserved. The simplest solution to preserve correctness is then to disable clause sharing [6]. Another (more complex) approach is to mark the clauses that must not be shared [17]. Clauses added for the division are initially marked. Then, the tag is propagated to each learnt clause that is deduced from at least one already marked clause.

When the search space division is performed using (ii), some decisions are forced. With this technique there is no sharing restrictions for any learnt clauses. This solution is often implemented using the assumption mechanisms [1, 2].

4   Implementation of a Divide-and-Conquer

This section presents the divide-and-conquer component we have built on top of the `Painless` framework. First, we recall the general architecture and operations of `Painless`. Then we describe the generic divide-and-conquer component's mechanisms. Finally we detail the different heuristics we have instantiated using this component.

4.1   About the Painless Framework

`Painless` [18] is a framework that aims at simplifying the implementation and evaluation of parallel SAT solvers for many-core environments. Thanks to its genericity and modularity, the components of `Painless` can be instantiated independently to produce new complete solvers.

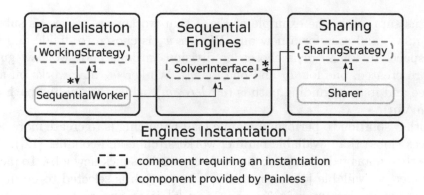

Fig. 3. Architecture of Painless

The main idea of the framework is to separate the technical components (*e.g.,* those dedicated to the management of concurrent programming aspects) from those implementing heuristics and optimizations embedded in a parallel SAT solver. Hence, the developer of a (new) parallel solver concentrates his efforts on the functional aspects, namely parallelisation and sharing strategies, thus delegating implementation issues (*e.g.,* data concurrent access protection mechanisms) to the framework.

Three main components arise when treating parallel SAT solvers: *sequential engines*, *parallelisation*, and *sharing*. These form the global architecture of Painless depicted in Fig. 3.

Sequential Engines. The core element considered in the framework is a sequential SAT solver. This can be any CDCL state-of-the art solver. Technically, these engines are operated through a generic interface providing basics of sequential solvers: *solve, interrupt, add clauses,* etc.

Thus, to instantiate Painless with a particular solver, one needs to implement the interface according to this engine.

Parallelisation. To build a parallel solver using the aforementioned engines, one needs to define and implement a parallelisation strategy. Portfolio and divide-and-conquer are the basic known ones. Also, they can be arbitrarily composed to form new strategies.

In Painless, a strategy is represented by a tree-structure of arbitrarily depth. The internal nodes of the tree represent parallelisation strategies, and leaves are core engines. Technically, the internal nodes are implemented using WorkingStrategy component and the leaves are instances of SequentialWorker component.

Hence, to develop its own parallelisation strategy, the user should create one or more strategies, and build the required tree-structure.

Sharing. In parallel SAT solving, the exchange of learnt clauses warrants a particular focus. Indeed, besides the theoretical aspects, a bad implementation of a good sharing strategy may dramatically impact the solver's efficiency.

In `Painless`, solvers can export (import) clauses to (from) the others during the resolution process. Technically, this is done by using lockfree queues [24]. The sharing of these learnt clauses is dedicated to particular components called `Sharers`. Each `Sharer` in charge of sets of producers and consumers and its behaviour reduces to a loop of sleeping and exchange phases.

Hence, the only part requiring a particular implementation is the exchange phase, that is user defined.

4.2 The Divide-and-Conquer Component in Painless

To implement divide-and-conquer solvers with `Painless`, we define a new component. It is based on a master/slaves architecture.

Figure 4 shows the architecture of our tool. It contains several entities. The *master* is a thread executing the only D&C instance of the `WorkingStrategy` class. The *workers* are slave threads executing instances of the `SequentialWorker` class. An instance of the `Sharing` class allows workers to share clauses.

The master and the workers interact asynchronously by means of events. In the initialisation phase, the master may send asynchronous events to himself too.

Master. The master (1) initialises the D&C component; (2) selects targets to divide their search spaces; (3) and operates the division along with the relaunch of the associated solvers. These actions are triggered by the events INIT, NEED_JOB, and READY_TO_DIV, respectively. In the remainder of this section we consider a configuration with N workers.

The master can be in two states: either it is sleeping, or it is currently processing an incoming event. Initially the master starts a first solver on the whole formula by sending it the SOLVE event. It then generates $N - 1$ NEED_JOB events to himself. This will provoke the division of the search space in N subspaces according the to implemented policy. At the end of this initialisation phase, it returns to its sleeping state. At this point, all workers are processing their subspaces.

Each time a worker needs a job, it notifies the master with a NEED_JOB event.

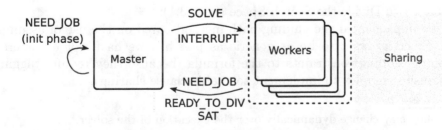

Fig. 4. Architecture of the divide-and-conquer SAT solver

All over its execution, the master reacts to the NEED_JOB event as follows:

1. it selects a target using the current policy[5], and requests this target to interrupt by sending an INTERRUPT event. Since this is an asynchronous communication, the master may process other events until it receives a READY_TO_DIV event;
2. once it receives a READY_TO_DIV event, the master proceeds to the effective division of the subspace of the worker which emitted the event. Both the worker which emitted the event and the one which requested a job are then invited to solve their new subspaces through the send of a SOLVE event.

The master may receive a SAT event from its workers. It means a solution has been computed and the whole execution must end. When a worker ends in an UNSAT situation, it makes a request for a new job (NEED_JOB event). When the master has no more division of the search space to perform, it states the SAT problem is UNSAT.

Slaves. A slave may be in three different states: *idle*, *work*, and *work_interrupt_requested*. Initially, it is *idle* until it receives a SOLVE request from the master. Then, it moves to the *work* state and starts to process its assigned subspace. It may:

- find a solution, then emit a SAT event to the master, and move back to *idle*;
- end processing of the subspace, with an UNSAT result, then it emits a NEED_JOB event to the master, and move back to *idle*;
- receive an INTERRUPT event from the master, then, it moves to the *work_interrupt_requested* state and continues its processing until it reaches a stable state[6] according to the underlying sequential engine implementation. Then, it sends a READY_TO_DIV event to the master prior to move back to *idle*.

4.3 Implemented Heuristics

The divide-and-conquer component presented in the previous section should be generic enough to allow the implementation of any of the state-of-the-art strategies presented in Sect. 3. We selected some strategies to be implemented, keeping in mind that at least one of each family should be retained:

1. Techniques to Divide the Search Space (Sect. 3.1):
   we have implemented the guiding path method based on the use of assumptions. Since we want to be as generic as possible, we have not considered techniques adding constraints to the formula (because they require tagging mechanisms complex to implement to enable clause sharing).

---

[5] This policy may change dynamically over the execution of the solver.

[6] For example, in Minisat-based solvers, a stable state could correspond to the configuration of the solver after a restart.

2. Choosing Division Variables (Sect. 3.1):
   the different division heuristics we have implemented in the `MapleCOMSPS` solver[7], are: VSIDS, number of flips, and propagation rate.
3. Load Balancing (Sect. 3.2):
   a work-stealing mechanism was implemented to operate dynamic load balancing. The master selects targets using a FIFO policy (as in `Dolius`) moderated by a minimum computation time (2 s) for the workers in order to let these acquire a sufficient knowledge of the subspace.

The exchange of learnt clauses (Sect. 3.3) on any of the strategies we implemented is not restricted. This allows to reuse any of the already off-the-shelf strategies provided by the `Painless` framework.

Another important issue deals with the way new subspaces are allocated to workers. We provide two strategies:

– **Reuse:** the worker reuses the same object-solver all over its execution and the master feeds it with guiding paths;
– **Clone:** each time a new subspace is assigned to a worker, the master clones the object-solver from the target and provides the copy to the idle worker. Thus, the idle worker will benefit form the knowledge (VSIDS, locally learned clauses, etc.) of the target worker.

Hence, our `Painless`-based `D&C` component can thus be instantiated to produces solvers over six orthogonal axes: (1) technique to divide the search space; (2) technique to choose the division variables; (3) load balancing strategy; (4) the sharing strategy; (5) the subspace allocation technique; (6) and the used underlying sequential solver.

By lack of time for experimentations, we select for this paper 6 solvers: all based on `MapleCOMSPS`, and sharing all learnt clauses which LBD ≤ 4 (this value has been experimentally deduced). Table 1 summarizes the implemented `D&C` solvers we have used for our experiments in the next section.

Table 1. The `D&C` solvers we use for experiments in this paper

	VSIDS	Number of flips	Propagation Rate
Reuse	`P-REUSE-VSIDS`	`P-REUSE-FLIPS`	`P-REUSE-PR`
Clone	`P-CLONE-VSIDS`	`P-CLONE-FLIPS`	`P-CLONE-PR`

5 Evaluation

This section presents the results of experiments done with the six `D&C` solvers we presented in Sect. 4.3. We also did comparative experiments with state-of-art `D&C` solvers (`Treengeling` [6] and `MapleAmpharos` [26]).

---

[7] We used the version that won the main track of the SAT Competition in 2016 [19].

Treengeling is a cube-and-conquer solver based on the Lingeling sequential solver. MapleAmpharos is an adaptive divide-and-conquer based on the solver Ampharos [2], and using MapleCOMSPS as sequential solver. Comparing our new solvers with state-of-the-art ones (*e.g.*, not implemented on Painless) is a way to assess if our solution is competitive despite the genericity introduced by Painless and ad-hoc optimizations implemented in other solvers.

All experiments were executed on a multi-core machine with 12 physical cores (2 x Intel Xeon E5645 @ 2.40 GHz), and 64 GB of memory. Hyper-threading has been activated porting the number of logical cores to 24. We used the 400 instances of the parallel track of the SAT Competition 2018[8]. All experiments have been conducted using the following settings:

- each solver has been run once on each instance with a time-out of 5000 s (as in the SAT Competition);
- the number of used cores is limited to 23 (the remaining core is booked to the operating system);
- instances that were trivially solved by a solver (at the preprocessing phase) were removed, indeed in this case the D&C component of solvers is not enabled, these instances are then irrelevant for our case study.

Results of these experiences are summarized in Table 2. The different columns represent respectively: the total number of solved instances, the number of UNSAT solved instances, the number of SAT solved instances, and the PAR-2 score[9].

Table 2. Results of the different solvers

Solver	ALL (360)	UNSAT	SAT	PAR-2
P-CLONE-FLIPS	198	87	111	1732696.65
P-CLONE-PR	183	73	110	1871614.48
P-CLONE-VSIDS	183	77	106	1880281.54
P-REUSE-FLIPS	190	83	107	1796426.72
P-REUSE-PR	180	72	108	1938621.48
P-REUSE-VSIDS	184	75	109	1868619.43
MapleAmpharos	153	29	124	2190680.55
Treengeling	200	84	116	1810471.56

5.1   Comparing the Implemented Divide-and-Conquer Solvers

Figure 5 presents the cactus plot of the performances of the different D&C solvers. These differ in two orthogonal axes: the used subspace allocation technique, and the used division heuristic. We analyse here each axe separately.

---

[8] http://sat2018.forsyte.tuwien.ac.at/benchmarks/Main.zip.
[9] The used measure in the annual SAT Competition.

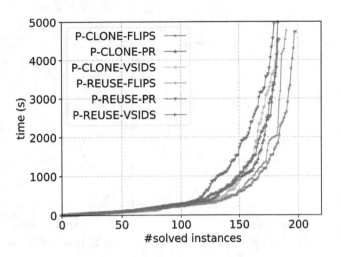

Fig. 5. Cactus plot of the different divide-and-conquer based solvers

When considering the allocation technique (clone *vs.* reuse), we can observe that the cloning based strategy is globally more efficient, even if it has a supplementary cost (due to the cloning phase). The scatter plots of Fig. 6 confirm this observation (most plots are below the diagonal, showing evidence of a better average performance). We believe this is due to the local knowledge that is implicitly shared between the (cloned) workers.

When considering the division heuristics (VSIDS, number of flips, and propagation rate), we observe that number of flips based approach is better than the two others. Both, by the number of solved instances and the PAR-2 measure. This is particularly true when considering the cloning based strategy. VSIDS and propagation rate based solvers are almost identical.

5.2   Comparison with State-of-the-Art Divide-and-Conquer

Figure 7 shows a cactus plot comparing our best divide-and-conquer (*i.e.,* P-CLO-NE-FLIPS) against `Treengeling` and `MapleAmpharos`.

The `MapleAmpharos` solver seems to be less efficient than our tool, and solves less instances. When considering only the 123 instances that both solvers were able to solve, we can calculate the cumulative execution time of this intersection (CTI) for `MapleAmpharos` and P-CLONE-FLIPS: it is, respectively, 24h33min and 14h34min.

Although our tool solves 2 less instances as `Treengeling`, it has better PAR-2 measure. The CTI calculated on the 169 instances solved by both solvers, is 49h14min and 22h23min, respectively for `Treengeling` and P-CLONE-FLIPS. We can say that even if both solve almost the same number of instances, our D&C solver is faster. We clearly observe this phenomenon in Fig. 7.

Thus, in addition to highlight the performance of our instantiation, this shows the effectiveness of the flip-based approach with respect to the well-proven cube-and-conquer strategies.

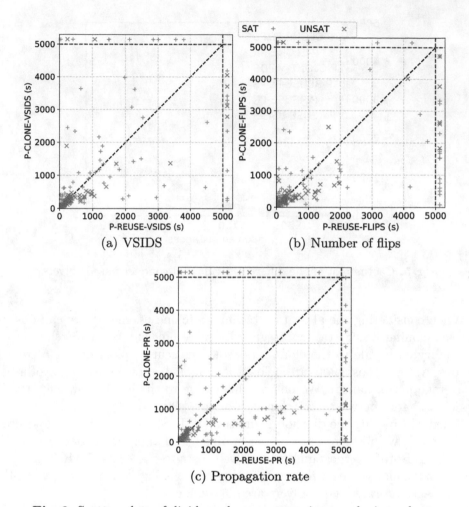

(a) VSIDS   (b) Number of flips

(c) Propagation rate

Fig. 6. Scatter plots of divide-and-conquer reusing *vs.* cloning solvers

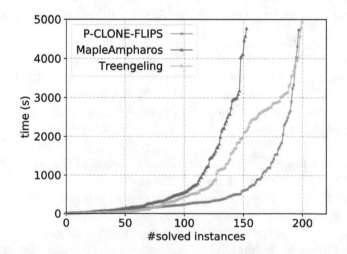

Fig. 7. Cactus plot of the best instantiated divide-and-conquer and state-of-the-art solvers

6   Conclusion

This paper proposed an optimal implementation of several parallel SAT solvers using the divide-and-conquer (D&C) strategy that handle parallelisms by performing successive divisions of the search space.

Such an implementation was performed on top of the `Painless` framework that allows to easily deal with variants of strategies. Our `Painless`-based implementation can be customized and adapted over six orthogonal axes: (1) technique to divide the search space; (2) technique to choose the division variables; (3) load balancing strategy; (4) the sharing strategy; (5) the subspace allocation technique; (6) and the used underlying sequential solver.

This work shows that we have now a modular and efficient framework to explore new D&C strategies along these six axes. We were then able to make a fair comparison between numerous strategies.

Among the numerous solvers we have available, we selected six of them for performance evaluation. Charts are provided to show how they competed, but also how they cope face to natively implemented D&C state-of-the-art solvers.

This study shows that the flip-based approach in association with the clone policy outperforms the other strategies whatever the used standard metrics is. Moreover, when compared with the state-of-the-art D&C-based solvers, our best solver shows to be very efficient and allows us to conclude the effectiveness of our modular platform based approach with respect to the well-competitive D&C solvers.

In the near future, we want to conduct more massive experiments to measure the impact of clauses sharing strategies in the D&C context, and evaluate the scalability of the various D&C approaches.

References

1. Audemard, G., Hoessen, B., Jabbour, S., Piette, C.: Dolius: a distributed parallel SAT solving framework. In: Pragmatics of SAT International Workshop (POS) at SAT, pp. 1–11. Citeseer (2014)
2. Audemard, G., Lagniez, J.-M., Szczepanski, N., Tabary, S.: An adaptive parallel SAT solver. In: Rueher, M. (ed.) CP 2016. LNCS, vol. 9892, pp. 30–48. Springer, Cham (2016). https://doi.org/10.1007/978-3-319-44953-1_3
3. Audemard, G., Simon, L.: Predicting learnt clauses quality in modern SAT solvers. In: Proceedings of the 21st International Joint Conferences on Artifical Intelligence (IJCAI), pp. 399–404. AAAI Press (2009)
4. Audemard, G., Simon, L.: Lazy clause exchange policy for parallel SAT solvers. In: Sinz, C., Egly, U. (eds.) SAT 2014. LNCS, vol. 8561, pp. 197–205. Springer, Cham (2014). https://doi.org/10.1007/978-3-319-09284-3_15
5. Balyo, T., Sanders, P., Sinz, C.: HordeSat: a massively parallel portfolio SAT solver. In: Heule, M., Weaver, S. (eds.) SAT 2015. LNCS, vol. 9340, pp. 156–172. Springer, Cham (2015). https://doi.org/10.1007/978-3-319-24318-4_12
6. Biere, A.: CaDiCaL, Lingeling, Plingeling, Treengeling and YalSAT entering the SAT competition 2018. In: Proceedings of SAT Competition 2018: Solver and Benchmark Descriptions, pp. 13–14. Department of Computer Science, University of Helsinki, Finland (2018)

7. Biere, A., Cimatti, A., Clarke, E., Zhu, Y.: Symbolic model checking without BDDs. In: Cleaveland, W.R. (ed.) TACAS 1999. LNCS, vol. 1579, pp. 193–207. Springer, Heidelberg (1999). https://doi.org/10.1007/3-540-49059-0_14

8. Biere, A., Heule, M., van Maaren, H.: Handbook of Satisfiability, vol. 185. IOS Press, Amsterdam (2009)

9. Davis, M., Logemann, G., Loveland, D.: A machine program for theorem-proving. Commun. ACM **5**(7), 394–397 (1962)

10. Davis, M., Putnam, H.: A computing procedure for quantification theory. J. ACM **7**(3), 201–215 (1960)

11. Hamadi, Y., Jabbour, S., Sais, L.: ManySAT: a parallel SAT solver. J. Satisfiability Boolean Model. Comput. **6**(4), 245–262 (2009)

12. Heule, M.J.H., Kullmann, O., Wieringa, S., Biere, A.: Cube and conquer: guiding CDCL SAT solvers by lookaheads. In: Eder, K., Lourenço, J., Shehory, O. (eds.) HVC 2011. LNCS, vol. 7261, pp. 50–65. Springer, Heidelberg (2012). https://doi.org/10.1007/978-3-642-34188-5_8

13. Hyvärinen, A.E.J., Junttila, T., Niemelä, I.: A distribution method for solving SAT in grids. In: Biere, A., Gomes, C.P. (eds.) SAT 2006. LNCS, vol. 4121, pp. 430–435. Springer, Heidelberg (2006). https://doi.org/10.1007/11814948_39

14. Hyvärinen, A.E.J., Manthey, N.: Designing scalable parallel SAT solvers. In: Cimatti, A., Sebastiani, R. (eds.) SAT 2012. LNCS, vol. 7317, pp. 214–227. Springer, Heidelberg (2012). https://doi.org/10.1007/978-3-642-31612-8_17

15. Jurkowiak, B., Li, C.M., Utard, G.: Parallelizing satz using dynamic workload balancing. Electron. Notes Discrete Math. **9**, 174–189 (2001)

16. Kautz, H.A., Selman, B., et al.: Planning as satisfiability. In: Proceedings of the 10th European Conference on Artificial Intelligence (ECAI), vol. 92, pp. 359–363 (1992)

17. Lanti, D., Manthey, N.: Sharing information in parallel search with search space partitioning. In: Nicosia, G., Pardalos, P. (eds.) LION 2013. LNCS, vol. 7997, pp. 52–58. Springer, Heidelberg (2013). https://doi.org/10.1007/978-3-642-44973-4_6

18. Le Frioux, L., Baarir, S., Sopena, J., Kordon, F.: PaInleSS: a framework for parallel SAT solving. In: Gaspers, S., Walsh, T. (eds.) SAT 2017. LNCS, vol. 10491, pp. 233–250. Springer, Cham (2017). https://doi.org/10.1007/978-3-319-66263-3_15

19. Liang, J.H., Oh, C., Ganesh, V., Czarnecki, K., Poupart, P.: MapleCOMSPS, mapleCOMSPS LRB, mapleCOMSPS CHB. In: Proceedings of SAT Competition 2016: Solver and Benchmark Descriptions, p. 52. Department of Computer Science, University of Helsinki, Finland (2016)

20. Lynce, I., Marques-Silva, J.: SAT in bioinformatics: making the case with haplotype inference. In: Biere, A., Gomes, C.P. (eds.) SAT 2006. LNCS, vol. 4121, pp. 136–141. Springer, Heidelberg (2006). https://doi.org/10.1007/11814948_16

21. Marques-Silva, J.P., Sakallah, K.: GRASP: a search algorithm for propositional satisfiability. IEEE Trans. Comput. **48**(5), 506–521 (1999)

22. Martins, R., Manquinho, V., Lynce, I.: Improving search space splitting for parallel SAT solving. In: Proceedings of the 22nd IEEE International Conference on Tools with Artificial Intelligence (ICTAI), vol. 1, pp. 336–343. IEEE (2010)

23. Massacci, F., Marraro, L.: Logical cryptanalysis as a SAT problem. J. Autom. Reasoning **24**(1), 165–203 (2000)

24. Michael, M.M., Scott, M.L.: Simple, fast, and practical non-blocking and blocking concurrent queue algorithms. In: Proceedings of the 15th ACM Symposium on Principles of Distributed Computing (PODC), pp. 267–275. ACM (1996)

25. Moskewicz, M.W., Madigan, C.F., Zhao, Y., Zhang, L., Malik, S.: Chaff: engineering an efficient SAT solver. In: Proceedings of the 38th Design Automation Conference (DAC), pp. 530–535. ACM (2001)

26. Nejati, S., et al.: A propagation rate based splitting heuristic for divide-and-conquer solvers. In: Gaspers, S., Walsh, T. (eds.) SAT 2017. LNCS, vol. 10491, pp. 251–260. Springer, Cham (2017). https://doi.org/10.1007/978-3-319-66263-3_16

27. Plaza, S., Markov, I., Bertacco, V.: Low-latency SAT solving on multicore processors with priority scheduling and XOR partitioning. In: the 17th International Workshop on Logic and Synthesis (IWLS) at DAC (2008)

28. Silva, J.P.M., Sakallah, K.A.: GRASP–a new search algorithm for satisfiability. In: Proceedings of the 16th IEEE/ACM International Conference on Computer-Aided Design (ICCAD), pp. 220–227. IEEE (1997)

29. Zhang, H., Bonacina, M.P., Hsiang, J.: PSATO: a distributed propositional prover and its application to quasigroup problems. J. Symb. Comput. **21**(4), 543–560 (1996)

30. Zhang, L., Madigan, C.F., Moskewicz, M.H., Malik, S.: Efficient conflict driven learning in a boolean satisfiability solver. In: Proceedings of the 20th IEEE/ACM International Conference on Computer-Aided Design (ICCAD), pp. 279–285. IEEE (2001)

WAPS: Weighted and Projected Sampling

Rahul Gupta[1]($\boxtimes$), Shubham Sharma[1], Subhajit Roy[1], and Kuldeep S. Meel[2]

[1] Indian Institute of Technology Kanpur, Kanpur, India
{grahul,smsharma,subhajit}@iitk.ac.in
[2] National University of Singapore, Singapore, Singapore
meel@comp.nus.edu.sg

Abstract. Given a set of constraints F and a user-defined weight function W on the assignment space, the problem of constrained sampling is to sample satisfying assignments of F conditioned on W. Constrained sampling is a fundamental problem with applications in probabilistic reasoning, synthesis, software and hardware testing. Consequently, the problem of sampling has been subject to intense theoretical and practical investigations over the years. Despite such intense investigations, there still remains a gap between theory and practice. In particular, there has been significant progress in the development of sampling techniques when W is a uniform distribution, but such techniques fail to handle general weight functions W. Furthermore, we are, often, interested in Σ_1^1 formulas, i.e., $G(X) := \exists Y F(X,Y)$ for some F; typically the set of variables Y are introduced as auxiliary variables during encoding of constraints to F. In this context, one wonders *whether it is possible to design sampling techniques whose runtime performance is agnostic to the underlying weight distribution and can handle Σ_1^1 formulas?*

The primary contribution of this work is a novel technique, called WAPS, for sampling over Σ_1^1 whose runtime is agnostic to W. WAPS is based on our recently discovered connection between knowledge compilation and uniform sampling. WAPS proceeds by compiling F into a well studied compiled form, d-DNNF, which allows sampling operations to be conducted in linear time in the size of the compiled form. We demonstrate that WAPS can significantly outperform existing state-of-the-art weighted and projected sampler WeightGen, by up to 3 orders of magnitude in runtime while achieving a geometric speedup of 296× and solving 564 more instances out of 773. The distribution generated by WAPS is statistically indistinguishable from that generated by an ideal weighted and projected sampler. Furthermore, WAPS is almost oblivious to the number of samples requested.

1   Introduction

Boolean satisfiability (SAT) has gathered applications in bounded model check-ing of hardware and software systems [5,7,51], classical planning [35] and scheduling [27]. Despite the worst-case hardness of SAT, the past few decades have witnessed a significant improvement in the runtime performance of the state-of-the-art SAT solvers [41]. This improvement has led to the usage of SAT solvers as oracles to handle problems whose complexity lies beyond NP. Among these problems, *constrained sampling*, that concerns with sampling from the space of solutions of a set of constraints F, subject to a user-defined weight func-tion W, has witnessed a surge of interest owing to the wide range of applications ranging from machine learning, probabilistic reasoning, software and hardware verification to statistical physics [3,32,39,45].

Not surprisingly, the problem of sampling is known to be computationally intractable. When the weight function W is fixed to a uniform distribution, the problem of constrained sampling is also known as uniform sampling. Uni-form sampling has witnessed a long-standing interest from theoreticians and practitioners alike [4,33,38,45]. The past few years, however, have witnessed a significant improvement in the runtime performance of the sampling tools when the weight function W is fixed to a uniform distribution owing to the rise of hashing-based paradigm [2,11,13,22]. While the significant progress for uniform sampling has paved the way for its usage in constrained random simulation [45], the restriction of uniform distribution is limiting, and several applications of constrained sampling require the underlying techniques to be able to handle a wide variety of distributions and related problem formulations as listed below:

Literal-Weighted Sampling. In case of literal-weighted sampling, we consider the weight function over assignments defined as the product of the weight of literals, which is specified using a weight function $W(\cdot)$ that assigns a non-negative weight to each literal l in a boolean formula F. As argued in [12], literal-weighted weight function suffices for most of the practical applica-tions ranging from constrained random simulation, probabilistic reasoning, and reliability of power-grids [10,14,21,45].

Projected Sampling. Typically, users define constraints in high-level model-ing languages such as Verilog [1], Bayesian networks [14] and configuration of grids [21] and then CNF encodings are employed to convert them into a CNF [6]. Commonly used schemes like *Tseitin encoding* [50] introduce auxil-iary variables during encoding; though the encoded formulas are equisatisfi-able, they typically do not preserve the number of satisfying assignments. In particular, given an initial set of constraints G expressed over a set of variables X, we obtain another formula F such that $G(X) = \exists Y F(X,Y)$. Therefore, we are concerned with sampling over solutions of F *projected over a subset of variables* (such as X in this case). In other words, we are concerned with sampling over Σ_1^1 formulas.

Conditioned Sampling. Given a boolean formula Φ and a partial assignment σ, conditioned sampling refers to sampling from the models of Φ *that satisfy σ*. Conditioning has interesting applications in testing where one is interested in fuzzing the system with inputs that satisfy certain patterns (preconditions). Conditioning has been applied in the past for fault diagnosis [23], conformant planning [46] and databases [15].

Typically, practical applications require sampling techniques that can handle all the above formulations. While techniques based on interval propagation, binary decision diagrams and random perturbation of solution space [22,25,44] cannot handle projection, conditioned, and weighted sampling efficiently, the hashing-based techniques have significantly improved the scalability of sampling techniques and are capable of handling projection and literal-weighted scheme [11,42]. However, the performance of hashing-based techniques is extremely limited in their ability to handle literal-weighted sampling, and one observes a drastic drop in their performance as the weight distribution shifts away from uniform. In this context, one wonders: *whether it is possible to design techniques which can handle projection, conditioned, and literal-weighted sampling without degradation in their performance?*

In this work, we answer the above question in affirmative: we extend our previously proposed knowledge compilation framework in the context of uniform sampling to handle all the three variants. We have implemented a prototype of our framework, named WAPS, and demonstrate that within a time limit of 1800 s, WAPS performs better than the current state-of-the-art weighted and projected sampler WeightGen [10], by up to 3 orders of magnitude in terms of runtime while achieving a geometric speedup of 296×. Out of the 773 benchmarks available, WAPS was able to sample from 588 benchmarks while WeightGen was able to sample from only 24 benchmarks. Furthermore, WAPS is almost oblivious to the number of samples requested.

A significant advantage of our framework is its simplicity: we show that our previously proposed framework in the context of uniform sampling, KUS [49], can be lifted to handle literal-weighted, projection and conditioned sampling. We demonstrate that unlike hashing-based techniques, the runtime performance of WAPS is not dependent on the underlying weight distribution. We want to assert that the simplicity of our framework, combined with its runtime performance and its ability to be agnostic to the underlying distribution is a significant novel contribution to the area of constrained sampling. Besides, an important contribution of our work is the theoretical analysis of sampling techniques that employ knowledge compilation.

The rest of the paper is organized as follows. We first discuss the related work in Sect. 2. We then introduce notations and preliminaries in Sect. 3. In Sect. 4 we present WAPS and do theoretical analysis of WAPS in Sect. 5. We then describe the experimental methodology and discuss results in Sect. 6. Finally, we conclude in Sect. 7.

2 Related Work

Weighted sampling is extensively studied in the literature with the objective of providing scalability while ensuring strong theoretical guarantees. Markov Chain Monte Carlo (MCMC) sampling [32,40] is the most popular technique for weighted sampling; several algorithms like Metropolis-Hastings and simulated annealing have been extensively studied in the literature [36,40]. While MCMC based sampling is guaranteed to converge to a target distribution under mild requirements, convergence is often impractically slow [31]. The practical adaptations for MCMC-based sampling in the context of constrained-random verification has been proposed in [37]. Unfortunately, practical MCMC based sampling tools use heuristics that destroy the theoretical guarantees. Interval-propagation and belief networks have also been employed for sampling [20,26,29], but, though these techniques are scalable, the generated distributions can deviate significantly from the uniform distribution, as shown in [38].

To bridge the wide gap between scalable algorithms and those that give strong guarantees of uniformity several hashing-based techniques have been proposed [10,11,24,28] for weighted sampling. The key idea behind hashing-based techniques is to employ random parity constraints as pairwise independent hash functions to partition the set of satisfying assignments of CNF formula into cells. The hashing-based techniques have achieved significant runtime performance improvement in case of uniform sampling but their scalability suffers for weight distribution and depends strongly on parameters such as *tilt*, which are unlikely to be small for most practical distributions [42].

In recent past, a significant amount of work has been done to compile propositional theory, often represented as a propositional formula in CNF into tractable knowledge representations. One of the prominent and earliest representations is Ordered Binary Decision Diagrams (OBDDs), which have been effectively used for circuit analysis and synthesis [9]. Another family of representations known as Deterministic Decomposable Negation Normal Form (d-DNNF) [19] have proved to be influential in many probabilistic reasoning applications [14,17,18]. Recently, another representation called as Sentential Decision Diagram (SDD) [16] was proposed which maintains canonicity and polytime support for boolean combinations and bridged the gap of succinctness between OBDDs and d-DNNFs. In our recent work [49], we were able to tackle the problem of uniform sampling by exploiting the properties of d-DNNF. Specifically, we were able to take advantage of recent advancements made in the field of knowledge compilation and use the compiled structure to generate uniform samples while competing with the state-of-the-art tools for uniform sampling.

3 Notations and Preliminaries

A literal is a boolean variable or its negation. A clause is a disjunction of a set of literals. A propositional formula F in conjunctive normal form (CNF) is a conjunction of clauses. Let $Vars(F)$ be the set of variables appearing in F. The set $Vars(F)$

is called *support* of F. A *satisfying assignment* or *witness* of F, denoted by σ, is an assignment of truth values to variables in its support such that F evaluates to true. We denote the set of all witnesses of F as R_F. Let $var(l)$ denote the variable of literal l, i.e., $var(l) = var(\neg l)$ and $F_{|l}$ denotes the formula obtained when literal l is set to true in F. Given an assignment σ over $Vars(F)$ and a set of variables $P \subseteq Vars(F)$, define $\sigma_P = \{l \mid l \in \sigma, var(l) \in P\}$ and $R_{F \downarrow P}$ to be the projection of R_F onto P, i.e., $R_{F \downarrow P} = \{\sigma_P | \sigma \in R_F\}$.

Given a propositional formula F and a weight function $W(\cdot)$ that assigns a non-negative weight to every literal, the weight of assignment σ denoted as $W(\sigma)$ is the product of weights of all the literals appearing in σ, i.e., $W(\sigma) = \prod_{l \in \sigma} W(l)$. The weight of a set of assignments Y is given by $W(Y) = \sum_{\sigma \in Y} W(\sigma)$. Note that, we have overloaded the definition of weight function $W(\cdot)$ to support different arguments – a literal, an assignment and a set of assignments. We want to highlight that the assumption about weight distribution being generated solely by a literal-weighted function stands well, as many real-world applications like probabilistic inference can be efficiently reduced to literal-weighted sampling [14]. Also, for notational convenience, whenever the formula F, weight function W and sampling set P is clear from the context, we omit mentioning it.

3.1   Weighted and Projected Generators

A *weighted and projected probabilistic generator* is a probabilistic algorithm that generates a witness from $R_{F \downarrow P}$ with respect to weight distribution generated by weight function W. A *weighted and projected generator* $\mathcal{G}^{wp}(\cdot, \cdot, \cdot)$ is a probabilistic generator that guarantees

$$\forall y \in R_{F \downarrow P}, \mathsf{Pr}\left[\mathcal{G}^{wp}(F, P, W) = y\right] = \frac{W(y)}{W(R_{F \downarrow P})},$$

An *almost weighted and projected generator* $\mathcal{G}^{awp}(\cdot, \cdot, \cdot)$ relaxes this requirement, ensuring that: given a tolerance $\varepsilon > 0$, $\forall y \in R_{F \downarrow P}$ we have

$$\frac{W(y)}{(1 + \varepsilon)W(R_{F \downarrow P})} \leq \mathsf{Pr}\left[\mathcal{G}^{awp}(F, P, W) = y\right] \leq \frac{(1 + \varepsilon)W(y)}{W(R_{F \downarrow P})},$$

Probabilistic generators are allowed to occasionally "fail" in the sense that no witness may be returned even if $R_{F \downarrow P}$ is non-empty. The failure probability for such generators must be bounded by a constant strictly less than 1.

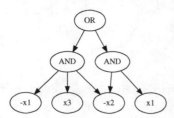

Fig. 1. Example of d-DNNF

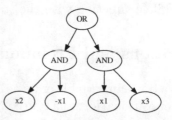

Fig. 2. The projected d-DNNF of Example 1

3.2   Deterministic Decomposable Negation Normal Form (d-DNNF)

To formally define d-DNNF, we first define the Negation Normal Form (NNF):

Definition 1 [19]. *Let X be the set of propositional variables. A sentence in NNF is a rooted, directed acyclic graph (DAG) where each leaf node i is labeled with true, false, x or $\neg x$, $x \in X$; and each internal node is labeled with $\vee$ or $\wedge$ and can have arbitrarily many children.*

d-DNNF further imposes that the representation is:

- **Deterministic:** An NNF is deterministic if the operands of $\vee$ in all well-formed boolean formula in the NNF are mutually inconsistent.
- **Decomposable:** An NNF is decomposable if the operands of $\wedge$ in all well-formed boolean formula in the NNF are expressed on a mutually disjoint set of variables.

The deterministic and decomposable properties are conveniently expressed by AND-OR graphs (DAGs) where a node is either an AND node, an OR node or a literal. The operands of AND/OR nodes appear as children of the node. Figure 1 shows an example of d-DNNF representation. For every node t, the subformula corresponding to t is the formula corresponding to d-DNNF obtained by removing all the nodes u such that there does not exist a path from t to u. $T(t)$ represents the set of all partial satisfying assignments for the subformula corresponding to t. The siblings of a node t are the children of the parent of t excluding t itself and the set of such children is given by $Siblings(t)$.

Decision-DNNF is a subset of d-DNNF where the deterministic OR nodes are decision nodes [18]. The state-of-the-art d-DNNF construction tools like C2D [18], DSHARP [43] and D4 [30], construct the Decision-DNNF representation where each OR node has exactly two children while an AND node may have multiple children. Since our framework WAPS employs modern d-DNNF compilers, we assume that the OR node has exactly two children. This assumption is only for the simplicity of exposition as our algorithms can be trivially adopted to the general d-DNNF representations.

4   Algorithm

In this section, we discuss our primary technical contribution: WAPS, weighted and projected sampler that samples from $R_{F\downarrow P}$ with respect to weight function W by employing the knowledge compilation techniques.

WAPS takes a CNF formula F, a set of sampling variables P, a function assigning weights to literals W and required number of samples s as inputs and returns SampleList, a list of size s which contain samples such that each sample is independently drawn from the weighted distribution generated by W over $R_{F\downarrow P}$.

Similar to KUS, WAPS (Algorithm 1) mainly comprises of three phases: Compilation, Annotation and Sampling. For d-DNNF compilation, WAPS invokes a specialized compilation routine PCompile over the formula F and the sampling set P (line 1). This is followed by the normalization of weights such that for any literal l, $W'(l) + W'(\neg l) = 1$, where W' is the normalized weight returned in line 2. Then for annotation, WAnnotate is invoked in line 3 which uses the weight function W' to annotate weights to all the nodes of the d-DNNF tree. Finally, subroutine Sampler (line 4) is invoked which returns s independently drawn samples over P following the weighted distribution generated by W over $R_{F\downarrow P}$. We now describe these three phases in detail.

4.1   Compilation

The compilation phase is performed using the subroutine PCompile. PCompile is a modified procedure over the component caching and clause learning based algorithm of the d-DNNF compiler DSHARP [43,47]. It is presented in Algorithm 2. The changes from the existing algorithm are underlined. The rest of the procedure which is similar to DSHARP is mentioned here for completeness. The description of PCompile is as follows:

PCompile takes in a CNF formula F in the clausal form and a set of sampling variables P as input and returns a d-DNNF over P. If the formula does not contain any variable from P, PCompile invokes SAT (line 2) which returns a *True* node if the formula is satisfiable, else it returns a *False* node. Otherwise, DecideLiteral is invoked to choose a literal appearing in F such that $var(l) \in P$ (line 3). This decision is then recursively propagated by invoking CompileBranch to create t_1, the d-DNNF of $F_{|l}$ (line 4) and t_2, the d-DNNF of $F_{|\neg l}$ (line 5). Disjoin is invoked in line 6 which takes t_1 and t_2 as input and returns t_2 if t_1 is *False* node, t_1 if t_2 is *False* node otherwise a new tree composed by an OR node as the parent of t_1 and t_2. The result of Disjoin is then stored in the cache (line 7) and returned as an output of PCompile (line 8).

We now discuss the subroutine CompileBranch. It is presented in Algorithm 3. It takes in a CNF formula F, set of sampling variables P and literal l as input and returns a d-DNNF tree of $F_{|l}$ on P. It first invokes BCP (Binary Constraint Propagation), with F, l and P which performs unit-propagation to return a tuple of reduced formula F' and a set of implied literals ($term$) projected over variables in P (line 1). Then CompileBranch checks if F' contains an empty clause and returns *False* node to indicate that $F_{|l}$ is not satisfiable, else the formula is solved using component decomposition as described below.

At line 6 it breaks the formula F' into separate components formed by disjoint set of clauses such that no two components share any variables. Then each component is solved independently (lines 8–15). For each component, it first examines the cache to see if this component has been solved earlier and is present in the cache (line 9). If cache lookup fails, it solves the component with a recursive call to PCompile (line 11). If any component is found to be unsatisfiable, *False* node is returned implying that the overall formula is unsatisfiable too, else CompileBranch simply conjoins the components' d-DNNFs together with the decided l and implied literals ($term$) and returns this after storing it in the cache for the formula $F_{|l}$ (lines 16–18).

We illustrate **PCompile** procedure on the following example formula F:

Example 1. $F = \{\{x_1, x_2\}, \{\neg x_3, \neg x_5, x_6\}, \{\neg x_2, x_4, \neg x_1\}, \{x_3, \neg x_6, \neg x_1\}, \{x_6, x_5, \neg x_1, x_3\}, \{x_3, x_6, \neg x_5, \neg x_1\}\}$

Figure 2 represents the d-DNNF of Example 1 on $P = \{x_1, x_2, x_3\}$. For detailed discussion about applying **PCompile** on F please refer to Appendix.

Algorithm 1. WAPS(F, P, W, s)

1: dag ← PCompile(F, P)
2: W' ← Normalize(W)
3: WAnnotate(dag.*root*, W')
4: SampleList ← Sampler(dag.*root*, s)
5: **return** SampleList

Algorithm 2. PCompile(F, P)

1: **if** $\underline{Vars(F) \cap P = \phi}$ **then**
2:     **return** $\underline{SAT(F)}$
3: $\underline{l \leftarrow \text{DecideLiteral}(F, P)}$
4: t_1 ← CompileBranch(F, P, l)
5: t_2 ← CompileBranch$(F, P, \neg l)$
6: t ← Disjoin(t_1, t_2)
7: CacheStore(F, t)
8: **return** t

Algorithm 3. CompileBranch(F, P, l)

1: $\underline{(F', term) \leftarrow \text{BCP}(F, l, P)}$
2: **if** $\emptyset \in F'$ **then**
3:     CacheStore$(F_{|l}, False)$
4:     **return** *False*   ▷ CDCL is done
5: **else**
6:     *Comps* ← DisjointComponents(F')
7:     *dcomps* ← {}
8:     **for** $C \leftarrow Comps$ **do**
9:         $ddnnf$ ← GetCache(C)
10:         **if** $ddnnf$ *is not found* **then**
11:             $ddnnf$ ← PCompile(C, P)
12:         $dcomps.Add(ddnnf)$
13:         **if** $ddnnf = False$ **then**
14:             CacheStore$(F_{|l}, False)$
15:             **return** *False*
16:     t = Conjoin$(l, term, dcomps)$
17:     CacheStore$(F_{|l}, t)$
18:     **return** t

4.2 Annotation

The subroutine WAnnotate is presented in Algorithm 4. WAnnotate takes in a d-DNNF dag and a weight function W as inputs and returns an annotated d-DNNF dag whose each node t is annotated with a weight, given by the sum of weights of all the partial assignments represented by subtree rooted at t. The weights subsequently annotated on children of an OR node indicate the probability with which it would be selected in the sampling phase.

WAnnotate performs a bottom up traversal on d-DNNF dag in a reverse topological order. For each node in the d-DNNF dag, WAnnotate maintains an attribute, weight, as per the label of the node given as follows:

Literal (lines 2–3): The weight of a literal node is taken as the weight of the literal given by the weight function W.

OR (lines 4–8): The weight of OR node is made equal to the sum of weights of both of its children.

AND (lines 9–13): The weight of AND node is made equal to the product of weights of all its children.

Algorithm 4. Bottom-Up Pass to annotate d-DNNF with weights on literals

---

1: **function** WAnnotate(t, W)
2:    **if** $label(t) = Literal$ **then**
3:        $t.weight \leftarrow W(t)$
4:    **else if** $label(t) = $ OR **then**
5:        $t.weight \leftarrow 0$
6:        **for** $c \in \{t.left, t.right\}$ **do**
7:            WAnnotate(c)
8:            $t.weight \leftarrow t.weight + c.weight$
9:    **else if** $label(t) = $ AND **then**
10:        $t.weight \leftarrow 1$
11:        **for** $c \in Childrens(t)$ **do**
12:            WAnnotate(c)
13:            $t.weight \leftarrow t.weight \times c.weight$

4.3 Sampling

Algorithm Sampler takes the annotated d-DNNF dag and the required number of samples s and returns SampleList, a list of s samples conforming to the distribution of their weights as governed by weight function W given to WAnnotate. The subroutine Sampler is very similar to the sampling procedure in our previous work [49] except that we take the annotated weight of the node instead of the annotated count in the previous work as the probability for Bernoulli trials. We refer the readers to Appendix for a detailed discussion.

4.4 Conditioned Sampling

The usage of samplers in testing environment necessitates sampling from F conditioned on fixing assignment to a subset of variables. The state of the art techniques, such as those based on universal hashing, treat every query as independent and are unable to reuse computation across different queries. In contrast, the compilation to d-DNNF allows WAPS to reuse the same d-DNNF. In particular, for a given conditioning expressed as conjunction of different literals, i.e., $\hat{C} = \bigwedge_i l_i$.

In particular, instead of modifying computationally expensive d-DNNF, we modify the weight function as follows:

$$\hat{W}(l) = \begin{cases} 0, & l \notin \hat{C} \\ W(l) & otherwise \end{cases}$$

5 Theoretical Analysis

We now present theoretical analysis of WAPS, which consists of two components: correctness of WAPS and analysis of behavior of Sampler on the underlying d-DNNF graph. First, we prove that WAPS is an exact weighted and projected sampler in Theorem 1. To this end, we prove the correctness of our projected d-DNNF dag compilation procedure PCompile in Lemma 1. In Lemma 2, we show that WAnnotate annotates each node of the d-DNNF with weights that represent the weight of assignments represented by subtree rooted at that node. This enables us to sample as per the weight distribution in the sampling phase which is proved in Theorem 1 using Lemmas 1 and 2. Secondly, further probing into the behavior of subroutine Sampler, we provide an analysis of the probability of visiting any node in the d-DNNF dag while sampling. For this, we first find a probability of visiting a node by following a particular path in Lemma 3 and then we use this result to prove an upper bound for the general case of visiting a node from all possible paths in Theorem 2. We believe that this analysis will motivate the researchers to find new ways to speed up or device new methods to find exact or approximate sampling techniques over a given compiled representation.

The proofs of Theorem 1 and Lemmas 1, 2 and 3 can be found in Appendix.

Lemma 1. *Given a formula F and set of sampling variables P, the tree returned by PCompile(F, P) is a d-DNNF dag which represents the set of satisfying assignments of the formula F projected over the set of sampling variables P.*

Lemma 2. *Every node t in the d-DNNF dag returned by WAnnotate is annotated by $W(T(t))$, where $T(t)$ is the set of all the partial assignments corresponding to the subtree rooted at t.*

Theorem 1. *For a given F, P and s, SampleList is the list of samples generated by WAPS. Let SampleList$[i]$ indicate the sample at the ith index of the list. Then for each $y \in R_{F \downarrow P}$, $\forall i \in [s]$, we have $\Pr[y = \text{SampleList}[i]] = \frac{W(y)}{W(R_{F \downarrow P})}$.*

Lemma 3. *For a given F and P, let fol(ρ) be the event of following a path ρ, which start at root and ends at node t, then $\Pr[\text{fol}(\rho)] = \frac{W(T(t)) \times c_\rho}{W(R_{F \downarrow P})}$ where c_ρ is the product of weight of all the OR nodes' siblings encountered in the path ρ from root to t and $T(t)$ is the set of all the partial satisfying assignments represented by subtree rooted at t.*

Theorem 2. *For a given F and P, let visit(t) be the event of visiting a node t to fetch one sample as per subroutine Sampler, then $\Pr[\text{visit}(t)] \leq \frac{W(\Gamma(t))}{W(R_{F \downarrow P})}$ where $\Gamma(t) = \{\sigma \mid \sigma \in R_{F \downarrow P}, \sigma_{\downarrow Vars(t)} \in T(t)\}$ and $T(t)$ is a set of all the partial satisfying assignments represented by subtree rooted at t.*

Proof. In Lemma 3 we have calculated the probability of visiting a node t by taking a particular path from root to node t. So the probability of visiting a node t will be the sum of probability of visiting t by all possible paths. Let $\mathcal{P} = \{\rho_1, \rho_2, \cdots, \rho_m\}$ be the set of all paths from root to node t and visit(t) be the event of visiting a node t in subroutine Sampler then,

$$\Pr[\text{visit}(t)] = \sum_{\rho \in \mathcal{P}} \Pr[\text{visit}(t) \mid \text{fol}(\rho)] \times \Pr[\text{fol}(\rho)] = \sum_{\rho \in \mathcal{P}} 1 \times \Pr[\text{fol}(\rho)]$$

From Lemma 3, $\Pr[\text{visit}(t)] = \sum_{\rho \in \mathcal{P}} \frac{W(T(t)) \times c_\rho}{W(R_{F \downarrow P})}$ where c_ρ is the product of the weight of all the OR nodes' siblings encountered in a path ρ from root to t. For any such path, we call $\{t_\rho^1, t_\rho^2, \cdots, t_\rho^n\}$ as the set of all the OR node siblings encountered on the path ρ. Now, let σ_ρ^{ext} be the set of assignments over P represented by path ρ. Therefore,

$$\sigma_\rho^{ext} = T(t_\rho^1) \times T(t_\rho^2) \cdots \times T(t_\rho^n) \times T(t)$$

where, $T(\cdot)$ are set of assignments and $\times$ is a cross product. Now, any tuple from σ_ρ^{ext} represents a satisfying assignment in the d-DNNF. Therefore, $\sigma_\rho^{ext} \subseteq R_{F \downarrow P}$. Note that, from Lemma 2, it follows that weight annotated by WAnnotate at t is equal to $W(T(t))$. Therefore,

$$c_\rho = W(T(t_\rho^1)) \times W(T(t_\rho^2)) \cdots \times W(T(t_\rho^n))$$

And, $W(\sigma_\rho^{ext}) = W(T(t)) \times c_\rho$. Notice that, $\sigma_\rho^{ext} \subseteq \Gamma(t)$ as σ_ρ^{ext} represents satisfying extensions of partial assignments contained in $T(t)$ itself. This is true $\forall \rho \in \mathcal{P}$. Therefore as $W(.)$ is an increasing function,

$$\bigcup_{\rho \in \mathcal{P}} \sigma_\rho^{ext} \subseteq \Gamma(t) \implies \sum_{\rho \in \mathcal{P}} W(T(t)) \times c_\rho \leq W(\Gamma(t))$$

Note that, the inequality indeed holds as the intersection of sets of partial assignments represented by t and any other node not lying on the path from root to t may not be ϕ (empty). Therefore,

$$\sum_{\rho \in \mathcal{P}} \frac{W(T(t)) \times c_\rho}{W(R_{F \downarrow P})} \leq \frac{W(\Gamma(t))}{W(R_{F \downarrow P})} \implies \Pr[\text{visit}(t)] \leq \frac{W(\Gamma(t))}{W(R_{F \downarrow P})}$$

6 Evaluation

In order to evaluate the runtime performance and analyze the quality of samples generated by WAPS, we implemented a prototype in Python. For d-DNNF compilation, our prototype makes use of DSHARP [43] when sampling set is available else we use D4 [30]. We would have preferred to use state-of-the-art d-DNNF compiler D4 but owing to its closed source implementation, we could not modify it as per our customized compilation procedure PCompile. Therefore, for projected compilation, we have modified DSHARP which has an open-source implementation. We have conducted our experiments on a wide range of publicly available benchmarks. In all, our benchmark suite consisted of 773 benchmarks arising from a wide range of real-world applications. Specifically, we used constraints arising from DQMR networks, bit-blasted versions of SMT-LIB (SMT) benchmarks, and ISCAS89 circuits [8] with parity conditions on randomly chosen subsets of outputs and nextstate variables [34, 48]. We assigned random weights to literals wherever weights were not already available in our benchmarks. All our experiments were conducted on a high performance compute cluster whose each node consists of E5-2690 v3 CPU with 24 cores and 96 GB of RAM. We utilized single core per instance of benchmark with a timeout of 1800 s.

Table 1. Run time (in seconds) for 1000 samples

Benchmark	Vars	Clauses	$|P|$	WeightGen	WAPS			Speedup
					Compile	A+S	Total	on WeightGen
s526a_3_2	366	944	24	490.34	15.37	1.96	17.33	28.29
LoginService	11511	41411	36	1203.93	15.02	0.75	15.77	76.34
blockmap_05_02	1738	3452	1738	1140.87	0.04	5.30	5.34	213.65
s526_3_2	365	943	24	417.24	0.06	0.67	0.73	571.56
or-100-5-4-UC-60	200	500	200	1795.52	0.01	0.74	0.74	2426.38
or-50-5-10-UC-40	100	250	100	1292.67	0.01	0.36	0.36	3590.75
blasted_case35	400	1414	46	TO	0.57	1.46	2.03	-
or-100-20-4-UC-50	200	500	200	TO	0.19	2.48	2.67	-

The objective of our evaluation was to answer the following questions:

1. How does WAPS perform in terms of runtime in comparison to WeightGen, the current state-of-the-art weighted and projected sampler?
2. How does WAPS perform for *incremental sampling* and scales when asked for different number of samples?
3. How does the distribution of samples generated by WAPS compare with the distribution generated by an ideal weighted and projected sampler?
4. How does WAPS perform for conditioning on arbitrary variables?
5. How does our knowledge compilation based sampling techniques perform in comparison to hashing based sampling techniques for the task of generalizing to arbitrary weight distributions?

Our experiment demonstrated that within a time limit of 1800 s, WAPS is able to significantly outperform existing state-of-the-art weighted and projected sampler WeightGen, by up to 3 orders of magnitude in terms of runtime while achieving a geometric speedup of 296×. Out of the 773 benchmarks available WAPS was able to sample from 588 benchmarks while WeightGen was able to sample from only 24 benchmarks. For *incremental sampling*, WAPS achieves a geometric speedup of 3.69. Also, WAPS is almost oblivious to the number of samples requested. Empirically, the distribution generated by WAPS is statistically indistinguishable from that generated by an ideal weighted and projected sampler. Also, while performing conditioned sampling in WAPS, we incur no extra cost in terms of runtime in most of the cases. Moreover, the performance of our knowledge compilation based sampling technique is found to be oblivious to weight distribution. We present results for only a subset of representative benchmarks here. Detailed data along with the expanded versions of all the tables presented here is available at https://github.com/meelgroup/waps.

Number of Instances Solved. We compared the runtime performance of WAPS with WeightGen [10] (state-of-the-art weighted and projected sampler) by generating 1000 samples from each tool with a timeout of 1800 s. Figure 3 shows the cactus plot for WeightGen and WAPS. We present the number of benchmarks on the

x−axis and the time taken on y−axis. A point (x, y) implies that x benchmarks took less than or equal to y seconds to sample. All our runtime statistics for WAPS include the time for the knowledge compilation phase (via D4 or DSHARP). From all the 773 available benchmarks WeightGen was able to sample from only 24 benchmarks while WAPS was able to sample from 588 benchmarks. Table 1 shows the runtimes of some of the benchmarks on the two tools. The columns in the table give the benchmark name, number of variables, number of clauses, size of sampling set, time taken in seconds by WeightGen and WAPS divided into time taken by Compilation and A+S: Annotation and Sampling followed by speedup of WAPS with respect to WeightGen. Table 1 clearly shows that WAPS outperforms WeightGen by upto 3 orders of magnitude. For all the 24 benchmarks that WeightGen was able to solve WAPS outperformed WeightGen with a geometric speedup of 296×.

Incremental Sampling. Incremental sampling involves fetching multiple, relatively small-sized samples until the objective (such as desired coverage or violation of property) is achieved. We benefit from pre-compiled knowledge representations in this scenario, as they allow us to perform repeated sampling as per varied distributions. If weights are changed, we simply Annotate the tree again followed by sampling, else, we directly move to the sampling phase, thus saving a significant amount of time by bypassing the compilation phase.

In our experiments, we have evaluated the time taken by WAPS for 1000 samples in 10 successive calls with same weights. The results are presented in Table 2 for a subset of benchmarks. The first column mentions the benchmark name with the number of variables, clauses and size of sampling set in subsequent columns. The time taken by WAPS for first run to fetch 1000 samples is given in the fifth column while the overall time taken for first run together with the subsequent 9 incremental runs is presented in sixth column. The final column shows the average gain in terms of speedup calculated by taking the ratio of time taken by WAPS for first run with the average time taken by WAPS for subsequent 9 incremental runs thus resulting in a total of 10000 samples. Overall, WAPS achieves a geometric speedup of 3.69× on our set of benchmarks.

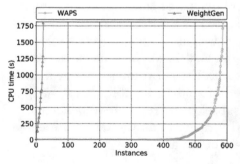

Benchmark	Vars	Clauses	$|P|$	WAPS 1000	WAPS 10,000	Speedup
case110	287	1263	287	1.14	9.28	1.26
or-70-10-10-UC-20	140	350	140	2.75	9.02	6.56
s526_7_4	383	1019	24	60.38	143.16	13.20
or-60-5-2-UC-10	120	300	120	12.10	20.35	16.50
s35932_15_7	17918	44709	1763	69.01	106.65	20.73
case121	291	975	48	35.85	51.41	20.73
s641_15_7	576	1399	54	729.38	916.83	35.01
squaring7	1628	5837	72	321.95	365.13	67.10
LoginService	11511	41411	36	15.89	18.12	64.13
ProjectService	3175	11019	55	184.51	195.25	154.61

Fig. 3. Cactus Plot comparing WeightGen and WAPS.

Table 2. Runtimes (in sec.) of WAPS for incremental sampling

Table 3. Runtime (in sec.) of WAPS to generate different size samples

Benchmark	Vars	Clauses	$\|P\|$	Sampling Size				
				1000	2000	4000	8000	10000
s1488_7_4	872	2499	14	0.5	0.75	1.29	2.2	2.9
s444_15_7	377	1072	24	0.74	1.29	1.91	3.46	4.12
s526_3_2	365	943	24	0.84	1.03	1.86	3.71	4.22
s820a_3_2	598	1627	23	0.63	1.03	2.04	3.92	4.81
case35	400	1414	46	2.38	3.22	5.31	9.38	11.41
LoginService	11511	41411	36	15.8	16.12	16.68	18.3	18.36
ProjectService	3175	11019	55	184.22	184.99	188.33	191.16	193.92
or-60-20-6-UC-10	120	300	120	1465.34	1458.23	1494.46	1499.67	1488.23

Effect of Number of Samples. To check how WAPS scales with different number of samples, we invoked WAPS for fetching different number of samples: 1000, 2000, 4000, 8000, 10000 with a timeout of 1800 s. Table 3 presents the runtime of WAPS for different samples on some benchmarks. The first column represents the benchmark name. Second, third and fourth columns represent the number of variables, clauses and size of sampling set. The next five columns represent the time taken by WAPS for 1000, 2000, 4000, 8000 and 10000 samples. Table 3 clearly demonstrates that WAPS is almost oblivious to the number of samples requested.

Uniform Sampling Generalized for Weighted Sampling. To explore the trend in performance between uniform and weighted sampling on the dimension of hashing based techniques pitched against our newly proposed sampling techniques based on knowledge compilation, we compared WAPS to KUS in a parallel comparison between WeightGen and UniGen2. Specifically, we ran WAPS for weighted sampling and KUS for uniform sampling without utilizing the sampling set as KUS does not support the sampling set. On the other hand, for hashing based sampling techniques, we compared WeightGen to UniGen2 while using the sampling set. Figure 4 shows the cactus plot for WeightGen and UniGen2 and Fig. 5 shows a cactus plot for WAPS and KUS. From all the 773 benchmarks, WeightGen was able to sample from only 24 benchmarks while UniGen2 was able to sample from 208 benchmarks. In comparison, WAPS was able to sample from 606 benchmarks while KUS was able to sample from 602 benchmarks. Our experiments demonstrated that the performance of hashing-based techniques is extremely limited in their ability to handle literal-weighted sampling and there is a drastic drop in their performance as the weight distribution shifts away from uniform. While for our knowledge compilation based sampling techniques we observe that their performance is oblivious to the weight distribution.

Distribution Comparison. We measure the distribution of WAPS vis-a-vis an *ideal weighted and projected sampler* (IS) and observed that WAPS is statistically indistinguishable from IS. Please refer to Appendix for more detailed discussion.

Effect of Conditioning on Variables. We evaluated the performance of WAPS in the context of conditioned sampling. We observed a slight improvement in average runtime as more and more variables get constrained. For detailed results, please refer to Appendix.

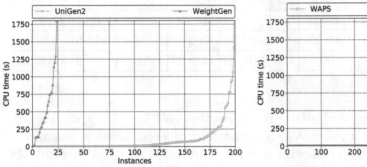

Fig. 4. Cactus Plot comparing WeightGen and UniGen2.

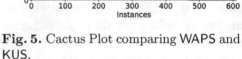

Fig. 5. Cactus Plot comparing WAPS and KUS.

7   Conclusion

In this paper, we designed a knowledge compilation-based framework, called WAPS, for literal-weighted, projected and conditional sampling. WAPS provides strong theoretical guarantees and its runtime performance upon the existing state-of-the-art weighted and projected sampler WeightGen, by up to 3 orders of magnitude in terms of runtime. Out of the 773 benchmarks available, WAPS is able to sample from 588 benchmarks while WeightGen is only able to sample from 24 benchmarks. WAPS achieves a geometric speedup of 3.69 for *incremental sampling*. It is worth noting that WeightGen has weaker guarantees than WAPS. Furthermore, WAPS is almost oblivious to the number of samples requested.

References

1. System Verilog (2015). http://www.systemverilog.org
2. Achlioptas, D., Hammoudeh, Z.S., Theodoropoulos, P.: Fast sampling of perfectly uniform satisfying assignments. In: Beyersdorff, O., Wintersteiger, C.M. (eds.) SAT 2018. LNCS, vol. 10929, pp. 135–147. Springer, Cham (2018). https://doi.org/10.1007/978-3-319-94144-8_9
3. Bacchus, F., Dalmao, S., Pitassi, T.: Algorithms and complexity results for #SAT and Bayesian inference. In: Proceedings of FOCS, pp. 340–351 (2003)

4. Bellare, M., Goldreich, O., Petrank, E.: Uniform generation of NP-witnesses using an NP-oracle. Inf. Comput. **163**(2), 510–526 (2000)
5. Biere, A., Cimatti, A., Clarke, E., Fujita, M., Zhu, Y.: Symbolic model checking using SAT procedures instead of BDDs. In: Proceedings of DAC, pp. 317–320 (1999)
6. Biere, A., Heule, M., van Maaren, H., Walsh, T.: Handbook of Satisfiability. IOS Press, Amsterdam (2009)
7. Bjesse, P., Leonard, T., Mokkedem, A.: Finding bugs in an Alpha microprocessor using satisfiability solvers. In: Berry, G., Comon, H., Finkel, A. (eds.) CAV 2001. LNCS, vol. 2102, pp. 454–464. Springer, Heidelberg (2001). https://doi.org/10.1007/3-540-44585-4_44
8. Brglez, F., Bryan, D., Kozminski, K.: Combinational profiles of sequential benchmark circuits. In: Proceedings of ISCAS, pp. 1929–1934 (1989)
9. Bryant, R.E.: Symbolic Boolean manipulation with ordered binary-decision diagrams. ACM Comput. Surv. (CSUR) **24**(3), 293–318 (1992)
10. Chakraborty, S., Fremont, D.J., Meel, K.S., Seshia, S.A., Vardi, M.Y.: Distribution-aware sampling and weighted model counting for SAT. In: Proceedings of AAAI, pp. 1722–1730 (2014)
11. Chakraborty, S., Fremont, D.J., Meel, K.S., Seshia, S.A., Vardi, M.Y.: On parallel scalable uniform SAT witness generation. In: Baier, C., Tinelli, C. (eds.) TACAS 2015. LNCS, vol. 9035, pp. 304–319. Springer, Heidelberg (2015). https://doi.org/10.1007/978-3-662-46681-0_25
12. Chakraborty, S., Fried, D., Meel, K.S., Vardi, M.Y.: From weighted to unweighted model counting. In: Proceedings of IJCAI, pp. 689–695 (2015)
13. Chakraborty, S., Meel, K.S., Vardi, M.Y.: A scalable and nearly uniform generator of SAT witnesses. In: Sharygina, N., Veith, H. (eds.) CAV 2013. LNCS, vol. 8044, pp. 608–623. Springer, Heidelberg (2013). https://doi.org/10.1007/978-3-642-39799-8_40
14. Chavira, M., Darwiche, A.: On probabilistic inference by weighted model counting. Artif. Intell. **172**(6), 772–799 (2008)
15. Dalvi, N.N., Schnaitter, K., Suciu, D.: Computing query probability with incidence algebras. In: Proceedings of PODS, pp. 203–214 (2010)
16. Darwiche, A.: SDD: a new canonical representation of propositional knowledge bases. In: Proceedings of 22nd International Joint Conference on Artificial Intelligence, pp. 819–826 (2011)
17. Darwiche, A.: On the tractable counting of theory models and its application to belief revision and truth maintenance. CoRR (2000)
18. Darwiche, A.: New advances in compiling CNF to decomposable negation normal form. In: Proceedings of ECAI, pp. 318–322 (2004)
19. Darwiche, A., Marquis, P.: A knowledge compilation map. J. Artif. Intell. Res. **17**, 229–264 (2002)
20. Dechter, R., Kask, K., Bin, E., Emek, R.: Generating random solutions for constraint satisfaction problems. In: Proceedings of AAAI, pp. 15–21 (2002)
21. Duenas-Osorio, L., Meel, K.S., Paredes, R., Vardi, M.Y.: Counting-based reliability estimation for power-transmission grids. In: Proceedings of AAAI (2017)
22. Dutra, R., Laeufer, K., Bachrach, J., Sen, K.: Efficient sampling of SAT solutions for testing. In: Proceedings of ICSE, pp. 549–559 (2018)
23. Elliott, P., Williams, B.: DNNF-based belief state estimation. In: Proceedings of AAAI, pp. 36–41 (2006)
24. Ermon, S., Gomes, C.P., Sabharwal, A., Selman, B.: Embed and project: discrete sampling with universal hashing. In: Proceedings of NIPS, pp. 2085–2093 (2013)

25. Ermon, S., Gomes, C.P., Selman, B.: Uniform solution sampling using a constraint solver as an Oracle. In: Proceedings of UAI, pp. 255–264 (2012)
26. Gogate, V., Dechter, R.: A new algorithm for sampling CSP solutions uniformly at random. In: Benhamou, F. (ed.) CP 2006. LNCS, vol. 4204, pp. 711–715. Springer, Heidelberg (2006). https://doi.org/10.1007/11889205_56
27. Gomes, C.P., Selman, B., McAloon, K., Tretkoff, C.: Randomization in backtrack search: exploiting heavy-tailed profiles for solving hard scheduling problems. In: Proceedings of AIPS (1998)
28. Ivrii, A., Malik, S., Meel, K.S., Vardi, M.Y.: On computing minimal independent support and its applications to sampling and counting. Constraints 21, 1–18 (2015). https://doi.org/10.1007/s10601-015-9204-z
29. Iyer, M.A.: RACE: a word-level ATPG-based constraints solver system for smart random simulation. In: Proceedings of ITC, pp. 299–308 (2003)
30. Lagniez, J.-M ., Marquis, P.: An improved decision-DNNF compiler. In: Proceedings of IJCAI, pp. 667–673 (2017)
31. Jerrum, M.R., Sinclair, A.: Approximating the permanent. SIAM J. Comput. 18(6), 1149–1178 (1989)
32. Jerrum, M.R., Sinclair, A.: The Markov Chain Monte Carlo method: an approach to approximate counting and integration. In: Hochbaum, D.S. (ed.) Approximation Algorithms for NP-Hard Problems, pp. 482–520. ACM, New York (1996)
33. Jerrum, M.R., Valiant, L.G., Vazirani, V.V.: Random generation of combinatorial structures from a uniform distribution. Theoret. Comput. Sci. 43(2–3), 169–188 (1986)
34. John, A.K., Chakraborty, S.: A quantifier elimination algorithm for linear modular equations and disequations. In: Gopalakrishnan, G., Qadeer, S. (eds.) CAV 2011. LNCS, vol. 6806, pp. 486–503. Springer, Heidelberg (2011). https://doi.org/10.1007/978-3-642-22110-1_39
35. Kautz, H., Selman, B.: Pushing the envelope: planning, propositional logic, and stochastic search. In: Proceedings of AAAI (1996)
36. Kirkpatrick, S., Gelatt, C.D., Vecchi, M.P.: Optimization by simulated annealing. Science 220(4598), 671–680 (1983)
37. Kitchen, N.: Markov Chain Monte Carlo stimulus generation for constrained random simulation. Ph.D. thesis, University of California, Berkeley (2010)
38. Kitchen, N., Kuehlmann, A.: Stimulus generation for constrained random simulation. In: Proceedings of ICCAD, pp. 258–265 (2007)
39. Madras, N., Piccioni, M.: Importance sampling for families of distributions. Ann. Appl. Probab. 9, 1202–1225 (1999)
40. Madras, N.: Lectures on Monte Carlo Methods, Fields Institute Monographs, vol. 16. American Mathematical Society, Providence (2002)
41. Malik, S., Zhang, L.: Boolean satisfiability from theoretical hardness topractical success. Commun. ACM 52(8), 76–82 (2009)
42. Meel, K.S.: Constrained counting and sampling: bridging the gap between theory and practice. Ph.D. thesis, Rice University (2017)
43. Muise, C., McIlraith, S.A., Beck, J.C., Hsu, E.I.: DSHARP: fast d-DNNF compilation with sharpSAT. In: Proceedings of AAAI, pp. 356–361 (2016)
44. Naveh, R., Metodi, A.: Beyond feasibility: CP usage in constrained-random functional hardware verification. In: Schulte, C. (ed.) CP 2013. LNCS, vol. 8124, pp. 823–831. Springer, Heidelberg (2013). https://doi.org/10.1007/978-3-642-40627-0_60
45. Naveh, Y., et al.: Constraint-based random stimuli generation for hardware verification. In: Proceedings of IAAI, pp. 1720–1727 (2006)

46. Palacios, H., Bonet, B., Darwiche, A., Geffner, H.: Pruning conformant plans by counting models on compiled d-DNNF representations. In: Proceedings of ICAPS, pp. 141–150 (2005)
47. Sang, T., Bacchus, F., Beame, P., Kautz, H.A., Pitassi, T.: Combining component caching and clause learning for effective model counting. In: Proceedings of SAT (2004)
48. Sang, T., Beame, P., Kautz, H.: Performing Bayesian inference by weighted model counting. In: Proceedings of AAAI, pp. 475–481 (2005)
49. Sharma, S., Gupta, R., Roy, S., Meel, K.S.: Knowledge compilation meets uniform sampling. In: Proceedings of LPAR-22, pp. 620–636 (2018)
50. Tseitin, G.S.: On the complexity of derivation in propositional calculus. In: Siekmann, J.H., Wrightson, G. (eds.) Automation of Reasoning. Symbolic Computation (Artificial Intelligence). Springer, Berlin, Heidelberg (1983). https://doi.org/10.1007/978-3-642-81955-1_28
51. Velev, M.N., Bryant, R.E.: Effective use of Boolean satisfiability procedures in the formal verification of superscalar and VLIW microprocessors. J. Symb. Comput. **2**, 73–106 (2003)

Extending a Brainiac Prover
to Lambda-Free Higher-Order Logic

Petar Vukmirović[1(✉)], Jasmin Christian Blanchette[1,2], Simon Cruanes[3],
and Stephan Schulz[4]

[1] Vrije Universiteit Amsterdam, Amsterdam, The Netherlands
p.vukmirovic@vu.nl
[2] Max-Planck-Institut für Informatik, Saarland Informatics Campus,
Saarbrücken, Germany
[3] Aesthetic Integration, Austin, TX, USA
[4] DHBW Stuttgart, Stuttgart, Germany

Abstract. Decades of work have gone into developing efficient proof calculi, data structures, algorithms, and heuristics for first-order automatic theorem proving. Higher-order provers lag behind in terms of efficiency. Instead of developing a new higher-order prover from the ground up, we propose to start with the state-of-the-art superposition-based prover E and gradually enrich it with higher-order features. We explain how to extend the prover's data structures, algorithms, and heuristics to λ-free higher-order logic, a formalism that supports partial application and applied variables. Our extension outperforms the traditional encoding and appears promising as a stepping stone towards full higher-order logic.

1   Introduction

Superposition-based provers, such as E [26], SPASS [33], and Vampire [18], are among the most successful first-order reasoning systems. They serve as backends in various frameworks, including software verifiers (Why3 [15]), automatic higher-order theorem provers (Leo-III [27], Satallax [12]), and "hammers" in proof assistants (HOLyHammer for HOL Light [17], Sledgehammer for Isabelle [21]). Decades of research have gone into refining calculi, devising efficient data structures and algorithms, and developing heuristics to guide proof search. This work has mostly focused on first-order logic with equality, with or without arithmetic.

Research on higher-order automatic provers has resulted in systems such as LEO [8], Leo-II [9], and Leo-III [27], based on resolution and paramodulation, and Satallax [12], based on tableaux. These provers feature a "cooperative" architecture, pioneered by LEO: They are full-fledged higher-order provers that regularly invoke an external first-order prover in an attempt to finish the proof quickly using only first-order reasoning. However, the first-order backend will succeed only if all the necessary higher-order reasoning has been performed, meaning that much of the first-order reasoning is carried out by the slower higher-order prover. As a result, this architecture leads to suboptimal performance on first-order problems and on problems with a large first-order component. For example, at the 2017 installment of the CADE ATP System Competition (CASC) [30], Leo-III, using E as one of its backends, proved 652 out of 2000 first-order problems in the Sledgehammer division, compared with 1185 for E on its own and 1433 for Vampire.

To obtain better performance, we propose to start with a competitive first-order prover and extend it to full higher-order logic one feature at a time. Our goal is a *graceful* extension, so that the system behaves as before on first-order problems, performs mostly like a first-order prover on typical, mildly higher-order problems, and scales up to arbitrary higher-order problems, in keeping with the zero-overhead principle: *What you don't use, you don't pay for.*

As a stepping stone towards full higher-order logic, we initially restrict our focus to a higher-order logic without λ-expressions (Sect. 2). Compared with first-order logic, its distinguishing features are partial application and applied variables. This formalism is rich enough to express the recursive equations of higher-order combinators, such as the map operation on finite lists:

$$\text{map } f \text{ nil} \approx \text{nil} \qquad \text{map } f \text{ (cons } x \text{ } xs) \approx \text{cons } (f \text{ } x) \text{ (map } f \text{ } xs)$$

Our vehicle is E, a prover developed primarily by Schulz. It is written in C and offers good performance, with the emphasis on "brainiac" heuristics rather than raw speed. E regularly scores among the top systems at CASC, and usually is the strongest open source[1] prover in the relevant divisions. It also serves as a backend for competitive higher-order provers. We refer to our extended version of E as Ehoh. It corresponds to E version 2.3 configured with `-enable-ho`. A prototype of Ehoh is described in Vukmirović's MSc thesis [31].

The three main challenges are generalizing the term representation (Sect. 3), the unification algorithm (Sect. 4), and the indexing data structures (Sect. 5). We also adapted the inference rules (Sect. 6) and the heuristics (Sect. 7). This paper explains the key ideas. Details, including correctness proofs, are given in a separate technical report [32].

A novel aspect of our work is *prefix optimization*. Higher-order terms contain twice as many proper subterms as first-order terms; for example, the term f (g a) b contains not only the argument subterms g a, a, b but also the "prefix" subterms f, f (g a), g. Using prefix optimization, the prover traverses subterms recursively in a first-order fashion, considering all the prefixes of the current subterm together, at no significant additional cost. Our experiments (Sect. 8) show that Ehoh is effectively as fast as E on first-order problems and can also prove higher-order problems that do not require synthesizing λ-terms. As a next step, we plan to add support for λ-terms and higher-order unification.

---

[1] http://wwwlehre.dhbw-stuttgart.de/~sschulz/WORK/E_DOWNLOAD/V_2.3/.

2   Logic

Our logic corresponds to the intensional λ-free higher-order logic (λfHOL) described by Bentkamp, Blanchette, Cruanes, and Waldmann [7, Sect. 2]. Another possible name for this logic would be "applicative first-order logic." Extensionality can be obtained by adding suitable axioms [7, Sect. 3.1].

A type is either an atomic type ι or a function type $\tau \to \upsilon$, where τ and υ are themselves types. Terms, ranged over by s, t, u, v, are either *variables* $x, y, z, \ldots$, (*function*) *symbols* a, b, c, d, f, g, $\ldots$ (often called "constants" in the higher-order literature), or binary applications $s\, t$. Application associates to the left, whereas $\to$ associates to the right. The typing rules are as for the simply typed λ-calculus. A term's *arity* is the number of extra arguments it can take; thus, if f has type $\iota \to \iota \to \iota$ and a has type ι, then f is binary, f a is unary, and f a a is nullary. Terms have a unique "flattened" decomposition of the form $\zeta\, s_1 \ldots s_m$, where ζ, the *head*, is a variable x or symbol f. We abbreviate tuples $(a_1, \ldots, a_m)$ to $\overline{a_m}$ or $\overline{a}$; abusing notation, we write $\zeta\, \overline{s_m}$ for the curried application $\zeta\, s_1 \ldots s_m$.

An equation $s \approx t$ corresponds to an unordered pair of terms. A literal L is an equation or its negation. Clauses C, D are finite multisets of literals, written $L_1 \vee \cdots \vee L_n$. E and Ehoh clausify the input as a preprocessing step.

A well-known technique to support λfHOL using first-order reasoning systems is to employ the *applicative encoding*. Following this scheme, every n-ary symbol is converted to a nullary symbol, and application is represented by a distinguished binary symbol @. For example, the λfHOL term f $(x$ a$)$ b is encoded as the first-order term @(@(f, @(x, a)), b). However, this representation is not graceful; it clutters data structures and impacts proof search in subtle ways, leading to poorer performance, especially on large benchmarks. In our empirical evaluation, we find that for some prover modes, the applicative encoding incurs a 15% decrease in success rate (Sect. 8). For these and further reasons (Sect. 9), it is not an ideal basis for higher-order reasoning.

3   Types and Terms

The term representation is a fundamental question when building a theorem prover. Delicate changes to E's term representation were needed to support partial application and especially applied variables. In contrast, the introduction of a higher-order type system had a less dramatic impact on the prover's code.

Types. For most of its history, E supported only untyped first-order logic. Cruanes implemented support for atomic types for E 2.0 [13, p. 117]. Symbols f are declared with a type signature: f : $\tau_1 \times \cdots \times \tau_m \to \tau$. Atomic types are represented by integers in memory, leading to efficient type comparisons.

In λfHOL, a type signature consists of types τ, in which the function type constructor $\to$ can be nested—e.g., $(\iota \to \iota) \to \iota \to \iota$. A natural way to represent such types is to mimic their recursive structures using tagged unions. However, this leads to memory fragmentation, and a simple operation such as querying the type of a function's ith argument would require dereferencing i pointers.

We prefer a flattened representation, in which a type $\tau_1 \to \cdots \to \tau_n \to \iota$ is represented by a single node labeled with $\to$ and pointing to the array $(\tau_1, \ldots, \tau_n, \iota)$. Applying $k \leq n$ arguments to a function of the above type yields a term of type $\tau_{k+1} \to \cdots \to \tau_n \to \iota$. In memory, this corresponds to skipping the first k array elements.

To speed up type comparisons, Ehoh stores all types in a shared bank and implements perfect sharing, ensuring that types that are structurally the same are represented by the same object in memory. Type equality can then be implemented as a pointer comparison.

Terms. In E, terms are represented as perfectly shared directed acyclic graphs. Each node, or *cell*, contains 11 fields, including f_code, an integer that identifies the term's head symbol (if ≥ 0) or variable (if < 0); arity, an integer corresponding to the number of arguments passed to the head symbol; args, an array of size arity consisting of pointers to argument terms; and binding, which possibly stores a substitution for a variable used for unification and matching.

In higher-order logic, variables may have function type and be applied, and symbols can be applied to fewer arguments than specified by their type signatures. A natural representation of λfHOL terms as tagged unions would distinguish between variables x, symbols f, and binary applications $s\ t$. However, this scheme suffers from memory fragmentation and linear-time access, as with the representation of types, affecting performance on purely or mostly first-order problems. Instead, we propose a flattened representation, as a generalization of E's existing data structures: Allow arguments to variables, and for symbols let arity be the number of *actual* arguments.

A side effect of the flattened representation is that prefix subterms are not shared. For example, the terms f a and f a b correspond to the flattened cells $f(a)$ and $f(a, b)$. The argument subterm a is shared, but not the prefix f a. Similarly, x and x b are represented by two distinct cells, $x()$ and $x(b)$, and there is no connection between the two occurrences of x. In particular, despite perfect sharing, their binding fields are unconnected, leading to inconsistencies.

A potential solution would be to systematically traverse a clause and set the binding fields of all cells of the form $x(\bar{s})$ whenever a variable x is bound, but this would be inefficient and inelegant. Instead, we implemented a hybrid approach: Variables are applied by an explicit application operator @, to ensure that they are always perfectly shared. Thus, x b c is represented by the cell $@(x, b, c)$, where x is a shared subcell. This is graceful, since variables never occur applied in first-order terms. The main drawback of this technique is that some normalization is necessary after substitution: Whenever a variable is instantiated by a term with a symbol head, the @ symbol must be eliminated. Applying the substitution $\{x \mapsto f\ a\}$ to the cell $@(x, b, c)$ must produce the cell $f(a, b, c)$ and not $@(f(a), b, c)$, for consistency with other occurrences of f a b c.

There is one more complication related to the binding field. In E, it is easy and useful to traverse a term as if a substitution has been applied, by following all set binding fields. In Ehoh, this is not enough, because cells must also be normalized. To avoid repeatedly creating the same normalized cells, we introduced a `binding_cache` field that connects a $@(x, \overline{s})$ cell with its substitution. However, this cache can easily become stale when the `binding` pointer is updated. To detect this situation, we store x's `binding` value in the $@(x, \overline{s})$ cell's `binding` field (which is otherwise unused). To find out whether the cache is valid, it suffices to check that the `binding` fields of x and $@(x, \overline{s})$ are equal.

Term Orders. Superposition provers rely on term orders to prune the search space. To ensure completeness, the order must be a simplification order that can be extended to a simplification order that is total on variable-free terms. The Knuth–Bendix order (KBO) and the lexicographic path order (LPO) meet this criterion. KBO is generally regarded as the more robust and efficient option for superposition. E implements both. In earlier work, Blanchette and colleagues have shown that only KBO can be generalized gracefully while preserving all the necessary properties for superposition [5]. For this reason, we focus on KBO.

E implements the linear-time algorithm for KBO described by Löchner [19], which relies on the tupling method to store intermediate results, avoiding repeated computations. It is straightforward to generalize the algorithm to compute the graceful λfHOL version of KBO [5]. The main difference is that when comparing two terms f $\overline{s_m}$ and f $\overline{t_n}$, because of partial application we may now have $m \neq n$; this required changing the implementation to perform a length-lexicographic comparison of the tuples $\overline{s_m}$ and $\overline{t_n}$.

4   Unification and Matching

Syntactic unification of λfHOL terms has a definite first-order flavor. It is decidable, and most general unifiers (MGUs) are unique up to variable renaming. For example, the unification constraint f $(y\ a) \stackrel{?}{=} y\ (f\ a)$ has the MGU $\{y \mapsto f\}$, whereas in full higher-order logic it would admit infinitely many independent solutions of the form $\{y \mapsto \lambda x.\, f\ (f\ (\cdots (f\ x)\cdots))\}$. Matching is a special case of unification where only the variables on the left-hand side can be instantiated.

An easy but inefficient way to implement unification and matching for λfHOL is to apply the applicative encoding (Sect. 1), perform first-order unification or matching, and decode the result. Instead, we propose to generalize the first-order unification and matching procedures to operate directly on λfHOL terms.

We present our unification procedure as a transition system, generalizing Baader and Nipkow [3]. A unification problem consists of a finite set S of unification constraints $s_i \stackrel{?}{=} t_i$, where s_i and t_i are of the same type. A problem is in *solved form* if it has the form $\{x_1 \stackrel{?}{=} t_1, \ldots, x_n \stackrel{?}{=} t_n\}$, where the x_i's are distinct and do not occur in the t_j's. The corresponding unifier is $\{x_1 \mapsto t_1, \ldots, x_n \mapsto t_n\}$. The transition rules attempt to bring the input constraints into solved form.

The first group of rules consists of operations that focus on a single constraint and replace it with a new (possibly empty) set of constraints:

Delete $\{t \stackrel{?}{=} t\} \uplus S \Longrightarrow S$

Decompose $\{f\ \overline{s_m} \stackrel{?}{=} f\ \overline{t_m}\} \uplus S \Longrightarrow S \cup \{s_1 \stackrel{?}{=} t_1, \ldots, s_m \stackrel{?}{=} t_m\}$

DecomposeX $\{x\ \overline{s_m} \stackrel{?}{=} u\ \overline{t_m}\} \uplus S \Longrightarrow S \cup \{x \stackrel{?}{=} u,\, s_1 \stackrel{?}{=} t_1, \ldots, s_m \stackrel{?}{=} t_m\}$
          if x and u have the same type and $m > 0$

Orient $\{f\ \overline{s} \stackrel{?}{=} x\ \overline{t}\} \uplus S \Longrightarrow S \cup \{x\ \overline{t} \stackrel{?}{=} f\ \overline{s}\}$

OrientXY $\{x\ \overline{s_m} \stackrel{?}{=} y\ \overline{t_n}\} \uplus S \Longrightarrow S \cup \{y\ \overline{t_n} \stackrel{?}{=} x\ \overline{s_m}\}$ if $m > n$

Eliminate $\{x \stackrel{?}{=} t\} \uplus S \Longrightarrow \{x \stackrel{?}{=} t\} \cup \{x \mapsto t\}(S)$ if $x \in \mathcal{V}ar(S) \setminus \mathcal{V}ar(t)$

The Delete, Decompose, and Eliminate rules are essentially as for first-order terms. The Orient rule is generalized to allow applied variables and complemented by a new OrientXY rule. DecomposeX, also a new rule, can be seen as a variant of Decompose that analyzes applied variables; the term u may be an application.

The rules belonging to the second group detect unsolvable constraints:

Clash $\{f\ \overline{s} \stackrel{?}{=} g\ \overline{t}\} \uplus S \Longrightarrow \bot$ if $f \neq g$

ClashTypeX $\{x\ \overline{s_m} \stackrel{?}{=} u\ \overline{t_m}\} \uplus S \Longrightarrow \bot$ if x and u have different types

ClashLenXF $\{x\ \overline{s_m} \stackrel{?}{=} f\ \overline{t_n}\} \uplus S \Longrightarrow \bot$ if $m > n$

OccursCheck $\{x \stackrel{?}{=} t\} \uplus S \Longrightarrow \bot$ if $x \in \mathcal{V}ar(t)$ and $x \neq t$

The derivations below demonstrate the computation of MGUs for the unification problems $\{f\ (y\ a) \stackrel{?}{=} y\ (f\ a)\}$ and $\{x\ (z\ b\ c) \stackrel{?}{=} g\ a\ (y\ c)\}$:

	$\{f\ (y\ a) \stackrel{?}{=} y\ (f\ a)\}$		$\{x\ (z\ b\ c) \stackrel{?}{=} g\ a\ (y\ c)\}$
$\Longrightarrow_{\text{Orient}}$	$\{y\ (f\ a) \stackrel{?}{=} f\ (y\ a)\}$	$\Longrightarrow_{\text{DecomposeX}}$	$\{x \stackrel{?}{=} g\ a,\, z\ b\ c \stackrel{?}{=} y\ c\}$
$\Longrightarrow_{\text{DecomposeX}}$	$\{y \stackrel{?}{=} f,\, f\ a \stackrel{?}{=} y\ a\}$	$\Longrightarrow_{\text{OrientXY}}$	$\{x \stackrel{?}{=} g\ a,\, y\ c \stackrel{?}{=} z\ b\ c\}$
$\Longrightarrow_{\text{Eliminate}}$	$\{y \stackrel{?}{=} f,\, f\ a \stackrel{?}{=} f\ a\}$	$\Longrightarrow_{\text{DecomposeX}}$	$\{x \stackrel{?}{=} g\ a,\, y \stackrel{?}{=} z\ b,\, c \stackrel{?}{=} c\}$
$\Longrightarrow_{\text{Delete}}$	$\{y \stackrel{?}{=} f\}$	$\Longrightarrow_{\text{Delete}}$	$\{x \stackrel{?}{=} g\ a,\, y \stackrel{?}{=} z\ b\}$

E stores open constraints in a double-ended queue. Constraints are processed from the front. New constraints are added at the front if they involve complex terms that can be dealt with swiftly by Decompose or Clash, or to the back if one side is a variable. Soundness and completeness proofs as well as the pseudocode for unification and matching algorithms are included in our report [32].

During proof search, E repeatedly needs to test a term s for unifiability not only with some other term t but also with t's subterms. Prefix optimization speeds up this test: The subterms of t are traversed in a first-order fashion; for each such subterm $\zeta\ \overline{t_n}$, at most one prefix $\zeta\ \overline{t_k}$, with $k \leq n$, is possibly unifiable with s, by virtue of their having the same arity. Using this technique, Ehoh is virtually as efficient as E on first-order terms.

5   Indexing Data Structures

Superposition provers like E work by saturation. Their main loop heuristically selects a clause and searches for potential inference partners among a possibly large set of other clauses. Mechanisms such as simplification and subsumption also require locating terms in a large clause set. For example, when E derives a new equation $s \approx t$, if s is larger than t according to the term order, it will rewrite all instances $\sigma(s)$ of s to $\sigma(t)$ in existing clauses.

To avoid iterating over all terms (including subterms) in large clause sets, superposition provers store the potential inference partners in indexing data structures. A term index stores a set of terms S. Given a *query term* t, a query returns all terms $s \in S$ that satisfy a given *retrieval condition*: $\sigma(s) = \sigma(t)$ (s and t are unifiable), $\sigma(s) = t$ (s generalizes t), or $s = \sigma(t)$ (s is an instance of t), for some substitution σ. *Perfect* indices return exactly the subset of terms satisfying the retrieval condition. In contrast, *imperfect* indices return a superset of eligible terms, and the retrieval condition needs to be checked for each candidate.

E relies on two term indexing data structures, perfect discrimination trees [20] and fingerprint indices [24], that needed to be generalized to λfHOL. It also uses feature vector indices [25] to speed up clause subsumption and related techniques, but these require no changes to work with λfHOL clauses.

Perfect Discrimination Trees. Discrimination trees [20] are tries in which every node is labeled with a symbol or a variable. A path from the root to a leaf node corresponds to a "serialized term"—a term expressed without parentheses and commas. Consider the following discrimination trees:

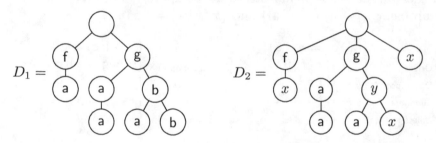

Assuming $\mathsf{a}, \mathsf{b}, x, y : \iota$, $\mathsf{f} : \iota \to \iota$, and $\mathsf{g} : \iota^2 \to \iota$, the trees D_1 and D_2 represent the term sets $\{\mathsf{f}(\mathsf{a}), \mathsf{g}(\mathsf{a},\mathsf{a}), \mathsf{g}(\mathsf{b},\mathsf{a}), \mathsf{g}(\mathsf{b},\mathsf{b})\}$ and $\{\mathsf{f}(x), \mathsf{g}(\mathsf{a},\mathsf{a}), \mathsf{g}(y,\mathsf{a}), \mathsf{g}(y,x), x\}$.

E uses perfect discrimination trees for finding generalizations of query terms. For example, if the query term is $\mathsf{g}(\mathsf{a},\mathsf{a})$, it would follow the path $\mathsf{g}.\mathsf{a}.\mathsf{a}$ in the tree D_1 and return $\{\mathsf{g}(\mathsf{a},\mathsf{a})\}$. For D_2, it would also explore paths labeled with variables, binding them as it proceeds, and return $\{\mathsf{g}(\mathsf{a},\mathsf{a}), \mathsf{g}(y,\mathsf{a}), \mathsf{g}(y,x), x\}$.

The data structure relies on the observation that serializing is unambiguous. Conveniently, this property also holds for λfHOL terms. Assume that two distinct λfHOL terms yield the same serialization. Clearly, they must disagree on parentheses; one will have the subterm $s\ t\ u$ where the other has $s\ (t\ u)$. However, these two subterms cannot both be well typed.

When generalizing the data structure to λfHOL, we face a slight complication due to partial application. First-order terms can only be stored in leaf nodes, but in Ehoh we must also be able to represent partially applied terms, such as f, g, or $\mathsf{g}\ \mathsf{a}$ (assuming, as above, that f is unary and g is binary). Conceptually, this can be solved by storing a Boolean on each node indicating whether it is an accepting state. In the implementation, the change is more subtle, because several parts of E's code implicitly assume that only leaf nodes are accepting.

The main difficulty specific to λfHOL concerns applied variables. To enumerate all generalizing terms, E needs to backtrack from child to parent nodes. To achieve this, it relies on two stacks that store subterms of the query term: `term_stack` stores the terms that must be matched in turn against the current subtree, and `term_proc` stores, for each node from the root to the current subtree, the corresponding processed term, including any arguments yet to be matched.

The matching procedure starts at the root with an empty substitution σ. Initially, `term_stack` contains the query term, and `term_proc` is empty. The procedure advances by moving to a suitable child node:

A. If the node is labeled with a symbol f and the top item t of `term_stack` is $f(\overline{t_n})$, replace t by n new items $t_1, \ldots, t_n$, and push t onto `term_proc`.
B. If the node is labeled with a variable x, there are two subcases. If x is already bound, check that $\sigma(x) = t$; otherwise, extend σ so that $\sigma(x) = t$. Next, pop a term t from `term_stack` and push it onto `term_proc`.

The goal is to reach an accepting node. If the query term and all the terms stored in the tree are first-order, `term_stack` will then be empty, and the entire query term will have been matched.

Backtracking works in reverse: Pop a term t from `term_proc`; if the current node is labeled with an n-ary symbol, discard `term_stack`'s topmost n items; finally, push t onto `term_stack`. Variable bindings must also be undone.

As an example, looking up $g(b, a)$ in the tree D_1 would result in the following succession of stack states, starting from the root ϵ along the path g.b.a:

	ϵ	g	g.b	g.b.a
`term_stack`:	$[g(b, a)]$	$[b, a]$	$[a]$	$[]$
`term_proc`:	$[]$	$[g(b, a)]$	$[b, g(b, a)]$	$[a, b, g(b, a)]$

(The notation $[a_1, \ldots, a_n]$ represents the n-item stack with a_1 on top.) Backtracking amounts to moving leftwards: When backtracking from the node g to the root, we pop $g(b, a)$ from `term_proc`, we discard two items from `term_stack`, and we push $g(b, a)$ onto `term_stack`.

To adapt the procedure to λfHOL, the key idea is that an applied variable is not very different from an applied symbol. A node labeled with an n-ary symbol or variable ζ matches a prefix t' of the k-ary term t popped from `term_stack` and leaves $n - k$ arguments $\overline{u}$ to be pushed back, with $t = t' \, \overline{u}$. If ζ is a variable, it must be bound to the prefix t'. Backtracking works analogously: Given the arity n of the node label ζ and the arity k of the term t popped from `term_proc`, we discard the topmost $n - k$ items $\overline{u}$ from `term_proc`.

To illustrate the procedure, we consider the tree D_2 but change y's type to $\iota \to \iota$. This tree represents the set $\{f \, x, \, g \, a \, a, \, g \, (y \, a), \, g \, (y \, x), \, x\}$. Let $g \, (g \, a \, b)$ be the query term. We have the following sequence of substitutions and stacks:

	ϵ	g	$g.y$	$g.y.x$
σ:	$\emptyset$	$\emptyset$	$\{y \mapsto g\,a\}$	$\{y \mapsto g\,a,\, x \mapsto b\}$
`term_stack:`	$[g\,(g\,a\,b)]$	$[g\,a\,b]$	$[b]$	$[\,]$
`term_proc:`	$[\,]$	$[g\,(g\,a\,b)]$	$[g\,a\,b,\, g\,(g\,a\,b)]$	$[b,\, g\,a\,b,\, g\,(g\,a\,b)]$

Finally, to avoid traversing twice as many subterms as in the first-order case, we can optimize prefixes: Given a query term $\zeta\,\overline{t_n}$, we can also match prefixes $\zeta\,\overline{t_k}$, where $k < n$, by allowing `term_stack` to be nonempty at the end.

Fingerprint Indices. Fingerprint indices [24] trade perfect indexing for a compact memory representation and more flexible retrieval conditions. The basic idea is to compare terms by looking only at a few predefined sample positions. If we know that term s has symbol f at the head of the subterm at 2.1 and term t has g at the same position, we can immediately conclude that s and t are not unifiable.

Let A ("at a variable"), B ("below a variable"), and N ("nonexistent") be distinguished symbols. Given a term t and a position p, the *fingerprint function* $\mathcal{G}\!fpf$ is defined as

$$\mathcal{G}\!fpf(t, p) = \begin{cases} f & \text{if } t|_p \text{ has a symbol head } f \\ A & \text{if } t|_p \text{ is a variable} \\ B & \text{if } t|_q \text{ is a variable for some proper prefix } q \text{ of } p \\ N & \text{otherwise} \end{cases}$$

Based on a fixed tuple of sample positions $\overline{p_n}$, the *fingerprint* of a term t is defined as $\mathcal{F}p(t) = \big(\mathcal{G}\!fpf(t, p_1), \ldots, \mathcal{G}\!fpf(t, p_n)\big)$. To compare two terms s and t, it suffices to check that their fingerprints are componentwise compatible using the following unification and matching matrices:

	f_1	f_2	A	B	N
f_1		✗			✗
A					✗
B					
N	✗	✗	✗		

	f_1	f_2	A	B	N
f_1		✗	✗	✗	✗
A				✗	✗
B					
N	✗	✗	✗	✗	

The rows and columns correspond to s and t, respectively. The metavariables f_1 and f_2 represent arbitrary distinct symbols. Incompatibility is indicated by ✗.

As an example, let $(\epsilon, 1, 2, 1.1, 1.2, 2.1, 2.2)$ be the sample positions, and let $s = f(a, x)$ and $t = f(g(x), g(a))$ be the terms to unify. Their fingerprints are

$$\mathcal{F}p(s) = (f, a, A, N, N, B, B) \qquad \mathcal{F}p(t) = (f, g, g, A, N, a, N)$$

Using the left matrix, we compute the compatibility vector $(-, ✗, -, ✗, -, -, -)$. The mismatches at positions 1 and 1.1 indicate that s and t are not unifiable.

A fingerprint index is a trie that stores a term set T keyed by fingerprint. The term $f(g(x), g(a))$ above would be stored in the node addressed by f.g.g.A.N.a.N, possibly together with other terms that share the same fingerprint. This organization makes it possible to unify or match a query term s against all the terms T in one traversal. Once a node storing the terms $U \subseteq T$ has been reached, due to overapproximation we must apply unification or matching on s and each $u \in U$.

When adapting this data structure to λfHOL, we must first choose a suitable notion of position in a term. Conventionally, higher-order positions are strings over $\{1, 2\}$ indicating, for each binary application $t_1 \, t_2$, which term t_i to follow. Given that this is not graceful, it seems preferable to generalize the first-order notion to flattened λfHOL terms—e.g., $x \, \mathsf{a} \, \mathsf{b} \, |_1 = \mathsf{a}$ and $x \, \mathsf{a} \, \mathsf{b} \, |_2 = \mathsf{b}$. However, this approach fails on applied variables. For example, although $x \, \mathsf{b}$ and $\mathsf{f} \, \mathsf{a} \, \mathsf{b}$ are unifiable (using $\{x \mapsto \mathsf{f} \, \mathsf{a}\}$), sampling position 1 would yield a clash between b and a. To ensure that positions remain stable under substitution, we propose to number arguments in reverse: $t|^\epsilon = t$ and $\zeta \, t_n \, \ldots \, t_1 |^{i \cdot p} = t_i |^p$ if $1 \le i \le n$.

Let $t \langle^p$ denote the subterm $t|^q$ such that q is the longest prefix of p for which $t|^q$ is defined. The λfHOL version of the fingerprint function is defined as follows:

$$\mathcal{G}\!\mathit{fpf}'(t, p) = \begin{cases} \mathsf{f} & \text{if } t|^p \text{ has a symbol head } \mathsf{f} \\ \mathsf{A} & \text{if } t|^p \text{ has a variable head} \\ \mathsf{B} & \text{if } t|^p \text{ is undefined but } t\langle^p \text{ has a variable head} \\ \mathsf{N} & \text{otherwise} \end{cases}$$

Except for the reversed numbering scheme, $\mathcal{G}\!\mathit{fpf}'$ coincides with $\mathcal{G}\!\mathit{fpf}$ on first-order terms. The fingerprint $\mathcal{F}p'(t)$ of a term t is defined analogously as before, and the same compatibility matrices can be used.

The most interesting new case is that of an applied variable. Given the sample positions $(\epsilon, 2, 1)$, the fingerprint of x is $(\mathsf{A}, \mathsf{B}, \mathsf{B})$ as before, whereas the fingerprint of $x \, \mathsf{c}$ is $(\mathsf{A}, \mathsf{B}, \mathsf{c})$. As another example, let $(\epsilon, 2, 1, 2.2, 2.1, 1.2, 1.1)$ be the sample positions, and let $s = x \, (\mathsf{f} \, \mathsf{b} \, \mathsf{c})$ and $t = \mathsf{g} \, \mathsf{a} \, (y \, \mathsf{d})$. Their fingerprints are

$$\mathcal{F}p(s) = (\mathsf{A}, \mathsf{B}, \mathsf{f}, \mathsf{B}, \mathsf{B}, \mathsf{b}, \mathsf{c}) \qquad \mathcal{F}p(t) = (\mathsf{g}, \mathsf{a}, \mathsf{A}, \mathsf{N}, \mathsf{N}, \mathsf{B}, \mathsf{d})$$

The terms are not unifiable due to the incompatibility at position 1.1 (c versus d).

We can easily support prefix optimization for both terms s and t being compared: We ensure that s and t are fully applied, by adding enough fresh variables as arguments, before computing their fingerprints.

6 Inference Rules

Saturating provers try to show the unsatisfiability of a set of clauses by systematically adding logical consequences (up to simplification and redundancy), eventually deriving the empty clause as an explicit witness of unsatisfiability. They employ two kinds of inference rules: *generating rules* produce new clauses and are necessary for completeness, whereas *simplification rules* delete existing clauses or replace them by simpler clauses. This simplification is crucial for success, and most modern provers spend a large part of their time on simplification.

Ehoh implements essentially the same logical calculus as E, except that it is generalized to λfHOL terms. The standard inference rules and completeness proof of superposition can be reused verbatim; the only changes concern the basic definitions of terms and substitutions [7, Sect. 1].

The Generating Rules. The superposition calculus consists of the following four core generating rules, whose conclusions are added to the proof state:

$$\frac{s \not\approx s' \vee C}{\sigma(C)} \text{ ER} \qquad\qquad \frac{s \approx t \vee s' \approx u \vee C}{\sigma(t \not\approx u \vee s \approx u \vee C)} \text{ EF}$$

$$\frac{s \approx t \vee C \qquad u[s'] \not\approx v \vee D}{\sigma(u[t] \not\approx v \vee C \vee D)} \text{ SN} \qquad\qquad \frac{s \approx t \vee C \qquad u[s'] \approx v \vee D}{\sigma(u[t] \approx v \vee C \vee D)} \text{ SP}$$

In each rule, σ denotes the MGU of s and s'. Not shown are order- and selection-based side conditions that restrict the rules' applicability.

Equality resolution and factoring (ER and EF) work on entire terms that occur on either side of a literal occurring in the given clause. To generalize them, it suffices to disable prefix optimization for our unification algorithm. By contrast, the rules for superposition into negative and positive literals (SN and SP) are more complex. As two-premise rules, they require the prover to find a partner for the given clause. There are two cases to consider.

To cover the case where the given clause acts as the left premise, the prover relies on a fingerprint index to compute a set of clauses containing terms possibly unifiable with a side s of a positive literal of the given clause. Thanks to our generalization of fingerprints, in Ehoh this candidate set is guaranteed to overapproximate the set of all possible inference partners. The unification algorithm is then applied to filter out unsuitable candidates. Thanks to prefix optimization, we can avoid gracelessly polluting the index with all prefix subterms.

For the case where the given clause is the right premise, the prover traverses its subterms s' looking for inference partners in another fingerprint index, which contains only entire left- and right-hand sides of equalities. Like E, Ehoh traverses subterms in a first-order fashion. If prefix unification succeeds, Ehoh determines the unified prefix and applies the appropriate inference instance.

The Simplifying Rules. Unlike generating rules, simplifying rules do not necessarily add conclusions to the proof state—they can also remove premises. E implements over a dozen simplifying rules, with unconditional rewriting and clause subsumption as the most significant examples. Here, we restrict our attention to a single rule, which best illustrates the challenges of supporting λfHOL:

$$\frac{s \approx t \qquad u[\sigma(s)] \approx u[\sigma(t)] \vee C}{s \approx t} \text{ ES}$$

Given an equation $s \approx t$, equality subsumption (ES) removes a clause containing a literal whose two sides are equal except that an instance of s appears on one side where the corresponding instance of t appears on the other side.

E maintains a perfect discrimination tree that stores clauses of the form $s \approx t$ indexed by s and t. When applying the ES rule, E considers each literal $u \approx v$ of the given clause in turn. It starts by taking the left-hand side u as a query term. If an equation $s \approx t$ (or $t \approx s$) is found in the tree, with $\sigma(s) = u$, the prover checks whether $\sigma'(t) = v$ for some extension σ' of σ. If so, ES is applicable. To consider nonempty contexts, the prover traverses the subterms u' and v' of u and v in lockstep, as long as they appear under identical contexts. Thanks to prefix optimization, when Ehoh is given a subterm u', it can find an equation $s \approx t$ in the tree such that $\sigma(s)$ is equal to some prefix of u', with n arguments $\overline{u_n}$ remaining as unmatched. Checking for equality subsumption then amounts to checking that $v' = \sigma'(t) \, \overline{u_n}$, for some extension σ' of σ.

For example, let f (g a b) $\approx$ f (h g b) be the given clause, and suppose that x a $\approx$ h x is indexed. Under context f [ ], Ehoh considers the subterms g a b and h x b. It finds the prefix g a of g a b in the tree, with $\sigma = \{x \mapsto g\}$. The prefix h g of h g b matches the indexed equation's right-hand side h x using the same substitution, and the remaining argument in both subterms, b, is identical.

7   Heuristics

E's heuristics are largely independent of the prover's logic and work unchanged for Ehoh. On first-order problems, Ehoh's behavior is virtually the same as E's. Yet, in preliminary experiments, we observed that some λfHOL benchmarks were proved quickly by E in conjunction with the applicative encoding (Sect. 1) but timed out with Ehoh. Based on these observations, we extended the heuristics.

Term Order Generation. The inference rules and the redundancy criterion are parameterized by a term order (Sect. 3). E can generate a *symbol weight* function (for KBO) and a *symbol precedence* (for KBO and LPO) based on criteria such as the symbols' frequencies and whether they appear in the conjecture.

In preliminary experiments, we discovered that the presence of an explicit application operator @ can be beneficial for some problems. With the applicative encoding, generation schemes can take the symbols $@_{\tau,\upsilon}$ into account, effectively exploiting the type information carried by such symbols. To simulate this behavior, we introduced four generation schemes that extend E's existing symbol-frequency-based schemes by partitioning the symbols by type. To each symbol, the new schemes assign a frequency corresponding to the sum of all symbol frequencies for its class. In addition, we designed four schemes that combine E's type-agnostic and Ehoh's type-aware approaches.

To generate symbol precedences, E can sort symbols by weight and use the symbol's position in the sorted array as the basis for precedence. To account for the type information introduced by the applicative encoding, we implemented four type-aware precedence generation schemes.

Literal Selection. The side conditions of the superposition rules (SN and SP, Sect. 6) allow the use of a literal selection function to restrict the set of *inference literals*, thereby pruning the search space. Given a clause, a literal selection function returns a (possibly empty) subset of its literals. For completeness, any nonempty subset selected must contain at least one negative literal. If no literal is selected, all *maximal* literals become inference literals. The most widely used function in E is probably `SelectMaxLComplexAvoidPosPred`, which we abbreviate to `SelectMLCAPP`. It selects at most one negative literal, based on size, groundness, and maximality of the literal in the clause. It also avoids negative literals that share a predicate symbol with a positive literal in the same clause.

Clause Selection. Selection of the given clause is a critical choice point. E heuristically assigns *clause priorities* and *clause weights* to the candidates. E's main loop visits, in round-robin fashion, a set of priority queues. From each queue, it selects a number of clauses with the highest priorities, breaking ties by preferring smaller weights.

E provides template weight functions that allow users to fine-tune parameters such as weights assigned to variables or function symbols. The most widely used template is `ConjectureRelativeSymbolWeight`. It computes term and clause weights according to eight parameters, notably *conj_mul*, a multiplier applied to the weight of conjecture symbols. We implemented a new type-aware template function, called `ConjectureRelativeSymbolTypeWeight`, that applies the *conj_mul* multiplier to all symbols whose type occurs in the conjecture.

Configurations and Modes. A combination of parameters—including term order, literal selection, and clause selection—is called a *configuration*. For years, E has provided an *auto* mode, which analyzes the input problem and chooses a configuration known to perform well on similar problems. More recently, E has been extended with an *autoschedule* mode, which applies a portfolio of configurations in sequence on the given problem. Configurations that perform well on a wide range of problems have emerged over time. One of them is the configuration that is most often chosen by E's *auto* mode. We call it *boa* ("best of *auto*").

8   Evaluation

In this section, we consider the following questions: How useful are Ehoh's new heuristics? And how does Ehoh perform compared with the previous version of E, 2.2, used directly or in conjunction with the applicative encoding, and compared with other provers? To answer the first question, we evaluated each new parameter independently. From the empirical results, we derived a new configuration optimized for λfHOL problems. To answer the second question, we compared Ehoh's success rate on λfHOL problems with native higher-order provers and with E's on their applicatively encoded counterparts. We also included first-order benchmarks to measure Ehoh's overhead with respect to E.

We set a CPU time limit of 60 s per problem. The experiments were performed on StarExec [28] nodes equipped with Intel Xeon E5-2609 0 CPUs clocked at 2.40 GHz and with 8192 MB of memory. Our raw data are publicly available.[2]

We used the *boa* configuration as the basis to evaluate the new heuristic schemes. For each heuristic parameter we tuned, we changed only its value while keeping the other parameters the same as for *boa*. All heuristic parameters were tested on a 5012 problem suite generated using Sledgehammer, consisting of four versions of the Judgment Day [11] suite. Our main findings are as follows:

- The combination of the weight generation scheme `invtypefreqrank` and the precedence generation scheme `invtypefreq` performs best.
- The literal selection heuristics `SelectMLCAPP`, `SelectMLCAPPPreferAppVar`, and `SelectMLCAPPAvoidAppVar` give virtually the same results.
- The clause selection function `ConjectureRelativeSymbolTypeWeight` with `ConstPrio` priority and an *appv_mul* factor of 1.41 performs best.

We derived a new configuration from *boa*, called *hoboa*, by enabling the features identified in the first and third points. Below, we present a more detailed evaluation of *hoboa*, along with other configurations, on a larger benchmark suite. The benchmarks are partitioned as follows: (1) 1147 first-order TPTP [29] problems belonging to the FOF (untyped) and TF0 (monomorphic) categories, excluding arithmetic; (2) 5012 Sledgehammer-generated problems from the Judgment Day [11] suite, targeting the monomorphic first-order logic embodied by TPTP TF0; (3) all 530 monomorphic higher-order problems from the TH0 category of the TPTP library belonging to the λfHOL fragment; (4) 5012 Judgment Day problems targeting the λfHOL fragment of TPTP TH0.

For the first group of benchmarks, we randomly chose 1000 FOF problems (out of 8172) and all monomorphic TFF problems that are parsable by E. Both groups of Sledgehammer problems include two subgroups of 2506 problems, generated to include 32 or 512 Isabelle lemmas (SH32 and SH512), to represent both smaller and larger problems arising in interactive verification. Each subgroup itself consists of two sub-subgroups of 1253 problems, generated by using either λ-lifting or SK-style combinators to encode λ-expressions.

We evaluated Ehoh against Leo-III and Satallax and a version of E, called @+E, that first performs the applicative encoding. Leo-III and Satallax have the advantage that they can instantiate higher-order variables by λ-terms. Thus, some formulas that are provable by these two systems may be nontheorems for @+E and Ehoh. A simple example is the conjecture $\exists f.\ \forall x\ y.\ f\ x\ y \approx \mathsf{g}\ y\ x$, whose proof requires taking $\lambda x\ y.\ \mathsf{g}\ y\ x$ as the witness for f.

We also evaluated E, @+E, Ehoh, and Leo-III on first-order benchmarks. The number of problems each system proved is given in Fig. 1. We considered the E modes *auto* (a) and *autoschedule* (as) and the configurations *boa* (b) and *hoboa* (hb).

---

[2] http://matryoshka.gforge.inria.fr/pubs/ehoh_results.tar.gz.

	First-order			Higher-order		
	TPTP	SH32	SH512	TPTP	SH32	SH512
E a	598	939	1234			
E as	**645**	950	**1311**			
E b	546	944	1243			
@+E a	526	943	1114	395	962	1119
@+E as	567	950	1151	397	965	1155
@+E b	538	942	1228	397	960	1272
Ehoh a	599	938	1233	396	962	1240
Ehoh as	644	949	1310	395	**973**	**1325**
Ehoh b	547	944	1243	396	966	1244
Ehoh hb	502	944	1231	393	968	1262
Leo-III	542	**951**	1126	**421**	963	1145
Satallax				406	768	790

Fig. 1. Number of proved problems

We observe the following:

- Comparing the Ehoh rows with the corresponding E rows, we see that Ehoh's overhead is barely noticeable—the difference is at most one problem. The raw evaluation data reveal that Ehoh's time overhead is about 3.7%.
- Ehoh generally outperforms the applicative encoding, on both first-order and higher-order problems. On Sledgehammer benchmarks, the best Ehoh mode (*autoschedule*) clearly outperforms all @+E modes and configurations. Despite this, there are problems that @+E proves faster than Ehoh.
- Especially on large benchmarks, the E variants are substantially more successful than Leo-III and Satallax. On the other hand, Leo-III emerges as the winner on the first-order SH32 benchmark set, presumably thanks to the combination of first-order backends (CVC4, E, and iProver) it depends on.
- The new *hoboa* configuration outperforms *boa* on higher-order problems, suggesting that it could be worthwhile to re-train *auto* and *autoschedule* based on λfHOL benchmarks and to design further heuristics.

9 Discussion and Related Work

Most higher-order provers were developed from the ground up. Two exceptions are Otter-λ by Beeson [6] and Zipperposition by Cruanes [14]. Otter-λ adds λ-terms and second-order unification to the superposition-based Otter. The approach is pragmatic, with little emphasis on completeness. Zipperposition is a superposition-based prover written in OCaml. It was initially designed for first-order logic but subsequently extended to higher-order logic. Its performance is a far cry from E's, but it is easier to modify. It is used by Bentkamp et al. [7] for experimenting with higher-order features. Finally, there is noteworthy preliminary work by the developers of Vampire [10] and of CVC4 and veriT [4].

Native higher-order reasoning was pioneered by Robinson [22], Andrews [1], and Huet [16]. TPS, by Andrews et al. [2], was based on expansion proofs and let users specify proof outlines. The Leo systems, developed by Benzmüller and his colleagues, are based on resolution and paramodulation. LEO [8] introduced the cooperative paradigm to integrate first-order provers. Leo-III [27] expands the cooperation with SMT (satisfiability modulo theories) solvers and introduces term orders. Brown's Satallax [12] is based on a higher-order tableau calculus, guided by a SAT solver; recent versions also cooperate with first-order provers.

An alternative to all of the above is to reduce higher-order logic to first-order logic by means of a translation. Robinson [23] outlined this approach decades before tools such as Sledgehammer [21] and HOLyHammer [17] popularized it in proof assistants. In addition to performing an applicative encoding, such translations must eliminate the λ-expressions and encode the type information.

By removing the need for the applicative encoding, our work reduces the translation gap. The encoding buries the λfHOL terms' heads under layers of @ symbols. Terms double in size, cluttering the data structures, and twice as many subterm positions must be considered for inferences. Moreover, encoding is incompatible with interpreted operators, notably for arithmetic. A further complication is that in a monomorphic logic, @ is not a single symbol but a type-indexed family of symbols $@_{\tau,\upsilon}$, which must be correctly introduced and recognized. Finally, the encoding must be undone in the generated proofs. While it should be possible to base a higher-order prover on such an encoding, the prospect is aesthetically and technically unappealing, and performance would likely suffer.

10   Conclusion

Despite considerable progress since the 1970s, higher-order automated reasoning has not yet assimilated some of the most successful methods for first-order logic with equality, such as superposition. We presented a graceful extension of a state-of-the-art first-order theorem prover to a fragment of higher-order logic devoid of λ-terms. Our work covers both theoretical and practical aspects. Experiments show promising results on λ-free higher-order problems and very little overhead for first-order problems, as we would expect from a graceful generalization.

The resulting Ehoh prover will form the basis of our work towards strong higher-order automation. Our aim is to turn it into a prover that excels on proof obligations emerging from interactive verification; in our experience, these tend to be large but only mildly higher-order. Our next steps will be to extend E's term data structure with λ-expressions and investigate techniques for computing higher-order unifiers efficiently.

Acknowledgment. We are grateful to the maintainers of StarExec for letting us use their service. We thank Ahmed Bhayat, Alexander Bentkamp, Daniel El Ouraoui, Michael Färber, Pascal Fontaine, Predrag Janičić, Robert Lewis, Tomer Libal, Giles Reger, Hans-Jörg Schurr, Alexander Steen, Mark Summerfield, Dmitriy Traytel, and the anonymous reviewers for suggesting many improvements to this text. We also want to thank the other members of the Matryoshka team, including Sophie Tourret and Uwe Waldmann, as well as Christoph Benzmüller, Andrei Voronkov, Daniel Wand, and Christoph Weidenbach, for many stimulating discussions.

Vukmirović and Blanchette's research has received funding from the European Research Council (ERC) under the European Union's Horizon 2020 research and innovation program (grant agreement No. 713999, Matryoshka). Blanchette has received funding from the Netherlands Organization for Scientific Research (NWO) under the Vidi program (project No. 016.Vidi.189.037, Lean Forward). He also benefited from the NWO Incidental Financial Support scheme.

References

1. Andrews, P.B.: Resolution in type theory. J. Symb. Log. **36**(3), 414–432 (1971)
2. Andrews, P.B., Bishop, M., Issar, S., Nesmith, D., Pfenning, F., Xi, H.: TPS: a theorem-proving system for classical type theory. J. Autom. Reason. **16**(3), 321–353 (1996)
3. Baader, F., Nipkow, T.: Term Rewriting and All That. Cambridge University Press, Cambridge (1998)
4. Barbosa, H., Reynolds, A., Fontaine, P., Ouraoui, D.E., Tinelli, C.: Higher-order SMT solving (work in progress). In: Dimitrova, R., D'Silva, V. (eds.) SMT 2018 (2018)
5. Becker, H., Blanchette, J.C., Waldmann, U., Wand, D.: A transfinite Knuth–Bendix order for lambda-free higher-order terms. In: de Moura, L. (ed.) CADE 2017. LNCS (LNAI), vol. 10395, pp. 432–453. Springer, Cham (2017). https://doi.org/10.1007/978-3-319-63046-5_27
6. Beeson, M.: Lambda logic. In: Basin, D., Rusinowitch, M. (eds.) IJCAR 2004. LNCS (LNAI), vol. 3097, pp. 460–474. Springer, Heidelberg (2004). https://doi.org/10.1007/978-3-540-25984-8_34
7. Bentkamp, A., Blanchette, J.C., Cruanes, S., Waldmann, U.: Superposition for lambda-free higher-order logic. In: Galmiche, D., Schulz, S., Sebastiani, R. (eds.) IJCAR 2018. LNCS (LNAI), vol. 10900, pp. 28–46. Springer, Cham (2018). https://doi.org/10.1007/978-3-319-94205-6_3
8. Benzmüller, C., Kohlhase, M.: System description: Leo—a higher-order theorem prover. In: Kirchner, C., Kirchner, H. (eds.) CADE 1998. LNCS (LNAI), vol. 1421, pp. 139–143. Springer, Heidelberg (1998). https://doi.org/10.1007/BFb0054256
9. Benzmüller, C., Sultana, N., Paulson, L.C., Theiss, F.: The higher-order prover LEO-II. J. Autom. Reason. **55**(4), 389–404 (2015)
10. Bhayat, A., Reger, G.: Set of support for higher-order reasoning. In: Konev, B., Urban, J., Rümmer, P. (eds.) PAAR-2018, CEUR Workshop Proceedings, vol. 2162, pp. 2–16. CEUR-WS.org (2018)
11. Böhme, S., Nipkow, T.: Sledgehammer: Judgement Day. In: Giesl, J., Hähnle, R. (eds.) IJCAR 2010. LNCS (LNAI), vol. 6173, pp. 107–121. Springer, Heidelberg (2010). https://doi.org/10.1007/978-3-642-14203-1_9
12. Brown, C.E.: Satallax: an automatic higher-order prover. In: Gramlich, B., Miller, D., Sattler, U. (eds.) IJCAR 2012. LNCS (LNAI), vol. 7364, pp. 111–117. Springer, Heidelberg (2012). https://doi.org/10.1007/978-3-642-31365-3_11
13. Cruanes, S.: Extending Superposition with Integer Arithmetic, Structural Induction, and Beyond. PhD thesis, École polytechnique (2015). https://who.rocq.inria.fr/Simon.Cruanes/files/thesis.pdf

14. Cruanes, S.: Superposition with structural induction. In: Dixon, C., Finger, M. (eds.) FroCoS 2017. LNCS (LNAI), vol. 10483, pp. 172–188. Springer, Cham (2017). https://doi.org/10.1007/978-3-319-66167-4_10
15. Filliâtre, J.-C., Paskevich, A.: Why3—where programs meet provers. In: Felleisen, M., Gardner, P. (eds.) ESOP 2013. LNCS, vol. 7792, pp. 125–128. Springer, Heidelberg (2013). https://doi.org/10.1007/978-3-642-37036-6_8
16. Huet, G.P.: A mechanization of type theory. In: Nilsson, N.J. (ed.) IJCAI-73, pp. 139–146. Morgan Kaufmann Publishers Inc., Burlington (1973)
17. Kaliszyk, C., Urban, J.: HOL(y)Hammer: online ATP service for HOL light. Math. Comput. Sci. **9**(1), 5–22 (2015)
18. Kovács, L., Voronkov, A.: First-order theorem proving and VAMPIRE. In: Sharygina, N., Veith, H. (eds.) CAV 2013. LNCS, vol. 8044, pp. 1–35. Springer, Heidelberg (2013). https://doi.org/10.1007/978-3-642-39799-8_1
19. Lochner, B.: Things to know when implementing KBO. J. Autom. Reason. **36**(4), 289–310 (2006)
20. McCune, W.: Experiments with discrimination-tree indexing and path indexing for term retrieval. J. Autom. Reason. **9**(2), 147–167 (1992)
21. Paulson, L.C., Blanchette, J.C.: Three years of experience with Sledgehammer, a practical link between automatic and interactive theorem provers. In: Sutcliffe, G., Schulz, S., Ternovska, E. (eds.) IWIL-2010. EPiC, vol. 2, pp. 1–11. EasyChair (2012)
22. Robinson, J.: Mechanizing higher order logic. In: Meltzer, B., Michie, D. (eds.) Machine Intelligence, vol. 4, pp. 151–170. Edinburgh University Press, Edinburgh (1969)
23. Robinson, J.: A note on mechanizing higher order logic. In: Meltzer, B., Michie, D. (eds.) Machine Intelligence, vol. 5, pp. 121–135. Edinburgh University Press, Edinburgh (1970)
24. Schulz, S.: Fingerprint indexing for paramodulation and rewriting. In: Gramlich, B., Miller, D., Sattler, U. (eds.) IJCAR 2012. LNCS (LNAI), vol. 7364, pp. 477–483. Springer, Heidelberg (2012). https://doi.org/10.1007/978-3-642-31365-3_37
25. Schulz, S.: Simple and efficient clause subsumption with feature vector indexing. In: Bonacina, M.P., Stickel, M.E. (eds.) Automated Reasoning and Mathematics. LNCS (LNAI), vol. 7788, pp. 45–67. Springer, Heidelberg (2013). https://doi.org/10.1007/978-3-642-36675-8_3
26. Schulz, S.: System description: E 1.8. In: McMillan, K., Middeldorp, A., Voronkov, A. (eds.) LPAR 2013. LNCS, vol. 8312, pp. 735–743. Springer, Heidelberg (2013). https://doi.org/10.1007/978-3-642-45221-5_49
27. Steen, A., Benzmüller, C.: The higher-order prover Leo-III. In: Galmiche, D., Schulz, S., Sebastiani, R. (eds.) IJCAR 2018. LNCS (LNAI), vol. 10900, pp. 108–116. Springer, Cham (2018). https://doi.org/10.1007/978-3-319-94205-6_8
28. Stump, A., Sutcliffe, G., Tinelli, C.: StarExec: a cross-community infrastructure for logic solving. In: Demri, S., Kapur, D., Weidenbach, C. (eds.) IJCAR 2014. LNCS (LNAI), vol. 8562, pp. 367–373. Springer, Cham (2014). https://doi.org/10.1007/978-3-319-08587-6_28
29. Sutcliffe, G.: The TPTP problem library and associated infrastructure. From CNF to TH0, TPTP v6.4.0. J. Autom. Reason. **59**(4), 483–502 (2017)
30. Sutcliffe, G.: The CADE-26 automated theorem proving system competition–CASC-26. AI Commun. **30**(6), 419–432 (2017)
31. Vukmirović, P.: Implementation of Lambda-Free Higher-Order Superposition. MSc thesis, Vrije Universiteit Amsterdam (2018). http://matryoshka.gforge.inria.fr/pubs/vukmirovic_msc_thesis.pdf

32. Vukmirović, P., Blanchette, J.C., Cruanes, S., Schulz, S.: Extending a brainiac prover to lambda-free higher-order logic (technical report). Technical report (2019). http://matryoshka.gforge.inria.fr/pubs/ehoh_report.pdf

33. Weidenbach, C., Dimova, D., Fietzke, A., Kumar, R., Suda, M., Wischnewski, P.: SPASS version 3.5. In: Schmidt, R.A. (ed.) CADE 2009. LNCS (LNAI), vol. 5663, pp. 140–145. Springer, Heidelberg (2009). https://doi.org/10.1007/978-3-642-02959-2_10

4

Computing Coupled Similarity

Benjamin Bisping[(✉)][iD] and Uwe Nestmann[iD]

Technische Universität Berlin, Berlin, Germany
{benjamin.bisping,uwe.nestmann}@tu-berlin.de

Abstract. *Coupled similarity* is a notion of equivalence for systems with internal actions. It has outstanding applications in contexts where internal choices must transparently be distributed in time or space, for example, in process calculi encodings or in action refinements. No tractable algorithms for the computation of coupled similarity have been proposed up to now. Accordingly, there has not been any tool support.

We present a *game-theoretic algorithm to compute coupled similarity*, running in cubic time and space with respect to the number of states in the input transition system. We show that one cannot hope for much better because deciding the coupled simulation preorder is at least as hard as deciding the weak simulation preorder.

Our results are backed by an *Isabelle/HOL* formalization, as well as by a parallelized implementation using the *Apache Flink* framework. Data or code related to this paper is available at: [2].

1 Introduction

Coupled similarity hits a sweet spot within the *linear-time branching-time spectrum* [9]. At that spot, one can encode between brands of process calculi [14, 22, 25], name a branching-time semantics for Communicating Sequential Processes [10], distribute synchronizations [23], and refine atomic actions [5, 28]. Weak bisimilarity is too strong for these applications due to the occurrence of situations with *partially commited states* like in the following example.

Example 1 (Gradually committing philosophers). Three philosophers A, B, and C want to eat pasta. To do so, they must first sit down on a bench s and grab a fork f. Unfortunately, only either A alone or the thinner B and C together can fit on the bench, and there is just one fork. From the outside, we are only interested in the fact which of them gets to eat. So we consider the whole bench-and-fork business internal to the system. The following CCS structure models the situation in the notation of [21]. The resources correspond to output actions (which can be consumed only once) and obtaining the resources corresponds to input actions.

$$P_g \stackrel{\text{def}}{=} \left(\bar{s} \mid \bar{f} \mid \text{s.f.A} \mid \text{s.}(\text{f.B} \mid \text{f.C}) \right) \setminus \{\text{s,f}\}$$

$$A \stackrel{\text{def}}{=} \text{aEats.A} \qquad B \stackrel{\text{def}}{=} \text{bEats.B}$$

$$C \stackrel{\text{def}}{=} \text{cEats.C}$$

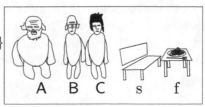

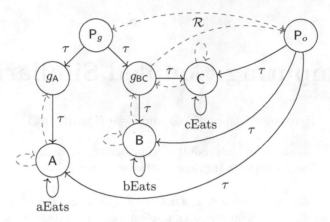

Fig. 1. A non-maximal weak/coupled simulation $\mathcal{R}$ on the philosopher system from Example 1. (Color figure online)

One might now be inclined to ponder that exactly one of the philosophers will get both resources and that we thus could merge s and f into a single resource sf:

$$\mathsf{P}_o \overset{\mathrm{def}}{=} \quad \left(\overline{\mathrm{sf}} \quad | \quad \mathrm{sf.A} \mid \mathrm{sf.B} \mid \mathrm{sf.C}\right) \setminus \{\mathrm{sf}\}$$

The structure of P_g and P_o has the transition system in Fig. 1 as its semantics. Notice that the internal communication concerning the resource allocation turns into internal τ-actions, which in P_g, g_A, and g_BC *gradually decide* who is going to eat the pasta, whereas P_o *decides in one step*.

P_g and P_o are mutually related by a weak simulation (blue dashed lines in Fig. 1) and hence *weakly similar*. However, there cannot be a *symmetric* weak simulation relating them because $\mathsf{P}_g \overset{\tau}{\to} g_\mathsf{BC}$ cannot be matched symmetrically by P_o as no other reachable state shares the weakly enabled actions of g_BC. Thus, they are *not weakly bisimilar*. This counters the intuition that weak bisimilarity ignores how much internal behavior happens between visible actions. There seems to be no good argument how an outside observer should notice the difference whether an internal choice is made in one or two steps.

So how to fix this overzealousness of weak bisimilarity? Falling back to weak similarity would be too coarse for many applications because it lacks the property of weak bisimilarity to coincide with strong bisimilarity on systems without internal behavior. This property, however, is present in notions that refine *contrasimilarity* [31]. There is an easy way to having the cake and eating it, here: *Coupled similarity* is precisely the intersection of contrasimilarity and weak similarity (Fig. 2). It can be defined by adding a weak form of symmetry (*coupling*) to weak simulation. The weak simulation in Fig. 1 fulfills coupling and thus is a coupled simulation. This shows that coupled similarity is coarse enough for situations with gradual commitments. At the same time, it is a close fit for weak bisimilarity, with which it coincides for many systems.

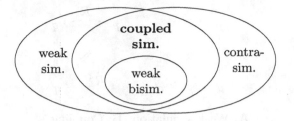

Fig. 2. Notions of equivalence for systems with internal actions.

Up to now, no algorithms and tools have been developed to enable a wider use of coupled similarity in automated verification settings. Parrow and Sjödin [24] have only hinted at an exponential-space algorithm and formulated as an open research question whether coupled similarity can be decided in **P**. For similarity and bisimilarity, polynomial algorithms exist. The best algorithms for weak bisimilarity [3,19,26] are slightly sub-cubic in time, $\mathcal{O}(|S|^2 \log |S|)$ for transition systems with $|S|$ states. The best algorithms for similarity [15,27], adapted for weak similarity, are cubic. Such a slope between similarity and bisimilarity is common [18]. As we show, coupled similarity inherits the higher complexity of weak similarity. Still, the closeness to weak bisimilarity can be exploited to speed up computations.

Contributions. This paper makes the following contributions.

- We prove that action-based single-relation *coupled similarity can be defined in terms of coupled delay simulation* (Subsect. 2.2).
- We *reduce weak similarity to coupled similarity*, thereby showing that deciding coupled similarity inherits the complexity of weak similarity (Subsect. 2.4).
- We present and verify a simple polynomial-time *coupled simulation fixed-point algorithm* (Sect. 3).
- We *characterize the coupled simulation preorder by a game and give an algorithm*, which runs in cubic time and can be nicely optimized (Sect. 4)
- We *implement the game algorithm for parallel computation using Apache Flink* and benchmark its performance (Sect. 5).

Technical details can be found in the first author's Master's thesis [1]. Isabelle/ HOL [32] proofs are available from https://coupledsim.bbisping.de/isabelle/.

2 Coupled Similarity

This section characterizes the coupled simulation preorder for transition systems with silent steps in terms of coupled delay simulation. We prove properties that are key to the correctness of the following algorithms.

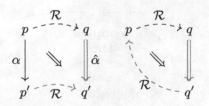

A: Weak simulation **B:** Coupling

Fig. 3. Illustration of weak simulation and coupling on transition systems (Definition 4, black part implies red part). (Color figure online)

2.1 Transition Systems with Silent Steps

Labeled transition systems capture a discrete world view, where there is a current state and a branching structure of possible state changes ("transitions") to future states.

Definition 1 (Labeled transition system). *A* labeled transition system *is a tuple* $\mathcal{S} = (S, \Sigma_\tau, \rightarrow)$ *where S is a set of* states, Σ_τ *is a set of* actions *containing a special* internal action $\tau \in \Sigma_\tau$, *and* $\rightarrow \subseteq S \times \Sigma_\tau \times S$ *is the* transition relation. *We call* $\Sigma := \Sigma_\tau \setminus \{\tau\}$ *the* visible actions.

  The weak transition relation $\overset{\hat{\ }}{\Rightarrow}$ *is defined as the reflexive transitive closure of internal steps* $\overset{\hat{\tau}}{\Rightarrow} := \overset{\tau}{\rightarrow}^*$ *combined with* $\overset{\hat{a}}{\Rightarrow} := \overset{\hat{\tau}}{\Rightarrow}\overset{a}{\rightarrow}\overset{\hat{\tau}}{\Rightarrow}$ *($a \in \Sigma$).*

As a shorthand for $\overset{\hat{\tau}}{\Rightarrow}$, we also write just $\Rightarrow$. We call an $\overset{\hat{a}}{\Rightarrow}$-step "weak" whereas an $\overset{\alpha}{\rightarrow}$-step is referred to as "strong" ($\alpha \in \Sigma_\tau$). A visible action $a \in \Sigma$ is said to be *weakly enabled* in p iff there is some p' such that $p \overset{\hat{a}}{\Rightarrow} p'$.

Definition 2 (Stability and divergence). *A state p is called* stable *iff it has no τ-transitions, $p \not\overset{\tau}{\rightarrow}$. A state p is called* divergent *iff it is possible to perform an infinite sequence of τ-transitions beginning in this state, $p \overset{\tau}{\rightarrow}^\omega$.*

2.2 Defining Coupled Similarity

Coupled simulation is often defined in terms of two *weak simulations*, but it is more convenient to use just a single one [10], which extends weak simulation with a weak form of symmetry, we shall call *coupling* (Fig. 3).

Definition 3 (Weak simulation). *A* weak simulation *is a relation $\mathcal{R} \subseteq S \times S$ such that, for all $(p, q) \in \mathcal{R}$, $p \overset{\alpha}{\rightarrow} p'$ implies that there is a q' such that $q \overset{\hat{\alpha}}{\Rightarrow} q'$ and $(p', q') \in \mathcal{R}$.*

Definition 4 (Coupled simulation). *A* coupled simulation *is a weak simulation $\mathcal{R} \subseteq S \times S$ such that, for all $(p, q) \in \mathcal{R}$, there exists a q' such that $q \Rightarrow q'$ and $(q', p) \in \mathcal{R}$ (coupling).*

The coupled simulation preorder *relates two processes,* $p \sqsubseteq_{CS} q$, *iff there is a coupled simulation* $\mathcal{R}$ *such that* $(p, q) \in \mathcal{R}$. Coupled similarity *relates two processes,* $p \equiv_{CS} q$, *iff* $p \sqsubseteq_{CS} q$ *and* $q \sqsubseteq_{CS} p$.

Adapting words from [10], $p \sqsubseteq_{CS} q$ intuitively does not only mean that "*p* is *ahead* of *q*" (weak simulation), but also that "*q* can *catch up* to *p*" (coupling). The weak simulation on the philosopher transition system from Example 1 is coupled.

Coupled similarity can also be characterized employing an effectively stronger concept than weak simulation, namely *delay simulation*. Delay simulations [11, 28] are defined in terms of a "shortened" weak step relation $\overset{\alpha}{\Rightarrow}$ where $\overset{\tau}{\Rightarrow} := \mathrm{id}$ and $\overset{a}{\Rightarrow} := \Rightarrow \overset{a}{\rightarrow}$. So the difference between $\overset{a}{\Rightarrow}$ and $\overset{\hat{a}}{\Rightarrow}$ lies in the fact that the latter can move on with τ-steps after the strong $\overset{a}{\rightarrow}$-step in its construction.

Definition 5 (Coupled delay simulation). *A coupled delay simulation is a relation* $\mathcal{R} \subseteq S \times S$ *such that, for all* $(p, q) \in \mathcal{R}$,

- $p \overset{\alpha}{\rightarrow} p'$ *implies there is a* q' *such that* $q \overset{\alpha}{\Rightarrow} q'$ *and* $(p', q') \in \mathcal{R}$ *(delay simulation),*
- *and there exists a* q' *such that* $q \Rightarrow q'$ *and* $(q', p) \in \mathcal{R}$ *(coupling).*

The only difference to Definition 4 is the use of $\overset{\alpha}{\Rightarrow}$ instead of $\overset{\hat{\alpha}}{\Rightarrow}$. Some coupled simulations are no (coupled) delay simulations, for example, consider $\mathcal{R} = \{(\mathrm{c}.\tau, \mathrm{c}.\tau), (\tau, \mathbf{0}), (\mathbf{0}, \tau), (\mathbf{0}, \mathbf{0})\}$ on CCS processes. Still, the *greatest* coupled simulation $\sqsubseteq_{CS}$ *is* a coupled delay simulation, which enables the following characterization:

Lemma 1. $p \sqsubseteq_{CS} q$ *precisely if there is a coupled delay simulation* $\mathcal{R}$ *such that* $(p, q) \in \mathcal{R}$.

2.3   Order Properties and Coinduction

Lemma 2. $\sqsubseteq_{CS}$ *forms a preorder, that is, it is reflexive and transitive. Coupled similarity* $\equiv_{CS}$ *is an equivalence relation.*

Lemma 3. *The coupled simulation preorder can be characterized coinductively by the rule:*

$$\frac{\forall p', \alpha.\ p \overset{\alpha}{\rightarrow} p' \longrightarrow \exists q'.\ q \overset{\alpha}{\Rightarrow} q' \wedge p' \sqsubseteq_{CS} q' \qquad \exists q'.\ q \Rightarrow q' \wedge q' \sqsubseteq_{CS} p}{p \sqsubseteq_{CS} q}.$$

This coinductive characterization motivates the fixed-point algorithm (Sect. 3) and the game characterization (Sect. 4) central to this paper.

Lemma 4. *If* $q \Rightarrow p$, *then* $p \sqsubseteq_{CS} q$.

Corollary 1. *If* p *and* q *are on a* τ-*cycle, that means* $p \Rightarrow q$ *and* $q \Rightarrow p$, *then* $p \equiv_{CS} q$.

Ordinary coupled simulation is blind to divergence. In particular, it cannot distinguish two states whose outgoing transitions only differ in an additional τ-loop at the second state:

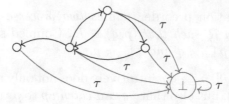

Fig. 4. Example for $\mathcal{S}^{\perp}$ from Theorem 1 ($\mathcal{S}$ in black, $\mathcal{S}^{\perp} \backslash \mathcal{S}$ in red). (Color figure online)

Lemma 5. *If* $p \xrightarrow{\alpha} p' \longleftrightarrow q \xrightarrow{\alpha} p' \vee p' = p \wedge \alpha = \tau$ *for all* α, p', *then* $p \equiv_{CS} q$.

Due to the previous two results, finite systems with divergence can be transformed into $\equiv_{CS}$-equivalent systems without divergence. This connects the original notion of stability-coupled similarity [23, 24] to our modern formulation and motivates the usefulness of the next lemma.

Coupling can be thought of as "weak symmetry." For a relation to be symmetric, $\mathcal{R}^{-1} \subseteq \mathcal{R}$ must hold whereas coupling means that $\mathcal{R}^{-1} \subseteq \Rightarrow\mathcal{R}$. This weakened symmetry of coupled similarity can guarantee weak bisimulation on steps to stable states:

Lemma 6. *Assume* $\mathcal{S}$ *is finite and has no* τ-*cycles. Then* $p \sqsubseteq_{CS} q$ *and* $p \xrightarrow{\hat{\alpha}} p'$ *with stable* p' *imply there is a stable* q' *such that* $q \xrightarrow{\hat{\alpha}} q'$ *and* $p' \equiv_{CS} q'$.

2.4   Reduction of Weak Simulation to Coupled Simulation

Theorem 1. *Every decision algorithm for the coupled simulation preorder in a system* $\mathcal{S}$, $\sqsubseteq_{CS}^{\mathcal{S}}$, *can be used to decide the weak simulation preorder*, $\sqsubseteq_{WS}^{\mathcal{S}}$, *(without relevant overhead with respect to space or time complexity).*

Proof. Let $\mathcal{S} = (S, \Sigma_\tau, \rightarrow)$ be an arbitrary transition system and $\perp \notin S$. Then

$$\mathcal{S}^{\perp} := \Big(S \cup \{\perp\}, \quad \Sigma_\tau, \quad \rightarrow \cup \{(p, \tau, \perp) \mid p \in S \cup \{\perp\}\} \Big)$$

extends $\mathcal{S}$ with a sink $\perp$ that can be reached by a τ-step from everywhere. For an illustration see Fig. 4. Note that for $p, q \neq \perp$, $p \sqsubseteq_{WS}^{\mathcal{S}} q$ exactly if $p \sqsubseteq_{WS}^{\mathcal{S}^{\perp}} q$. On $\mathcal{S}^{\perp}$, coupled simulation preorder and weak simulation preorder coincide, $\sqsubseteq_{WS}^{\mathcal{S}^{\perp}} = \sqsubseteq_{CS}^{\mathcal{S}^{\perp}}$, because $\perp$ is τ-reachable everywhere, and, for each p, $\perp \sqsubseteq_{CS}^{\mathcal{S}^{\perp}} p$ discharges the coupling constraint of coupled simulation.

Because $\sqsubseteq_{WS}^{\mathcal{S}}$ can be decided by deciding $\sqsubseteq_{CS}^{\mathcal{S}^{\perp}}$, a decision procedure for $\sqsubseteq_{CS}$ also induces a decision procedure for $\sqsubseteq_{WS}$. The transformation has linear time in terms of state space size $|S|$ and adds only one state to the problem size.

```
1  def fp_step_(S,Σ_τ,→)(R):
2      return  {(p,q) ∈ R |
3          (∀p', α.  p →ᵅ p' ⟶ ∃q'. (p',q') ∈ R ∧ q ⇒ᵅ q')
4          ∧ (∃q'. q ⇒ q' ∧ (q',p) ∈ R)}
5  def fp_compute_cs(S = (S, Σ_τ, →)):
6      R := S × S
7      while fp_step_S(R) ≠ R:
8        |   R := fp_step_S(R)
9      return R
```

Algorithm 1: Fixed-point algorithm for the coupled simulation preorder.

3   Fixed-Point Algorithm for Coupled Similarity

The coinductive characterization of $\sqsubseteq_{CS}$ in Lemma 3 induces an extremely simple polynomial-time algorithm to compute the coupled simulation preorder as a *greatest fixed point*. This section introduces the algorithm and proves its correctness.

3.1   The Algorithm

Roughly speaking, the algorithm first considers the universal relation between states, $S \times S$, and then proceeds by removing every pair of states from the relation that would contradict the coupling or the simulation property. Its pseudo code is depicted in Algorithm 1.

fp_step plays the role of removing the tuples that would immediately violate the simulation or coupling property from the relation. Of course, such a pruning might invalidate tuples that were not rejected before. Therefore, fp_compute_cs repeats the process until $\text{fp\_step}_S(\mathcal{R}) = \mathcal{R}$, that is, until $\mathcal{R}$ is a fixed point of fp_step_S.

3.2   Correctness and Complexity

It is quite straight-forward to show that Algorithm 1 indeed computes $\sqsubseteq_{CS}$ because of the resemblance between fp_step and the coupled simulation property itself, and because of the monotonicity of fp_step.

Lemma 7. *If $\mathcal{R}$ is the greatest fixed point of* fp_step, *then* $\mathcal{R} = \sqsubseteq_{CS}$.

On finite labeled transition systems, that is, with finite S and $\rightarrow$, the while loop of fp_compute_cs is guaranteed to terminate at the greatest fixed point of fp_step (by a dual variant of the Kleene fixed-point theorem).

Lemma 8. *For finite $\mathcal{S}$,* fp_compute_cs($\mathcal{S}$) *computes the greatest fixed point of* fp_step_S.

Theorem 2. *For finite S, fp_compute_cs(S) returns $\sqsubseteq_{CS}^{S}$.*

We verified the proof using Isabelle/HOL. Due to its simplicity, we can trust implementations of Algorithm 1 to faithfully return sound and complete $\sqsubseteq_{CS}$-relations. Therefore, we use this algorithm to generate reliable results within test suites for the behavior of other $\sqsubseteq_{CS}$-implementations.

The space complexity, given by the maximal size of $\mathcal{R}$, clearly is in $\mathcal{O}(|S|^2)$. Time complexity takes some inspection of the algorithm. For our considerations, we assume that $\overset{\cdot}{\Rightarrow}$ has been pre-computed, which can slightly increase the space complexity to $\mathcal{O}(|\Sigma||S|^2)$.

Lemma 9. *The running time of fp_compute_cs is in $\mathcal{O}(|\Sigma||S|^6)$.*

Proof. Checking the simulation property for a tuple $(p, q) \in \mathcal{R}$ means that for all $\mathcal{O}(|\Sigma||S|)$ outgoing $p\overset{\cdot}{\rightarrow}$-transitions, each has to be matched by a $q\overset{\cdot}{\Rightarrow}$-transition with identical action, of which there are at most $|S|$. So, simulation checking costs $\mathcal{O}(|\Sigma||S|^2)$ time per tuple. Checking the coupling can be approximated by $\mathcal{O}(|S|)$ per tuple. Simulation dominates coupling. The amount of tuples that have to be checked is in $\mathcal{O}(|S|^2)$. Thus, the overall complexity of one invocation of fp_step is in $\mathcal{O}(|\Sigma||S|^4)$.

Because every invocation of fp_step decreases the size of $\mathcal{R}$ or leads to termination, there can be at most $\mathcal{O}(|S|^2)$ invocations of fp_step in fp_compute_cs. Checking whether fp_step changes $\mathcal{R}$ can be done without notable overhead. In conclusion, we arrive at an overall time complexity of $\mathcal{O}(|\Sigma||S|^6)$.

Now, it does not take much energy to spot that applying the filtering in fp_step to each and every tuple in $\mathcal{R}$ in every step, would not be necessary. Only after a tuple (p, q) has been removed from $\mathcal{R}$, the algorithm does really need to find out whether this was the last witness for the $\exists$-quantification in the clause of another tuple. While this observation could inspire various improvements, let us fast-forward to the game-theoretic approach in the next section, which elegantly explicates the witness structure of a coupled similarity problem.

4   Game Algorithm for Coupled Similarity

Checking whether two states are related by a (bi-)simulation preorder $\sqsubseteq_X$ can be seen as a *game* along the lines of coinductive characterizations [30]. One player, the *attacker*, challenges that $p \sqsubseteq_X q$, while the other player, the *defender*, has to name witnesses for the existential quantifications of the definition.

Based on the coinductive characterization from Lemma 3, we here define such a game for the coupled simulation preorder and transform it into an algorithm, which basically only amounts to a more clever way of computing the fixed point of the previous section. We show how this additional layer of abstraction enables optimizations.

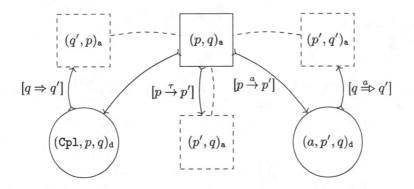

Fig. 5. Schematic coupled simulation game. Boxes stand for attacker nodes, circles for defender nodes, arrows for moves. From the dashed boxes, the moves are analogous to the ones of the solid box.

4.1 The Coupled Simulation Game

The *coupled simulation game* proceeds as follows: For $p \sqsubseteq_{CS} q$, the attacker may question that simulation holds by selecting p' and $a \in \Sigma$ with $p \xrightarrow{a} p'$. The defender then has to name a q' with $q \xRightarrow{a} q'$, whereupon the attacker may go on to challenge $p' \sqsubseteq_{CS} q'$. If $p \xrightarrow{\tau} p'$, the attacker can directly skip to question $p' \sqsubseteq_{CS} q$. For coupled simulation, the attacker may moreover demand the defender to name a coupling witness q' with $q \Rightarrow q'$ whereafter $q' \sqsubseteq_{CS} p$ stands to question. If the defender runs out of answers, they lose; if the game continues forever, they win. This can be modeled by a simple game, whose schema is given in Fig. 5, as follows.

Definition 6 (Games). *A simple game* $\mathcal{G}[p_0] = (G, G_d, \rightarrowtail, p_0)$ *consists of*

- *a (countable) set of* game positions G,
  - *partitioned into a set of* defender positions $G_d \subseteq G$
  - *and* attacker positions $G_a := G \setminus G_d$,
- *a graph of* game moves $\rightarrowtail \subseteq G \times G$, *and*
- *an* initial position $p_0 \in G$.

Definition 7 ($\sqsubseteq_{CS}$ game). *For a transition system* $\mathcal{S} = (S, \Sigma_\tau, \rightarrow)$, *the coupled simulation game* $\mathcal{G}^{\mathcal{S}}_{CS}[p_0] = (G, G_d, \rightarrowtail, p_0)$ *consists of*

- *attacker nodes* $(p, q)_a \in G_a$ *with* $p, q \in S$,
- *simulation defender nodes* $(a, p, q)_d \in G_d$ *for situations where a simulation challenge for* $a \in \Sigma$ *has been formulated, and*
- *coupling defender nodes* $(\mathtt{Cpl}, p, q)_d \in G_d$ *when coupling is challenged,*

and five kinds of moves

- *simulation challenges* $(p, q)_a \rightarrowtail (a, p', q)_d$ *if* $p \xrightarrow{a} p'$ *with* $a \neq \tau$,
- *simulation internal moves* $(p, q)_a \rightarrowtail (p', q)_a$ *if* $p \xrightarrow{\tau} p'$,

  – simulation answers $(a, p', q)_d \rightarrowtail (p', q')_a$ *if* $q \overset{a}{\Rightarrow} q'$,
  – coupling challenges $(p, q)_a \rightarrowtail (\mathrm{Cpl}, p, q)_d$, *and*
  – coupling answers $(\mathrm{Cpl}, p, q)_d \rightarrowtail (q', p)_a$ *if* $q \Rightarrow q'$.

Definition 8 (Plays and wins). *We call the paths $p_0 p_1 ... \in G^\infty$ with $p_i \rightarrowtail p_{i+1}$ plays of $\mathcal{G}[p_0]$. The defender wins all infinite plays. If a finite play $p_0 \ldots p_n$ is stuck, that is, if $p_n \nrightarrow$, then the stuck player loses: The defender wins if $p_n \in G_a$, and the attacker wins if $p_n \in G_d$.*

Definition 9 (Strategies and winning strategies). *A defender strategy is a (usually partial) mapping from initial play fragments to next moves $f \subseteq \{(p_0 ... p_n, p') \mid p_n \in G_d \wedge p_n \rightarrowtail p'\}$. A play p follows a strategy f iff, for each move $p_i \rightarrowtail p_{i+1}$ with $p_i \in G_d$, $p_{i+1} = f(p_0 ... p_i)$. If every such play is won by the defender, f is a winning strategy for the defender. The player with a winning strategy for $\mathcal{G}[p_0]$ is said to win $\mathcal{G}[p_0]$.*

Definition 10 (Winning regions and determinacy). *The winning region W_σ of player $\sigma \in \{a, d\}$ for a game $\mathcal{G}$ is the set of states p_0 from which player σ wins $\mathcal{G}[p_0]$.*

Let us now see that the defender's winning region of $\mathcal{G}^{\mathcal{S}}_{CS}$ indeed corresponds to $\sqsubseteq^{\mathcal{S}}_{CS}$. To this end, we first show how to construct winning strategies for the defender from a coupled simulation, and then establish the opposite direction.

Lemma 10. *Let $\mathcal{R}$ be a coupled delay simulation and $(p_0, q_0) \in \mathcal{R}$. Then the defender wins $\mathcal{G}^{\mathcal{S}}_{CS}[(p_0, q_0)_a]$ with the following positional strategy:*

  – *If the current play fragment ends in a simulation defender node $(a, p', q)_d$, move to some attacker node $(p', q')_a$ with $(p', q') \in \mathcal{R}$ and $q \overset{a}{\Rightarrow} q'$;*
  – *if the current play fragment ends in a coupling defender node $(\mathrm{Cpl}, p, q)_d$, move to some attacker node $(q', p)_a$ with $(q', p) \in \mathcal{R}$ and $q \Rightarrow q'$.*

Lemma 11. *Let f be a winning strategy for the defender in $\mathcal{G}^{\mathcal{S}}_{CS}[(p_0, q_0)_a]$. Then $\{(p, q) \mid$ some $\mathcal{G}^{\mathcal{S}}_{CS}[(p_0, q_0)_a]$-play fragment consistent with f ends in $(p, q)_a\}$ is a coupled delay simulation.*

Theorem 3. *The defender wins $\mathcal{G}^{\mathcal{S}}_{CS}[(p, q)_a]$ precisely if $p \sqsubseteq_{CS} q$.*

4.2   Deciding the Coupled Simulation Game

It is well-known that the winning regions of finite simple games can be computed in linear time. Variants of the standard algorithm for this task can be found in [12] and in our implementation [1]. Intuitively, the algorithm first assumes that the defender wins everywhere and then sets off a chain reaction beginning in defender deadlock nodes, which "turns" all the nodes won by the attacker. The algorithm runs in linear time of the game moves because every node can only turn once.

```
1  def game_compute_cs(S):
2      G^S_CS = (G, G_a, ↣) := obtain_cs_game(S)
3      win := compute_winning_region(G^S_CS)
4      R := {(p, q) | (p, q)_a ∈ G_a ∧ win[(p, q)_a] = d}
5      return R
```

Algorithm 2: Game algorithm for the coupled simulation preorder $\sqsubseteq_{CS}$.

With such a winning region algorithm for simple games, referred to as compute_winning_region in the following, it is only a matter of a few lines to determine the coupled simulation preorder for a system S as shown in game_compute_cs in Algorithm 2. One starts by constructing the corresponding game G^S_{CS} using a function obtain_cs_game, we consider given by Definition 7. Then, one calls compute_winning_region and collects the attacker nodes won by the defender for the result.

Theorem 4. *For a finite labeled transition systems* S, game_compute_cs(S) *from Algorithm 2 returns* $\sqsubseteq^S_{CS}$.

Proof. Theorem 3 states that the defender wins $G^S_{CS}[(p, q)_a]$ exactly if $p \sqsubseteq^S_{CS} q$. As compute_winning_region(G^S_{CS}), according to [12], returns where the defender wins, line 4 of Algorithm 2 precisely assigns $R = \sqsubseteq^S_{CS}$.

The complexity arguments from [12] yield linear complexity for deciding the game by compute_winning_region.

Proposition 1. *For a game* $G = (G, G_a, ↣)$, compute_winning_region *runs in* $\mathcal{O}(|G| + |↣|)$ *time and space.*

In order to tell the overall complexity of the resulting algorithm, we have to look at the size of G^S_{CS} depending on the size of S.

Lemma 12. *Consider the coupled simulation game* $G^S_{CS} = (G, G_a, ↣)$ *for varying* $S = (S, \Sigma_\tau, \rightarrow)$. *The growth of the game size* $|G| + |↣|$ *is in* $\mathcal{O}(|\Rightarrow||S|)$.

Proof. Let us reexamine Definition 7. There are $|S|^2$ attacker nodes. Collectively, they can formulate $\mathcal{O}(|\rightarrow||S|)$ simulation challenges including internal moves and $|S|^2$ coupling challenges. There are $\mathcal{O}(|\Rightarrow||S|)$ simulation answers and $\mathcal{O}(|\Rightarrow||S|)$ coupling answers. Of these, $\mathcal{O}(|\Rightarrow||S|)$ dominates the others.

Lemma 13. game_compute_cs *runs in* $\mathcal{O}(|\Rightarrow||S|)$ *time and space.*

Proof. Proposition 1 and Lemma 12 already yield that line 3 is in $\mathcal{O}(|\Rightarrow||S|)$ time and space. Definition 7 is completely straight-forward, so the complexity of building G^S_{CS} in line 2 equals its output size $\mathcal{O}(|\Rightarrow||S|)$, which coincides with the complexity of computing $\Rightarrow$. The filtering in line 4 is in $\mathcal{O}(|S|^2)$ (upper bound for attacker nodes) and thus does not influence the overall complexity.

4.3   Tackling the τ-closure

We have mentioned that there can be some complexity to computing the τ-closure $\Rightarrow \, = \, \xrightarrow{\tau}{}^*$ and the derived $\dot{\Rightarrow}$. In theory, both the weak delay transition relation $\dot{\Rightarrow}$ and the conventional transition relation $\xrightarrow{}$ are bounded in size by $|\Sigma_\tau| \, |S|^2$. But for most transition systems, the weak step relations tend to be much bigger in size. Sparse $\xrightarrow{}$-graphs can generate dense $\Rightarrow$-graphs. The computation of the transitive closure also has significant time complexity. Algorithms for transitive closures usually are cubic, even though the theoretical bound is a little lower.

There has been a trend to skip the construction of the transitive closure in the computation of weak forms of bisimulation [3, 13, 19, 26]. With the game approach, we can follow this trend. The transitivity of the game can emulate the transitivity of $\dot{\Rightarrow}$ (for details see [1, Sec. 4.5.4]). With this trick, the game size, and thus time and space complexity, reduces to $\mathcal{O}(|\Sigma_\tau| \, |\xrightarrow{\tau}| \, |S| + |\xrightarrow{}| \, |S|)$. Though this is practically better than the bound from Lemma 13, both results amount to cubic complexity $\mathcal{O}(|\Sigma| \, |S|^3)$, which is in line with the reduction result from Theorem 1 and the time complexity of existing similarity algorithms.

4.4   Optimizing the Game Algorithm

The game can be downsized tremendously once we take additional over- and under-approximation information into account.

Definition 11. *An* over-approximation *of* $\sqsubseteq_{CS}$ *is a relation* $\mathcal{R}_O$ *of that we know that* $\sqsubseteq_{CS} \subseteq \mathcal{R}_O$. *Conversely, an* under-approximation *of* $\sqsubseteq_{CS}$ *is a relation* $\mathcal{R}_U$ *where* $\mathcal{R}_U \subseteq \sqsubseteq_{CS}$.

Regarding the game, over-approximations tell us where the defender *can* win, and under-approximations tell us where the attacker is doomed to lose. They can be used to eliminate "boring" parts of the game. Given an over-approximation $\mathcal{R}_O$, when unfolding the game, it only makes sense to add moves from defender nodes to attacker nodes $(p, q)_a$ if $(p, q) \in \mathcal{R}_O$. There just is no need to allow the defender moves we already know cannot be winning for them. Given an under-approximation $\mathcal{R}_U$, we can ignore all the outgoing moves of $(p, q)_a$ if $(p, q) \in \mathcal{R}_U$. Without moves, $(p, q)_a$ is sure to be won by the defender, which is in line with the claim of the approximation.

Corollary 2. $\Rightarrow^{-1}$ *is an under-approximation of* $\sqsubseteq_{CS}$. *(Cf. Lemma 4)*

Lemma 14. $\{(p, q) \mid$ *all actions weakly enabled in* p *are weakly enabled in* $q\}$ *is an over-approximation of* $\sqsubseteq_{CS}$.

The fact that coupled simulation is "almost bisimulation" on steps to stable states in finite systems (Lemma 6) can be used for a comparably cheap and precise over-approximation. The idea is to compute strong bisimilarity for the system $\mathcal{S}_{\Rightarrow|} = (S, \Sigma_\tau, \Rightarrow|)$, where *maximal weak steps*, $p \xrightarrow{\alpha}| \, p'$, exist iff $p \xRightarrow{\hat{\alpha}} p'$ and p' is stable, that is, $p' \xrightarrow{\tau}\!\!\!\!/\,$. Let $\equiv_{\Rightarrow|}$ be the biggest symmetric relation where $p \equiv_{\Rightarrow|} q$ and $p \xrightarrow{\alpha}| \, p'$ implies there is q' such that $p' \equiv_{\Rightarrow|} q'$ and $q \xrightarrow{\alpha}| \, q'$.

Lemma 15. $\mathcal{R}_{\Rightarrow\mid} = \{(p,q) \mid \forall p'. p \overset{\alpha}{\Rightarrow}\mid p' \longrightarrow q \overset{\alpha}{\Rightarrow}\mid \equiv_{\Rightarrow\mid} p'\}$ *is an over-approxima-tion of* $\sqsubseteq_{CS}$ *on finite systems.*

Computing $\equiv_{\Rightarrow\mid}$ can be expected to be cheaper than computing weak bisimilarity $\equiv_{WB}$. After all, $\Rightarrow\mid$ is just a subset of $\overset{\hat{}}{\Rightarrow}$. However, filtering $S \times S$ using subset checks to create $\mathcal{R}_{\Rightarrow\mid}$ might well be *quartic,* $\mathcal{O}(|S|^4)$, or worse. Nevertheless, one can argue that with a reasonable algorithm design and for many real-world examples, $\overset{\alpha}{\Rightarrow}\mid \equiv_{\Rightarrow\mid}$ will be sufficiently bounded in branching degree, in order for the over-approximation to do more good than harm.

For everyday system designs, $\mathcal{R}_{\Rightarrow\mid}$ is a tight approximation of $\sqsubseteq_{CS}$. On the philosopher system from Example 1, they even coincide. In some situations, $\mathcal{R}_{\Rightarrow\mid}$ degenerates to the shared enabledness relation (Lemma 14), which is to say it becomes comparably useless. One example for this are the systems created by the reduction from weak simulation to coupled simulation in Theorem 1 after τ-cycle removal. There, all $\Rightarrow\mid$-steps are bound to end in the same one τ-sink state $\bot$.

5 A Scalable Implementation

The experimental results by Ranzato and Tapparo [27] suggest that their simulation algorithm and the algorithm by Henzinger, Henzinger, and Kopke [15] only work on comparably small systems. The necessary data structures quickly consume gigabytes of RAM. So, the bothering question is not so much whether some highly optimized C++-implementation can do the job in milliseconds for small problems, but how to implement the algorithm such that large-scale systems are feasible at all.

To give first answers, we implemented a scalable and distributable prototype of the coupled simulation game algorithm using the stream processing framework *Apache Flink* [4] and its *Gelly* graph API, which enable computations on large data sets built around a universal data-flow engine. Our implementation can be found on https://coupledsim.bbisping.de/code/flink/.

5.1 Prototype Implementation

We base our implementation on the game algorithm and optimizations from Sect. 4. The implementation is a vertical prototype in the sense that every feature to get from a transition system to its coupled simulation preorder is present, but there is no big variety of options in the process. The phases are:

Import Reads a CSV representation of the transition system $\mathcal{S}$.
Minimize Computes an equivalence relation under-approximating $\equiv_{CS}$ on the transition system and builds a quotient system $\mathcal{S}_M$. This stage should at least compress τ-cycles if there are any. The default minimization uses a parallelized signature refinement algorithm [20,33] to compute delay bisimilarity ($\equiv_{DB}^{\mathcal{S}}$).

Table 1. Sample systems, sizes, and benchmark results.

system	S	$\rightarrow$	$\Rightarrow$	$S_{/\equiv_{DB}}$	$\rightarrowtail$	$\rightarrowtail_{\sigma\cdot}$	$S_{/\equiv_{CS}}$	$\sqsubseteq_{CS}^{S_{/\equiv_{CS}}}$	time/s
phil	10	14	86	6	234	201	5	11	5.1
ltbts	88	98	2,599	27	4,100	399	25	38	5.5
vasy_0_1	289	1,224	52,641	9	543	67	9	9	5.7
vasy_1_4	1,183	4,464	637,585	4	73	30	4	4	5.3
vasy_5_9	5,486	9,676	1,335,325	112	63,534	808	112	112	6.0
cwi_1_2	1,952	2,387	593,734	67	29,049	1,559	67	137	6.9
cwi_3_14	3,996	14,552	15,964,021	2	15	10	2	2	7.8
vasy_8_24	8,879	24,411	2,615,500	170	225,555	3,199	169	232	6.7
vasy_8_38	8,921	38,424	46,232,423	193	297,643	2,163	193	193	6.7
vasy_10_56	10,849	56,156	842,087	2,112	o.o.m.	72,617	2,112	3,932	13.8
vasy_25_25	25,217	25,216	50,433	25,217	o.o.m.	126,083	25,217	25,217	117.4

Compute over-approximation Determines an equivalence relation over-approximating $\equiv_{CS}^{S_M}$. The result is a mapping σ from states to *signatures* (sets of colors) such that $p \sqsubseteq_{CS}^{S_M} q$ implies $\sigma(p) \subseteq \sigma(q)$. The prototype uses the maximal weak step equivalence $\equiv_{\Rightarrow\mid}$ from Subsect. 4.4.

Build game graph Constructs the τ-closure-free coupled simulation game $\mathcal{G}_{CS}^{S_M}$ for $\mathcal{S}_M$ with attacker states restricted according to the over-approximation signatures σ.

Compute winning regions Decides for $\mathcal{G}_{CS}^{S_M}$ where the attacker has a winning strategy following the scatter-gather scheme [16]. If a game node is discovered to be won by the attacker, it *scatters* the information to its predecessors. Every game node *gathers* information on its winning successors. Defender nodes count down their degrees of freedom starting at their game move out-degrees.

Output Finally, the results can be output or checked for soundness. The winning regions directly imply $\sqsubseteq_{CS}^{S_M}$. The output can be de-minimized to refer to the original system $\mathcal{S}$.

5.2 Evaluation

Experimental evaluation shows that the approach can cope with the smaller examples of the "Very Large Transition Systems (VLTS) Benchmark Suite" [6] (vasy_* and cwi_* up to 50,000 transitions). On small examples, we also tested that the output matches the return values of the verified fixed-point $\sqsubseteq_{CS}$-algorithm from Sect. 3. These samples include, among others, the philosopher system phil containing P_g and P_o from Example 1 and ltbts, which consists of the finitary separating examples from the linear-time branching-time spectrum [9, p. 73].

Table 1 summarizes the results for some of our test systems with pre-minimization by delay bisimilarity and over-approximation by maximal weak step equivalence. The first two value columns give the system sizes in number of states

S and transitions $\xrightarrow{\cdot}$. The next two columns present derived properties, namely an upper estimate of the size of the (weak) delay step relation $\xRightarrow{\cdot}$, and the number of partitions with respect to delay bisimulation $S_{/\equiv_{DB}}$. The next columns list the sizes of the game graphs without and with maximal weak step over-approximation ($\rightarrowtail$ and $\rightarrowtail_\sigma$, some tests without the over-approximation trick ran out of memory, "o.o.m."). The following columns enumerate the sizes of the resulting coupled simulation preorders represented by the partition relation pair $(S_{/\equiv_{CS}}, \sqsubseteq_{CS}^{S_{/\equiv_{CS}}})$, where $S_{/\equiv_{CS}}$ is the partitioning of S with respect to coupled similarity $\equiv_{CS}$, and $\sqsubseteq_{CS}^{S_{/\equiv_{CS}}}$ the coupled simulation preorder projected to this quotient. The last column reports the running time of the programs on an Intel i7-8550U CPU with four threads and 2 GB Java Virtual Machine heap space.

The systems in Table 1 are a superset of the VLTS systems for which Ranzato and Tapparo [27] report their algorithm SA to terminate. Regarding complexity, SA is the best simulation algorithm known. In the [27]-experiments, the C++ implementation ran out of 2 GB RAM for vasy_10_56 and vasy_25_25 but finished much faster than our setup for most smaller examples. Their time advantage on small systems comes as no surprise as the start-up of the whole Apache Flink pipeline induces heavy overhead costs of about 5 s even for tiny examples like phil. However, on bigger examples such as vasy_18_73 their and our implementation both fail. This is in stark contrast to *bi*-simulation implementations, which usually cope with much larger systems single-handedly [3, 19].

Interestingly, for all tested VLTS systems, the weak bisimilarity quotient system $S_{/\equiv_{WB}}$ equals $S_{/\equiv_{CS}}$ (and, with the exception of vasy_8_24, $S_{/\equiv_{DB}}$). The preorder $\sqsubseteq_{CS}^{S_{/\equiv_{CS}}}$ also matches the identity in 6 of 9 examples. This observation about the effective closeness of coupled similarity and weak bisimilarity is two-fold. On the one hand, it brings into question how meaningful coupled similarity is for minimization. After all, it takes a lot of space and time to come up with the output that the cheaper delay bisimilarity already minimized everything that could be minimized. On the other hand, the observation suggests that the considered VLTS samples are based around models that do not need—or maybe even do avoid—the expressive power of weak bisimilarity. This is further evidence for the case from the introduction that coupled similarity has a more sensible level of precision than weak bisimilarity.

6   Conclusion

The core of this paper has been to present a game-based algorithm to compute coupled similarity in cubic time and space. To this end, we have formalized coupled similarity in Isabelle/HOL and merged two previous approaches to defining coupled similarity, namely using single relations with weak symmetry [10] and the relation-pair-based coupled delay simulation from [28], which followed the older tradition of two weak simulations [24, 29]. Our characterization seems to be the most convenient. We used the entailed coinductive characterization to devise a game characterization and an algorithm. Although we could show that deciding coupled similarity is as hard as deciding weak similarity, our Apache Flink implementation is able to exploit the closeness between coupled similarity and weak bisimilarity to at least handle slightly bigger systems than comparable similarity algorithms. Through the application to the VLTS suite, we have established that coupled similarity and weak bisimilarity match for the considered systems. This points back to a line of thought [11] that, for many applications, branching, delay and weak bisimilarity will coincide with coupled similarity. Where they do not, usually coupled similarity or a coarser notion of equivalence is called for. To gain deeper insights in that direction, real-world case studies—and maybe an embedding into existing tool landscapes like FDR [8], CADP [7], or LTSmin [17]—would be necessary.

References

1. Bisping, B.: Computing coupled similarity. Master's thesis, Technische Universität Berlin (2018). https://coupledsim.bbisping.de/bisping_computingCoupledSimilarity_thesis.pdf
2. Bisping, B.: Isabelle/HOL proof and Apache Flink program for TACAS 2019 paper: Computing Coupled Similarity (artifact). Figshare (2019). https://doi.org/10.6084/m9.figshare.7831382.v1
3. Boulgakov, A., Gibson-Robinson, T., Roscoe, A.W.: Computing maximal weak and other bisimulations. Formal Aspects Comput. **28**(3), 381–407 (2016). https://doi.org/10.1007/s00165-016-0366-2
4. Carbone, P., Katsifodimos, A., Ewen, S., Markl, V., Haridi, S., Tzoumas, K.: Apache Flink: stream and batch processing in a single engine. In: Bulletin of the IEEE Computer Society Technical Committee on Data Engineering, vol. 36, no. 4 (2015)
5. Derrick, J., Wehrheim, H.: Using coupled simulations in non-atomic refinement. In: Bert, D., Bowen, J.P., King, S., Waldén, M. (eds.) ZB 2003. LNCS, vol. 2651, pp. 127–147. Springer, Heidelberg (2003). https://doi.org/10.1007/3-540-44880-2_10
6. Garavel, H.: The VLTS benchmark suite (2017). https://doi.org/10.18709/perscido.2017.11.ds100. Jointly created by CWI/SEN2 and INRIA/VASY as a CADP resource
7. Garavel, H., Lang, F., Mateescu, R., Serwe, W.: CADP 2011: a toolbox for the construction and analysis of distributed processes. Int. J. Softw. Tools Technol. Transfer **15**(2), 89–107 (2013). https://doi.org/10.1007/s10009-012-0244-z
8. Gibson-Robinson, T., Armstrong, P., Boulgakov, A., Roscoe, A.W.: FDR3 — a modern refinement checker for CSP. In: Ábrahám, E., Havelund, K. (eds.) TACAS 2014. LNCS, vol. 8413, pp. 187–201. Springer, Heidelberg (2014). https://doi.org/10.1007/978-3-642-54862-8_13
9. van Glabbeek, R.J.: The linear time — branching time spectrum II. In: Best, E. (ed.) CONCUR 1993. LNCS, vol. 715, pp. 66–81. Springer, Heidelberg (1993). https://doi.org/10.1007/3-540-57208-2_6
10. van Glabbeek, R.J.: A branching time model of CSP. In: Gibson-Robinson, T., Hopcroft, P., Lazić, R. (eds.) Concurrency, Security, and Puzzles. LNCS, vol. 10160, pp. 272–293. Springer, Cham (2017). https://doi.org/10.1007/978-3-319-51046-0_14

11. van Glabbeek, R.J., Weijland, W.P.: Branching time and abstraction in bisimula-
    tion semantics. J. ACM (JACM) **43**(3), 555–600 (1996). https://doi.org/10.1145/
    233551.233556
12. Grädel, E.: Finite model theory and descriptive complexity. In: Grädel, E., et al.
    (eds.) Finite Model Theory and Its Applications. Texts in Theoretical Computer
    Science an EATCS Series, pp. 125–130. Springer, Heidelberg (2007). https://doi.
    org/10.1007/3-540-68804-8_3
13. Groote, J.F., Jansen, D.N., Keiren, J.J.A., Wijs, A.J.: An $\mathcal{O}(m \log n)$ algorithm for
    computing stuttering equivalence and branching bisimulation. ACM Trans. Com-
    put. Logic (TOCL) **18**(2), 13:1–13:34 (2017). https://doi.org/10.1145/3060140
14. Hatzel, M., Wagner, C., Peters, K., Nestmann, U.: Encoding CSP into CCS. In:
    Proceedings of the Combined 22th International Workshop on Expressiveness in
    Concurrency and 12th Workshop on Structural Operational Semantics, and 12th
    Workshop on Structural Operational Semantics, EXPRESS/SOS, pp. 61–75 (2015).
    https://doi.org/10.4204/EPTCS.190.5
15. Henzinger, M.R., Henzinger, T.A., Kopke, P.W.: Computing simulations on finite
    and infinite graphs. In: 36th Annual Symposium on Foundations of Computer
    Science, Milwaukee, Wisconsin, pp. 453–462 (1995). https://doi.org/10.1109/SFCS.
    1995.492576
16. Kalavri, V., Vlassov, V., Haridi, S.: High-level programming abstractions for dis-
    tributed graph processing. IEEE Trans. Knowl. Data Eng. **30**(2), 305–324 (2018).
    https://doi.org/10.1109/TKDE.2017.2762294
17. Kant, G., Laarman, A., Meijer, J., van de Pol, J., Blom, S., van Dijk, T.: LTSmin:
    high-performance language-independent model checking. In: Baier, C., Tinelli, C.
    (eds.) TACAS 2015. LNCS, vol. 9035, pp. 692–707. Springer, Heidelberg (2015).
    https://doi.org/10.1007/978-3-662-46681-0_61
18. Kučera, A., Mayr, R.: Why is simulation harder than bisimulation? In: Brim, L.,
    Křetínský, M., Kučera, A., Jančar, P. (eds.) CONCUR 2002. LNCS, vol. 2421, pp.
    594–609. Springer, Heidelberg (2002). https://doi.org/10.1007/3-540-45694-5_39
19. Li, W.: Algorithms for computing weak bisimulation equivalence. In: Third IEEE
    International Symposium on Theoretical Aspects of Software Engineering, 2009.
    TASE 2009, pp. 241–248. IEEE (2009). https://doi.org/10.1109/TASE.2009.47
20. Luo, Y., de Lange, Y., Fletcher, G.H.L., De Bra, P., Hidders, J., Wu, Y.: Bisimula-
    tion reduction of big graphs on MapReduce. In: Gottlob, G., Grasso, G., Olteanu,
    D., Schallhart, C. (eds.) BNCOD 2013. LNCS, vol. 7968, pp. 189–203. Springer,
    Heidelberg (2013). https://doi.org/10.1007/978-3-642-39467-6_18
21. Milner, R.: Communication and Concurrency. Prentice-Hall Inc., Upper Saddle
    River (1989)
22. Nestmann, U., Pierce, B.C.: Decoding choice encodings. Inf. Comput. **163**(1), 1–59
    (2000). https://doi.org/10.1006/inco.2000.2868
23. Parrow, J., Sjödin, P.: Multiway synchronization verified with coupled simulation.
    In: Cleaveland, W.R. (ed.) CONCUR 1992. LNCS, vol. 630, pp. 518–533. Springer,
    Heidelberg (1992). https://doi.org/10.1007/BFb0084813
24. Parrow, J., Sjödin, P.: The complete axiomatization of Cs-congruence. In: Enjal-
    bert, P., Mayr, E.W., Wagner, K.W. (eds.) STACS 1994. LNCS, vol. 775, pp.
    555–568. Springer, Heidelberg (1994). https://doi.org/10.1007/3-540-57785-8_171
25. Peters, K., van Glabbeek, R.J.: Analysing and comparing encodability criteria.
    In: Proceedings of the Combined 22th International Workshop on Expressive-
    ness in Concurrency and 12th Workshop on Structural Operational Semantics,
    EXPRESS/SOS, pp. 46–60 (2015). https://doi.org/10.4204/EPTCS.190.4

26. Ranzato, F., Tapparo, F.: Generalizing the Paige-Tarjan algorithm by abstract interpretation. Inf. Comput. **206**(5), 620–651 (2008). https://doi.org/10.1016/j.ic. 2008.01.001. Special Issue: The 17th International Conference on Concurrency Theory (CONCUR 2006)

27. Ranzato, F., Tapparo, F.: An efficient simulation algorithm based on abstract interpretation. Inf. Comput. **208**(1), 1–22 (2010). https://doi.org/10.1016/j.ic.2009.06. 002

28. Rensink, A.: Action contraction. In: Palamidessi, C. (ed.) CONCUR 2000. LNCS, vol. 1877, pp. 290–305. Springer, Heidelberg (2000). https://doi.org/10.1007/3-540-44618-4_22

29. Sangiorgi, D.: Introduction to Bisimulation and Coinduction. Cambridge University Press, New York (2012). https://doi.org/10.1017/CBO9780511777110

30. Stirling, C.: Modal and Temporal Properties of Processes. Springer, New York (2001). https://doi.org/10.1007/978-1-4757-3550-5

31. Voorhoeve, M., Mauw, S.: Impossible futures and determinism. Inf. Process. Lett. **80**(1), 51–58 (2001). https://doi.org/10.1016/S0020-0190(01)00217-4

32. Wenzel, M.: The Isabelle/Isar Reference Manual (2018). https://isabelle.in.tum. de/dist/Isabelle2018/doc/isar-ref.pdf

33. Wimmer, R., Herbstritt, M., Hermanns, H., Strampp, K., Becker, B.: Sigref – a symbolic bisimulation tool box. In: Graf, S., Zhang, W. (eds.) ATVA 2006. LNCS, vol. 4218, pp. 477–492. Springer, Heidelberg (2006). https://doi.org/10. 1007/11901914_35

Parallel SAT Simplification on GPU Architectures

Muhammad Osama[✉] [iD] and Anton Wijs[✉] [iD]

Eindhoven University of Technology, 5600 MB Eindhoven, The Netherlands
{o.m.m.muhammad,a.j.wijs}@tue.nl

Abstract. The growing scale of applications encoded to Boolean Satisfiability (SAT) problems imposes the need for accelerating SAT simplifications or preprocessing. Parallel SAT preprocessing has been an open challenge for many years. Therefore, we propose novel parallel algorithms for variable and subsumption elimination targeting Graphics Processing Units (GPUs). Benchmarks show that the algorithms achieve an acceleration of 66× over a state-of-the-art SAT simplifier (SatELite). Regarding SAT solving, we have conducted a thorough evaluation, combining both our GPU algorithms and SatELite with MiniSat to solve the simplified problems. In addition, we have studied the impact of the algorithms on the solvability of problems with Lingeling. We conclude that our algorithms have a considerable impact on the solvability of SAT problems.

Keywords: Satisfiability · Variable elimination ·
Subsumption elimination · Parallel SAT preprocessing · GPU

1 Introduction

Algorithms to solve propositional Boolean Satisfiability (SAT) problems are being used extensively for various applications, such as artificial intelligence, circuit design, automatic test pattern generation, automatic theorem proving, and bounded model checking. Of course, SAT being NP-complete, scalability of these algorithms is an issue. Simplifying SAT problems prior to solving them has proven its effectiveness in modern conflict-driven clause learning (CDCL) SAT solvers [6, 9], particularly when applied on real-world applications relevant to software and hardware verification [8, 12, 17, 19]. It tends to produce reasonable reductions in acceptable processing time. Many techniques based on, e.g., variable elimination, clause elimination, and equivalence reasoning are being used to simplify SAT problems, whether prior to the solving phase (preprocessing) [8, 10, 12, 15, 16, 24] or during the search (inprocessing) [3, 18]. However, applying variable and clause elimination iteratively to large problems (in terms of the number of literals) can be a performance bottleneck in the whole SAT solving procedure, or even increase the number of literals, negatively impacting the solving time.

Recently, the authors of [2,11] discussed the current main challenges in parallel SAT solving. One of these challenges concerns the parallelisation of SAT simplification in modern SAT solvers. Massively parallel computing systems such as Graphics Processing Units (GPUs) offer great potential to speed up computations, but to achieve this, it is crucial to engineer new parallel algorithms and data structures from scratch to make optimal use of those architectures. GPU platforms have become attractive for general-purpose computing with the availability of the Compute Unified Device Architecture (CUDA) programming model [20]. CUDA is widely used to accelerate applications that are computationally intensive w.r.t. data processing and memory access. In recent years, for instance, we have applied GPUs to accelerate explicit-state model checking [26,27,30], state space decomposition [28,29] and minimisation [25], meta-heuristic SAT solving [31], and SAT-based test generation [22].

In this paper, we introduce the first parallel algorithms for various techniques widely used in SAT simplification and discuss the various performance aspects of the proposed implementations and data structures. Also, we discuss the main challenges in CPU-GPU memory management and how to address them. In a nutshell, we aim to effectively simplify SAT formulas, even if they are extremely large, in only a few seconds using the massive computing capabilities of GPUs.

Contributions. We propose novel parallel algorithms to simplify SAT formulas using GPUs, and experimentally evaluate them, i.e., we measure both their runtime efficiency and their effect on the overall solving time, for a large benchmark set of SAT instances encoding real-world problems. We show how multiple variables can be eliminated simultaneously on a GPU while preserving the original satisfiability of a given formula. We call this technique Bounded Variable-Independent Parallel Elimination (BVIPE). The eliminated variables are elected first based on some criteria using the proposed algorithm Least-Constrained Variable Elections (LCVE). The variable elimination procedure includes both the so-called *resolution rule* and *gate equivalence reasoning*. Furthermore, we propose an algorithm for *parallel subsumption elimination* (PSE), covering both *subsumption elimination* and *self-subsuming resolution*.

The paper is organised as follows: Sect. 2 introduces the preliminaries. The main GPU challenges for SAT simplification are discussed in Sect. 3, and the proposed algorithms are explained in Sect. 4. Section 5 presents our experimental evaluation. Section 6 discusses related work, and Sect. 7 provides a conclusion and suggests future work.

2   Preliminaries

All SAT formulas in this paper are in conjunctive normal form (CNF). A CNF formula is a conjunction of clauses $\bigwedge_{i=1}^{m} C_i$ where each clause C_i is a disjunction of literals $\bigvee_{j=1}^{k} \ell_j$ and a literal is a Boolean variable x or its complement $\neg x$, which we refer to as $\bar{x}$. We represent clauses by sets of literals $C = \{\ell_1, \ldots, \ell_k\}$, i.e., $\{\ell_1, \ldots, \ell_k\}$ represents the formula $\ell_1 \vee \ldots \vee \ell_k$, and a SAT formula by a set of clauses $\{C_1, \ldots, C_m\}$, i.e., $\{C_1, \ldots, C_m\}$ represents the formula $C_1 \wedge \ldots \wedge C_m$.

Variable Elimination. Variables can be removed from clauses by either applying the *resolution rule* or *gate-equivalence reasoning*. Concerning the former, we represent application of the resolution rule w.r.t. some variable x using a *resolving operator* $\otimes_x$ on C_1 and C_2. The result of applying the rule is called the *resolvent* [24]. It is defined as $C_1 \otimes_x C_2 = C_1 \cup C_2 \setminus \{x, \bar{x}\}$, and can be applied iff $x \in C_1$, $\bar{x} \in C_2$. The $\otimes_x$ operator can be extended to resolve sets of clauses w.r.t. variable x. For a formula S, let $S_x \subseteq S$, $S_{\bar{x}} \subseteq S$ be the set of all clauses in S containing x and $\bar{x}$, respectively. The new resolvents are defined as $R_x(S) = \{C_1 \otimes_x C_2 \mid C_1 \in S_x \wedge C_2 \in S_{\bar{x}} \wedge \neg \exists y.\{y, \bar{y}\} \subseteq C_1 \otimes_x C_2\}$. The last condition addresses that a resolvent should not be a *tautology*, i.e. a self-satisfied clause in which a variable and its negation exist. The set of non-tautology resolvents can replace S, producing an equivalent SAT formula.

Gate-Equivalence Reasoning. This technique substitutes eliminated variables with deduced logical equivalent expressions. In this work, we focus on the reasoning of AND-OR gates since they are common in SAT-encoded problems and OR gates are likely to be found if AND-equivalence reasoning fails. In general, gate-equivalence reasoning can also be applied using other logical gates. A logical AND gate with k inputs $\ell_1, \ldots, \ell_k$ and output x can be captured by the two implications $x \implies \ell_1 \wedge \ldots \wedge \ell_k$ and $\ell_1 \wedge \ldots \wedge \ell_k \implies x$. In turn, these two implications can be encoded in SAT clauses $\{\{\bar{x}, \ell_1\}, \ldots, \{\bar{x}, \ell_k\}\}$ and $\{\{x, \bar{\ell}_1, \ldots, \bar{\ell}_k\}\}$, respectively. Similarly, the implications of an OR gate $x \implies \ell_1 \vee \ldots \vee \ell_k$ and $\ell_1 \vee \ldots \vee \ell_k \implies x$ are expressed by the SAT clauses $\{\{x, \bar{\ell}_1\}, \ldots, \{x, \bar{\ell}_k\}\}$ and $\{\{\bar{x}, \ell_1, \ldots, \ell_k\}\}$, respectively.

For instance, consider the following formula:

$$S = \{\{x, \bar{a}, \bar{b}\}, \{\bar{x}, a\}, \{\bar{x}, b\}, \{x, c\}, \{\bar{x}, \bar{b}\}, \{y, f\}, \{\bar{y}, d, e\}, \{y, \bar{d}\}, \{y, \bar{e}\}\}$$

The first three clauses in S capture the AND gate (x, a, b) and the last three clauses capture the OR gate (y, d, e). By substituting $a \wedge b$ for x and $d \vee e$ for y in the fourth, fifth, and sixth clauses, a new formula $\{\{a, c\}, \{b, c\}, \{\bar{a}, \bar{b}\}, \{d, e, f\}\}$ can be constructed. Combining AND/OR-gate equivalence reasoning with the resolution rule tends to result in smaller formulas compared to only applying the resolution rule [8, 23].

Subsumption Elimination. A clause C_2 is said to *subsume* clause C_1 iff $C_2 \subseteq C_1$. The subsumed clause C_1 is redundant and can be deleted from the original SAT equation. A special form of subsumption is called *self-subsuming resolution*. It is applicable for two clauses C_1, C_2 iff for some variable x, we have $C_1 = C_1' \cup \{x\}$, $C_2 = C_2' \cup \{\bar{x}\}$, and $C_2' \subseteq C_1'$. Consider the clauses: $C_1 = \{x, a, b\}$ and $C_2 = \{\bar{x}, b\}$; C_2 self-subsumes C_1 since $x \in C_1$, $\bar{x} \in C_2$ and $\{b\} \subseteq \{a, b\}$. The self-subsuming literal x can be discarded, producing clause $\check{C}_1 = \{a, b\}$. In other words, we say that C_1 is *strengthened* by C_2.

3 GPU Challenges: Memory and Data

GPU Architecture. CUDA is a programming model developed by NVIDIA [20] to provide a general-purpose programming paradigm and allow using the massive capabilities of GPU resources to accelerate applications. Regarding the processing hardware, a GPU consists of multiple streaming multiprocessors (SMs) and each SM resembles an array of streaming processors (SPs) where every SP can execute multiple threads grouped together in 32-thread scheduling units called *warps.* On the programming level, a program can launch a *kernel* (GPU global function) to be executed by thousands of threads packed in thread *blocks* of up to 1,024 threads or 32 warps. All threads together form a *grid.* The GPU manages the execution of a launched kernel by evenly distributing the launched blocks to the available SMs through a hardware warp scheduler.

Concerning the memory hierarchy, a GPU has multiple types of memory:

- *Global memory* is accessible by all threads with high bandwidth but also high latency. The CPU (host) can access it as an interface to the GPU.
- *Shared memory* is on-chip memory shared by the threads in a block; it is smaller in size and has lower latency than global memory. It can be used to efficiently communicate data between threads in a block.
- *Registers* provide thread-local storage and provide the fastest memory.

To make optimal use of global memory bandwidth and hide its latency, using *coalesced accesses* is one of the best practices in global memory optimisation. When the threads in a warp try to access a consecutive block of 32-bit words, their accesses are combined into a single (coalesced) memory access. Uncoalesced memory accesses can for instance be caused by data sparsity or misalignment.

Regarding atomicity, a GPU is capable of executing *atomic* operations on both global and shared memory. A GPU *atomic* function typically performs a *read-modify-write* memory operation on one 32-bit or 64-bit word.

Memory Management. When small data packets need to be accessed frequently, both on the host (CPU) and device (GPU) side (which is the case in the current work), *unified memory* can play a crucial role in boosting the transfer rates by avoiding excessive memory copies. Unified memory creates a pool of managed memory that is shared between the CPU and GPU. This pool is accessible to both sides using a single pointer. Another advantage of unified memory is that it allows the CPU to allocate multidimensional pointers referencing global memory locations or nested structures. However, if a memory pool is required to be reallocated (resized), one must maintain memory coherency between the CPU-side and GPU-side memories. A reallocation procedure is necessary for our variable elimination algorithm, to make memory available when producing resolvents and reduce the memory use when removing clauses.

To better explain the coherency problem in reallocation, suppose there is an array A allocated and loaded with some data X, then X is visible from both the CPU and GPU memories. When A is reallocated from the host side, the memory is not physically allocated until it is first accessed, particularly when using an NVIDIA GPU with the Pascal architecture [20]. Once new data Y is written to A from the device side, both sides will observe a combination of X and Y, leading to memory corruptions and page faults. To avoid this problem, A must be reset on the host side directly after memory reallocation to assert the physical allocation. After that, each kernel may store its own data safely in the global memory. In the proposed algorithms, we introduce two types of optimisations addressing memory space and latency.

Regarding memory space optimisation, allocating memory dynamically each time a clause is added is not practical on a GPU while variables are eliminated in parallel. To resolve this, we initially launch a GPU kernel to calculate an upper bound for the number of resolvents to be added before the elimination procedure starts (Sect. 4.1). After this, reallocation is applied to store the new resolvents. Furthermore, a global counter is implemented inside our CNF data structure to keep track of new clauses. This counter is incremented atomically by each thread when adding a clause.

Concerning memory latency optimisation, when thread blocks produce resolvents, these can initially be stored in shared memory. Checking for tautologies can then be done by accessing shared memory, and non-tautologies can be written back to the global memory in a new CNF formula. Also, the definitions of AND-OR gates can be stored in shared memory, to be used later when applying clause substitution (see Sect. 4.1). This has the advantage of reducing the number of global memory accesses. Nevertheless, the size of shared memory in a GPU is very limited (48 KB in most architectures). If the potential size of a resolvent is larger than the amount pre-allocated for a single clause, our BVIPE algorithm automatically switches to the global memory and the resolvent is directly added to the new CNF formula. This mechanism reduces the global memory latency when applicable and deals with the shared memory size limitation dynamically.

Data Structures. The efficiency of state-of-the-art sequential SAT solving and preprocessing is to a large extent due to the meticulously coded data structures. When considering SAT simplification on GPUs, new data structures have to be tailored from scratch. In this work, we need two of them, one for the SAT formula in CNF form (which we refer to as *CNF*) and another for the literal *occurrence table* (*occurTAB*), via which one can efficiently iterate over all clauses containing a particular literal. In CPU implementations, typically, they are created using *heaps* and *auto-resizable vectors*, respectively. However, heaps and vectors are not suitable for GPU parallelisation, since data is inserted, reallocated and sorted dynamically. The best GPU alternative is to create a nested data structure with arrays using unified memory (see Fig. 1). The *CNF* contains a raw pointer (linear array) to store CNF literals and a child structure *Clause* to store clause info. Each clause has a *head pointer* referring to its first literal. The *occurTAB* structure has a raw pointer to store the clause occurrences (array pointers) for each literal in the formula and a child structure *occurList*. The creation of an *occurList* instance is done in parallel per literal using atomic operations. For each clause C, a thread is launched to insert the occurrences of C's literals in the associated *occurLists*. One important remark is that two threads storing the occurrences of different literals do not have to wait for each other. For instance, *occurTAB* in Fig. 1 shows two different atomic insertions executed at the same time for literals 2 and –1 (if an integer i represents a literal x, then $-i$ represents $\bar{x}$). This minimises the performance penalty of using atomics.

The advantages of the proposed data structures are: as mentioned above, *occurTAB* instances can be constructed in parallel. Furthermore, coalesced access is guaranteed since pointers are stored consecutively (the gray arrows in Fig. 1), and no explicit memory copying is done (host and device pointers are identical) making it easier to integrate the data structures with any sequential or parallel code.

4   Algorithm Design and Implementation

4.1   Parallel Variable Elimination

In order to eliminate Boolean variables simultaneously in SAT formulas without altering the original satisfiability, a set of variables should be selected for elimination checking that contains only variables that are *independent* of each other. The LCVE algorithm we propose is responsible for electing such a subset from a set of authorised candidates. The remaining variables relying on the elected ones are frozen.

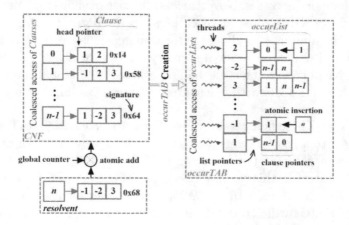

Fig. 1. An example of *CNF* and *occurTAB* data structures.

Algorithm 1: Constructing $\mathcal{A}$ - *GPU*

    Input : __global__ $S[]$, n, μ
    Output: __global__ $\mathcal{A}[]$

1 $h \leftarrow$ histogram(S, n);
2 $\mathcal{A} \leftarrow []$; *scores* $\leftarrow []$;
3 $\mathcal{A}$, *scores* $\leftarrow$ assignScores(h, $\mathcal{A}$, *scores*);
4 $\mathcal{A} \leftarrow$ prune(sort($\mathcal{A}$, *scores*), h, μ);

Definition 1 (Authorised candidates). *Given a CNF formula S, we call $\mathcal{A}$ the set of* authorised candidates: $\mathcal{A} = \{x \mid 1 \leq h[x] \leq \mu \vee 1 \leq h[\bar{x}] \leq \mu\}$, *where*

- h is a histogram array ($h[x]$ is the number of occurrences of x in S)
- μ denotes a given maximum number of occurrences allowed for both x and its complement, representing the cut-off point for the LCVE algorithm

Definition 2 (Candidate Dependency Relation). *We call a relation* $\mathcal{D}$: $\mathcal{A} \times \mathcal{A}$ *a candidate dependency relation iff* $\forall x, y \in \mathcal{A}$, $x \mathcal{D} y$ *implies that* $\exists C \in S.(x \in C \vee \bar{x} \in C) \wedge (y \in C \vee \bar{y} \in C)$

Definition 3 (Elected candidates). *Given a set of authorised candidates* $\mathcal{A}$, *we call a set* $\varphi \subseteq \mathcal{A}$ *a set of* elected candidates *iff* $\forall x, y \in \varphi. \neg(x \mathcal{D} y)$

Definition 4 (Frozen candidates). *Given the sets* $\mathcal{A}$ *and* φ, *the set of* frozen candidates $\mathcal{F} \subseteq \mathcal{A}$ *is defined as* $\mathcal{F} = \{x \mid x \in \mathcal{A} \wedge \exists y \in \varphi. x \mathcal{D} y\}$

Before LCVE is executed, a sorted list of the variables in the CNF formula needs to be created, ordered by the number of occurrences in the formula, in ascending order (following the same rule as in [8]). From this list, the authorised candidates $\mathcal{A}$ can be straightforwardly derived, using μ as a cut-off point. Construction of this list can be done efficiently on a GPU using Algorithms 1 and 2. Algorithm 1 is labelled *GPU*, indicating that each individual step can be launched as a GPU computation. In contrast, algorithms providing kernel code, i.e., that describe the steps each individual GPU thread should perform as part of a GPU computation, such as Algorithm 2, are labelled *GPU kernel*.

Algorithm 2: Assign Scores to SAT formula variables - *GPU kernel*

Input : __global__ $h[]$, $\mathcal{A}[]$, $scores[]$
Output: __global__ $\mathcal{A}[]$, $scores[]$

```
1  tid ← xThread + blockDim × xBlock; stride ← gridDim × blockDim;
2  while tid < n do
3  │   x ← tid + 1;
4  │   A[tid] ← x;
5  │   if h[x] = 0 ∨ h[x̄] = 0 then
6  │   └   scores[x] ← max(h[x], h[x̄])
7  │   else
8  │   └   scores[x] ← h[x] × h[x̄]
9  │   tid ← tid + stride
```

As input, Algorithm 1 requires a SAT formula S as an instance of *CNF*. Furthermore, it requires the number of variables n occurring in S and a cut-off point μ. At line 1, a histogram array h, providing for each literal the number of occurrences in S, is constructed. This histogram can be constructed on the GPU using the histogram method offered by the *Thrust* library [4,5]. At line 2, memory is allocated for the arrays $\mathcal{A}$ and *scores*. With h, these are input for the kernel *assignScores*. Once the kernel execution has terminated, at line 4, the candidates in $\mathcal{A}$ are sorted on the GPU based on their scores in *scores* and μ is used on the GPU to prune candidates with too many occurrences. We used the radix-sort algorithm as provided in the Thrust library [5].

In the kernel of Algorithm 2, at line 1, the *tid* variable refers to the thread identifier in the launched grid where *xThread* is the thread index inside a block of size *blockDim* and *xBlock* is the block index inside the entire grid of size *gridDim*.

The *stride* variable is used to determine the distance between variables that have to be processed by the same thread. In the subsequent **while** loop (lines 2–9), the thread index is used as a variable index (variable indices start at 1), jumping ahead *stride* variables at the end of each iteration. At lines 5–8, a score is computed for the currently considered variable x. This score should be indicative of the number of resolvents produced when eliminating x, which depends on the number of occurrences of both x and $\bar{x}$, and can be approximated by the formula $h[x] \times h[\bar{x}]$. To avoid score zero in case exactly one of the two literals does not occur in S, we consider that case separately. On average, Algorithm 1 outperforms the sequential counterpart 52×, when considering our benchmark set of problems [21].

LCVE Algorithm. Next, Algorithm 3 is executed on the host, given S, $\mathcal{A}$, h and an instance of *occurTAB* named OT. This algorithm accesses $2 \cdot |\mathcal{A}|$ number of *occurList* instances and parts of S. The use of unified memory significantly improves the rates of the resulting transfers and avoids explicitly copying entire data structures to the host side. The output is φ, implemented as a list. Function **abs** is defined as follows: $\textbf{abs}(x) = x$ and $\textbf{abs}(\bar{x}) = x$. The algorithm considers all variables x in $\mathcal{A}$ (line 2). If x has not yet been frozen (line 3), it adds x to φ (line 4). Next, the algorithm needs to identify all variables that depend on x. For this, the algorithm iterates over all clauses containing either x or $\bar{x}$ (line 5), and each literal ℓ in those clauses is compared to x (lines 6–8). If ℓ refers to a different variable v, and v is an authorised candidate, then v must be frozen (line 9).

Algorithm 3: The LCVE algorithm - *CPU*

    Input : $S[\,], \mathcal{A}[\,], h[\,], OT[\,]$
    Output: φ

1 $\mathcal{F} \leftarrow [\,]$;
2 **foreach** $x \in \mathcal{A}$ **do**
3   **if** $\neg \mathcal{F}[x]$ **then**
4          $\varphi \leftarrow \varphi \mathbin{+\!\!+} x$;
5   **foreach** $C \in S[OT[x]] \cup S[OT[\bar{x}]]$ **do**
6   **foreach** $\ell \in C$ **do**
7                  $v \leftarrow \textbf{abs}(\ell)$;
8   **if** $v \neq x \wedge v \in \mathcal{A}$ **then**
9                     $\mathcal{F}[v] \leftarrow$ **true**;

BVIPE GPU Algorithm. After φ has been constructed, a kernel is launched to compute an upper bound for the number of resolvents (excluding tautologies) that may be produced by eliminating variables in φ. This kernel accumulates the number of resolvents of each variable using parallel reduction in shared memory within thread blocks. The resulting values (resident in shared memory) of all blocks are added up by atomic operations, resulting in the final output, stored in global memory (denoted by $|\tilde{S}|$). Afterwards, the *CNF* is reallocated according to the extra memory needed. The parallel variable elimination kernel (Algorithm 4) is now ready to be performed on the GPU, considering both the *resolution rule* and *gate-equivalence reasoning* (Sect. 2).

In Algorithm 4, first, each thread selects a variable in φ, based on *tid* (line 4). The *eliminated* array marks the variables that have been eliminated. It is used to distinguish eliminated and non-eliminated variabels when executing Algorithm 6.

Each thread checks the control condition at line 5 to determine whether the number of resolvents ($h[x] \times h[\bar{x}]$) of x will be less than the number of deleted clauses ($h[x]+h[\bar{x}]$). If the condition evaluates to **true**, a list *resolvents* is created in shared memory, which is then added to the simplified formula $\tilde{S}$ in global memory after discarding tautologies (line 8). The *markDeleted* routine marks resolved clauses as deleted. They are actually deleted on the host side, once the algorithm has terminated.

At line 10, definitions of AND and OR gates are deduced by the *gateReasoning* routine, and stored in shared memory in the lists α and β, respectively. If at least one gate definition is found, the *clauseSubstitution* routine substitutes the involved variable with the underlying definition (line 11), creating the resolvents.

In some situations, even if $h[x]$ or $h[\bar{x}]$ is greater than 1, the number of resolvents can be smaller than the deleted clauses, due to the fact that some resolvents may be tautologies that are subsequently discarded. For this reason, we provide a third alternative to lookahead for tautologies in order to conclusively decide whether to resolve a variable if the conditions at lines 5 and 10 both evaluate to **false**. This third option (line 15) has lower priority than gate equivalence reasoning (line 10), since the latter in practice tends to perform more reduction than the former.

Algorithm 4: The BVIPE algorithm - *GPU kernel*

Input : __global__ $S, \varphi[], h, OT[], eliminated[]$
Input : __shared__ $resolvents[], \alpha[], \beta[]$
Output: __global__ $\tilde{S}$

1 $tid \leftarrow xThread + blockDim \times xBlock;$
2 $stride \leftarrow gridDim \times blockDim;$
3 **while** $tid < |\varphi|$ **do**
4      $x \leftarrow \varphi[tid], eliminated[x] \leftarrow$ **false**, $numTautologies \leftarrow 0;$
5   **if** $h[x] = 1 \vee h[\bar{x}] = 1$ **then**
6          $resolvents \leftarrow$ resolve$(x, S, OT[x], OT[\bar{x}]);$ /* computes $R_x(S)$ */
7   markDeleted$(S, OT[x], OT[\bar{x}]);$
8          $\tilde{S} \leftarrow S \cup resolvents;$
9          $eliminated[x] \leftarrow$ **true**;
10   **else if** $(\alpha, \beta) \leftarrow$ gateReasoning$(x, S, OT[x], OT[\bar{x}]) \neq (\emptyset, \emptyset)$ **then**
11         $resolvents \leftarrow$ clauseSubstitution$(x, S, OT[x], OT[\bar{x}], \alpha, \beta);$
12   markDeleted$(S, OT[x], OT[\bar{x}]);$
13         $\tilde{S} \leftarrow S \cup resolvents;$
14         $eliminated[x] \leftarrow$ **true**;
15   **else**
16         $numTautologies \leftarrow$ tautologyLookahead$(x, S, OT[x], OT[\bar{x}]);$
17         $numResolvents \leftarrow h[x] \times h[\bar{x}], numDeleted \leftarrow h[x] + h[\bar{x}];$
18   **if** $(numResolvents - numTautologies) < numDeleted$ **then**
19             $resolvents \leftarrow$ resolve$(x, S, OT[x], OT[\bar{x}]);$
20   markDeleted$(S, OT[x], OT[\bar{x}]);$
21             $\tilde{S} \leftarrow S \cup resolvents;$
22             $eliminated[x] \leftarrow$ **true**;
23     $tid \leftarrow tid + stride;$

The sequential running time of Algorithm 4 is $\mathcal{O}(k \cdot |\varphi|)$, where k is the maximum length of a resolved clause in S. In practice, k often ranges between 2 and 10. Therefore, the worst case is linear w.r.t. $|\varphi|$. Consequently, the parallel complexity is $\mathcal{O}(|\varphi|/p)$, where p is the number of threads. Since a GPU is capable of launching thousands of threads, that is, $p \approx |\varphi|$, the parallel complexity is an amortised constant $\mathcal{O}(1)$. Our empirical results show an average speedup of $32\times$ compared to the sequential alternative [21].

4.2 Parallel Subsumption Elimination

Algorithm 5 presents our PSE algorithm. Notice that the subsumption check (lines 6–7) has a higher priority than self-subsumption (lines 8–12) because the former often results in deleting more clauses. We apply PSE on the *most constrained variables*, that is, the variables that occur most frequently in S, to maximise parallelism on the GPU. For each literal ℓ, the PSE algorithm is launched on a *two-dimensional* GPU grid, in which threads and blocks have two identifiers. Each thread compares the two clauses in $OT[\ell]$ that are associated with the thread coordinates in the grid. At line 4, those two clauses are obtained. At line 5, it is checked whether subsumption or self-subsumption may be applicable. For this to be the case, the length of one clause needs to be larger than the other. The *sig* routine compares the identifiers of two clauses. The identifier of a clause is computed by hashing its literals to a 64-bit value [8]. It has the property of refuting many non-subsuming clauses, but not all of them since hashing collisions may occur. At line 6, the *isSubset* routine runs a set intersection algorithm in linear time $\mathcal{O}(k)$ assuming that both clauses are sorted. If one clause is indeed a subset of the other, the latter clause is marked for deletion later (line 7).

Algorithm 5: The PSE algorithm - *GPU kernel*

    Input: __global__ $S, \ell, OT[\,]$

1    $tx \leftarrow xThread + blockDim \times xBlock$, $ty \leftarrow yThread + blockDim \times yBlock$;
2    $stride \leftarrow gridDim \times blockDim$;
3   **while** $ty < |OT[\ell]| \wedge tx < |OT[\ell]|$ **do**
4       $C \leftarrow S[OT[\ell][ty]]$; $\acute{C} \leftarrow S[OT[\ell][tx]]$;
5   **if** $|\acute{C}| < |C| \wedge sig(\acute{C}, C) \neq 0$ **then**
6   **if** $isSubset(\acute{C}, C)$ **then**
7           $markDeleted(C)$;
8   **else if** $|C| > 1$ **then**
9           $litPos \leftarrow isSelfSub(\acute{C}, C)$;
10   **if** $litPos > -1$ **then**
11            $atomicStrengthen(C, litPos)$;
12            $markSelfSub(C)$;

13     $ty \leftarrow ty + stride$, $tx \leftarrow tx + stride$;

As an alternative, the applicability of self-subsumption is checked at line 8. If C is not a unit clause, i.e., $|C| > 1$, then self-subsumption can be considered. We exclude unit clauses, because they cannot be reduced in size; instead, they should be propagated over the entire formula before being removed (doing so is planned for future work). If applicable, the routine *isSelfSub* returns the position in C of the literal to be removed, otherwise -1 is returned. This literal is marked for removal in C, using an atomic operation, to avoid race conditions on writing and reading the literal. Finally, the clause is marked as being altered by self-subsumption (line 12), as after execution of the algorithm, the marked literals need to be removed, and the clause resized accordingly.

Finally, following the concept of thread reuse, each thread jumps ahead *stride* variables in both dimensions at the end of each **while** loop iteration (line 13). Sequential subsumption elimination has time complexity $\mathcal{O}(k \cdot |OT[\ell]|^2)$. By launching enough threads in both dimensions (i.e., $|OT[\ell]|^2 \approx p$), the parallel complexity becomes $\mathcal{O}(k)$. In practice, the average speedup of PSE compared to sequential SE is $9\times$ [21].

Correctly Strenghtening Clauses in PSE. Strengthening self-subsumed clauses cannot be done directly at line 9 of Algorithm 5. Instead, clauses need to be altered in-place. Consider the case that a clause C can be self-subsumed by two different clauses C_1, C_2 on two different self-subsuming literals, and that this is detected by two different threads at the exact same time. We call this phenomenon the parallel-effect of self-subsumption. Notice that the same result can be obtained by applying self-subsumption sequentially in two successive rounds. In the first round, C is checked against C_1, while in the second round, what is left of C is checked against C_2. If C would be removed by t_1 and replaced by a new, strengthened clause, then t_2 may suddenly be accessing unallocated memory. Instead, C is atomically strengthened in-place at line 11; t marks the self-subsumed literal using an atomic Compare-And-Swap operation. At the end, all clauses marked as self-subsumed have to be shrunk in size, in essence, overwriting reset positions. This is performed in a separate kernel call.

Algorithm 6: The PHSE algorithm - *GPU kernel*

Input: __global__ $S, \varphi[\,], eliminated[\,], OT[\,]$
Input: __shared__ $sh\_C[\,]$

```
1   tid ← xThread + blockDim × xBlock, stride ← gridDim × blockDim;
2   while tid < |φ| do
3       x ← φ[tid];
4       if ¬eliminated[x] then
5           foreach C ∈ S[OT[x]] do
6               sh_C ← C;
7               foreach C' ∈ S[OT[x̄]] do
8                   if |C'| < |C| ∧ sig(C', C) ≠ 0 ∧ isSelfSub(C', sh_C) then
9                       strengthenWT(C, sh_C, x);
10                  else if |C'| = |C| ∧ sig(C', C) ≠ 0 ∧ isSelfSub(C', sh_C) then
11                      strengthenWT(C, sh_C, x);
12                      markDeleted(C');
13              foreach C'' ∈ S[OT[x]] do
14                  if |C''| < |C| ∧ sig(C'', C) ≠ 0 ∧ isSubset(C'', sh_C) then
15                      markDeleted(C);
16      tid ← tid + stride;
```

Parallel Hybrid Subsumption Elimination (PHSE). PHSE is executed on elected variables that could not be eliminated earlier by variable elimination.

(Self)-subsumption elimination tends to reduce the number of occurrences of these non-eliminated variables as they usually eliminate many literals. After performing PHSE (Algorithm 6), the BVIPE algorithm can be executed again, after which PHSE can be executed, and so on, until no more literals can be removed.

Unlike PSE, the parallelism in the PHSE kernel is achieved on the variable level. In other words, each thread is assigned to a variable when executing PHSE. At line 4, previously eliminated variables are skipped. At line 6, a new clause is loaded, referenced by $OT[x]$, into shared memory (we call it the *shared clause, sh_C*).

The shared clause is then compared in the loop at lines 7–12 to all clauses referenced by $OT[\bar{x}]$ to check whether x is a self-subsuming literal. If so, both the original clause C, which resides in the global memory, and sh_C must be strengthened (via the *strengthenWT* function). Subsequently, the strengthened sh_C is used for subsumption checking in the loop at lines 13–15.

Regarding the complexity of Algorithm 6, the worst-case is that a variable x occurs in all clauses of S. However, in practice, the number of occurrences of x is bounded by the threshold value μ (see Definition 1). The same applies for its complement. Therefore, worst case, a variable and its complement both occur μ times. As PHSE considers all variables in φ and worst case has to traverse each loop μ times, its sequential worst-case complexity is $\mathcal{O}(|\varphi| \cdot \mu^2)$ and its parallel worst-case complexity is $\mathcal{O}(\mu^2)$.

5   Benchmarks

We implemented the proposed algorithms in CUDA C++ using CUDA toolkit v9.2. We conducted experiments using an NVIDIA Titan Xp GPU which has 30 SMs (128 cores each), 12 GB global memory and 48 KB shared memory. The machine equipped with the GPU was running Linux Mint v18. All GPU SAT simplifications were executed in four phases iteratively. Every two phases, the resulting CNF was reallocated to discard removed clauses. In general, the number of iterations can be configured, and the reallocation frequency can be also set to a desired value.

We selected 214 SAT problems from the industrial track of the 2013, 2016 and 2017 SAT competitions [13]. This set consists of almost all problems from those tracks that are more than 1 MB in file size. The largest size of problems occurring in this set is 1.2 GB. These problems have been encoded from 31 different real-world applications that have a whole range of dissimilar logical properties. Before applying any simplifications using the experimental tools, any occurring unit clauses were propagated. The presence of unit clauses immediately leads to simplification of the formula. By only considering formulas without unit clauses, the benchmark results directly indicate the true impact of our preprocessing algorithms.

In the benchmark experiments, besides the implementations of our new GPU algorithms, we involved the SatELite preprocessor [8], and the MiniSat and Lingeling [6] SAT solvers for the solving of problems, and executed these on the compute nodes of the DAS-5 cluster [1]. Each problem was analysed in isolation on a separate computing node. Each computing node had an Intel Xeon E5-2630 CPU running at a core clock speed of 2.4 GHz with 128 GB of system memory, and runs on the CentOS 7.4 operating system. We performed the equivalent of 6 months and 22 days of uninterrupted processing on a single node to measure how GPU SAT simplification impacts SAT solving in comparison to using sequential simplification or no simplification. The time out for solving experiments and simplification experiments was set to 24 h and 5,000 s, respectively. Time outs are marked 'T' in the tables in this section. Out-of-memory cases are marked 'M' in the tables.

Table 1 gives the MiniSat solving performance summed over the CNF families for both the original and simplified problems produced by GPU SAT simplification and SatELite. The $ve+$ and ve modes in GPU simplification represent variable elimination with and without PHSE, respectively. The all mode involves both $ve+$ and PSE. The numbers between brackets of columns 2 to 7 denote the number of solved instances at each family. Bold results in column 6 indicate that the combination of GPU SAT simplification and MiniSat reduced the net solution times (preprocessing + solving), or allowed more problems to be solved compared to the ve column of SatElite + MiniSat (column 3). Likewise, the all column for our results (column 7) is compared to column 4. The final four columns summarise the number of instances solved faster by MiniSat when using GPU SAT simplification (GPU+M) compared to not using GPU SAT simplification, and compared to using SatElite for simplification (SatElite+M). Numbers in bold indicate that 50% or more of the CNF formulas were solved faster.

The final row accumulates all problems solved faster. The percentage expresses the induced improvement by GPU SAT simplification over MiniSat and SatElite. Similarly, Table 2 gives the performance of solving the problems with Lingeling and GPU SAT simplification+Lingeling (GPU+L). Since SatELite is the groundwork of preprocessing in Lingeling, there is no reason to apply it again.[1]

The presented data shows that GPU+L solved many instances faster than SatElite with Lingeling, especially for the $ak128$, $blockpuzzle$, and $sokoban$ problems. In addition, GPU SAT simplification allowed Lingeling to solve more instances of the $hwmcc$, $velev$, and $sncf$ models. This effect did not occur for MiniSat.

Table 3 provides an evaluation of the achieved simplifications with GPU SAT simplification and SatELite, where V, C, L are the number of variables, clauses, and literals (in thousands), respectively, and $t(s)$ is the runtime in seconds. In case of GPU SAT simplification, t includes the transfer time between host and device. Bold results indicate significant improvements in reductions on literals for more than 50% of the instances.

On average, SatElite managed to eliminate more variables and clauses at the expense of literals explosion. Regarding scalability, GPU SAT simplification is able to preprocess extremely large problems (e.g., the $esawn$ problem, $sokoban$-$p20.sas.ex.23$, and the high-depth $sncf$ model) in only a few seconds while SatElite failed. For our benchmark set of SAT problems, GPU SAT

---

[1] The full tables with all obtained results are available at [21].

Table 1. MiniSat solving of original and simplified formulas (time in seconds).

Family (#CNF)	Minisat	SatElite + Minisat		GPU + Minisat			GPU+M vs MiniSat		GPU+M vs SatElite+M	
		ve	all	ve	ve+	all	ve+	all	ve+	all
dspam(8)	726(8)	143(8)	86(8)	194(8)	**127(8)**	**51(8)**	**6**	3	6	7
ACG(4)	10146(4)	5376(4)	2813(4)	9597(4)	4139(4)	3558(4)	4	4	3	1
ak128(30)	17353(11)	19604(11)	52185(11)	54302(11)	**34001(12)**	**5045(12)**	**12**	7	12	12
hwmcc(27)	291885(10)	294646(12)	408184(14)	205099(12)	145182(11)	262539(12)	11	11	8	7
UCG(3)	3048(3)	1467(3)	1022(3)	2186(3)	1831(3)	**725(3)**	2	3	1	3
UR(3)	12648(3)	12233(3)	4221(3)	27547(3)	**6431(3)**	20240(3)	3	1	2	0
UTI(1)	4594(1)	916(1)	1908(1)	2350(1)	4192(1)	**1244(1)**	1	1	0	1
itox(6)	7(6)	78(6)	151(6)	4.2(6)	**5.7(6)**	**12(6)**	**3**	0	6	6
manol-pipe(10)	1978(10)	3909(10)	3106(10)	1432(10)	**1239(10)**	**1213(10)**	**7**	7	5	5
blockpuzzle(14)	43584(13)	177545(13)	99569(10)	36698(14)	**55250(14)**	**55317(14)**	**7**	5	12	13
26-stack-cas(1)	0.9(1)	110(1)	110(1)	0.67(1)	**0.8(1)**	**2.81(1)**	**1**	0	1	1
9dlx-vliw(10)	14093(3)	141993(5)	133859(5)	76716(4)	33306(3)	**112862(5)**	1	4	0	4
dated(1)	3711(1)	4699(1)	3711(1)	3894(1)	**4553(1)**	3833(1)	0	0	1	0
podwr001(1)	14.5(1)	22(1)	53(1)	15.7(1)	**18(1)**	23(1)	0	0	1	1
transport(3)	2935(3)	1967(3)	2804(3)	5109(3)	2366(3)	7649(3)	1	1	0	1
valves(1)	3120(1)	770(1)	702(1)	1202(1)	1237(1)	873(1)	1	1	0	0
mizh-md5(6)	7492(6)	3272(6)	5091(6)	7519(6)	4457(6)	5805(6)	4	5	2	3
synthesis-aes(6)	15868(5)	10443(6)	54348(6)	7271(6)	**7645(6)**	8797(6)	5	5	3	5
test-c1-s(6)	32277(5)	86955(6)	23596(5)	23044(5)	28716(5)	81727(5)	4	5	1	2
cube-11-h13(1)	625(1)	324(1)	1173(1)	319(1)	**318(1)**	**122(1)**	1	1	1	1
esawn-uw3(1)	224(1)	M	M	426(1)	**563(1)**	**610(1)**	0	0	1	1
ibm-2002(1)	385(1)	66(1)	169(1)	61(1)	195(1)	**73(1)**	1	1	0	1
sin2(2)	38542(2)	44691(2)	39246(2)	45981(2)	54442(2)	**38016(2)**	1	1	1	2
traffic(1)	134(1)	133(1)	206(1)	133(1)	**41(1)**	282(1)	1	0	1	0
partial(8)	1696(1)	348(1)	605(1)	7062(2)	735(1)	T	1	0	0	0
newton(4)	24926(4)	6152(4)	5464(4)	15477(4)	19645(4)	13783(4)	4	4	2	2
safe(4)	5.5(4)	27(4)	102(4)	4.5(4)	**4.2(4)**	**20(4)**	2	0	4	4
arcfour(8)	1531(3)	831(3)	2196	1010(3)	1046(3)	**1051(3)**	3	3	0	1
sokoban(33)	127523(15)	116562(19)	91555(11)	119958(16)	101166(17)	**147564(18)**	11	11	8	13
#CNF solved faster (Percentage %)							98/135(73)	84/139(61)	82/140(59)	97/142(68)

Table 2. Lingeling solving of original and simplified formulas (time in seconds).

Family (#CNF)	Lingeling	GPU + Lingeling			GPU+L vs Lingeling	
		ve	ve+	all	ve+	all
dspam(8)	35(8)	52(8)	79(8)	65(8)	1	0
ACG(4)	1426(4)	1685(4)	1457(4)	**1392(4)**	3	3
ak128(30)	35692(16)	2602(16)	**41275(17)**	**2649(16)**	15	8
hwmcc15(27)	115970(27)	95530(27)	**96329(27)**	**109925(27)**	18	16
UCG(3)	605(3)	679(3)	762(3)	691(3)	0	1
UR(3)	2029(3)	1199(3)	2709(3)	**1739(3)**	1	2
UTI(1)	469(1)	412(1)	**402(1)**	**362(1)**	1	1
itox(6)	195(6)	153(6)	**92(6)**	**106(6)**	3	3
manol-pipe(10)	631(10)	662(10)	713(10)	659(10)	1	2
blockpuzzle(14)	30391(14)	57559(14)	57895(14)	**15328(14)**	7	7
26-stack-cas(1)	7(1)	1(1)	**1(1)**	**3(1)**	1	1
9dlx-vliw(10)	4287(10)	4713(10)	4579(10)	5121(10)	3	4
dated(1)	800(1)	704(1)	**751(1)**	**657(1)**	1	1
podwr001(1)	111(1)	108(1)	171(1)	**93(1)**	0	1
transport(3)	2526(3)	2246(3)	**1012(3)**	**2025(3)**	2	1
valves(1)	1536(1)	1501(1)	**1288(1)**	**1455(1)**	1	1
velev(2)	11717(2)	10645(2)	**10695(2)**	**9381(2)**	2	2
mizh-md5(6)	34104(6)	33327(6)	**32589(6)**	**23096(6)**	3	5
synthesis-aes(6)	49679(6)	16494(6)	**31927(6)**	**16151(6)**	3	6
test-c1-s(6)	84807(6)	55512(6)	17284(5)	4450(4)	3	2
cube-11-h13(1)	1495(1)	2022(1)	**1217(1)**	**813(1)**	1	1
esawn-uw3(1)	107(1)	271(1)	239(1)	463(1)	0	0
ibm-2002(1)	150(1)	191(1)	**129(1)**	194(1)	1	0
sin2(2)	4(1)	7(1)	4.2(1)	20(1)	0	0
traffic(1)	355(1)	694(1)	505(1)	869(1)	0	0
partial(8)	4691(2)	16026(2)	**1276(2)**	6735(2)	2	1
newton(4)	825(4)	913(4)	908(4)	861(4)	2	2
safe(4)	49(4)	57(4)	51(4)	63(4)	1	0
sncf-model(8)	73690(4)	135683(5)	T	**131301(5)**	0	4
arcfour(8)	1293(3)	1338(3)	1319(3)	1451(3)	0	1
sokoban(33)	339236(26)	139509(23)	248439(24)	166542(24)	**14**	**17**
#CNF solved faster (Percentage %)					90/179(50)	93/179(52)

simplification methods *ve+* and *all* achieve on average a speedup of 66× and 12× compared to SatElite *ve* and *all*, respectively [21].

Our appendix [21] presents larger tables, providing all our results related to Tables 1, 2 and 3. In addition, it presents a comparison between our GPU simplification algorithms and directly ported to the CPU versions of the algorithms, to provide more insight into the contribution of the GPU parallelisation. On average, subsumption elimination is performed 9× faster on the GPU, hybrid

Table 3. Comprehensive evaluation of simplification impact on original CNF size

CNF (Original)				SatElite								GPU							
				ve				all				ve+				all			
Name	V	C	L	V	C	L	t(s)	V	C	L	t(s)	V	C	L	t(s)	V	C	L	t(s)
dspam_dump_vc1103	275	920	2464	161	722	2190	12.9	155	695	2092	15.53	164	729	2182	0.69	164	729	2178	3.52
ACG-20-10p1	325	1316	3140	272	1293	3544	10.4	250	1194	3154	20.95	287	1243	3135	0.32	287	1242	3134	5.94
ak128astepbg2asisc	260	844	2144	130	681	2176	4.95	98	552	1853	11.32	162	617	1722	0.32	162	617	1722	1.12
hwmcc15deep-intel032	426	882	2051	69	334	1235	88.1	45	226	856	114.8	104	391	1171	0.47	104	390	1164	1.51
UCG-15-10p1	151	757	1845	119	739	2132	5.78	102	666	1849	13.51	122	700	1838	0.23	122	700	1837	3.50
UR-20-5p1	178	938	2320	140	918	2661	6.83	121	833	2332	15.97	145	874	2317	0.32	145	874	2317	9.37
UTI-20-10p1	203	1075	2656	160	1051	3042	7.74	138	954	2666	18.17	166	1001	2651	0.29	166	1001	2650	11.8
itox_vc1033	111	339	898	35	176	639	12.2	28	132	434	19.92	42	195	629	0.56	42	194	620	1.42
manol-pipe-f10ni	368	1100	2567	56	458	1855	15.2	56	456	1844	17.94	102	508	1590	0.75	102	508	1589	5.69
blockpuzzle_8x8_s1f4	3	311	625	3	305	987	0.91	3	303	794	3.42	3	311	632	0.08	3	311	632	6.83
blockpuzzle_9x9_s1f7	5	692	1389	5	681	2179	1.84	5	678	1764	8.53	5	691	1414	0.13	5	691	1414	6.18
26_stack_cas_longest	1505	3799	11287	1	11	44	110	1	10	39	110.4	3	15	43	0.84	3	14	41	2.80
9dlx_vliw_at_b_iq8	371	7170	20872	303	7042	22708	136	303	6994	21690	607.8	333	7098	21071	5.80	333	7069	20408	48.8
dated-10-17-u	177	813	1914	134	740	2074	8.49	67	425	1112	15.96	127	678	1764	0.43	127	678	1764	4.22
valves-gates-1-k617	970	3062	7842	302	1777	6027	30.9	249	1368	4454	52.40	371	1680	4970	1.21	366	1655	4856	18.5
velev-pipe-oun-1.1-05	236	7676	22782	143	7491	23933	45.0	143	7488	23914	84.85	178	7561	22683	11.5	178	7557	22530	109
velev-vliw-uns-2.0-uq5	151	2465	7141	120	2407	7653	41.2	120	2391	7388	99.17	131	2424	7181	1.55	130	2411	6963	20.3
esawn_uw3_debugged	12200	48049	133127	n/a	n/a	n/a	M	n/a	n/a	n/a	M	7361	36184	108331	16.0	7385	36189	108187	333
mizh-md5-12	69	226	585	28	171	576	1.53	28	163	552	2.17	37	163	482	0.07	37	163	482	0.32
mizh-md5-48-5	61	238	689	34	193	641	1.36	26	157	533	2.31	26	167	563	0.12	26	167	563	2.05
slp-synthesis-aes-top30	97	304	745	37	211	1110	41.9	37	191	1043	90.04	42	215	658	0.07	42	196	599	1.71
ibm-2002-23r-k90	209	864	2176	80	601	2179	9.93	72	523	1796	17.74	107	652	1899	0.38	107	645	1834	5.26
newton.2.3.i.smt2-cvc4	302	1309	3625	193	1116	3669	19.5	183	1025	3320	29.79	215	1079	3193	0.77	215	1074	3160	7.12
partial-10-19-s	269	1282	3033	207	1175	3293	13.0	168	995	2750	25.59	198	1089	2845	0.56	198	1089	2845	7.64
safe029	62	305	1048	41	261	1204	7.92	40	251	1095	23.66	56	291	1025	0.27	56	290	932	3.01
sin2.c.20.smt2-cvc4	1962	7954	21638	1063	6684	22579	136	867	5647	19591	306	1196	6072	18167	3.24	1196	6056	18057	35.2
sncf_model_depth_07	814	2641	6565	n/a	n/a	n/a	T	n/a	n/a	n/a	T	423	1778	5089	1.97	424	1778	5084	7.82
test_s18160	411	1831	5104	266	1595	5170	23.0	266	1595	5102	30.2	306	1607	4770	0.75	306	1599	4731	10.6
traffic_3_uc_sat	142	1312	4558	141	1311	4556	3.15	141	1311	4556	3.22	141	1311	4557	1.06	141	1310	4554	28.5
arcfour_6_14	105	404	1172	60	316	1365	4.99	60	316	1364	6.13	72	341	1114	0.09	72	341	1114	1.21
sokoban-p17.sas.ex.11	606	876	2312	6	151	1023	49.1	6	134	718	179	34	283	1180	0.53	34	282	1026	2.44
sokoban-p20.sas.ex.23	3632	7258	48119	111	2929	40787	11.0	n/a	n/a	n/a	T	276	3716	41536	0.34	276	3714	38205	5.96

subsumption elimination is performed 15× faster on the GPU, and BVE is conducted 32× faster on the GPU.

6 Related Work

Subbarayan and Pradhan [24] provided the first Bounded Variable Elimination (BVE) technique, called NiVER, based on the resolution rule of Davis-Putnam-Logemann-Loveland (DPLL) [7]. Eén and Biere [8] extended NiVER with subsumption elimination and clause substitution. However, the subsumption check is only performed on the clauses resulting from variable elimination, hence no reductions are obtained if there are no variables to resolve.

Heule *et al.* [14,16] introduced several approaches for clause elimination that can be effective in SAT simplifications, such as Blocked Clause Elimination. Bao *et al.* [3], on the other hand, have presented an efficient implementation of Common Sub-clause Elimination (CSE) performed periodically during SAT solving. CSE trims the search space, thereby decreasing the solving time, and is stable, i.e., the outcome of CSE does not depend on the chosen clause ordering. Gebhardt and Manthey [10] presented the first attempt to parallelise SAT preprocessing on a multi-core CPU using a locking scheme to prevent threads corrupting the SAT formula. However, they reported only a very limited speedup of on average 1.88× when running on eight cores.

All the above methods apply sound simplifications, but none are tailored for GPU parallelisation. They may consume considerable time when processing large problems.

Finally, it should be noted that BVE, as introduced in [8,10,16,24], is not confluent, as noted by the authors of [16]. Due to dependency between variables, altering the elimination order of these variables may result in different simplified formulas. This drawback is circumvented by our LCVE algorithm, which makes it possible to perform parallel variable elimination while achieving the confluence property.

7 Conclusion

We have shown that SAT simplifications can be performed efficiently on many-core systems, producing impactful reductions in a fraction of a second, even for larger problems consisting of millions of variables and tens of millions of clauses. The proposed BVIPE algorithm provides the first methodology to eliminate multiple variables in parallel while preserving satisfiability. Finally, PSE and PHSE have proven their effectiveness in removing many clauses and literals in a reasonable amount of time.

Concerning future work, the results of this work motivate us to take the capabilities of GPU SAT simplification further by supporting more simplification techniques or balancing the workload on multiple GPUs.

References

1. Bal, H., et al.: A medium-scale distributed system for computer science research: infrastructure for the long term. IEEE Comput. **49**(5), 54–63 (2016)
2. Balyo, T., Sinz, C.: Parallel satisfiability. In: Hamadi, Y., Sais, L. (eds.) Handbook of Parallel Constraint Reasoning, pp. 3–29. Springer, Cham (2018). https://doi.org/10.1007/978-3-319-63516-3_1
3. Bao, F.S., Gutierrez, C., Charles-Blount, J.J., Yan, Y., Zhang, Y.: Accelerating boolean satisfiability (SAT) solving by common subclause elimination. Artif. Intell. Rev. **49**(3), 439–453 (2018)
4. Bell, N., Hoberock, J.: Thrust: a productivity-oriented library for CUDA. In: GPU computing gems Jade edition, pp. 359–371. Elsevier, Atlanta (2012)
5. Bell, N., Hoberock, J.: A parallel algorithms library. Thrust Github (2018). https://thrust.github.io/
6. Biere, A.: Lingeling, plingeling and treengeling entering the SAT competition 2013. In: Proceedings of SAT Competition, pp. 51–52 (2013)
7. Davis, M., Logemann, G., Loveland, D.: A machine program for theorem-proving. Commun. ACM **5**(7), 394–397 (1962)
8. Eén, N., Biere, A.: Effective preprocessing in SAT through variable and clause elimination. In: Bacchus, F., Walsh, T. (eds.) SAT 2005. LNCS, vol. 3569, pp. 61–75. Springer, Heidelberg (2005). https://doi.org/10.1007/11499107_5
9. Eén, N., Sörensson, N.: An extensible SAT-solver. In: Giunchiglia, E., Tacchella, A. (eds.) SAT 2003. LNCS, vol. 2919, pp. 502–518. Springer, Heidelberg (2004). https://doi.org/10.1007/978-3-540-24605-3_37
10. Gebhardt, K., Manthey, N.: Parallel variable elimination on CNF formulas. In: Timm, I.J., Thimm, M. (eds.) KI 2013. LNCS (LNAI), vol. 8077, pp. 61–73. Springer, Heidelberg (2013). https://doi.org/10.1007/978-3-642-40942-4_6
11. Hamadi, Y., Wintersteiger, C.: Seven challenges in parallel SAT solving. AI Mag. **34**(2), 99 (2013)
12. Han, H., Somenzi, F.: Alembic: an efficient algorithm for CNF preprocessing. In: Proceedings of 44th ACM/IEEE Design Automation Conference, pp. 582–587. IEEE (2007)
13. Heule, M., Järvisalo, M., Balyo, T., Balint, A., Belov, A.: SAT Competition, vol. 13, pp. 16–17 (2018). https://satcompetition.org/
14. Heule, M., Järvisalo, M., Biere, A.: Clause elimination procedures for CNF formulas. In: Fermüller, C.G., Voronkov, A. (eds.) LPAR 2010. LNCS, vol. 6397, pp. 357–371. Springer, Heidelberg (2010). https://doi.org/10.1007/978-3-642-16242-8_26
15. Heule, M., Järvisalo, M., Lonsing, F., Seidl, M., Biere, A.: Clause elimination for SAT and QSAT. J. Artif. Intell. Res. **53**, 127–168 (2015)
16. Järvisalo, M., Biere, A., Heule, M.: Blocked clause elimination. In: Esparza, J., Majumdar, R. (eds.) TACAS 2010. LNCS, vol. 6015, pp. 129–144. Springer, Heidelberg (2010). https://doi.org/10.1007/978-3-642-12002-2_10
17. Järvisalo, M., Biere, A., Heule, M.J.: Simulating circuit-level simplifications on CNF. J. Autom. Reasoning **49**(4), 583–619 (2012)
18. Järvisalo, M., Heule, M.J.H., Biere, A.: Inprocessing rules. In: Gramlich, B., Miller, D., Sattler, U. (eds.) IJCAR 2012. LNCS (LNAI), vol. 7364, pp. 355–370. Springer, Heidelberg (2012). https://doi.org/10.1007/978-3-642-31365-3_28
19. Jin, H., Somenzi, F.: An incremental algorithm to check satisfiability for bounded model checking. ENTCS **119**(2), 51–65 (2005)

20. NVIDIA: CUDA C Programming Guide (2018). https://docs.nvidia.com/cuda/cuda-c-programming-guide/index.html

21. Osama, M., Wijs, A.: Parallel SAT Simplification on GPU Architectures -Appendix (2019). http://www.win.tue.nl/~awijs/suppls/pss-app.pdf

22. Osama, M., Gaber, L., Hussein, A.I., Mahmoud, H.: An efficient SAT-based test generation algorithm with GPU accelerator. J. Electron. Test. **34**(5), 511–527 (2018)

23. Ostrowski, R., Grégoire, É., Mazure, B., Saïs, L.: Recovering and exploiting structural knowledge from CNF formulas. In: Van Hentenryck, P. (ed.) CP 2002. LNCS, vol. 2470, pp. 185–199. Springer, Heidelberg (2002). https://doi.org/10.1007/3-540-46135-3_13

24. Subbarayan, S., Pradhan, D.K.: NiVER: non-increasing variable elimination resolution for preprocessing SAT instances. In: Hoos, H.H., Mitchell, D.G. (eds.) SAT 2004. LNCS, vol. 3542, pp. 276–291. Springer, Heidelberg (2005). https://doi.org/10.1007/11527695_22

25. Wijs, A.: GPU accelerated strong and branching bisimilarity checking. In: Baier, C., Tinelli, C. (eds.) TACAS 2015. LNCS, vol. 9035, pp. 368–383. Springer, Heidelberg (2015). https://doi.org/10.1007/978-3-662-46681-0_29

26. Wijs, A.: BFS-based model checking of linear-time properties with an application on GPUs. In: Chaudhuri, S., Farzan, A. (eds.) CAV 2016. LNCS, vol. 9780, pp. 472–493. Springer, Cham (2016). https://doi.org/10.1007/978-3-319-41540-6_26

27. Wijs, A., Bošnački, D.: Many-core on-the-fly model checking of safety properties using GPUs. Int. J. Softw. Tools Technol. Transfer **18**(2), 169–185 (2016)

28. Wijs, A., Katoen, J.-P., Bošnački, D.: GPU-based graph decomposition into strongly connected and maximal end components. In: Biere, A., Bloem, R. (eds.) CAV 2014. LNCS, vol. 8559, pp. 310–326. Springer, Cham (2014). https://doi.org/10.1007/978-3-319-08867-9_20

29. Wijs, A., Katoen, J.P., Bošnački, D.: Efficient GPU algorithms for parallel decomposition of graphs into strongly connected and maximal end components. Formal Methods Syst. Des. **48**(3), 274–300 (2016)

30. Wijs, A., Neele, T., Bošnački, D.: GPUexplore 2.0: unleashing GPU explicit-state model checking. In: Fitzgerald, J., Heitmeyer, C., Gnesi, S., Philippou, A. (eds.) FM 2016. LNCS, vol. 9995, pp. 694–701. Springer, Cham (2016). https://doi.org/10.1007/978-3-319-48989-6_42

31. Youness, H., Ibraheim, A., Moness, M., Osama, M.: An efficient implementation of ant colony optimization on GPU for the satisfiability problem. In: 2015 23rd Euromicro International Conference on Parallel, Distributed, and Network-Based Processing, pp. 230–235, March 2015

6

Quantitative Verification of Masked Arithmetic Programs Against Side-Channel Attacks

Pengfei Gao[1], Hongyi Xie[1], Jun Zhang[1], Fu Song[1(✉)], and Taolue Chen[2]

[1] School of Information Science and Technology,
ShanghaiTech University, Shanghai, China
`songfu@shanghaitech.edu.cn`
[2] Department of Computer Science and Information Systems,
Birkbeck, University of London, London, UK

Abstract. Power side-channel attacks, which can deduce secret data via statistical analysis, have become a serious threat. Masking is an effective countermeasure for reducing the statistical dependence between secret data and side-channel information. However, designing masking algorithms is an error-prone process. In this paper, we propose a hybrid approach combing type inference and model-counting to verify masked arithmetic programs against side-channel attacks. The type inference allows an efficient, lightweight procedure to determine most observable variables whereas model-counting accounts for completeness. In case that the program is not perfectly masked, we also provide a method to quantify the security level of the program. We implement our methods in a tool QMVERIF and evaluate it on cryptographic benchmarks. The experiment results show the effectiveness and efficiency of our approach.

1 Introduction

Side-channel attacks aim to infer secret data (e.g. cryptographic keys) by exploiting statistical dependence between secret data and non-functional observations such as execution time [33], power consumption [34], and electromagnetic radiation [46]. They have become a serious threat in application domains such as cyber-physical systems. As a typical example, the power consumption of a device executing the instruction $c = p \oplus k$ usually depends on the secret k, and this can be exploited via *differential power analysis* (DPA) [37] to deduce k.

Masking is one of the most widely-used and effective countermeasure to thwart side-channel attacks. Masking is essentially a randomization technique for reducing the statistical dependence between secret data and side-channel information (e.g. power consumption). For example, using Boolean masking scheme, one can mask the secret data k by applying the exclusive-or ($\oplus$) operation with a random variable r, yielding a masked secret data $k \oplus r$. It can be readily verified that the distribution of $k \oplus r$ is independent of the value of k when r is uniformly distributed. Besides Boolean masking scheme, there are other masking schemes such as additive masking schemes (e.g. $(k + r) \bmod n$) and multiplicative masking schemes (e.g. $(k \times r) \bmod n$). A variety of masking implementations such as AES and its non-linear components (S-boxes) have been published over the years. However, designing effective and efficient masking schemes is still a notoriously difficult task, especially for non-linear functions. This has motivated a large amount of work on verifying whether masked implementations, as either (hardware) circuits or (software) programs, are statistically independent of secret inputs. Typically, masked hardware implementations are modeled as (probabilistic) Boolean programs where all variables range over the Boolean domain (i.e. $GF(2)$), while masked software implementations, featuring a richer set of operations, require to be modeled as (probabilistic) arithmetic programs.

Verification techniques for masking schemes can be roughly classified into type system based approaches [3–5,14,16,19,38] and model-counting based approaches [24,25,50]. The basic idea of type system based approaches is to infer a *distribution type* for observable variables in the program that are potentially exposed to attackers. From the type information one may be able to show that the program is secure. This class of approaches is generally very efficient mainly because of their static analysis nature. However, they may give inconclusive answers as most existing type systems do not provide completeness guarantees.

Model-counting based approaches, unsurprisingly, encode the verification problem as a series of model-counting problems, and typically leverage SAT/SMT solvers. The main advantage of this approach is its completeness guarantees. However, the size of the model-counting constraint is usually exponential in the number of (bits of) random variables used in masking, hence the approach poses great challenges to its scalability. We mention that, within this category, some work further exploits Fourier analysis [11,15], which considers the Fourier expansion of the Boolean functions. The verification problem can then be reduced to checking whether certain coefficients of the Fourier expansion are zero or not. Although there is no hurdle in principle, to our best knowledge currently model-counting based approaches are limited to Boolean programs only.

While verification of masking for Boolean programs is well-studied [24,50], generalizing them to arithmetic programs brings additional challenges. First of all, arithmetic programs admit more operations which are absent from Boolean programs. A typical example is field multiplication. In the Boolean domain, it is nothing more than $\oplus$ which is a bit operation. However for $GF(2^n)$ (typically $n = 8$ in cryptographic algorithm implementations), the operation is nontrivial which prohibits many optimization which would otherwise be useful for Boolean domains. Second, verification of arithmetic programs often suffers from serious scalability issues, especially when the model-counting based approaches are applied. We note that transforming arithmetic programs into equivalent Boolean versions is theoretically possible, but suffer from several deficiencies: (1) one has to encode complicated arithmetic operations (e.g. finite field multiplication) as bitwise operations; (2) the resulting Boolean program needs to be checked against higher-order attacks which are supposed to observe multiple observations simultaneously. This is a far more difficult problem. Because of this, we believe such as approach is practically, if not infeasible, unfavourable.

Perfect masking is ideal but not necessarily holds when there are flaws or only a limited number of random variables are allowed for efficiency consideration. In case that the program is not perfectly masked (i.e., a potential side channel does exist), naturally one wants to tell how severe it is. For instance, one possible measure is the resource the attacker needs to invest in order to infer the secret from the side channel. For this purpose, we adapt the notion of *Quantitative Masking Strength*, with which a correlation of the number of power traces to successfully infer secret has been established empirically [26, 27].

Main Contributions. We mainly focus on the verification of masked *arithmetic* programs. We advocate a hybrid verification method combining type system based and model-counting based approaches, and provide additional quantitative analysis. We summarize the main contributions as follows.

- We provide a hybrid approach which integrates type system based and model-counting based approaches into a framework, and support a sound and complete reasoning of masked arithmetic programs.
- We provide quantitative analysis in case when the masking is not effective, to calculate a quantitative measure of the information leakage.
- We provide various heuristics and optimized algorithms to significantly improve the scalability of previous approaches.
- We implement our approaches in a software tool and provide thorough evaluations. Our experiments show orders of magnitude of improvement with respect to previous verification methods on common benchmarks.

We find, perhaps surprisingly, that for model-counting, the widely adopted approaches based on SMT solvers (e.g. [24, 25, 50]) may not be the best approach, as our experiments suggest that an alternative brute-force approach is comparable for Boolean programs, and significantly outperforms for arithmetic programs.

Related Work. The d-threshold probing model is the de facto standard leakage model for order-d power side-channel attacks [32]. This paper focuses on the case that $d = 1$. Other models like noise leakage model [17, 45], bounded moment model [6], and threshold probing model with transitions/glitch [15, 20] could be reduced to the threshold probing model, at the cost of introducing higher orders [3]. Other work on side channels such as execution-time, faults, and cache do exist ([1, 2, 7, 8, 12, 28, 31, 33] to cite a few), but is orthogonal to our work.

Type systems have been widely used in the verification of side channel attacks with early work [9, 38], where masking compilers are provided which can transform an input program into a functionally equivalent program that is resistant to first-order DPA. However, these systems either are limited to certain operations (i.e., $\oplus$ and table look-up), or suffer from unsoundness and incompleteness under the threshold probing model. To support verification of higher-order masking, Barthe et al. introduced the notion of noninterference (NI, [3]), and strong t-noninterference (SNI, [4]), which were extended to give a unified framework for both software and hardware implementations in `maskVerif` [5]. Further work along this line includes improvements for efficiency [14, 19], generalization for assembly-level code [15], and extensions with glitches for hardware programs [29]. As mentioned earlier, these approaches are incomplete, i.e., secure programs may fail to pass their verification.

[24,25] proposed a model-counting based approach for Boolean programs by leveraging SMT solvers, which is complete but limited in scalability. To improve efficiency, a hybrid approach integrating type-based and model-counting based approaches [24,25] was proposed in [50], which is similar to the current work in spirit. However, it is limited to Boolean programs and qualitative analysis only. [26,27] extended the approach of [24,25] for quantitative analysis, but is limited to Boolean programs. The current work not only extends the applicability but also achieves significant improvement in efficiency even for Boolean programs (cf. Sect. 5). We also find that solving model-counting via SMT solvers [24,50] may not be the best approach, in particular for arithmetic programs.

Our work is related to quantitative information flow (QIF) [13,35,43,44,49] which leverages notions from information theory (typically Shannon entropy and mutual information) to measure the flow of information in programs. The QIF framework has also been specialized to side-channel analysis [36,41,42]. The main differences are, first of all, QIF targets fully-fledged programs (including branching and loops) so program analysis techniques (e.g. symbolic execution) are needed, while we deal with more specialized (transformed) masked programs in straight-line forms; second, to measure the information leakage quantitatively, our measure is based on the notion QMS which is correlated with the number of power traces needed to successfully infer the secret, while QIF is based on a more general sense of information theory; third, for calculating such a measure, both works rely on model-counting. In QIF, the constraints over the input are usually linear, but the constraints in our setting involve arithmetic operations in rings and fields. Randomized approximate schemes can be exploited in QIF [13] which is not suitable in our setting. Moreover, we mention that in QIF, input variables should in principle be partitioned into public and private variables, and the former of which needs to be existentially quantified. This was briefly mentioned in, e.g., [36], but without implementation.

2 Preliminaries

Let us fix a bounded integer domain $\mathbb{D} = \{0, \cdots, 2^n - 1\}$, where n is a fixed positive integer. Bit-wise operations are defined over $\mathbb{D}$, but we shall also consider arithmetic operations over $\mathbb{D}$ which include $+, -, \times$ modulo 2^n for which $\mathbb{D}$ is consider to be a ring and the Galois field multiplication $\odot$ where $\mathbb{D}$ is isomorphic to $\mathbb{GF}(2)[x]/(p(x))$ (or simply $\mathbb{GF}(2^n)$) for some irreducible polynomial p. For instance, in AES one normally uses $\mathbb{GF}(2^8)$ and $p(x) = x^8 + x^4 + x^3 + x^2 + 1$.

2.1 Cryptographic Programs

We focus on programs written in C-like code that implement cryptographic algorithms such as AES, as opposed to arbitrary software programs. To analyze such programs, it is common to assume that they are given in straight-line forms (i.e., branching-free) over $\mathbb{D}$ [3, 24]. The syntax of the program under consideration is given as follows, where $c \in \mathbb{D}$.

Operation: $\mathcal{O} \ni \circ ::= \oplus \mid \wedge \mid \vee \mid \odot \mid + \mid - \mid \times$

Expression: $e ::= c \mid x \mid e \circ e \mid \neg e \mid e \ll c \mid e \gg c$

Statememt: $\mathtt{stmt} ::= x \leftarrow e \mid \mathtt{stmt}; \mathtt{stmt}$

Program: $P(X_p, X_k, X_r) ::= \mathtt{stmt}; \mathtt{return}\ x_1, ..., x_m$

A program P consists of a sequence of assignments followed by a return statement. An assignment $x \leftarrow e$ assigns the value of the expression e to the variable x, where e is built up from a set of variables and constants using (1) bit-wise operations *negation* ($\neg$), *and* ($\wedge$), *or* ($\vee$), *exclusive-or* ($\oplus$), *left shift* $\ll$ and *right shift* $\gg$; (2) modulo 2^n arithmetic operations: *addition* ($+$), *subtraction* ($-$), *multiplication* ($\times$); and (3) finite-field *multiplication* ($\odot$) (over $\mathbb{GF}(2^n)$)[1]. We denote by $\mathcal{O}^*$ the extended set $\mathcal{O} \cup \{\ll, \gg\}$ of operations.

Given a program P, let $X = X_p \uplus X_k \uplus X_i \uplus X_r$ denote the set of variables used in P, where X_p, X_k and X_i respectively denote the set of public input, private input and internal variables, and X_r denotes the set of (uniformly distributed) random variables for *masking* private variables. We assume that the program is given in the *single static assignment* (SSA) form (i.e., each variable is defined exactly once) and each expression uses at most one operator. (One can easily transform an arbitrary straight-line program into an equivalent one satisfying these conditions.) For each assignment $x \leftarrow e$ in P, **the computation $\mathcal{E}(x)$ of** x is an expression obtained from e by iteratively replacing all the occurrences of the internal variables in e by their defining expressions in P. SSA form guarantees that $\mathcal{E}(x)$ is well-defined.

Semantics. A *valuation* is a function $\sigma : X_p \cup X_k \to \mathbb{D}$ assigning to each variable $x \in X_p \cup X_k$ a value $c \in \mathbb{D}$. Let Θ denote the set of all valuations. Two valuations $\sigma_1, \sigma_2 \in \Theta$ are *Y-equivalent*, denoted by $\sigma_1 \approx_Y \sigma_2$, if $\sigma_1(x) = \sigma_2(x)$ for all $x \in Y$.

Given an expression e in terms of $X_p \cup X_k \cup X_r$ and a valuation $\sigma \in \Theta$, we denote by $e(\sigma)$ the expression obtained from e by replacing all the occurrences of variables $x \in X_p \cup X_k$ by their values $\sigma(x)$, and denote by $\llbracket e \rrbracket_\sigma$ the distribution of e (with respect to the uniform distribution of random variables $e(\sigma)$ may contain). Concretely, $\llbracket e \rrbracket_\sigma(v)$ is the probability of the expression $e(\sigma)$ being evaluated to v for each $v \in \mathbb{D}$. For each variable $x \in X$ and valuation $\sigma \in \Theta$, we denote by $\llbracket x \rrbracket_\sigma$ the distribution $\llbracket \mathcal{E}(x) \rrbracket_\sigma$. The semantics of the program P is defined as a (partial) function $\llbracket P \rrbracket$ which takes a valuation $\sigma \in \Theta$ and an internal variable $x \in X_i$ as inputs, returns the distribution $\llbracket x \rrbracket_\sigma$ of x.

Threat Models and Security Notions. We assume that the adversary has access to public input X_p, but not to private input X_k or random variables X_r, of a program P. However, the adversary may have access to an internal variable $x \in X_i$ via side-channels. Under these assumptions, the goal of the adversary is to deduce the information of X_k.

---

[1] Note that addition/subtraction over Galois fields is essentially bit-wise exclusive-or.

```
1 Cube(k, r₀, r₁){        6    x₃ = x₁ ⊙ x;        11    x₈ = x₁ ⊙ r₀;
2    x = k ⊕ r₀;          7    x₄ = r₁ ⊕ x₂;       12    x₉ = x₈ ⊕ x₅;
3    x₀ = x ⊙ x;          8    x₅ = x₄ ⊕ x₃;       13    return (x₇, x₉);
4    x₁ = r₀ ⊙ r₀;        9    x₆ = x₀ ⊙ x;        14 }
5    x₂ = x₀ ⊙ r₀;        10   x₇ = x₆ ⊕ r₁;
```

Fig. 1. A buggy version of Cube from [47]

Definition 1. *Let P be a program. For every internal variable $x \in X_i$,*

- *x is* uniform *in P, denoted by x-**UF**, if $[\![P]\!](\sigma)(x)$ is uniform for all $\sigma \in \Theta$.*
- *x is* statistically independent *in P, denoted by x-**SI**, if $[\![P]\!](\sigma_1)(x) = [\![P]\!](\sigma_2)(x)$ for all $(\sigma_1, \sigma_2) \in \Theta^2_{X_p}$, where $\Theta^2_{X_p} := \{(\sigma_1, \sigma_2) \in \Theta \times \Theta \mid \sigma_1 \approx_{X_p} \sigma_2\}$.*

Proposition 1. *If the program P is x-**UF**, then P is x-**SI**.*

Definition 2. *For a program P, a variable x is* perfectly masked *(a.k.a. secure under 1-threshold probing model [32]) in P if it is x-**SI**, otherwise x is* leaky.
    P is perfectly masked *if all internal variables in P are perfectly masked.*

2.2 Quantitative Masking Strength

When a program is not perfectly masked, it is important to quantify how secure it is. For this purpose, we adapt the notion of *Quantitative Masking Strength* (QMS) from [26, 27] to quantify the strength of masking countermeasures.

Definition 3. *The* quantitative masking strength *QMS_x of a variable $x \in X$, is defined as: $1 - \max_{(\sigma_1, \sigma_2) \in \Theta^2_{X_p}, c \in \mathbb{D}} \left([\![x]\!]_{\sigma_1}(c) - [\![x]\!]_{\sigma_2}(c) \right)$.*
    Accordingly, the quantitative masking strength *of the program P is defined by $\mathsf{QMS}_P := \min_{x \in X_i} \mathsf{QMS}_x$.*

The notion of QMS generalizes that of perfect masking, i.e., P is x-**SI** iff $\mathsf{QMS}_x = 1$. The importance of QMS has been highlighted in [26, 27] where it is empirically shown that, for Boolean programs the number of power traces needed to determine the secret key is exponential in the QMS value. This study suggests that computing an *accurate* QMS value for leaky variables is highly desirable.

Example 1. Let us consider the program in Fig. 1, which implements a buggy Cube in $\mathbb{GF}(2^8)$ from [47]. Given a secret key k, to avoid first-order side-channel attacks, k is masked by a random variable r_0 leading to two shares $x = k \oplus r_0$ and r_0. Cube(k, r_0, r_1) returns two shares x_7 and x_9 such that $x_7 \oplus x_9 = k^3 := k \odot k \odot k$, where r_1 is another random variable.

Cube computes $k \odot k$ by $x_0 = x \odot x$ and $x_1 = r_0 \odot r_0$ (Lines 3–4), as $k \odot k = x_0 \oplus x_1$. Then, it computes k^3 by a secure multiplication of two pairs of shares (x_0, x_1) and (x, r_0) using the random variable r_1 (Lines 5–12). However, this program is vulnerable to first-order side-channel attacks, as it is neither x_2-**SI** nor x_3-**SI**. As shown in [47], we shall refresh (x_0, x_1) before computing $k^2 \odot k$ by inserting

$x_0 = x_0 \oplus r_2$ and $x_1 = x_1 \oplus r_2$ after Line 4, where r_2 is a random variable. We use this buggy version as a running example to illustrate our techniques.

As setup for further use, we have: $X_p = \emptyset$, $X_k = \{k\}$, $X_r = \{r_0, r_1\}$ and $X_i = \{x, x_0, \cdots, x_9\}$. The computations $\mathcal{E}(\cdot)$ of internal variables are:

$\mathcal{E}(x) = k \oplus r_0$ $\mathcal{E}(x_0) = (k \oplus r_0) \odot (k \oplus r_0)$ $\mathcal{E}(x_1) = r_0 \odot r_0$

$\mathcal{E}(x_2) = ((k \oplus r_0) \odot (k \oplus r_0)) \odot r_0$ $\mathcal{E}(x_3) = (r_0 \odot r_0) \odot (k \oplus r_0)$

$\mathcal{E}(x_4) = r_1 \oplus (((k \oplus r_0) \odot (k \oplus r_0)) \odot r_0)$ $\mathcal{E}(x_6) = ((k \oplus r_0) \odot (k \oplus r_0)) \odot (k \oplus r_0)$

$\mathcal{E}(x_5) = (r_1 \oplus ((k \oplus r_0) \odot (k \oplus r_0)) \odot r_0) \oplus ((r_0 \odot r_0) \odot (k \oplus r_0))$

$\mathcal{E}(x_7) = (((k \oplus r_0) \odot (k \oplus r_0)) \odot (k \oplus r_0)) \oplus r_1$ $\mathcal{E}(x_8) = (r_0 \odot r_0) \odot r_0$

$\mathcal{E}(x_9) = ((r_0 \odot r_0) \odot r_0) \oplus ((r_1 \oplus ((k \oplus r_0) \odot (k \oplus r_0) \odot r_0)) \oplus ((r_0 \odot r_0) \odot (k \oplus r_0)))$

3   Three Key Techniques

In this section, we introduce three key techniques: type system, model-counting based reasoning and reduction techniques, which will be used in our algorithm.

3.1   Type System

We present a type system for formally inferring *distribution types* of internal variables, inspired by prior work [3, 14, 40, 50]. We start with some basic notations.

Definition 4 (Dominant variables). *Given an expression e, a random variable r is called a* dominant variable *of e if the following two conditions hold: (i) r occurs in e exactly once, and (ii) each operator on the path between the leaf r and the root in the abstract syntax tree of e is from either $\{\oplus, \neg, +, -\}$ or $\{\odot\}$ such that one of the children of the operator is a non-zero constant.*

Remark that in Definition 4, for efficiency consideration, we take a purely syntactic approach meaning that we do not simplify e when checking the condition (i) that r occurs once. For instance, x is *not* a dominant variable in $((x \oplus y) \oplus x) \oplus x$, although intuitively e is equivalent to $y \oplus x$.

Given an expression e, let $\mathsf{Var}(e)$ be the set of variables occurring in e, and $\mathsf{RVar}(e) := \mathsf{Var}(e) \cap X_r$. We denote by $\mathsf{Dom}(e) \subseteq \mathsf{RVar}(e)$ the set of all dominant random variables of e, which can be computed in linear time in the size of e.

Proposition 2. *Given a program P with $\mathcal{E}(x)$ defined for each variable x of P, if $\mathsf{Dom}(\mathcal{E}(x)) \neq \emptyset$, then P is x-**UF**.*

Definition 5 (Distribution Types). *Let $\mathcal{T} = \{\mathsf{RUD}, \mathsf{SID}, \mathsf{SDD}, \mathsf{UKD}\}$ be the set of distribution types, where for each variable $x \in X$,*

- *$\mathcal{E}(x) : \mathsf{RUD}$ meaning that the program is x-**UF**;*
- *$\mathcal{E}(x) : \mathsf{SID}$ meaning that the program is x-**SI**;*
- *$\mathcal{E}(x) : \mathsf{SDD}$ meaning that the program is not x-**SI**;*
- *$\mathcal{E}(x) : \mathsf{UKD}$ meaning that the distribution type of x is unknown.*

where RUD is a subtype of SID (cf. Proposition 1).

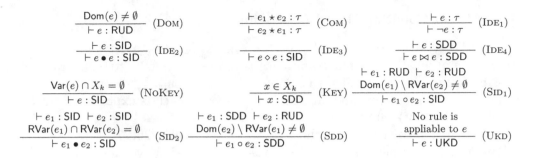

$$\frac{\mathrm{Dom}(e) \neq \emptyset}{\vdash e : \mathsf{RUD}} \; (\mathrm{Dom}) \qquad \frac{\vdash e_1 \star e_2 : \tau}{\vdash e_2 \star e_1 : \tau} \; (\mathrm{Com}) \qquad \frac{\vdash e : \tau}{\vdash \neg e : \tau} \; (\mathrm{IDE}_1)$$

$$\frac{\vdash e : \mathsf{SID}}{\vdash e \bullet e : \mathsf{SID}} \; (\mathrm{IDE}_2) \qquad \frac{}{\vdash e \diamond e : \mathsf{SID}} \; (\mathrm{IDE}_3) \qquad \frac{\vdash e : \mathsf{SDD}}{\vdash e \bowtie e : \mathsf{SDD}} \; (\mathrm{IDE}_4)$$

$$\frac{\mathrm{Var}(e) \cap X_k = \emptyset}{\vdash e : \mathsf{SID}} \; (\mathrm{NoKey}) \qquad \frac{x \in X_k}{\vdash x : \mathsf{SDD}} \; (\mathrm{Key}) \qquad \frac{\vdash e_1 : \mathsf{RUD} \; \vdash e_2 : \mathsf{RUD} \quad \mathrm{Dom}(e_1) \setminus \mathrm{RVar}(e_2) \neq \emptyset}{\vdash e_1 \circ e_2 : \mathsf{SID}} \; (\mathrm{SID}_1)$$

$$\frac{\vdash e_1 : \mathsf{SID} \; \vdash e_2 : \mathsf{SID} \quad \mathrm{RVar}(e_1) \cap \mathrm{RVar}(e_2) = \emptyset}{\vdash e_1 \bullet e_2 : \mathsf{SID}} \; (\mathrm{SID}_2) \qquad \frac{\vdash e_1 : \mathsf{SDD} \; \vdash e_2 : \mathsf{RUD} \quad \mathrm{Dom}(e_2) \setminus \mathrm{RVar}(e_1) \neq \emptyset}{\vdash e_1 \circ e_2 : \mathsf{SDD}} \; (\mathrm{SDD}) \qquad \frac{\text{No rule is appliable to } e}{\vdash e : \mathsf{UKD}} \; (\mathrm{UKD})$$

Fig. 2. Type inference rules, where $\star \in \mathcal{O}$, $\circ \in \{\wedge, \vee, \odot, \times\}$, $\bullet \in \mathcal{O}^*$, $\bowtie \in \{\wedge, \vee\}$ and $\diamond \in \{\oplus, -\}$.

Type judgements, as usual, are defined in the form of $\vdash e : \tau$, where e is an expression in terms of $X_r \cup X_k \cup X_p$, and $\tau \in \mathcal{T}$ denotes the distribution type of e. A type judgement $\vdash e : \mathsf{RUD}$ (resp. $\vdash e : \mathsf{SID}$ and $\vdash e : \mathsf{SDD}$) is valid iff P is x-**UF** (resp. x-**SI** and not x-**SI**) for all variables x such that $\mathcal{E}(x) = e$. A sound proof system for deriving valid type judgements is given in Fig. 2.

Rule (Dom) states that e containing some dominant variable has type RUD (cf. Proposition 2). Rule (Com) captures the commutative law of operators $\star \in \mathcal{O}$. Rules (IDE_i) for $i = 1, 2, 3, 4$ are straightforward. Rule (NoKey) states that e has type SID if e does not use any private input. Rule (Key) states that each private input has type SDD. Rule (SID_1) states that $e_1 \circ e_2$ for $\circ \in \{\wedge, \vee, \odot, \times\}$ has type SID, if both e_1 and e_2 have type RUD, and e_1 has a dominant variable r which is not used by e_2. Indeed, $e_1 \circ e_2$ can be seen as $r \circ e_2$, then for each valuation $\eta \in \Theta$, the distributions of r and $e_2(\eta)$ are independent. Rule (SID_2) states that $e_1 \bullet e_2$ for $\bullet \in \mathcal{O}^*$ has type SID, if both e_1 and e_2 have type SID (as well as its subtype RUD), and the sets of random variables used by e_1 and e_2 are disjoint. Likewise, for each valuation $\eta \in \Theta$, the distributions on $e_1(\eta)$ and $e_2(\eta)$ are independent. Rule (SDD) states that $e_1 \circ e_2$ for $\circ \in \{\wedge, \vee, \odot, \times\}$ has type SDD, if e_1 has type SDD, e_2 has type RUD, and e_2 has a dominant variable r which is not used by e_1. Intuitively, $e_1 \circ e_2$ can be safely seen as $e_1 \circ r$.

Finally, if no rule is applicable to an expression e, then e has unknown distribution type. Such a type is needed because our type system is—by design—incomplete. However, we expect—and demonstrate empirically—that for cryptographic programs, most internal variables have a definitive type other than UKD. As we will show later, to resolve UKD-typed variables, one can resort to model-counting (cf. Sect. 3.2).

Theorem 1. *If $\vdash \mathcal{E}(x) : \mathsf{RUD}$ (resp. $\vdash \mathcal{E}(x) : \mathsf{SID}$ and $\vdash \mathcal{E}(x) : \mathsf{SDD}$) is valid, then P is x-**UF** (resp. x-**SI** and not x-**SI**).*

Example 2. Consider the program in Fig. 1, we have:

$$\vdash \mathcal{E}(x) : \mathsf{RUD}; \quad \vdash \mathcal{E}(x_0) : \mathsf{SID}; \quad \vdash \mathcal{E}(x_1) : \mathsf{SID}; \quad \vdash \mathcal{E}(x_2) : \mathsf{UKD};$$
$$\vdash \mathcal{E}(x_3) : \mathsf{UKD}; \quad \vdash \mathcal{E}(x_4) : \mathsf{RUD}; \quad \vdash \mathcal{E}(x_5) : \mathsf{RUD}; \quad \vdash \mathcal{E}(x_6) : \mathsf{UKD};$$
$$\vdash \mathcal{E}(x_7) : \mathsf{RUD}; \quad \vdash \mathcal{E}(x_8) : \mathsf{SID}; \quad \vdash \mathcal{E}(x_9) : \mathsf{RUD}.$$

3.2   Model-Counting Based Reasoning

Recall that for $x \in X_i$, $\mathrm{QMS}_x := 1 - \max_{(\sigma_1, \sigma_2) \in \Theta^2_{X_p}, c \in \mathbb{D}}(\llbracket x \rrbracket_{\sigma_1}(c) - \llbracket x \rrbracket_{\sigma_2}(c))$.

To compute QMS_x, one naive approach is to use brute-force to enumerate all possible valuations σ and then to compute distributions $\llbracket x \rrbracket_\sigma$ again by enumerating the assignments of random variables. This approach is exponential in the number of (bits of) variables in $\mathcal{E}(x)$.

Another approach is to lift the SMT-based approach [26,27] from Boolean setting to the arithmetic one. We first consider a "decision" version of the problem, i.e., checking whether $\mathrm{QMS}_x \geq q$ for a given rational number $q \in [0,1]$. It is not difficult to observe that this can be reduced to checking the satisfiability of the following logic formula:

$$\exists \sigma_1, \sigma_2 \in \Theta^2_{X_p}. \exists c \in \mathbb{D}. \big(\sharp(c = \llbracket x \rrbracket_{\sigma_1}) - \sharp(c = \llbracket x \rrbracket_{\sigma_2}) \big) > \Delta^q_x, \tag{1}$$

where $\sharp(c = \llbracket x \rrbracket_{\sigma_1})$ and $\sharp(c = \llbracket x \rrbracket_{\sigma_2})$ respectively denote the number of satisfying assignments of $c = \llbracket x \rrbracket_{\sigma_1}$ and $c = \llbracket x \rrbracket_{\sigma_2}$, $\Delta^q_x = (1-q) \times 2^m$, and m is the number of bits of random variables in $\mathcal{E}(x)$.

We further encode (1) as a (quantifier-free) first-order formula Ψ^q_x to be solved by an off-the-shelf SMT solver (e.g. Z3 [23]):

$$\Psi^q_x := \big(\bigwedge\nolimits_{f: \mathsf{RVar}(\mathcal{E}(x)) \to \mathbb{D}} (\Theta_f \wedge \Theta'_f) \big) \wedge \Theta_{\mathsf{b2i}} \wedge \Theta'_{\mathsf{b2i}} \wedge \Theta^q_{\mathsf{diff}}$$

where

- **Program logic** (Θ_f and Θ'_f): for every $f : \mathsf{RVar}(\mathcal{E}(x)) \to \mathbb{D}$, Θ_f encodes $c_f = \mathcal{E}(x)$ into a logical formula with each occurrence of a random variable $r \in \mathsf{RVar}(\mathcal{E}(x))$ being replaced by its value $f(r)$, where c_f is a fresh variable. There are $|\mathbb{D}|^{|\mathsf{RVar}(\mathcal{E}(x))|}$ distinct copies, but share the same X_p and X_k. Θ'_f is similar to Θ_f except that all variables $k \in X_k$ and c_f are replaced by fresh variables k' and c'_f respectively.
- **Boolean to integer** (Θ_{b2i} and Θ'_{b2i}): $\Theta_{\mathsf{b2i}} := \bigwedge_{f: \mathsf{RVar}(\mathcal{E}(x)) \to \mathbb{D}} I_f = (c = c_f) ? 1 : 0$. It asserts that for each $f : \mathsf{RVar}(\mathcal{E}(x)) \to \mathbb{D}$, a fresh integer variable I_f is 1 if $c = c_f$, otherwise 0. Θ'_{b2i} is similar to Θ_{b2i} except that I_f and c_f are replaced by I'_f and c'_f respectively.
- **Different sums** (Θ^q_{diff}): $\sum_{f: \mathsf{RVar}(\mathcal{E}(x)) \to \mathbb{D}} I_f - \sum_{f: \mathsf{RVar}(\mathcal{E}(x)) \to \mathbb{D}} I'_f > \Delta^q_x$.

Theorem 2. Ψ^q_x *is unsatisfiable iff* $\mathrm{QMS}_x \geq q$, *and the size of* Ψ^q_x *is polynomial in* $|P|$ *and exponential in* $|\mathsf{RVar}(\mathcal{E}(x))|$ *and* $|\mathbb{D}|$.

Based on Theorem 2, we present an algorithm for computing QMS_x in Sect. 4.2.

Note that the qualitative variant of Ψ^q_x (i.e. $q = 1$) can be used to decide whether x is statistically independent by checking whether $\mathrm{QMS}_x = 1$ holds. This will be used in Algorithm 1.

Example 3. By applying the model-counting based reasoning to the program in Fig. 1, we can conclude that x_6 is perfectly masked, while x_2 and x_3 are leaky. This cannot be done by our type system or the ones in [3,4]. To give a sample encoding, consider the variable x_3 for $q = \frac{1}{2}$ and $\mathbb{D} = \{0, 1, 2, 3\}$. We have that $\Psi^{\frac{1}{2}}_{x_3}$ is

$$\begin{pmatrix} c_0 = (0 \odot 0) \odot (k \oplus 0) \quad \wedge \quad c_0' = (0 \odot 0) \odot (k' \oplus 0) \quad \wedge \\ c_1 = (1 \odot 1) \odot (k \oplus 1) \quad \wedge \quad c_1' = (1 \odot 1) \odot (k' \oplus 1) \quad \wedge \\ c_2 = (2 \odot 2) \odot (k \oplus 2) \quad \wedge \quad c_2' = (2 \odot 2) \odot (k' \oplus 2) \quad \wedge \\ c_3 = (3 \odot 3) \odot (k \oplus 3) \quad \wedge \quad c_3' = (3 \odot 3) \odot (k' \oplus 3) \quad \wedge \end{pmatrix}$$

$$\begin{pmatrix} I_0 = (c = c_0) \ ? \ 1 : 0 \quad \wedge \quad I_1 = (c = c_1) \ ? \ 1 : 0 \quad \wedge \\ I_2 = (c = c_2) \ ? \ 1 : 0 \quad \wedge \quad I_3 = (c = c_3) \ ? \ 1 : 0 \quad \wedge \end{pmatrix}$$

$$\begin{pmatrix} I_0' = (c = c_0') \ ? \ 1 : 0 \quad \wedge \quad I_1' = (c = c_1') \ ? \ 1 : 0 \quad \wedge \\ I_2' = (c = c_2') \ ? \ 1 : 0 \quad \wedge \quad I_3' = (c = c_3') \ ? \ 1 : 0 \quad \wedge \end{pmatrix}$$
$$(I_0 + I_1 + I_2 + I_3) - (I_0' + I_1' + I_2' + I_3') > (1 - \tfrac{1}{2})^2$$

3.3   Reduction Heuristics

In this section, we provide various heuristics to reduce the size of formulae. These can be both applied to type inference and model-counting based reasoning.

Ineffective Variable Elimination. A variable x is *ineffective* in an expression e if for all functions $\sigma_1, \sigma_2 : \mathsf{Var}(e) \to \mathbb{D}$ that agree on their values on the variables $\mathsf{Var}(e) \setminus \{x\}$, e has same values under σ_1 and σ_2. Otherwise, we say x is *effective* in e. Clearly if x is ineffective in e, then e and $e[c/x]$ are equivalent for any $c \in \mathbb{D}$ while $e[c/x]$ contains less variables, where $e[c/x]$ is obtained from e by replacing all occurrences of x with c. Checking whether x is effective or not in e can be performed by a satisfiability checking of the logical formula: $e[c/x] \neq e[c'/x]$. Obviously, $e[c/x] \neq e[c'/x]$ is satisfiable iff x is effective in e.

Algebraic Laws. For every sub-expression e' of the form $e_1 \oplus e_1, e_2 - e_2, e \circ 0$ or $0 \circ e$ with $\circ \in \{\times, \odot, \wedge\}$ in the expression e, it is safe to replace e' by 0, namely, e and $e[0/e']$ are equivalent. Note that the constant 0 is usually introduced by instantiating ineffective variables by 0 when eliminating ineffective variables.

Dominated Subexpression Elimination. Given an expression e, if e' is a r-dominated sub-expression in e and r does not occur in e elsewhere, then it is safe to replace each occurrence of e' in e by the random variable r. Intuitively, e' as a whole can be seen as a random variable when evaluating e. Besides this elimination, we also allow to add mete-theorems specifying forms of sub-expressions e' that can be replaced by a fresh variable. For instance, $r \oplus ((2 \times r) \wedge e'')$ in e, when the random variable r does not appear elsewhere, can be replaced by the random variable r.

Let $\hat{e}$ denote the expression obtained by applying the above heuristics on the expression e.

Transformation Oracle. We suppose there is an oracle Ω which, whenever possible, transforms an expression e into an equivalent expression $\Omega(e)$ such that the type inference can give a non-UKD type to $\Omega(e)$.

Lemma 1. $\mathcal{E}(x)(\sigma)$ *and* $\widehat{\mathcal{E}(x)}(\sigma)$ *have same distribution for any* $\sigma \in \Theta$.

Example 4. Consider the variable x_6 in the program in Fig. 1, $(k \oplus r_0)$ is r_0-dominated sub-expression in $\mathcal{E}(x_6) = ((k \oplus r_0) \odot (k \oplus r_0)) \odot (k \oplus r_0)$, then, we can simplify $\mathcal{E}(x_6)$ into $\widehat{\mathcal{E}(x_6)} = r_0 \odot r_0 \odot r_0$. Therefore, we can deduce that $\vdash \mathcal{E}(x_6) : \mathsf{SID}$ by applying the NoKey rule on $\widehat{\mathcal{E}(x_6)}$.

Algorithm 1. PMCHECKING(P, X_p, X_k, X_r, X_i)

---

1 **Function** PMCHECKING(P, X_p, X_k, X_r, X_i)
2   **foreach** $x \in X_i$ **do**
3   **if** $\vdash \mathcal{E}(x) :$ UKD *is valid* **then**
4   **if** $\vdash \widehat{\mathcal{E}(x)} :$ UKD *is valid* **then**
5   **if** $\Omega(\widehat{\mathcal{E}(x)})$ *exists* **then**
6   Let $\vdash \mathcal{E}(x) : \tau$ be valid for valid $\vdash \Omega(\widehat{\mathcal{E}(x)}) : \tau$;
7   **else if** ModelCountingBasedSolver$(\widehat{\mathcal{E}(x)})$=SAT **then**
8   Let $\vdash \mathcal{E}(x) :$ SDD be valid;
9   **else** Let $\vdash \mathcal{E}(x) :$ SID be valid;
10   **else** Let $\vdash \mathcal{E}(x) : \tau$ be valid for valid $\vdash \widehat{\mathcal{E}(x)} : \tau$;

---

4 Overall Algorithms

In this section, we present algorithms to check perfect masking and to compute the QMS values.

4.1 Perfect Masking Verification

Given a program P with the sets of public (X_p), secret (X_k), random (X_r) and internal (X_i) variables, PMCHECKING, given in Algorithm 1, checks whether P is perfectly masked or not. It iteratively traverses all the internal variables. For each variable $x \in X_i$, it first applies the type system to infer its distribution type. If $\vdash \mathcal{E}(x) : \tau$ for $\tau \neq$ UKD is valid, then the result is conclusive. Otherwise, we will simplify the expression $\mathcal{E}(x)$ and apply the type inference to $\widehat{\mathcal{E}(x)}$.

If it fails to resolve the type of x and $\Omega(\widehat{\mathcal{E}(x)})$ does not exist, we apply the model-counting based (SMT-based or brute-force) approach outlined in Sect. 3.2, in particular, to check the expression $\widehat{\mathcal{E}(x)}$. There are two possible outcomes: either $\widehat{\mathcal{E}(x)}$ is SID or SDD. We enforce $\mathcal{E}(x)$ to have the same distributional type as $\widehat{\mathcal{E}(x)}$ which might facilitate the inference for other expressions.

Theorem 3. *P is perfectly masked iff* $\vdash \mathcal{E}(x) :$ SDD *is not valid for any* $x \in X_i$, *when Algorithm 1 terminates.*

We remark that, if the model-counting is disabled in Algorithm 1 where UKD-typed variables are interpreted as potentially leaky, Algorithm 1 would degenerate to a type inference procedure that is fast and potentially more accurate than the one in [3], owing to the optimization introduced in Sect. 3.3.

4.2 QMS Computing

After applying Algorithm 1, each internal variable $x \in X_i$ is endowed by a distributional type of either SID (or RUD which implies SID) or SDD. In the former case, x is perfectly masked meaning observing x would gain nothing for

---

Algorithm 2. Procedure QMSComputing(P, X_p, X_k, X_r, X_i)

---

1 **Function** QMSComputing(P, X_p, X_k, X_r, X_i)
2   PMChecking(P, X_p, X_k, X_r, X_i);
3   **foreach** $x \in X_i$ **do**
4   **if** $\vdash \mathcal{E}(x) : $ SID *is valid* **then** QMS$_x := 1$;
5   **else**
6   **if** RVar$(\widehat{\mathcal{E}(x)}) = \emptyset$ **then** QMS$_x := 0$;
7   **else**
8   low $:= 0$; high $:= 2^{n \times |\mathsf{RVar}(\widehat{\mathcal{E}(x)})|}$;
9   **while** low $<$ high **do**
10   mid $:= \lceil \frac{\text{low+high}}{2} \rceil$; $q := \frac{\text{mid}}{2^{n \times |\mathsf{RVar}(\widehat{\mathcal{E}(x)})|}}$;
11   **if** SMTSolver$(\widehat{\Psi}_x^q) =$ SAT **then** high $:=$ mid $- 1$;
12   **else** low $:=$ mid;
13   QMS$_x := \frac{\text{low}}{2^{n \times |\mathsf{RVar}(\widehat{\mathcal{E}(x)})|}}$;

---

side-channel attackers. In the latter case, however, x becomes a side-channel and it is natural to ask how many power traces are required to infer secret from x of which we have provided a measure formalized via QMS.

QMSComputing, given in Algorithm 2, computes QMS$_x$ for each $x \in X_i$. It first invokes the function PMChecking for perfect masking verification. For SID-typed variable $x \in X_i$, we can directly infer that QMS$_x$ is 1. For each leaky variable $x \in X_i$, we first check whether $\widehat{\mathcal{E}(x)}$ uses any random variables or not. If it does not use any random variables, we directly deduce that QMS$_x$ is 0. Otherwise, we use either the brute-force enumeration or an SMT-based binary search to compute QMS$_x$. The former one is trivial, hence not presented in Algorithm 2. The latter one is based on the fact that QMS$_x = \frac{i}{2^{n \cdot |\mathsf{RVar}(\widehat{\mathcal{E}(x)})|}}$ for some integer $0 \leq i \leq 2^{n \cdot |\mathsf{RVar}(\widehat{\mathcal{E}(x)})|}$. Hence the while-loop in Algorithm 2 executes at most $\mathbf{O}(n \cdot |\mathsf{RVar}(\widehat{\mathcal{E}(x)})|)$ times for each x.

Our SMT-based binary search for computing QMS values is different from the one proposed by Eldib et al. [26,27]. Their algorithm considers Boolean programs *only* and computes QMS values by directly binary searching the QMS value q between 0 to 1 with a pre-defined step size ϵ ($\epsilon = 0.01$ in [26,27]). Hence, it only *approximate* the actual QMS value and the binary search iterates $\mathbf{O}(\log(\frac{1}{\epsilon}))$ times for each internal variable. Our approach works for more general arithmetic programs and computes the accurate QMS value.

5   Practical Evaluation

We have implemented our methods in a tool named QMVerif, which uses Z3 [23] as the underlying SMT solver (fixed size bit-vector theory). We conducted experiments perfect masking verification and QMS computing on both Boolean and arithmetic programs. Our experiments were conducted on a server with 64-bit Ubuntu 16.04.4 LTS, Intel Xeon CPU E5-2690 v4, and 256 GB RAM.

Table 1. Results on masked Boolean programs for perfect masking verification.

Name	$|X_i|$	♯SDD	♯Count	QMVERIF SMT	QMVERIF B.F.	SCINFER [50]
P12	197k	0	0	2.9s	**2.7s**	3.8s
P13	197k	4.8k	4.8k	2m 8s	**2m 6s**	47m 8s
P14	197k	3.2k	3.2k	1m 58s	**1m 45s**	53m 40s
P15	198k	1.6k	3.2k	**2m 25s**	2m 43s	69m 6s
P16	197k	4.8k	4.8k	1m 50s	**1m 38s**	61m 15s
P17	205k	17.6k	12.8k	1m 24s	**1m 10s**	121m 28s

5.1 Experimental Results on Boolean Programs

We use the benchmarks from the publicly available cryptographic software implementations of [25], which consists of 17 Boolean programs (P1-P17). We conducted experiments on P12-P17, which are the regenerations of MAC-Keccak reference code submitted to the SHA-3 competition held by NIST. (We skipped tiny examples P1-P11 which can be verified in less than 1 second.) P12-P17 are transformed into programs in straight-line forms.

Perfect Masking Verification. Table 1 shows the results of perfect masking verification on P12-P17, where Columns 2–4 show basic statistics, in particular, they respectively give the number of internal variables, leaky internal variables, and internal variables which required model-counting based reasoning. Columns 5–6 respectively show the total time of our tool QMVERIF using SMT-based and brute-force methods. Column 7 shows the total time of the tool SCINFER [50].

We can observe that: (1) our reduction heuristics significantly improve performance compared with SCINFER [50] (generally 22–104 times faster for imperfect masked programs; note that SCINFER is based on SMT model-counting), and (2) the performance of the SMT-based and brute-force counting methods for verifying perfect masking of Boolean programs is largely comparable.

Computing QMS. For comparison purposes, we implemented the algorithm of [24, 25] for computing QMS values of leaky internal variables. Table 2 shows the results of computing QMS values on P13-P17 (P12 is excluded because it does not contain any leaky internal variable), where Column 2 shows the number of leaky internal variables, Columns 3–7 show the total number of iterations in the binary search (cf. Sect. 4.2), time, the minimal, maximal and average of QMS values using the algorithm from [24, 25]. Similarly, Columns 8–13 shows statistics of our tool QMVERIF, in particular, Column 9 (resp. Column 10) shows the time of using SMT-based (resp. brute-force) method. The time reported in Table 2 *excludes* the time used for perfect masking checking.

We can observe that (1) the brute-force method outperforms the SMT-based method for computing QMS values, and (2) our tool QMVERIF using SMT-based methods takes significant less iterations and time, as our binary search step

Table 2. Results of masked Boolean programs for computing QMS Values.

Name	♯SDD	SC Sniffer [26, 27]					QMVERIF					
		♯Iter	Time	Min	Max	Avg.	♯Iter	SMT	B.F.	Min	Max	Avg.
P13	4.8k	480k	97m 23s	0.00	1.00	0.98	**0**	0	0	0.00	1.00	0.98
P14	3.2k	160k	40m 13s	0.51	1.00	0.99	9.6k	2m 56s	**39s**	0.50	1.00	0.99
P15	1.6k	80k	23m 26s	0.51	1.00	1.00	4.8k	1m 36s	**1m 32s**	0.50	1.00	1.00
P16	4.8k	320k	66m 27s	0.00	1.00	0.98	6.4k	1m 40s	**8s**	0.00	1.00	0.98
P17	17.6k	1440k	337m 46s	0.00	1.00	0.93	4.8k	51s	**1s**	0.00	1.00	0.94

Table 3. Results of masked arithmetic programs, where P.M.V. denotes perfect masking verification, B.F. denotes brute-force, 12 S.F. denotes that Z3 emits segmentation fault after verifying 12 internal variables.

Description	$|X_i|$	♯SDD	♯Count	P.M.V.		QMS		
				SMT	B.F.	SMT	B.F.	Value
SecMult [47]	11	0	0	≈0s	≈0s	-	-	1
Sbox (4) [22]	66	0	0	≈0s	≈0s	-	-	1
B2A [30]	8	**0**	**1**	17s	**2s**	-	-	1
A2B [30]	46	0	0	≈0s	≈0s	-	-	1
B2A [21]	82	0	0	≈0s	≈0s	-	-	1
A2B [21]	41	0	0	≈0s	≈0s	-	-	1
B2A [18]	11	**0**	**1**	**1m 35s**	10m 59s	-	-	1
B2A [10]	16	0	0	≈0s	≈0s	-	-	1
Sbox [47]	45	0	0	≈0s	≈0s	-	-	1
Sbox [48]	772	**2**	**1**	≈0s	≈0s	0.9s	≈0s	0
k^3	11	2	2	96m 59s	**0.2s**		32s	0.988
k^{12}	15	2	2	101m 34s	**0.3s**		27s	0.988
k^{15}	21	4	4	93m 27s (12 S.F.)	**28m 17s**		≈64h	0.988, 0.980
k^{240}	23	4	4	93m 27s (12 S.F.)	**30m 9s**		≈64h	0.988, 0.980
k^{252}	31	4	4	93m 27s (12 S.F.)	**32m 58s**		≈64h	0.988, 0.980
k^{254}	39	4	4	93m 27s (12 S.F.)	**30m 9s**		≈64h	0.988, 0.980

depends on the number of bits of random variables, but not a pre-defined value (e.g. 0.01) as used in [24, 25]. In particular, the QMS values of leaky variables whose expressions contain no random variables, e.g., P13 and P17, do not need binary search.

5.2 Experimental Results on Arithmetic Programs

We collect arithmetic programs which represent non-linear functions of masked cryptographic software implementations from the literature. In Table 3, Column 1 lists the name of the functions under consideration, where $k^3, \ldots, k^{254}$ are buggy fragments of first-order secure exponentiation [47] without the first RefreshMask function; A2B and B2A are shorthand for ArithmeticToBoolean and BooleanToArithmetic, respectively. Columns 2–4 show basic statistics. For all the experiments, we set $\mathbb{D} = \{0, \cdots, 2^8 - 1\}$.

Perfect Masking Verification. Columns 5–6 in Table 3 show the results of perfect masking verification on these programs using SMT-based and brute-force methods respectively.

We observe that (1) some UKD-typed variables (e.g., in B2A [30], B2A [18] and Sbox [48], meaning that the type inference is inconclusive in these cases) are resolved (as SID-type) by model-counting, and (2) on the programs (except B2A [18]) where model-counting based reasoning is required (i.e., $\sharp$Count is non-zero), the brute-force method is significantly faster than the SMT-based method. In particular, for programs $k^{15}, \ldots, k^{254}$, Z3 crashed with segment fault after verifying 12 internal variables in 93 min, while the brute-force method comfortably returns the result. To further explain the performance of these two classes of methods, we manually examine these programs and find that the expressions of the UKD-typed variable (using type inference) in B2A [18] (where the SMT-based method is faster) only use exclusive-or ($\oplus$) operations and one subtraction ($-$) operation, while the expressions of the other UKD-typed variables (where the brute-force method is faster) involve the finite field multiplication ($\odot$).

We remark that the transformation oracle and meta-theorems (cf. Sect. 3.3) are only used for A2B [30] by manually utilizing the equations of Theorem 3 in [30]. We have verified the correctness of those equations by SMT solvers. In theory model-counting based reasoning could verify A2B [30]. However, in our experiments both SMT-based and brute-force methods failed to terminate in 3 days, though brute-force methods had verified more internal variables. For instance, on the expression $((2 \times r_1) \oplus (x - r) \oplus r_1) \wedge r$ where x is a private input and r, r_1 are random variables, Z3 cannot terminate in 2 days, while brute-force methods successfully verified in a few minutes. We also tested the SMT solver Boolector [39] (the winner of SMT-COMP 2018 on QF-BV, Main Track), which crashed with being out of memory. Undoubtedly more systematic experiments are required in the future, but our results suggest that, contrary to the common belief, currently SMT-based approaches are not promising, which calls for more scalable techniques.

Computing QMS. Columns 7–9 in Table 3 show the results of computing QMS values, where Column 7 (resp. Column 8) shows the time of the SMT-based (resp. brute-force) method for computing QMS values (*excluding* the time for perfect masking verification) and Column 9 shows QMS values of all leaky variables (note that duplicated values are omitted).

6 Conclusion

We have proposed a hybrid approach combing type inference and model-counting to verify masked arithmetic programs against first-order side-channel attacks. The type inference allows an efficient, lightweight procedure to determine most observable variables whereas model-counting accounts for completeness, bringing the best of two worlds. We also provided model-counting based methods to quantify the amount of information leakage via side channels. We have presented the tool support QMVERIF which has been evaluated on standard cryptographic benchmarks. The experimental results showed that our method significantly out-performed state-of-the-art techniques in terms of both accuracy and scalability.

Future work includes further improving SMT-based model counting tech-niques which currently provide no better, if not worse, performance than the naïve brutal-force approach. Furthermore, generalizing the work in the current paper to the verification of higher-order masking schemes remains to be a very challenging task.

References

1. Almeida, J.B., Barbosa, M., Barthe, G., Dupressoir, F., Emmi, M.: Verify-ing constant-time implementations. In: USENIX Security Symposium, pp. 53–70 (2016)
2. Antonopoulos, T., Gazzillo, P., Hicks, M., Koskinen, E., Terauchi, T., Wei, S.: Decomposition instead of self-composition for proving the absence of timing chan-nels. In: ACM SIGPLAN Conference on Programming Language Design and Imple-mentation, pp. 362–375 (2017)
3. Barthe, G., Belaïd, S., Dupressoir, F., Fouque, P.-A., Grégoire, B., Strub, P.-Y.: Verified proofs of higher-order masking. In: Oswald, E., Fischlin, M. (eds.) EURO-CRYPT 2015. LNCS, Part I, vol. 9056, pp. 457–485. Springer, Heidelberg (2015). https://doi.org/10.1007/978-3-662-46800-5_18
4. Barthe, G., et al.: Strong non-interference and type-directed higher-order masking. In: ACM Conference on Computer and Communications Security, pp. 116–129 (2016)
5. Barthe, G., Belaïd, S., Fouque, P., Grégoire, B.: maskVerif: a formal tool for ana-lyzing software and hardware masked implementations. IACR Cryptology ePrint Archive 2018:562 (2018)
6. Barthe, G., Dupressoir, F., Faust, S., Grégoire, B., Standaert, F.-X., Strub, P.-Y.: Parallel implementations of masking schemes and the bounded moment leakage model. In: Coron, J.-S., Nielsen, J.B. (eds.) EUROCRYPT 2017. LNCS, Part I, vol. 10210, pp. 535–566. Springer, Cham (2017). https://doi.org/10.1007/978-3-319-56620-7_19
7. Barthe, G., Dupressoir, F., Fouque, P., Grégoire, B., Zapalowicz, J.: Synthesis of fault attacks on cryptographic implementations. In: Proceedings of the ACM SIGSAC Conference on Computer and Communications Security, pp. 1016–1027 (2014)
8. Barthe, G., Köpf, B., Mauborgne, L., Ochoa, M.: Leakage resilience against con-current cache attacks. In: Abadi, M., Kremer, S. (eds.) POST 2014. LNCS, vol. 8414, pp. 140–158. Springer, Heidelberg (2014). https://doi.org/10.1007/978-3-642-54792-8_8
9. Bayrak, A.G., Regazzoni, F., Novo, D., Ienne, P.: Sleuth: automated verification of software power analysis countermeasures. In: Bertoni, G., Coron, J.-S. (eds.) CHES 2013. LNCS, vol. 8086, pp. 293–310. Springer, Heidelberg (2013). https://doi.org/10.1007/978-3-642-40349-1_17
10. Bettale, L., Coron, J., Zeitoun, R.: Improved high-order conversion from boolean to arithmetic masking. IACR Trans. Cryptogr. Hardw. Embed. Syst. **2018**(2), 22–45 (2018)

11. Bhasin, S., Carlet, C., Guilley, S.: Theory of masking with codewords in hardware: low-weight dth-order correlation-immune boolean functions. IACR Cryptology ePrint Archive 2013:303 (2013)
12. Biham, E., Shamir, A.: Differential fault analysis of secret key cryptosystems. In: Kaliski, B.S. (ed.) CRYPTO 1997. LNCS, vol. 1294, pp. 513–525. Springer, Heidelberg (1997). https://doi.org/10.1007/BFb0052259
13. Biondi, F., Enescu, M.A., Heuser, A., Legay, A., Meel, K.S., Quilbeuf, J.: Scalable approximation of quantitative information flow in programs. In: Dillig, I., Palsberg, J. (eds.) VMCAI 2018. LNCS, vol. 10747, pp. 71–93. Springer, Cham (2018). https://doi.org/10.1007/978-3-319-73721-8_4
14. Bisi, E., Melzani, F., Zaccaria, V.: Symbolic analysis of higher-order side channel countermeasures. IEEE Trans. Comput. **66**(6), 1099–1105 (2017)
15. Bloem, R., Gross, H., Iusupov, R., Könighofer, B., Mangard, S., Winter, J.: Formal verification of masked hardware implementations in the presence of glitches. In: Nielsen, J.B., Rijmen, V. (eds.) EUROCRYPT 2018. LNCS, Part II, vol. 10821, pp. 321–353. Springer, Cham (2018). https://doi.org/10.1007/978-3-319-78375-8_11
16. Breier, J., Hou, X., Liu, Y.: Fault attacks made easy: differential fault analysis automation on assembly code. Cryptology ePrint Archive, Report 2017/829 (2017). https://eprint.iacr.org/2017/829
17. Chari, S., Jutla, C.S., Rao, J.R., Rohatgi, P.: Towards sound approaches to counteract power-analysis attacks. In: Wiener, M. (ed.) CRYPTO 1999. LNCS, vol. 1666, pp. 398–412. Springer, Heidelberg (1999). https://doi.org/10.1007/3-540-48405-1_26
18. Coron, J.-S.: High-order conversion from boolean to arithmetic masking. In: Fischer, W., Homma, N. (eds.) CHES 2017. LNCS, vol. 10529, pp. 93–114. Springer, Cham (2017). https://doi.org/10.1007/978-3-319-66787-4_5
19. Coron, J.-S.: Formal verification of side-channel countermeasures via elementary circuit transformations. In: Preneel, B., Vercauteren, F. (eds.) ACNS 2018. LNCS, vol. 10892, pp. 65–82. Springer, Cham (2018). https://doi.org/10.1007/978-3-319-93387-0_4
20. Coron, J.-S., Giraud, C., Prouff, E., Renner, S., Rivain, M., Vadnala, P.K.: Conversion of security proofs from one leakage model to another: a new issue. In: Schindler, W., Huss, S.A. (eds.) COSADE 2012. LNCS, vol. 7275, pp. 69–81. Springer, Heidelberg (2012). https://doi.org/10.1007/978-3-642-29912-4_6
21. Coron, J.-S., Großschädl, J., Vadnala, P.K.: Secure conversion between boolean and arithmetic masking of any order. In: Batina, L., Robshaw, M. (eds.) CHES 2014. LNCS, vol. 8731, pp. 188–205. Springer, Heidelberg (2014). https://doi.org/10.1007/978-3-662-44709-3_11
22. Coron, J.-S., Prouff, E., Rivain, M., Roche, T.: Higher-order side channel security and mask refreshing. In: Moriai, S. (ed.) FSE 2013. LNCS, vol. 8424, pp. 410–424. Springer, Heidelberg (2014). https://doi.org/10.1007/978-3-662-43933-3_21
23. de Moura, L., Bjørner, N.: Z3: An efficient SMT solver. In: Ramakrishnan, C.R., Rehof, J. (eds.) TACAS 2008. LNCS, vol. 4963, pp. 337–340. Springer, Heidelberg (2008). https://doi.org/10.1007/978-3-540-78800-3_24
24. Eldib, H., Wang, C., Schaumont, P.: Formal verification of software countermeasures against side-channel attacks. ACM Trans. Softw. Eng. Methodol. **24**(2), 11 (2014)
25. Eldib, H., Wang, C., Schaumont, P.: SMT-based verification of software countermeasures against side-channel attacks. In: Ábrahám, E., Havelund, K. (eds.) TACAS 2014. LNCS, vol. 8413, pp. 62–77. Springer, Heidelberg (2014). https://doi.org/10.1007/978-3-642-54862-8_5

26. Eldib, H., Wang, C., Taha, M., Schaumont, P.: QMS: evaluating the side-channel resistance of masked software from source code. In: ACM/IEEE Design Automation Conference, vol. 209, pp. 1–6 (2014)

27. Eldib, H., Wang, C., Taha, M.M.I., Schaumont, P.: Quantitative masking strength: quantifying the power side-channel resistance of software code. IEEE Trans. CAD Integr. Circ. Syst. **34**(10), 1558–1568 (2015)

28. Eldib, H., Wu, M., Wang, C.: Synthesis of fault-attack countermeasures for cryptographic circuits. In: Chaudhuri, S., Farzan, A. (eds.) CAV 2016. LNCS, Part II, vol. 9780, pp. 343–363. Springer, Cham (2016). https://doi.org/10.1007/978-3-319-41540-6_19

29. Faust, S., Grosso, V., Pozo, S.M.D., Paglialonga, C., Standaert, F.: Composable masking schemes in the presence of physical defaults and the robust probing model. IACR Cryptology ePrint Archive 2017:711 (2017)

30. Goubin, L.: A sound method for switching between boolean and arithmetic masking. In: Koç, Ç.K., Naccache, D., Paar, C. (eds.) CHES 2001. LNCS, vol. 2162, pp. 3–15. Springer, Heidelberg (2001). https://doi.org/10.1007/3-540-44709-1_2

31. Guo, S., Wu, M., Wang, C.: Adversarial symbolic execution for detecting concurrency-related cache timing leaks. In: Proceedings of the ACM SIGSOFT Symposium on the Foundations of Software Engineering, pp. 377–388 (2018)

32. Ishai, Y., Sahai, A., Wagner, D.: Private circuits: securing hardware against probing attacks. In: Boneh, D. (ed.) CRYPTO 2003. LNCS, vol. 2729, pp. 463–481. Springer, Heidelberg (2003). https://doi.org/10.1007/978-3-540-45146-4_27

33. Kocher, P.C.: Timing attacks on implementations of Diffie-Hellman, RSA, DSS, and other systems. In: Koblitz, N. (ed.) CRYPTO 1996. LNCS, vol. 1109, pp. 104–113. Springer, Heidelberg (1996). https://doi.org/10.1007/3-540-68697-5_9

34. Kocher, P., Jaffe, J., Jun, B.: Differential power analysis. In: Wiener, M. (ed.) CRYPTO 1999. LNCS, vol. 1666, pp. 388–397. Springer, Heidelberg (1999). https://doi.org/10.1007/3-540-48405-1_25

35. Malacaria, P., Heusser, J.: Information theory and security: quantitative information flow. In: Aldini, A., Bernardo, M., Di Pierro, A., Wiklicky, H. (eds.) SFM 2010. LNCS, vol. 6154, pp. 87–134. Springer, Heidelberg (2010). https://doi.org/10.1007/978-3-642-13678-8_3

36. Malacaria, P., Khouzani, M.H.R., Pasareanu, C.S., Phan, Q., Luckow, K.S.: Symbolic side-channel analysis for probabilistic programs. In: Proceedings of the 31st IEEE Computer Security Foundations Symposium (CSF), pp. 313–327 (2018)

37. Moradi, A., Barenghi, A., Kasper, T., Paar, C.: On the vulnerability of FPGA bitstream encryption against power analysis attacks: extracting keys from xilinx virtex-ii fpgas. In: Proceedings of ACM Conference on Computer and Communications Security (CCS), pp. 111–124 (2011)

38. Moss, A., Oswald, E., Page, D., Tunstall, M.: Compiler assisted masking. In: Prouff, E., Schaumont, P. (eds.) CHES 2012. LNCS, vol. 7428, pp. 58–75. Springer, Heidelberg (2012). https://doi.org/10.1007/978-3-642-33027-8_4

39. Niemetz, A., Preiner, M., Biere, A.: Boolector 2.0 system description. J. Satisf. Boolean Model. Comput. **9**, 53–58 (2014). (published 2015)

40. Ouahma, I.B.E., Meunier, Q., Heydemann, K., Encrenaz, E.: Symbolic approach for side-channel resistance analysis of masked assembly codes. In: Security Proofs for Embedded Systems (2017)

41. Pasareanu, C.S., Phan, Q., Malacaria, P.: Multi-run side-channel analysis using symbolic execution and Max-SMT. In: Proceedings of the IEEE 29th Computer Security Foundations Symposium (CSF), pp. 387–400 (2016)

42. Phan, Q., Bang, L., Pasareanu, C.S., Malacaria, P., Bultan, T.: Synthesis of adaptive side-channel attacks. In: Proceedings of the 30th IEEE Computer Security Foundations Symposium (CSF), pp. 328–342 (2017)

43. Phan, Q., Malacaria, P.: Abstract model counting: a novel approach for quantification of information leaks. In: Proceedings of the 9th ACM Symposium on Information, Computer and Communications Security (ASIACCS), pp. 283–292 (2014)

44. Phan, Q., Malacaria, P., Pasareanu, C.S., d'Amorim, M.: Quantifying information leaks using reliability analysis. In: Proceedings of 2014 International Symposium on Model Checking of Software (SPIN), pp. 105–108 (2014)

45. Prouff, E., Rivain, M.: Masking against side-channel attacks: a formal security proof. In: Johansson, T., Nguyen, P.Q. (eds.) EUROCRYPT 2013. LNCS, vol. 7881, pp. 142–159. Springer, Heidelberg (2013). https://doi.org/10.1007/978-3-642-38348-9_9

46. Quisquater, J.-J., Samyde, D.: ElectroMagnetic Analysis (EMA): measures and counter-measures for smart cards. In: Attali, I., Jensen, T. (eds.) E-smart 2001. LNCS, vol. 2140, pp. 200–210. Springer, Heidelberg (2001). https://doi.org/10.1007/3-540-45418-7_17

47. Rivain, M., Prouff, E.: Provably secure higher-order masking of AES. In: Mangard, S., Standaert, F.-X. (eds.) CHES 2010. LNCS, vol. 6225, pp. 413–427. Springer, Heidelberg (2010). https://doi.org/10.1007/978-3-642-15031-9_28

48. Schramm, K., Paar, C.: Higher order masking of the AES. In: Pointcheval, D. (ed.) CT-RSA 2006. LNCS, vol. 3860, pp. 208–225. Springer, Heidelberg (2006). https://doi.org/10.1007/11605805_14

49. Val, C.G., Enescu, M.A., Bayless, S., Aiello, W., Hu, A.J.: Precisely measuring quantitative information flow: 10k lines of code and beyond. In: Proceedings of IEEE European Symposium on Security and Privacy (EuroS&P), pp. 31–46 (2016)

50. Zhang, J., Gao, P., Song, F., Wang, C.: SCInfer: refinement-based verification of software countermeasures against side-channel attacks. In: Chockler, H., Weissenbacher, G. (eds.) CAV 2018. LNCS, Part II, vol. 10982, pp. 157–177. Springer, Cham (2018). https://doi.org/10.1007/978-3-319-96142-2_12

7

Encoding Redundancy for Satisfaction-Driven Clause Learning

Marijn J. H. Heule[1], Benjamin Kiesl[2,3], and Armin Biere[4(✉)]

[1] Department of Computer Science, The University of Texas, Austin, USA
[2] Institute of Logic and Computation, TU Wien, Vienna, Austria
[3] CISPA Helmholtz Center for Information Security, Saarbrücken, Germany
[4] Institute for Formal Models and Verification,
Johannes Kepler University, Linz, Austria
armin.biere@jku.at

Abstract. Satisfaction-Driven Clause Learning (SDCL) is a recent SAT solving paradigm that aggressively trims the search space of possible truth assignments. To determine if the SAT solver is currently exploring a dispensable part of the search space, SDCL uses the so-called positive reduct of a formula: The positive reduct is an easily solvable propositional formula that is satisfiable if the current assignment of the solver can be safely pruned from the search space. In this paper, we present two novel variants of the positive reduct that allow for even more aggressive pruning. Using one of these variants allows SDCL to solve harder problems, in particular the well-known Tseitin formulas and mutilated chessboard problems. For the first time, we are able to generate and automatically check clausal proofs for large instances of these problems.

1 Introduction

Conflict-driven clause learning (CDCL) [26,28] is the most successful paradigm for solving satisfiability (SAT) problems and therefore CDCL solvers are pervasively used as reasoning engines to construct and verify systems. However, CDCL solvers still struggle to handle some important applications within reasonable time. These applications include the verification of arithmetic circuits, challenges from cryptanalysis, and hard combinatorial problems. There appears to be a theoretical barrier to dealing with some of these applications efficiently.

At its core, CDCL is based on the resolution proof system, which means that the same limitations that apply to resolution also apply to CDCL. Most importantly, there exist only exponentially large resolution proofs for several seemingly easy problems [15,33], implying that CDCL solvers require exponential time to solve them. A recent approach to breaking this exponential barrier is the *satisfaction-driven clause learning* (SDCL) paradigm [20], which can automatically find short proofs of pigeon-hole formulas in the PR proof system [19].

SDCL extends CDCL by pruning the search space of truth assignments more aggressively. While a pure CDCL solver learns only clauses that can be efficiently derived via resolution, an SDCL solver also learns stronger clauses. The initial approach to learning these clauses is based on the so-called *positive reduct*: Given a formula and a partial truth assignment, the positive reduct is a simple propositional formula encoding the question of whether the assignment can be pruned safely from the search space. In cases where the positive reduct is satisfiable, the solver performs the pruning by learning a clause that blocks the assignment.

Although the original SDCL paradigm can solve the hard pigeon-hole formulas, we observe that it is not sophisticated enough to deal with other hard formulas that require exponential-size resolution proofs, such as Tseitin formulas over expander graphs [32,33] or mutilated chessboard problems [1,13,27]. In this paper, we deal with this issue and present techniques that improve the SDCL paradigm. In particular, we introduce new variants of the above-mentioned positive reduct that allow SDCL to prune the search space even more aggressively.

In a first step, we explicitly formalize the notion of a *pruning predicate*: For a formula F and a (partial) assignment α, a pruning predicate is a propositional formula that is satisfiable if α can be pruned in a satisfiability-preserving way. Ideally, a pruning predicate is easily solvable while still pruning the search space as much as possible. We then present two novel pruning predicates of which one, the *filtered positive reduct*, is easier to solve and arguably more useful in practice while the other, the PR *reduct*, allows for stronger pruning.

In many applications, it is not enough that a solver just provides a simple yes/no answer. Especially when dealing with mathematical problems or safety-critical systems, solvers are required to provide automatically checkable proofs that certify the correctness of their answers. The current state of the art in proof generation and proof checking is to focus on *clausal proofs*, which are specific sequences of clause additions and clause removals. Besides the requirement that SAT solvers in the main track of the SAT competition must produce such clausal proofs, there also exist corresponding proof checkers whose correctness has been verified by theorem provers, as first proposed in a seminal TACAS'17 paper [12].

We implemented a new SDCL solver, called SADiCAL, that can solve the pigeon-hole formulas, the Tseitin formulas, and the mutilated chessboard problems due to using the filtered positive reduct. Our solver also produces PR proofs [19]. We certify their correctness by translating them via DRAT proofs [17] to LRAT proofs, which are then validated by a formally verified proof checker [18].

Existing approaches to solving the Tseitin formulas are based on symmetry breaking [14] or algebraic reasoning, in particular Gaussian elimination [3,9, 21,31]. However, the respective tools do not output machine-checkable proofs. Moreover, approaches based on symmetry breaking and Gaussian elimination depend strongly on the syntactic structure of formulas to identify symmetries and cardinality constraints, respectively. They are therefore vulnerable to syntactic changes that do not affect the semantics of a formula. In contrast, SDCL reasons on the semantic level, making it less prone to syntactic changes.

The main contributions of this paper are as follows: (1) We explicitly formulate the notion of a pruning predicate, which was used only implicitly in the original formulation of SDCL. (2) We present two novel pruning predicates that generalize the positive reduct. (3) We implemented a new SDCL solver, called SADICAL, that uses one of our new pruning predicates. (4) We show by an experimental evaluation that this new pruning predicate enables SADICAL to produce short proofs (without new variables) of Tseitin formulas and of mutilated chessboard problems.

2 Preliminaries

Propositional logic. We consider propositional formulas in *conjunctive normal form* (CNF), which are defined as follows. A *literal* is defined to be either a variable x (a *positive literal*) or the negation $\overline{x}$ of a variable x (a *negative literal*). The *complement* $\overline{l}$ of a literal l is defined as $\overline{l} = \overline{x}$ if $l = x$ and $\overline{l} = x$ if $l = \overline{x}$. Accordingly, for a set L of literals, we define $\overline{L} = \{\overline{l} \mid l \in L\}$. A *clause* is a disjunction of literals. A *formula* is a conjunction of clauses. We view clauses as sets of literals and formulas as sets of clauses. For a set L of literals and a formula F, we define $F_L = \{C \in F \mid C \cap L \neq \emptyset\}$. By $var(F)$ we denote the variables of a literal, clause, or formula F. For convenience, we treat $var(F)$ as a variable if F is a literal, and as a set of variables otherwise.

Satisfiability. An *assignment* is a function from a set of variables to the truth values 1 (*true*) and 0 (*false*). An assignment is *total* w.r.t. a formula F if it assigns a truth value to all variables $var(F)$ occurring in F; otherwise it is *partial*. A literal l is *satisfied* by an assignment α if l is positive and $\alpha(var(l)) = 1$ or if it is negative and $\alpha(var(l)) = 0$. A literal is *falsified* by an assignment α if its complement is satisfied by α. A clause is satisfied by an assignment α if it contains a literal that is satisfied by α. Finally, a formula is satisfied by an assignment α if all its clauses are satisfied by α. A formula is *satisfiable* if there exists an assignment that satisfies it. We often denote assignments by sequences of the literals they satisfy. For instance, $x\,\overline{y}$ denotes the assignment that assigns 1 to x and 0 to y. For an assignment α, $var(\alpha)$ denotes the variables assigned by α. For a set L of non-contradictory literals, we denote by α_L the assignment obtained from α by making all literals in L true and assigning the same value as α to other variables not in $var(L)$.

Formula simplification. We refer to the empty clause by $\bot$. Given an assignment α and a clause C, we define $C{\restriction}\alpha = \top$ if α satisfies C; otherwise, $C{\restriction}\alpha$ denotes the result of removing from C all the literals falsified by α. For a formula F, we define $F{\restriction}\alpha = \{C{\restriction}\alpha \mid C \in F \text{ and } C{\restriction}\alpha \neq \top\}$. We say that an assignment α *touches* a clause C if $var(\alpha) \cap var(C) \neq \emptyset$. A *unit clause* is a clause with only one literal. The result of applying the *unit clause rule* to a formula F is the formula

$F \upharpoonright l$ where (l) is a unit clause in F. The iterated application of the unit clause rule to a formula F, until no unit clauses are left, is called *unit propagation*. If unit propagation yields the empty clause $\perp$, we say that unit propagation applied to F derived a *conflict*.

```
    SDCL ( formula F )
1   α := ∅
2   forever do
3     α := UnitPropagate (F, α)
4     if α falsifies a clause in F then
5       C := AnalyzeConflict()
6       F := F ∧ C
7       if C is the empty clause ⊥ then return UNSAT
8       α := BackJump(C, α)
9     else if the pruning predicate Pα(F) is satisfiable then
10      C := AnalyzeWitness()
11      F := F ∧ C
12      α := BackJump(C, α)
13    else
14      if all variables are assigned then return SAT
15      l := Decide ()
16      α := α ∪ {l}
```

Fig. 1. SDCL algorithm [20]. The lines 9 to 12 extend CDCL [26].

Formula relations. Two formulas are *logically equivalent* if they are satisfied by the same total assignments. Two formulas are *equisatisfiable* if they are either both satisfiable or both unsatisfiable. Furthermore, by $F \vdash G$ we denote that for every clause $(l_1 \vee \cdots \vee l_n) \in G$, unit propagation applied to $F \wedge (\bar{l}_1) \wedge \cdots \wedge (\bar{l}_n)$ derives a conflict. If $F \vdash G$, we say that F implies G via unit propagation. For example, $(\bar{a} \vee c) \wedge (\bar{b} \vee \bar{c})$ implies $(\bar{a} \vee \bar{b})$ via unit propagation since unit propagation derives a conflict on $(\bar{a} \vee c) \wedge (\bar{b} \vee \bar{c}) \wedge (a) \wedge (b)$.

Conflict-Driven Clause Learning (CDCL). To determine whether a formula is satisfiable a CDCL solver iteratively performs the following operations (obtained from the pseudo code in Fig. 1 by removing the lines 9 to 12): First, the solver performs unit propagation until either it derives a conflict or the formula contains no more unit clauses. If it derives a conflict, it analyzes the conflict to learn a clause that prevents it from repeating similar (bad) decisions in the future ("clause learning"). If this learned clause is the (unsatisfiable) empty clause $\perp$, the solver can conclude that the formula is unsatisfiable. In case it is not the empty clause, the solver revokes some of its variable assignments ("backjumping") and then repeats the whole procedure again by performing unit propagation. If, however, the solver does not derive a conflict, there are two options: Either all variables are assigned, in which case the solver can conclude that the formula is satisfiable, or there are still unassigned variables, in which case the solver first assigns a truth value to an unassigned variable (the actual variable and the truth value are chosen based on a so-called *decision heuristic*) and then continues by again performing unit propagation. For more details see the chapter on CDCL [25] in the Handbook of Satisfiability [7].

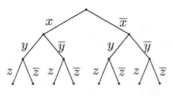

Fig. 2. By learning the clause $\overline{x} \vee y$, a solver prunes all branches where x is true and y is false from the search space. SDCL can prune satisfying branches too (unlike CDCL).

Satisfaction-Driven Clause Learning (SDCL). The SDCL algorithm [20], shown in Fig. 1, is a generalization of CDCL that is obtained by adding lines 9 to 12 to the CDCL algorithm. In CDCL, if unit propagation does not derive a conflict, the solver picks a variable and assigns a truth value to it. In contrast, an SDCL solver does not necessarily assign a new variable in this situation. Instead, it first checks if the current assignment can be pruned from the search space without affecting satisfiability. If so, the solver prunes the assignment by learning a new clause (Fig. 2 illustrates how clause learning can prune the search space). This clause is returned by the AnalyzeWitness() function and usually consists of the decision literals of the current assignment (although other ways of computing the clause are possible, c.f. [20]). If the assignment cannot be pruned, the solver proceeds by assigning a new variable—just as in CDCL. To check if the current assignment can be pruned, the solver produces a propositional formula that should be easier to solve than the original formula and that can only be satisfiable if the assignment can be pruned. Thus, an SDCL solver solves several easier formulas in order to solve a hard formula. In this paper, we call these easier formulas *pruning predicates*. We first formalize the pruning predicate used in the original SDCL paper before we introduce more powerful pruning predicates.

3   Pruning Predicates and Redundant Clauses

As already explained informally, a pruning predicate is a propositional formula whose satisfiability guarantees that an assignment can be pruned from the search space. The actual pruning is then performed by adding the clause that *blocks* the assignment (or a subclause of this clause, as explained in detail later):

Definition 1. *Given an assignment* $\alpha = a_1 \ldots a_k$, *the clause* $(\overline{a}_1 \vee \cdots \vee \overline{a}_k)$ *is the clause that* blocks α.

The clause that blocks α is thus the unique maximal clause falsified by α. Based on this notion, we define pruning predicates as follows:

Definition 2. *Let F be a formula and C the clause that blocks a given (partial) assignment α. A pruning predicate for F and α is a formula $P_\alpha(F)$ such that the following holds: if $P_\alpha(F)$ is satisfiable, then F and $F \wedge C$ are equisatisfiable.*

Thus, if a pruning predicate for a formula F and an assignment α is satisfiable, we can add the clause that blocks α to F without affecting satisfiability. We thus say that this clause is *redundant* with respect to F. In the paper that introduces SDCL [20], the so-called *positive reduct* (see Definition 3 below) is used as a pruning predicate. The positive reduct is obtained from satisfied clauses of the original formula by removing unassigned literals.

In the following, given a clause C and an assignment α, we write $\mathsf{touched}_\alpha(C)$ to denote the subclause of C that contains exactly the literals assigned by α. Analogously, we denote by $\mathsf{untouched}_\alpha(C)$ the subclause of C that contains the literals *not* assigned by α [20].

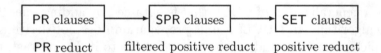

Fig. 3. Relationship between types of redundant clauses and the corresponding pruning predicates. An arrow from X to Y means that X is a superset of Y.

Definition 3. *Let F be a formula and α an assignment. Then, the positive reduct $\mathsf{p}_\alpha(F)$ of F and α is the formula $G \wedge C$ where C is the clause that blocks α and $G = \{\mathsf{touched}_\alpha(D) \mid D \in F \text{ and } D{\restriction}\alpha = \top\}$.*

Example 1. Let $F = (x \vee \overline{y} \vee z) \wedge (w \vee \overline{y}) \wedge (\overline{w} \vee \overline{z})$ and $\alpha = x\,y\,\overline{z}$. Then, the positive reduct $\mathsf{p}_\alpha(F)$ of F w.r.t. α is the formula $(x \vee \overline{y} \vee z) \wedge (\overline{z}) \wedge (\overline{x} \vee \overline{y} \vee z)$.

The positive reduct is satisfiable if and only if the clause blocked by α is a *set-blocked clause* [23], short **SET** clause, with respect to F. Since the addition of set-blocked clauses to a formula preserves satisfiability, it follows that the positive reduct is a pruning predicate. Moreover, since the problem of deciding whether a given clause is a set-blocked clause is NP-complete, it is natural to use a SAT solver for finding set-blocked clauses.

Although set-blocked clauses can be found efficiently with the positive reduct, there are more general kinds of clauses whose addition can prune the search space more aggressively, namely *propagation-redundant clauses* (**PR** clauses) and their subclass of *set-propagation-redundant clauses* (**SPR** clauses) [19].

In the following, we thus introduce two different kinds of pruning predicates. Given a formula F and an assignment α, the first pruning predicate, called the *filtered positive reduct*, is satisfiable if and only if the clause that blocks α is an

SPR clause in F. The second pruning predicate, called PR *reduct*, is satisfiable if and only if the clause that blocks α is a PR clause; it allows us to prune more assignments than the filtered positive reduct but it is also harder to solve. The relationship between the redundant clause types and pruning predicates is shown in Fig. 3. According to [19], the definition of PR clauses is as follows:

Definition 4. *Let F be a formula, C a clause, and α the assignment blocked by C. Then, C is* propagation redundant (PR) *with respect to F if there exists an assignment ω such that $F\restriction\alpha \vdash_1 F\restriction\omega$ and ω satisfies C.*

The clause C can be seen as a constraint that prunes all assignments that extend α from the search space. Since $F\restriction\alpha$ implies $F\restriction\omega$ via unit propagation, every assignment that satisfies $F\restriction\alpha$ also satisfies $F\restriction\omega$, and so we say that F is *at least as satisfiable* under ω as it is under α. Moreover, since ω satisfies C, it must disagree with α. Consider the following example [19]:

Example 2. Let $F = (x \vee y) \wedge (\overline{x} \vee y) \wedge (\overline{x} \vee z)$ be a formula, $C = (x)$ a clause, and $\omega = x\,z$ an assignment. Then, $\alpha = \overline{x}$ is the assignment blocked by C. Now, consider $F\restriction\alpha = (y)$ and $F\restriction\omega = (y)$. Since unit propagation clearly derives a conflict on $F\restriction\alpha \wedge (\overline{y}) = (y) \wedge (\overline{y})$, we have $F\restriction\alpha \vdash_1 F\restriction\omega$ and thus C is propagation redundant with respect to F.

The key property of propagation-redundant clauses is that their addition to a formula preserves satisfiability [19]. A strict subclass of propagation-redundant clauses are set-propagation-redundant clauses, which have the additional requirement that ω must assign the same variables as α. For the following definition, recall (from the preliminaries) that α_L denotes the assignment obtained from α by assigning 1 to the literals in L [19]:

Definition 5. *Let F be a formula, C a clause, and α the assignment blocked by C. Then, C is* set-propagation redundant (SPR) *with respect to F if it contains a non-empty set L of literals such that $F\restriction\alpha \vdash_1 F\restriction\alpha_L$.*

If $F\restriction\alpha \vdash_1 F\restriction\alpha_L$, we say C is SPR *by L* with respect to F.

Example 3. Let $F = (x \vee y) \wedge (x \vee \overline{y} \vee z) \wedge (\overline{x} \vee z) \wedge (\overline{x} \vee u) \wedge (\overline{u} \vee x)$, $C = x \vee u$, and $L = \{x, u\}$. Then, $\alpha = \overline{x}\,\overline{u}$ is the assignment blocked by C, and $\alpha_L = x\,u$. Now, consider $F\restriction\alpha = (y) \wedge (\overline{y} \vee z)$ and $F\restriction\alpha_L = (z)$. Clearly, $F\restriction\alpha \vdash_1 F\restriction\alpha_L$ and so C is set-propagation redundant by L with respect to F.

Most known types of redundant clauses are SPR clauses [19]. This includes *blocked clauses* [24], *set-blocked clauses* [23], *resolution asymmetric tautologies* (RATs) [22], and many more. By introducing pruning predicates that allow us to add SPR clauses and even PR clauses to a formula, we thus allow for more effective pruning than with the positive reduct originally used in SDCL. We start by presenting our new *filtered* positive reduct.

4   The Filtered Positive Reduct

The original positive reduct of a formula F and an assignment α is obtained by first taking all clauses of F that are satisfied by α and then removing from these clauses the literals that are not touched (assigned) by α. The resulting clauses are then conjoined with the clause C that blocks α. We obtain the *filtered* positive reduct by not taking *all* satisfied clauses of F but only those for which the untouched part is not implied by $F\upharpoonright\alpha$ via unit propagation:

Definition 6. *Let F be a formula and α an assignment. Then, the* filtered *positive reduct $f_\alpha(F)$ of F and α is the formula $G \wedge C$ where C is the clause that blocks α and $G = \{\text{touched}_\alpha(D) \mid D \in F \text{ and } F\upharpoonright\alpha \not\vdash_1 \text{untouched}_\alpha(D)\}$.*

Clearly the filtered positive reduct is a subset of the positive reduct because $F\upharpoonright\alpha \not\vdash_1 \text{untouched}_\alpha(D)$ implies $D\upharpoonright\alpha = \top$. To see this, suppose $D\upharpoonright\alpha \neq \top$. Then, $D\upharpoonright\alpha$ is contained in $F\upharpoonright\alpha$ and since $\text{untouched}_\alpha(D) = D\upharpoonright\alpha$, it follows that $F\upharpoonright\alpha \vdash_1 \text{untouched}_\alpha(D)$. Therefore, the filtered positive reduct is obtained from the positive reduct by removing ("filtering") every clause $D' = \text{touched}_\alpha(D)$ such that $F\upharpoonright\alpha \vdash_1 \text{untouched}_\alpha(D)$.

The following example illustrates how the filtered positive reduct allows us to prune assignments that cannot be pruned when using only the positive reduct:

Example 4. Let $F = (x \vee y) \wedge (\overline{x} \vee y)$ and consider the assignment $\alpha = x$. The positive reduct $p_\alpha(F) = (x) \wedge (\overline{x})$ is unsatisfiable and so it does not allow us to prune α. In contrast, the filtered positive reduct $f_\alpha(F) = (\overline{x})$, obtained by filtering out the clause (x), is satisfied by the assignment $\overline{x}$. The clause (x) is not contained in the filtered reduct because $\text{untouched}_\alpha(x \vee y) = (y)$ and $F\upharpoonright\alpha = (y)$, which implies $F\upharpoonright\alpha \vdash_1 \text{untouched}_\alpha(x \vee y)$. Note that the clause $(\overline{x})$ is contained both in the positive reduct and in the filtered positive reduct since it blocks α.

The filtered positive reduct has a useful property: If a non-empty assignment α falsifies a formula F, then the filtered positive reduct $f_\alpha(F)$ is satisfiable. To see this, observe that $\bot \in F\upharpoonright\alpha$ and so $F\upharpoonright\alpha \vdash_1 \text{untouched}_\alpha(D)$ for every clause $D \in F$ because unit propagation derives a conflict on $F\upharpoonright\alpha$ alone (note that this also holds if $\text{untouched}_\alpha(D)$ is the empty clause $\bot$). Therefore, $f_\alpha(F)$ contains only the clause that blocks α, which is clearly satisfiable. The ordinary positive reduct does not have this property.

Note that the filtered positive reduct contains only variables of $var(\alpha)$. Since it also contains the clause that blocks α, any satisfying assignment of the filtered positive reduct must disagree with α on at least one literal. Hence, every satisfying assignment of the filtered positive reduct is of the form α_L where L is a set of literals that are contained in the clause that blocks α. With the filtered positive reduct, we can identify exactly the clauses that are set-propagation redundant with respect to a formula:

Theorem 1. *Let F be a formula, α an assignment, and C the clause that blocks α. Then, C is SPR by an $L \subseteq C$ with respect to F if and only if the assignment α_L satisfies the filtered positive reduct $f_\alpha(F)$.*

Proof. For the "only if" direction, suppose C is SPR by an $L \subseteq C$ in F, meaning that $F{\restriction}\alpha \vdash_1 F{\restriction}\alpha_L$. We show that α_L satisfies all clauses of $\mathsf{f}_\alpha(F)$. Let therefore $D' \in \mathsf{f}_\alpha(F)$. By definition, D' is either the clause that blocks α or it is of the form $\mathsf{touched}_\alpha(D)$ for some clause $D \in F$ such that $F{\restriction}\alpha \nvdash_1 \mathsf{untouched}_\alpha(D)$. In the former case, D' is clearly satisfied by α_L since α_L must disagree with α. In the latter case, since $F{\restriction}\alpha \vdash_1 F{\restriction}\alpha_L$, it follows that either $F{\restriction}\alpha \vdash_1 D{\restriction}\alpha_L$ or α_L satisfies D. Now, if $D{\restriction}\alpha_L \neq \top$, it cannot be the case that $F{\restriction}\alpha \vdash_1 D{\restriction}\alpha_L$ since $var(\alpha_L) = var(\alpha)$ and thus $D{\restriction}\alpha_L = \mathsf{untouched}_\alpha(D)$, which would imply $F{\restriction}\alpha \vdash_1 \mathsf{untouched}_\alpha(D)$. Therefore, α_L must satisfy D. But then α_L must satisfy $D' = \mathsf{touched}_\alpha(D)$, again since $var(\alpha_L) = var(\alpha)$.

For the "if" direction, assume that α_L satisfies the filtered positive reduct $\mathsf{f}_\alpha(F)$. We show that $F{\restriction}\alpha \vdash_1 F{\restriction}\alpha_L$. Let $D{\restriction}\alpha_L \in F{\restriction}\alpha_L$. Since $D{\restriction}\alpha_L$ is contained in $F{\restriction}\alpha_L$, we know that α_L does not satisfy D and so it does not satisfy $\mathsf{touched}_\alpha(D)$. Hence, $\mathsf{touched}_\alpha(D)$ cannot be contained in $\mathsf{f}_\alpha(F)$, implying that $F{\restriction}\alpha \vdash_1 \mathsf{untouched}_\alpha(D)$. But, $D{\restriction}\alpha_L = \mathsf{untouched}_\alpha(D)$ since $var(\alpha_L) = var(\alpha)$ and thus it follows that $F{\restriction}\alpha \vdash_1 D{\restriction}\alpha_L$. □

When the (ordinary) positive reduct is used for SDCL solving, the following property holds [20]: Assume the solver has a current assignment $\alpha = \alpha_d \cup \alpha_u$ where α_d consists of all the assignments that were made by the decision heuristic and α_u consists of all assignments that were derived via unit propagation. If the solver then finds that the positive reduct of its formula and the assignment α is satisfiable, it can learn the clause that blocks α_d instead of the longer clause that blocks α, thus pruning the search space more effectively. This is allowed because the clause that blocks α_d is guaranteed to be propagation redundant.

The same holds for the filtered positive reduct and the argument is analogous to the earlier one [20]: Assume the filtered positive reduct of F and $\alpha = \alpha_d \cup \alpha_u$ is satisfiable. Then, the clause that blocks α is set-propagation redundant with respect to F and thus there exists an assignment α_L such that $F{\restriction}\alpha \vdash_1 F{\restriction}\alpha_L$. But then, since unit propagation derives all the assignments of α_u from $F{\restriction}\alpha_d$, it must also hold that $F{\restriction}\alpha_d \vdash_1 F{\restriction}\alpha_L$, and so the clause that blocks α_d is propagation redundant with respect to F and (witness) assignment $\omega = \alpha_L$.

Finally, observe that the filtered positive reducts $\mathsf{f}_{\alpha_d}(F)$ and $\mathsf{f}_\alpha(F)$ are not always equisatisfiable. To see this, consider the formula $F = (\overline{x} \vee y) \wedge (x \vee \overline{y})$ and the assignments $\alpha = x\,y$ and $\alpha_d = x$. Clearly, the unit clause y is derived from $F{\restriction}\alpha_d$. Now, observe that $\mathsf{f}_\alpha(F)$ is satisfiable while $\mathsf{f}_{\alpha_d}(F)$ is unsatisfiable. It thus makes sense to first compute the filtered positive reduct with respect to α and then—in case it is satisfiable—remove the propagated literals to obtain a shorter clause.

5   The PR Reduct

We showed in the previous section that the filtered positive reduct characterizes precisely the set-propagation-redundant clauses. Since set-propagation-redundant clauses are a subset of propagation-redundant clauses [19], it is natural to search for an encoding that characterizes the propagation-redundant clauses, which could possibly lead to an even more aggressive pruning of the search space. As we will see in the following, such an encoding must necessarily be large because it has to reason over all possible clauses of a formula. We thus believe that it is hardly useful for practical SDCL solving.

The positive reduct and the filtered positive reduct yield small formulas that can be easily solved in practice. The downside, however, is that nothing can be learned from their unsatisfiability. This is different for a pruning predicate that encodes propagation redundancy:

Theorem 2. *If a clause $l_1 \vee \cdots \vee l_k$ is not propagation redundant with respect to a formula F, then F implies $\bar{l}_1 \wedge \cdots \wedge \bar{l}_k$.*

Proof. Assume $l_1 \vee \cdots \vee l_k$ is not propagation redundant with respect to F, or equivalently that all assignments ω with $F\lceil \bar{l}_1 \ldots \bar{l}_k \vdash F\lceil \omega$ agree with $\bar{l}_1 \ldots \bar{l}_k$. Then, no assignment that disagrees with $\bar{l}_1 \ldots \bar{l}_k$ can satisfy F. As a consequence, F implies $\bar{l}_1 \wedge \cdots \wedge \bar{l}_k$. $\qquad \square$

By solving a pruning predicate for propagation-redundant clauses, we thus not only detect if the current assignment can be pruned (in case the predicate is satisfiable), but also if the formula can only possibly be satisfied by extensions of the current assignment (in case the predicate is unsatisfiable). This is in contrast to the positive reduct and the filtered positive reduct, which often only need to consider a small subpart of the original formula. We thus believe that such an encoding is not useful in practice. In the following, we present a possible encoding which—due to the above reasons—we did not evaluate in practice. Nevertheless, performing such an evaluation is still part of our future work.

In the definition of propagation-redundant clauses, the assignment ω does not necessarily assign the same variables as α. To deal with this, we use the idea of the so-called *dual-rail encoding* [8,10,30]. In the dual-rail encoding, a given variable x is replaced by two new variables x^p and x^n. The intuitive idea is that x^p is true whenever the original variable x is supposed to be true and x^n is true whenever x is supposed to be false. If both x^p and x^n are false, then x is supposed to be unassigned. Finally, x^p and x^n cannot be true at the same time. Thus, the *dual-rail encodings* of a clause are defined as follows: Let $C = P \vee N$ be a clause with $P = x_1 \vee \cdots \vee x_k$ containing only positive literals and $N = \bar{x}_{k+1} \vee \cdots \vee \bar{x}_m$ containing only negative literals. Further, let $x_1^p, x_1^n, \ldots, x_m^p, x_m^n$ be new variables. Then, the *positive dual-rail encoding* C^p of C is the clause

$$x_1^p \vee \cdots \vee x_k^p \vee x_{k+1}^n \vee \cdots \vee x_m^n,$$

and the *negative dual-rail encoding* C^n of C is the clause

$$x_1^n \vee \cdots \vee x_k^n \vee x_{k+1}^p \vee \cdots \vee x_m^p.$$

We can now define the PR reduct as follows:

Definition 7. *Let F be a formula and α an assignment. Then, the* PR *reduct* $\mathsf{pr}_\alpha(F)$ *of F and α is the formula $G \wedge C$ where C is the clause that blocks α and G is the union of the following sets of clauses where all the s_i are new variables:*

$$\{\overline{x^p} \vee \overline{x^n} \mid x \in var(F) \setminus var(\alpha)\},$$

$$\{\overline{s_i} \vee \mathsf{touched}_\alpha(D_i) \vee \mathsf{untouched}_\alpha(D_i)^p \mid D_i \in F\},$$

$$\{\overline{L^n} \vee s_i \mid D_i \in F \ \text{ and } \ L \subseteq \mathsf{untouched}_\alpha(D_i)$$
$$\text{such that } F{\restriction}\alpha \not\models \mathsf{untouched}_\alpha(D_i) \setminus L\}.$$

In the last set, if L is empty, we obtain a unit clause with the literal s_i.

We thus keep all the variables assigned by α but introduce the dual-rail variants for variables of F not assigned by α. The clauses of the form $\overline{x^p} \vee \overline{x^n}$ ensure that for a variable x, the two variables x^p and x^n cannot be true at the same time.

The main idea is that satisfying assignments of the PR reduct correspond to assignments of the formula F: from a satisfying assignment τ of the PR reduct we obtain an assignment ω over the variables of the original formula F as follows:

$$\omega(x) = \begin{cases} \tau(x) & \text{if } x \in var(\tau) \cap var(F), \\ 1 & \text{if } \tau(x^p) = 1, \\ 0 & \text{if } \tau(x^n) = 1. \end{cases}$$

Analogously, we obtain from ω a satisfying assignment τ of the filtered positive reduct $\mathsf{pr}_\alpha(F)$ as follows:

$$\tau(x) = \begin{cases} \omega(x) & \text{if } x \in var(\alpha); \\ 1 & \text{if } x = x^p \text{ and } \omega(x) = 1, \text{ or} \\ & \text{if } x = x^n \text{ and } \omega(x) = 0, \text{ or} \\ & \text{if } x = s_i \text{ and } \omega \text{ satisfies } D_i; \\ 0 & \text{otherwise.} \end{cases}$$

To prove that the clause that blocks an assignment α is propagation redundant w.r.t. a formula F if the PR reduct of F and α is satisfiable, we use the following:

Lemma 1. *Let F be a formula and let α and ω be two assignments such that $F{\restriction}\alpha \models F{\restriction}\omega$. Then, $F{\restriction}\alpha \models F{\restriction}\omega x$ for every literal x such that $var(x) \in var(\alpha)$.*

Proof. Let $D{\restriction}\omega x \in F{\restriction}\omega x$. We show that $F{\restriction}\alpha \models D{\restriction}\omega x$. Clearly, $x \notin D$ for otherwise $D{\restriction}\omega x = \top$, which would imply $D{\restriction}\omega x \notin F{\restriction}\omega x$. Therefore, the only possible difference between $D{\restriction}\omega$ and $D{\restriction}\omega x$ is that $\overline{x}$ is contained in $D{\restriction}\omega$ but not in $D{\restriction}\omega x$. Now, since $var(x) \in var(\alpha)$, we know that $var(x) \notin F{\restriction}\alpha$. But then, $F{\restriction}\alpha \models D{\restriction}\omega x$ if and only if $F{\restriction}\alpha \models D{\restriction}\omega$ and thus $F{\restriction}\alpha \models F{\restriction}\omega x$. $\qquad\square$

We can now show that the PR reduct precisely characterizes the propagation-redundant clauses:

Theorem 3. *Let F be a formula, α an assignment, and C the clause that blocks α. Then, C is propagation redundant with respect to F if and only if the PR reduct $\mathsf{pr}_\alpha(F)$ of F and α is satisfiable.*

Proof. For the "only if" direction, assume that C is propagation redundant with respect to F, meaning that there exists an assignment ω such that ω satisfies C and $F\lceil\alpha \vdash F\lceil\omega$. By Lemma 1, we can without loss of generality assume that $var(\alpha) \subseteq var(\omega)$. Now consider the assignment τ that corresponds to ω as explained before Lemma 1. We show that τ satisfies $\mathsf{pr}_\alpha(F)$. Since the clause C that blocks α is in $\mathsf{pr}_\alpha(F)$, it must be satisfied by ω. Since ω satisfies C, τ satisfies C. Also, by construction, τ never satisfies both x^p and x^n for a variable x and so it satisfies the clauses $\overline{x^p} \vee \overline{x^n}$. If, for a clause $\overline{s}_i \vee \mathsf{touched}_\alpha(D_i) \vee \mathsf{untouched}_\alpha(D_i)^p$, τ satisfies s_i, then we know that ω satisfies D_i and thus τ must satisfy $\mathsf{touched}_\alpha(D_i) \vee \mathsf{untouched}_\alpha(D_i)^p$.

It remains to show that τ satisfies the clause $\overline{L^n} \vee s_i$ for every $D_i \in F$ and every set $L \subseteq \mathsf{untouched}_\alpha(D_i)$ such that $F\lceil\alpha \nvdash \mathsf{untouched}_\alpha(D_i) \setminus L$. Assume to the contrary that, for such a clause, $\tau(s_i) = 0$ and τ falsifies all literals in $\overline{L^n}$. Then, ω does not satisfy D_i and it falsifies all literals in L. But, from $var(\alpha) \subseteq var(\omega)$ we know that $D_i\lceil\omega \subseteq \mathsf{untouched}_\alpha(D_i)$ and thus it follows that $D_i\lceil\omega \subseteq \mathsf{untouched}_\alpha(D_i)\setminus L$. Hence, since $F\lceil\alpha \nvdash \mathsf{untouched}_\alpha(D_i)\setminus L$, we conclude that $F\lceil\alpha \nvdash D_i\lceil\omega$, a contradiction.

For the "if" direction, assume that there exists a satisfying assignment τ of $\mathsf{pr}_\alpha(F)$ and consider the assignment ω that corresponds to τ as explained before Lemma 1. Since $C \in \mathsf{pr}_\alpha(F)$, ω must satisfy C. It remains to show that $F\lceil\alpha \vdash F\lceil\omega$. Let $D_i\lceil\omega \in F\lceil\omega$. Then, ω does not satisfy D_i and so $\mathsf{touched}_\alpha(D_i) \vee \mathsf{untouched}_\alpha(D_i)^p$ is falsified by τ, implying that τ must falsify s_i. As $var(\alpha) \subseteq var(\omega)$, we know that $D_i\lceil\omega \subseteq \mathsf{untouched}_\alpha(D_i)$, meaning that $D_i\lceil\omega$ is of the form $\mathsf{untouched}_\alpha(D_i) \setminus L$ for some set $L \subseteq \mathsf{untouched}_\alpha(D_i)$ such that ω falsifies L. But then the clause $\overline{L^n} \vee s_i$ cannot be contained in $\mathsf{pr}_\alpha(F)$ since it would be falsified by τ. We thus conclude that $F\lceil\omega \vdash \mathsf{untouched}_\alpha(D_i) \setminus L$ and so $F\lceil\omega \vdash D_i\lceil\omega$. □

Note that the last set of clauses of the PR reduct, in principle has exponentially many clauses w.r.t. the length of the largest original clause. We leave it to future work to answer the question whether non-exponential encodings exist. But even if a polynomial encoding can be found, we doubt its usefulness in practice.

6　Implementation

We implemented a clean-slate SDCL solver, called SADiCaL, that can learn PR clauses using either the positive reduct or the filtered positive reduct. It consists of around 3K lines of C and is based on an efficient CDCL engine using state-of-the-art algorithms, data structures, and heuristics, including a variable-move-to-front decision heuristic [4], a sophisticated restart policy [5], and aggressive clause-data-based reduction [2]. Our implementation provides a simple but efficient framework to evaluate new SDCL-inspired ideas and heuristics.

The implementation closely follows the pseudo-code shown in Fig. 1 and computes the pruning predicate before every decision. This is costly in general, but allows the solver to detect PR clauses as early as possible. Our goal is to determine whether short PR proofs can be found automatically. The solver produces PR proofs and we verified all the presented results using proof checkers. The source code of SADICAL is available at http://fmv.jku.at/sadical.

Two aspects of SDCL are crucial: the pruning predicate and the decision heuristics. For the pruning predicate we ran experiments with both the positive reduct and the filtered positive reduct. The initially proposed decision heuristics for SDCL [20] are as follows: Pick the variable that occurs most frequently in short clauses. Also, apart from the root-node branch, assign only literals that occur in clauses that are touched but not satisfied by the current assignment.

We added another restriction: whenever a (filtered) positive reduct is satisfiable, make all literals in the witness (i.e., the satisfying assignment of the pruning predicate) that disagree with the current assignment more important than any other literal in the formula. This restriction is removed when the solver backtracks to the root node (i.e., when a unit clause is learned) and added again when a new PR clause is found. The motivation of this restriction is as follows: we observed that literals in the witness that disagree with the current assignment typically occur in short PR clauses; making them more important than other literals increases the likelihood of learning short PR clauses.

7 Evaluation

In the following, we demonstrate that the filtered positive reduct allows our SDCL solver to prove unsatisfiability of formulas well-known for having only exponential-size resolution proofs. We start with Tseitin formulas [11,32]. In short, a Tseitin formula represents the following graph problem: Given a graph with 0/1-labels for each vertex such that an odd number of vertices has label 1, does there exist a subset of the edges such that (after removing edges not in the subset) every vertex with label 0 has an even degree and every vertex with label 1 has an odd degree? The answer is *no* as the sum of all degrees is always even. The formula is therefore unsatisfiable by construction. Tseitin formulas defined over expander graphs require resolution proofs of exponential size [33] and also appear hard for SDCL when using the ordinary positive reduct as pruning predicate. We compare three settings, all with proof logging:

    (1) plain CDCL,
    (2) SDCL with the positive reduct $p_\alpha(F)$, and
    (3) SDCL with the filtered positive reduct $f_\alpha(F)$.

Additionally, we include the winner of the 2018 SAT Competition: the CDCL-based solver MapleLCMDistChronoBT (short MLBT) [29]. The results are shown in Table 1. The last column shows the proof-validation times by the formally verified checker in ACL2. To verify the proofs for all our experiments, we did the following: We started with the PR proofs produced by our SDCL solver using the filtered positive reduct. We then translated them into DRAT proofs using the `pr2drat` tool [17]. Finally, we used the `drat-trim` checker to optimize the proofs (i.e., to remove redundant proof parts) and to convert them into the LRAT format, which is the format supported by the formally verified proof checker.

Table 1 shows the performance on small (Urquhart-s3*), medium (Urquhart-s4*), and large (Urquhart-s5*) Tseitin formulas running on a Xeon E5-2690 CPU 2.6 GHz with 64 GB memory.[1] Only our solver with the filtered positive reduct is able to efficiently prove unsatisfiability of all these instances. Notice that with the ordinary positive reduct it is impossible to solve any of the formulas. There may actually be a theoretical barrier here. The LSDCL solver also uses the positive reduct, but only for assignments with at most two decision literals. As a consequence, the overhead of the positive reduct is small. In the future we plan to develop meaningful limits for SaDiCaL as well.

Table 1. Runtime Comparison (in Seconds) on the Tseitin Benchmarks [11,33].

formula	MLBT [29]	LSDCL [20]	plain	$p_\alpha(F)$	$f_\alpha(F)$	ACL2
Urquhart-s3-b1	2.95	5.86	16.31	> 3600	**0.02**	0.09
Urquhart-s3-b2	1.36	2.4	2.82	> 3600	**0.03**	0.13
Urquhart-s3-b3	2.28	19.94	2.08	> 3600	**0.03**	0.16
Urquhart-s3-b4	10.74	32.42	7.65	> 3600	**0.03**	0.17
Urquhart-s4-b1	86.11	583.96	> 3600	> 3600	**0.32**	2.37
Urquhart-s4-b2	154.35	1824.95	183.77	> 3600	**0.11**	0.78
Urquhart-s4-b3	258.46	> 3600	129.27	> 3600	**0.16**	1.12
Urquhart-s4-b4	> 3600	> 3600	> 3600	> 3600	**0.14**	1.17
Urquhart-s5-b1	> 3600	> 3600	> 3600	> 3600	**1.27**	9.86
Urquhart-s5-b2	> 3600	> 3600	> 3600	> 3600	**0.58**	4.38
Urquhart-s5-b3	> 3600	> 3600	> 3600	> 3600	**1.67**	17.99
Urquhart-s5-b4	> 3600	> 3600	> 3600	> 3600	**2.91**	24.24

Table 2. Runtime Comparison (in Seconds) on the Pigeon-Hole Formulas.

formula	MLBT [29]	LSDCL [20]	plain	$p_\alpha(F)$	$f_\alpha(F)$	ACL2
hole20	> 3600	1.13	> 3600	**0.22**	0.55	6.78
hole30	> 3600	8.81	> 3600	**1.71**	4.30	87.58
hole40	> 3600	43.10	> 3600	**7.94**	20.38	611.24
hole50	> 3600	149.67	> 3600	**25.60**	68.46	2792.39

We also ran experiments with the pigeon-hole formulas. Although these formulas are hard for resolution, they can be solved efficiently with SDCL using

---

[1] Log files, benchmarks and source code are available at http://fmv.jku.at/sadical.

the positive reduct [20]. Table 2 shows a runtime comparison, again including PR proof logging, for pigeon-hole formulas of various sizes. Notice that the computational costs of the solver with the filtered positive reduct are about 3 to 4 times as large compared to the solver with the positive reduct. This is caused by the overhead of computing the filtering. The sizes of the PR proofs produced by both versions are similar. Our solver with the positive reduct is about four times as fast compared to the SDCL version (only positive reduct) of LINGELING [20], in short LSDCL. As the heuristics and proof sizes of our solver and LSDCL are similar, the better performance is due to our dedicated SDCL implementation.

Finally, we performed experiments with the recently released 2018 SAT Competition benchmarks. We expected slow performance on most benchmarks due to the high overhead of solving pruning predicates before making decisions. However, our solver outperformed the participating solvers on mutilated chessboard problems [27] which were contributed by Alexey Porkhunov (see Table 3).

For example, our solver can prove unsatisfiability of the 18×18 mutilated chessboard in 43.88 seconds. The filtered positive reduct was crucial to obtain this result. The other solvers, apart from CADICAL solving it in 828 seconds, timed out after 5000 seconds during the competition (on competition hardware). Resolution proofs of mutilated chessboard problems are exponential in size [1], which explains the poor performance of CDCL solvers. On these problems, like on the Tseitin formulas, our solver performed much better with the filtered positive reduct than with the positive reduct. The results are robust with respect to partially and completely scrambling formulas as suggested by [6], with the exception of the pigeon hole formulas, which needs to be investigated.

Table 3. Runtime Comparison (in Seconds) on the Mutilated Chessboard Formulas.

formula	MLBT [29]	LSDCL [20]	plain	$p_\alpha(F)$	$f_\alpha(F)$	ACL2
mchess_15	51.53	1473.11	2480.67	> 3600	**13.14**	29.12
mchess_16	380.45	> 3600	2115.75	> 3600	**15.52**	36.86
mchess_17	2418.35	> 3600	> 3600	> 3600	**25.54**	57.83
mchess_18	> 3600	> 3600	> 3600	> 3600	**43.88**	100.71

8 Conclusion

We introduced two new SAT encodings for pruning the search space in satisfaction-driven clause learning (SDCL). The first encoding, called the filtered positive reduct, is easily solvable and prunes the search space more aggressively than the positive reduct (which was used when SDCL was initially introduced). The second encoding, called the PR reduct, might not be useful in practice though it precisely characterizes propagation redundancy.

Based on the filtered positive reduct, we implemented an SDCL solver and our experiments show that the solver can efficiently prove the unsatisfiability of the Tseitin formulas, the pigeon-hole formulas, and the mutilated chessboard problems. For all these formulas, CDCL solvers require exponential time due to theoretical restrictions. Moreover, to the best of our knowledge, our solver is the first to generate machine-checkable proofs of unsatisfiability of these formulas. We certified our results using a formally verified proof checker.

Although our SDCL solver can already produce proofs of formulas that are too hard for CDCL solvers, it is still outperformed by CDCL solvers on many simpler formulas. This seems to suggest that also in SAT solving, there is no free lunch. Nevertheless, we believe that the performance of SDCL on simple formulas can be improved by tuning the solver more carefully, e.g., by only learning propagation-redundant clauses when this is really beneficial, or by coming up with a dedicated decision heuristic. To deal with these problems, we are currently investigating an approach based on reinforcement learning.

Considering our results, we believe that SDCL is a promising SAT-solving paradigm for formulas that are too hard for ordinary CDCL solvers. Finally, proofs of challenging problems can be enormous in size, such as the 2 petabytes proof of Schur Number Five [16]; SDCL improvements have the potential to produce proofs that are substantially smaller and faster to verify.

References

1. Alekhnovich, M.: Mutilated chessboard problem is exponentially hard for resolution. Theoret. Comput. Sci. **310**(1–3), 513–525 (2004)
2. Audemard, G., Simon, L.: Predicting learnt clauses quality in modern SAT solvers. In: Proceedings of the 21st International Joint Conference on Artificial Intelligence (IJCAI 2019), pp. 399–404 (2009)
3. Biere, A.: Splatz, Lingeling, Plingeling, Treengeling, YalSAT entering the SAT competition 2016. In: Proceedings of SAT Competition 2016 - Solver and Benchmark Descriptions. Department of Computer Science Series of Publications B, vol. B-2016-1, pp. 44–45. University of Helsinki (2016)
4. Biere, A., Fröhlich, A.: Evaluating CDCL variable scoring schemes. In: Heule, M.J.H., Weaver, S. (eds.) SAT 2015. LNCS, vol. 9340, pp. 405–422. Springer, Cham (2015)
5. Biere, A., Fröhlich, A.: Evaluating CDCL restart schemes. In: Proceedings of the 6th Pragmatics of SAT Workshop (PoS 2015). EPiC Series in Computing, vol. 59, pp. 1–17 (2019)
6. Biere, A., Heule, M.J.H.: The effect of scrambling CNFs. In: Proceedings of the 9th Pragmatics of SAT Workshop (PoS 2018) (2018, to be published)
7. Biere, A., Heule, M.J.H., van Maaren, H., Walsh, T. (eds.): Handbook of Satisfiability. IOS Press, Amsterdam (2009)
8. Bonet, M.L., Buss, S., Ignatiev, A., Marques-Silva, J., Morgado, A.: MaxSAT resolution with the dual rail encoding. In: Proceedings of the 32nd AAAI Conference on Artificial Intelligence (AAAI 2018). AAAI Press (2018)
9. Brickenstein, M., Dreyer, A.: PolyBoRi: a framework for Gröbner-basis computations with boolean polynomials. J. Symbolic Comput. **44**(9), 1326–1345 (2009). Effective Methods in Algebraic Geometry

10. Bryant, R.E., Beatty, D., Brace, K., Cho, K., Sheffler, T.: COSMOS: a compiled simulator for MOS circuits. In: Proceedings of the 24th ACM/IEEE Design Automation Conference (DAC 87), pp. 9–16. ACM (1987)

11. Chatalic, P., Simon, L.: Multi-resolution on compressed sets of clauses. In: Proceedings of the 12th IEEE International Conference on Tools with Artificial Intelligence (ICTAI 2000), pp. 2–10 (2000)

12. Cruz-Filipe, L., Marques-Silva, J., Schneider-Kamp, P.: Efficient certified resolution proof checking. In: Legay, A., Margaria, T. (eds.) TACAS 2017. LNCS, vol. 10205, pp. 118–135. Springer, Heidelberg (2017)

13. Dantchev, S.S., Riis, S.: "Planar" tautologies hard for resolution. In: Proceedings of the 42nd Annual Symposium on Foundations of Computer Science (FOCS 2001), pp. 220–229. IEEE Computer Society (2001)

14. Devriendt, J., Bogaerts, B., Bruynooghe, M., Denecker, M.: Improved static symmetry breaking for SAT. In: Creignou, N., Le Berre, D. (eds.) SAT 2016. LNCS, vol. 9710, pp. 104–122. Springer, Cham (2016)

15. Haken, A.: The intractability of resolution. Theoret. Comput. Sci. **39**, 297–308 (1985)

16. Heule, M.J.H.: Schur number five. In: Proceedings of the 32nd AAAI Conference on Artificial Intelligence (AAAI 2018). AAAI Press (2018)

17. Heule, M.J.H., Biere, A.: What a difference a variable makes. In: Beyer, D., Huisman, M. (eds.) TACAS 2018. LNCS, vol. 10806, pp. 75–92. Springer, Cham (2018)

18. Heule, M.J.H., Hunt Jr., W.A., Kaufmann, M., Wetzler, N.: Efficient, verified checking of propositional proofs. In: Ayala-Rincón, M., Muñoz, C.A. (eds.) ITP 2017. LNCS, vol. 10499, pp. 269–284. Springer, Cham (2017)

19. Heule, M.J.H., Kiesl, B., Biere, A.: Short proofs without new variables. In: de Moura, L. (ed.) CADE 2017. LNCS (LNAI), vol. 10395, pp. 130–147. Springer, Cham (2017)

20. Heule, M.J.H., Kiesl, B., Seidl, M., Biere, A.: PRuning through satisfaction. In: Strichman, O., Tzoref-Brill, R. (eds.) HVC 2017. LNCS, vol. 10629, pp. 179–194. Springer, Cham (2017)

21. Heule, M.J.H., van Maaren, H.: Aligning CNF- and equivalence-reasoning. In: Hoos, H.H., Mitchell, D.G. (eds.) SAT 2004. LNCS, vol. 3542, pp. 145–156. Springer, Heidelberg (2005)

22. Järvisalo, M., Heule, M.J.H., Biere, A.: Inprocessing rules. In: Gramlich, B., Miller, D., Sattler, U. (eds.) IJCAR 2012. LNCS (LNAI), vol. 7364, pp. 355–370. Springer, Heidelberg (2012)

23. Kiesl, B., Seidl, M., Tompits, H., Biere, A.: Super-blocked clauses. In: Olivetti, N., Tiwari, A. (eds.) IJCAR 2016. LNCS (LNAI), vol. 9706, pp. 45–61. Springer, Cham (2016)

24. Kullmann, O.: On a generalization of extended resolution. Discrete Appl. Math. **96–97**, 149–176 (1999)

25. Marques-Silva, J., Lynce, I., Malik, S.: Conflict-driven clause learning SAT solvers. In: Biere, A., Heule, M.J.H., van Maaren, H., Walsh, T. (eds.) Handbook of Satisfiability, pp. 131–153. IOS Press, Amsterdam (2009)

26. Marques Silva, J.P., Sakallah, K.A.: GRASP: a search algorithm for propositional satisfiability. IEEE Trans. Comput. **48**(5), 506–521 (1999)

27. McCarthy, J.: A tough nut for proof procedures. Memo 16, Stanford Artificial Intelligence Project, July 1964

28. Moskewicz, M.W., Madigan, C.F., Zhao, Y., Zhang, L., Malik, S.: Chaff: engineering an efficient SAT solver. In: Proceedings of the 38th Design Automation Conference (DAC 2001), pp. 530–535. ACM (2001)

29. Nadel, A., Ryvchin, V.: Chronological backtracking. In: Beyersdorff, O., Winter-steiger, C.M. (eds.) SAT 2018. LNCS, vol. 10929, pp. 111–121. Springer, Cham (2018)
30. Palopoli, L., Pirri, F., Pizzuti, C.: Algorithms for selective enumeration of prime implicants. Artif. Intell. **111**(1), 41–72 (1999)
31. Soos, M., Nohl, K., Castelluccia, C.: Extending SAT solvers to cryptographic problems. In: Kullmann, O. (ed.) SAT 2009. LNCS, vol. 5584, pp. 244–257. Springer, Heidelberg (2009)
32. Tseitin, G.S.: On the complexity of derivation in propositional calculus. In: Siekmann, J.H., Wrightson, G. (eds.) Automation of Reasoning: 2: Classical Papers on Computational Logic 1967–1970, pp. 466–483. Springer, Heidelberg (1983)
33. Urquhart, A.: Hard examples for resolution. J. ACM **34**(1), 209–219 (1987)

8

The Axiom Profiler: Understanding and Debugging SMT Quantifier Instantiations

Nils Becker, Peter Müller, and Alexander J. Summers[✉]

Department of Computer Science, ETH Zurich, Zurich, Switzerland
nbecker@student.ethz.ch, {peter.mueller,alexander.summers}@inf.ethz.ch

Abstract. SMT solvers typically reason about universal quantifiers via E-matching: syntactic matching patterns for each quantifier prescribe shapes of ground terms whose presence in the SMT run will trigger quantifier instantiations. The effectiveness and performance of the SMT solver depend crucially on well-chosen patterns. Overly restrictive patterns cause relevant quantifier instantiations to be missed, while overly permissive patterns can cause performance degradation including non-termination if the solver gets stuck in a matching loop. Understanding and debugging such instantiation problems is an overwhelming task, due to the typically large number of quantifier instantiations and their non-trivial interactions with each other and other solver aspects. In this paper, we present the Axiom Profiler, a tool that enables users to analyse instantiation problems effectively, by filtering and visualising rich logging information from SMT runs. Our tool implements novel techniques for automatically detecting matching loops and explaining why they repeat indefinitely. We evaluated the tool on the full test suites of five existing program verifiers, where it discovered and explained multiple previously-unknown matching loops.

1 Introduction

SMT solvers are in prevalent use for a wide variety of applications, including constraint solving, program synthesis, software model checking, test generation and program verification. They combine highly-efficient propositional reasoning with natively supported theories and first-order quantifiers. Quantifiers are used frequently, for instance, to model additional mathematical theories and other domain-specific aspects of an encoded problem. In a program verification setting, for example, one might model a factorial function using an uninterpreted function `fact` from integers to integers and (partially) defining its meaning by means of quantified formulas such as $\forall i\texttt{:Int} :: i > 1 \Rightarrow \texttt{fact}(i) = i * \texttt{fact}(i-1)$.

The support for quantifiers in SMT is not without a price; satisfiability of SMT assertions with quantifiers is undecidable in general. SMT solvers employ a range of heuristics for quantifier instantiation, the most widely-used (and the one focused on in this paper) being *E-matching* [7]. The E-matching approach attaches syntactic *patterns* to each universal quantifier, prescribing shapes of ground terms which, when encountered during the SMT solver's run, will trigger[1] a quantifier instantiation. For example, the pattern {fact(i)} on the quantifier above would indicate that a quantifier instantiation should be made whenever a function application fact(t) (for some term t) is encountered; the term t then prescribes the corresponding instantiation for the quantified variable.

The success of E-matching as a quantifier instantiation strategy depends crucially on well-chosen patterns: poorly chosen patterns can result in *too few* quantifier instantiations and failure to prove unsatisfiability of a formula, or *too many* quantifier instantiations, leading to poor and unpredictable performance, and even non-termination. For the factorial example above, a ground term fact(n) will match the pattern {fact(i)}, yielding an instantiation of the quantifier body, which includes the ground term fact(n-1); this term again matches the pattern, and, if it is never *provable* that $n - x > 1$ is definitely false, this process continues generating terms and quantifier instantiations indefinitely, in a *matching loop*.

Choosing suitable matching patterns is one of the main difficulties in using E-matching effectively [14, 16]. It is extremely difficult to analyse *how* and *why* quantifier instantiations misbehave, especially for SMT problems with a large number of quantifiers[2]. Some solvers report high-level statistics (e.g. total number of quantifier instantiations); these are insufficient to determine whether quantifiers were instantiated as intended, and what the root causes of unintended instantiations are. SMT problems with poor performance are typically highly *brittle* with respect to changes in the input (due to internal pseudo-random heuristics), making performance problems difficult to reproduce or minimise; altering the example often unpredictably changes its behaviour. Conversely, problems with poor quantifier instantiation behaviour are not *always* slow; slowdowns typically manifest only when sufficiently many *interactions* with other aspects of the solver (e.g. theory reasoning) arise: extending problematic examples can cause sudden performance degradation, while the underlying cause existed in the original problem. There is therefore a clear need for tool support for uncovering, understanding and debugging quantifier instantiations made during SMT queries.

In this paper, we present the *Axiom Profiler*, a tool that addresses these challenges, providing comprehensive support for the manual and automated analysis of the quantifier instantiations performed by an SMT solver run, enabling a user to uncover and explain the underlying causes for quantifier-related problems. Our tool takes a log file generated by an SMT solver (in our case, Z3 [6]), interprets it, and provides a wide array of features and algorithms for displaying, navigating and analysing the data. Specifically, we present the following key contributions:

---

[1] In some tools, patterns are themselves alternatively called *triggers*.

[2] Such problems are common in e.g. program verification: for example, queries generated from Dafny's [13] test suite include an average of 2,500 quantifiers; it is not uncommon for hundreds to be instantiated hundreds of times for a single query: *cf.* Sect. 7.

1. We propose a *debugging recipe*, identifying the essential information needed and typical steps performed to analyse quantifier-related problems (Sect. 3).
2. We devise and present detailed *justifications* for each quantifier instantiation, including equality reasoning steps that enable the pattern match (Sect. 4).
3. We define an *instantiation graph* which reflects the causal relationships between quantifier instantiations, that is, which instantiations generate terms or equalities used to trigger which other instantiations (Sect. 5).
4. We present a novel automatic analysis over the causal graph which detects matching loops and explains why they occur (Sect. 6).
5. We provide an implementation. Our evaluation on test suites from five existing program verifiers reveals and explains (confirmed) previously-unknown matching loops (Sect. 7).

Our implementation extends the *VCC Axiom Profiler* [16], developed during the VCC [3] project at Microsoft Research. While this older tool (as well as the prior logging mechanism implemented for Z3) has been invaluable as a basis for our implementation, the features and contributions presented in this paper did not exist in the prior tool (aside from a basic explanation of single instantiations, omitting, e.g., equality reasoning steps used to justify a match). Our tool is open source and is available at https://bitbucket.org/viperproject/axiom-profiler/.

2   Background and Running Example

SMT Solving. SMT solvers handle input problems expressed as first-order logic assertions, including both *uninterpreted* function symbols and combinations of natively-supported *interpreted theories* (e.g., integers or reals). SMT problems can contain free uninterpreted symbols (e.g., unknown constants); the problem of SMT solving is to decide whether some interpretation for these symbols results in a model of the assertion (the assertion is *satisfiable*), or not (it is *unsatisfiable*).

The core of an SMT solver is a boolean SAT solving engine, which searches for a model by case-splitting on boolean literals, building up a *candidate model*. This core engine natively represents only quantifier-free propositional logic (including uninterpreted function symbols and equality). Transitive reasoning about equalities, as well as congruence closure properties (i.e., $a = b \Rightarrow f(a) = f(b)$ for functions f), is handled using an *E-graph* data structure [7], which efficiently represents the equivalence classes induced by currently-assumed equality facts (and represents disequality facts) over terms in the candidate model.

Running Example. Figure 1 shows our running example, an SMT query including a simplified modelling of program heaps and arrays, along with assertions (facts) encoding several properties: injectivity of the slot mapping (from integers to array locations), meaning of a next function (C-style pointer increment), and sortedness of an array a. The last two assertions represent an index i being somewhere early in array a, and an attempt to *prove* that the next array entry cannot be smaller than that at i; this proof goal is negated: any model found by the SMT solver is a counterexample to the proof goal. The check-sat command tells the solver to try to find a model for the conjunction of the assertions.

```
 1   ; ... uninterpreted sorts: Heap, Loc, Arr
 2   (declare-fun slot (Arr Int) Loc)          ; heap location for array slot
 3   (declare-fun lookup (Heap Loc) Int)       ; dereference on the heap
 4   (declare-fun next (Loc) Loc)              ; next slot: pointer increment
 5   (assert ∀ar:Arr, i: Int, k:Int :: {slot(ar,i),slot(ar,k)}
 6    i = k ∨ slot(ar,i) != slot(ar,k))        ; injectivity of slot (Q_inj)
 7   (assert ∀ar:Arr, i: Int :: {slot(ar,i)}
 8    next(slot(ar,i)) = slot(ar,i+1))         ; definition of next (Q_nxt)
 9   ; ... declare uninterpreted constants h : Heap, a : Arr, len,j : Int
10   (assert ∀i: Int. {lookup(h, slot(a,i))}  ; sortedness property (Q_srt)
11    i < 0 ∨ i >= len ∨ lookup(h, slot(a,i)) >= lookup(h, next(slot(a,i))))
12   (assert 0 <= j ∧ j+100 < len) ; avoids trivial models (e.g., len = 0)
13   (assert (not (lookup(h, slot(a,j)) > (lookup(h, next(slot(a,j)))))))
14   (check-sat)
```

Fig. 1. Running example: a simple SMT encoding of a problem with heaps and arrays. We use pseudocode roughly based on the smtlib format, with presentational liberties.

Quantifier Instantiation via E-matching. The most commonly-employed method for supporting first-order quantifiers in an SMT solver is *E-matching* [7]. Each ∀-quantified subformula (after conversion to negation normal form) must be equipped with at least one *pattern*: a set of terms to pattern-match against in order to trigger a quantifier instantiation. We write patterns in braces preceding a quantifier body, such as {slot(ar,i)} in line 7 of Fig. 1. This pattern prescribes instantiating the quantifier when a ground term of the form slot(ar',i') is present (for some terms ar', i') in the E-graph. In this instantiation, ar is bound to (replaced by) ar' and i to i'. Patterns may contain multiple terms (e.g. {slot(ar,i),slot(ar,k)} in line 5), meaning that the quantifier is instantiated only if the E-graph contains a matching term for *each* of these pattern terms. It is also possible to specify multiple (alternative) patterns for the same quantifier.

The choice of patterns is critical to the behaviour of the SMT solver. Since quantifier instantiations will *only* be considered when matching terms are encountered, overly restrictive patterns cause relevant quantifier instantiations to be missed (in the extreme case, if *no* ground term matching the pattern is encountered, the solver will behave as if the quantified formula were not present). But overly *permissive* patterns can cause too many quantifier instantiations, resulting in bad performance and even non-termination. The example in Fig. 1 performs around 5000 quantifier instantiations before *unknown* is reported, indicating that the solver can neither deduce unsatisfiability, nor confirm that its candidate model is correct (the solver cannot be certain whether the candidate model could be ruled out by extra quantifier instantiations not allowed by the patterns).

Why are so many quantifier instantiations made, for such a simple problem? One issue is the quantifier labelled Q_{nxt}, with a matching term slot(ar',i'). The resulting instantiation yields the assertion next(slot(ar',i')) = slot(ar',i'+1), in which the (new) ground term slot(ar',i'+1) occurs; when added to the E-graph, this will trigger a new match, in a sequence which can continue indefinitely (the solver terminates only because we bound the depth to 100). Such a repeating instantiation pattern is called a *matching loop*, and is a key cause of poorly performing solver runs. We will show in the next sections how we can systematically discover this matching loop and other quantifier-related problems in our example.

As illustrated by the quantifier Q_{srt}, terms in patterns may include nested function applications. Matching of ground terms against such patterns is not purely syntactic, but is performed modulo the *equalities* in the candidate model. For example, adding `x = slot(a,3) ∧ lookup(h, x) = 42` to the example will trigger a match against the pattern `{lookup(h, slot(a,j))}`. The application of `lookup` can be rewritten via the assumed equality to `lookup(h, slot(a,3))`, which matches the pattern. Thus, understanding an instantiation requires knowledge not only of the available terms, but also of the equalities derived by the solver.

3   A Debugging Recipe for SMT Quantifiers

Even with input problems as simple as that of Fig. 1, undesirable quantifier instantiations easily occur; realistic problems generated by, for instance, program verification tools typically include many hundreds of quantifiers, thousands of terms, and a complex mixture of propositional and theory-specific constraints. Diagnosing and understanding performance problems is further complicated by the fact that the observed slow-downs may not be due to the quantifier instantiations alone; quantifier instantiations may generate many additional theory-specific terms which slow theory reasoning in the SMT solver, and disjunctive formulas which slow the case-splitting boolean search.

In order to systematically understand a quantifier-related SMT problem, we identify (based on our experience) the following sequence of debugging questions:

1. *Are there suspicious numbers of quantifier instantiations?* If not, poor performance is due to other causes, such as non-linear arithmetic reasoning.
2. *Which quantifiers exist in the given SMT problem, and what are their patterns?* The answer to this question is crucial for the subsequent steps and is by no means trivial: in many SMT applications, some quantifiers may be generated by client tools, the SMT solver itself may preprocess input formulas heavily (and heuristically select missing patterns), and nested quantifiers may be added only when outer quantifiers are instantiated.
3. *Which quantifiers are instantiated many times?* Our experience shows that most quantifier instantiation problems are caused by relatively few quantifiers. The quantifiers identified here will be further examined in the next steps.
4. To identify problematic quantifiers, it is often useful to explore the interactions between several quantifiers by asking:
   (a) *Does the causal relationship between quantifier instantiations exhibit high branching: that is, a single quantifier instantiation leads directly to many subsequent instantiations?* A typical example is when an instantiation produces new terms that lead to a combinatorial explosion of matches for another quantifier. Once we have identified such a situation, we analyse the involved quantifiers according to step 5.

(b) *Are there long sequences of instantiations causing one another?* Long sequences often indicate matching loops. To determine whether that's the case, we ask: *Is there a repeating sequence which indicates a matching loop?* If so, we analyse the involved quantifiers (as described in step 5) to determine whether and how this sequence can repeat indefinitely.

5. Once we have identified potentially problematic quantifiers, we analyse their individual instantiations by asking:

(a) *Which pattern of the instantiated quantifier is matched, and to which terms?* The answer is needed to understand the cause of the instantiation, and particularly for identifying overly-permissive matching patterns.

(b) *What do these terms mean with respect to the input problem?* SMT terms can often get very large and, thus, difficult to understand; tracing them back to the original problems facilitates the analysis.

(c) *Is the match triggered via equality reasoning? Where do the necessary terms and equalities originate from?* Such matches are difficult to detect by manually inspecting the input problem because the patterns and the matching terms look syntactically different; instantiation problems that involve equality reasoning are especially difficult to debug by hand.

Except for the very first step in this recipe, efficiently answering these questions is impractical without tool support; our Axiom Profiler now provides this support.

4   Visualising Quantifier Instantiations

The Axiom Profiler takes as input a log file produced by Z3 and provides a wide range of features for analysing the performed quantifier instantiations. In this section, we show the key features for visualising and navigating the data from the log file. In the subsequent sections, we demonstrate how to analyse quantifier instantiation problems, both manually and automatically.

Figure 2 shows a screenshot for the example from Fig. 1. The tool shows in the middle panel raw data on quantifier instantiations from the log file plus some summary statistics, in the right-hand panel an instantiation graph with causal relationships between instantiations, and in the left-hand panel details of selected instantiations. We describe the three panels in the following.

Raw Data. The middle panel displays the raw data on quantifier instantiations, organised per quantifier as an (XML-like) hierarchy of fields; we inherited this view from the VCC Axiom Profiler [16]. The top-level statistics are useful as an overview for steps 1–3 of our debugging recipe (Sect. 3). Each line corresponds to an individual quantifier and shows its total number of instantiations ("#instances"). Manually navigating the underlying raw data is possible, but typically impractical.

In our example 11 quantifiers are listed: the first 3 are from our input problem; the remaining 8 are generated internally by Z3 (they are never instantiated, and we ignore them for our discussion). We can see there are more than 5000 quantifier instantiations in total; all three quantifiers are instantiated many times.

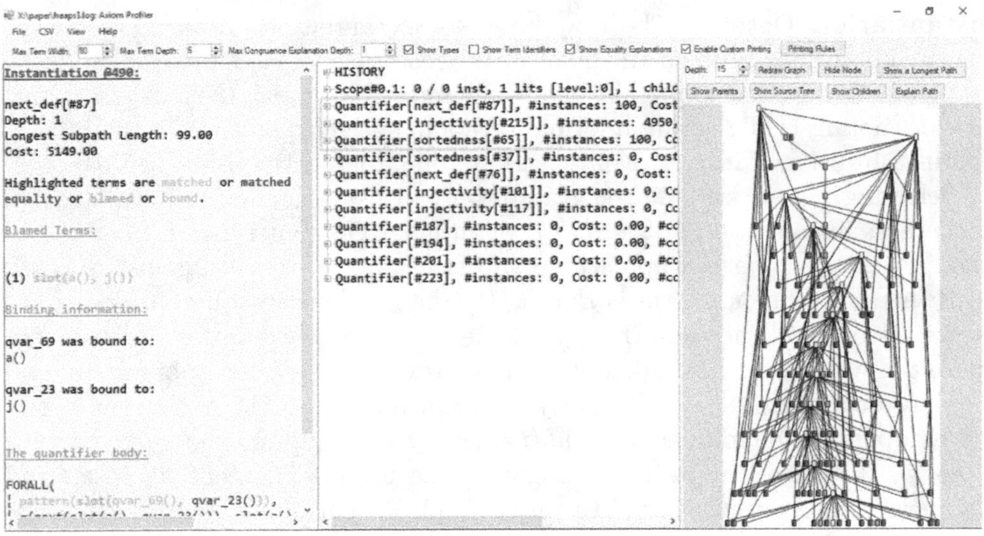

Fig. 2. A visualisation of the quantifier instantiations for the example in Fig. 1. (Colour figure online)

Instantiation Graph. The right-hand panel is one of the most important features of our tool. The *instantiation graph* visualises *causal relationships* between quantifier instantiations, which allows us to identify the high-branching and long-sequence scenarios described in step 4 of our debugging recipe. The nodes in the graph represent quantifier instantiations; a (directed) edge indicates that the source node provides either a term which was matched in order to trigger the successor node, or an equality used to trigger the match. Information about equalities is important for step 5c of our recipe, as we will discuss in Sect. 5.

Graph nodes are coloured, where each colour indicates a different quantifier; all instantiations of the same quantifier are coloured identically. The colours make it easy to spot prevalent quantifiers, and to visually identify patterns such as repeating sequences down a long path, which often indicate a matching loop.

Since instantiation graphs can get very large, we provide various filters, for instance, to control the maximum depth to which the graph is displayed, or to expand and collapse the children of a node. It is also possible to display the nodes with the highest number of children (to detect high branching, see step 4a) or the nodes starting the longest paths, as well as longest path starting from a node, which are features especially useful for detecting matching loops.

Our running example contains several instantiation problems. For instance, the instantiation graph in Fig. 2 shows a very large number of purple nodes (the quantifier labelled Q_{inj} in Fig. 1) and two sequences of yellow (the Q_{nxt} quantifier) and green (Q_{srt}) nodes, which indicate potential matching loops. Whereas the *number* of instantiations is also visible from the raw data, identifying such groupings and patterns is made possible by the instantiation graph.

Instantiation Details. The raw data and instantiation graph allow one to identify potentially-problematic quantifiers according to the first four steps of our debugging recipe. To support the analysis described in step 5, the left-hand panel provides details of all relevant information about specific quantifier instantiations. The instantiation of interest can be selected in either of the other two panels.

Selecting the top node in the graph from our example yields an explanation of the first instantiation of the (Q_{nxt}) quantifier. The panel lists *blamed terms*: that is, terms in the E-graph whose subterms were matched against the patterns; here, the blamed term is `slot(a,j)` (the numbers in square brackets are explained below). The subterm of a blamed term matched against the pattern (here, the whole term) is highlighted in gold, while the nested subterms bound to quantified variables (here, a and j) are shown in blue. The panel then shows the bindings per quantified variable (named by a unique number prefixed with "`qvar_`"), the quantifier itself (highlighting the pattern matched against), and any new resulting terms added to the E-graph. In particular, the bound terms and pattern matched against provide the information needed for step 5a of the debugging recipe.

In realistic examples, presenting the relevant terms readably can be a challenge, for which we provide a variety of features. Since the E-graph often contains only partial information about interpreted literals, it can be useful to annotate function applications and constants with a numeric *term identifier* (shown in square brackets); these identifiers are generated by Z3. For example, all integer-typed terms are simply represented by `Int()` here; the term identifiers allow us to identify identical terms, even though their precise meanings are unknown. Since identifiers can also make large terms harder to read, enabling them is optional.

For some problems, the relevant terms can get extremely large. To present terms in a meaningful form (see step 5b of our recipe), our tool provides facilities for defining custom printing rules. Typical use cases include simplifying names, and rendering those representing operators (such as a list append function) with infix syntax. In addition, our tool allows one to choose the depth to which terms are printed; we use ... to replace subterms below this depth.

5   Manual Analysis of Instantiation Problems

In this section, we demonstrate on the example from Fig. 1 how to use the features of the Axiom Profiler to manually analyse and debug quantifier instantiation problems. The *automatic* analyses provided by our tool will be discussed in Sect. 6.

Simple Matching Loops. Since all three quantifiers in our example lead to many instantiations, we start narrowing down the problem by looking for matching loops (step 4b in the recipe). Filtering for nodes starting the longest paths displays the sub-graph on the left of Fig. 3. One can see two parallel sequences of instantiations; an initial one of yellow (Q_{nxt}) instantiations, and a second of green (Q_{srt}) instantiations. Since the (Q_{nxt}) sequence is self-contained (there are

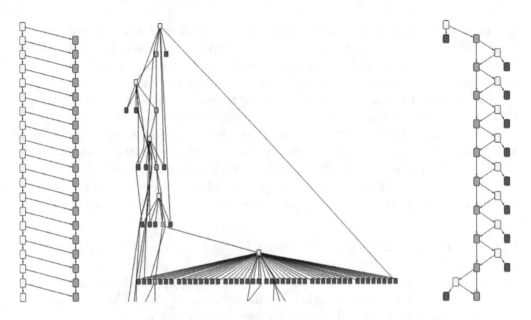

Fig. 3. Sub-graphs of the instantiation graph for the example in Fig. 1 showing the simple matching loop, high branching, and the matching loop with equality reasoning. Instantiations of Q_{nxt} are yellow, Q_{srt} is green, and Q_{inj} is purple. (Colour figure online)

no incoming edges from outside of these nodes), we investigate this one first. By selecting and inspecting the details of these instantiations (in the left-hand panel) in turn, we see that all after the first look very similar: each blames a term of the shape `slot(a, Int() + j)` (`Int()` abstracts all constants from the integer theory) and produces (among others) a new term of this same shape. The term identifiers show that the new term from each instantiation is the one blamed by the next, indicating a matching loop. In Sect. 6, we will show how the Axiom Profiler can perform this entire analysis automatically.

The detected matching loop for Q_{nxt} is the one we discussed in Sect. 2. It can be fixed by selecting a more restrictive pattern for the Q_{nxt} quantifier, namely `{next(slot(a,i))}`, only allowing instantiations when the `next` function is applied to an array slot. In particular, instantiating the quantifier does not produce a new term of this shape, which breaks the matching loop. Re-running Z3 on the fixed example reduces the number of quantifier instantiations to around 1400.

High Branching. Besides long paths, high branching may point to potentially problematic quantifiers (see step 4a of our debugging recipe). Once we have fixed the matching loop described above, we use the "Most Children" filter (available from "Redraw Graph") to identify the nodes with highest branching factor; subsequently using "Show Children" on one of these nodes results in the sub-graph in the middle of Fig. 3. This node has 42 child nodes, of which 41 are instantiations of the injectivity property (Q_{inj}). The pattern for this quantifier is `{slot(a,i),slot(a,k)}`, so each instantiation requires two applications of the `slot` function. Examining the instantiation details reveals that the 41 instantiations all share one of the two `slot` terms, while the other varies. The common term is produced by the parent node, and then combined with many previously-existing terms to trigger the instantiation 41 times.

The underlying problem is that the pattern yields a number of instantiations that is quadratic in the number of `slot` terms. This is a known "anti-pattern" for expressing injectivity properties; an alternative is to add an inverse function and axioms expressing this fact [5], which can then match linearly in the number of `slot` terms. For simple injectivity axioms such as that from our example, Z3 will even perform this rewriting for us; we disabled this option for the sake of illustration. Enabling this reduces the number of quantifier instantiations to 152.

Equality Explanations. The remaining instantiations in our example form a long path, which may indicate another matching loop. As shown on the right of Fig. 3, the path alternates the quantifiers Q_{nxt} and Q_{srt}. Unlike for the simple matching loop we uncovered earlier in this section, neither of the two quantifiers now produces a term that *directly* matches the pattern for Q_{srt}. Instead, subsequent instantiations are triggered by rewriting terms via equalities.

The Axiom Profiler explains the required rewriting steps to support step 5c of the recipe. In particular, the instantiation details shown include, besides the blamed terms, the equalities used and how they can yield a term that matches the necessary pattern. In our example, the very first instantiation blames a term `lookup(h, next(slot(a, j)))` and shows the following relevant equality:

```
(2)  next(slot(a, j))
     = (next_def[#56])
     slot(a, +(Int(), j))
```

where `(2)` is a number for this equality, and the (`next_def[#56]`) annotation after the equality symbol is the *justification* for the equality; in this case, it names a quantifier (the Q_{nxt} quantifier in Fig. 1). In general, equality justifications can be more complex; we contributed code for Z3 to log relevant information, letting us reconstruct transitive equality steps, theory-generated equalities, and congruence closure steps (for which a recursive equality explanation can also be generated).

By inspecting each node's blamed terms and relevant equality information, it is possible to indeed uncover a matching loop still present in this version of our example. In brief: instantiating the Q_{srt} quantifier produces a term that triggers an instantiation of the Q_{nxt} quantifier, which produces equality (2). This equality is then used to rewrite the same term, resulting in another match for the Q_{srt} quantifier, and so on. Matching up all relevant terms and assembling the details of this explanation manually remains somewhat laborious; in the next section, we show a more detailed explanation which our tool produces *automatically*.

6   Automated Explanation of Matching Loops

The previous section illustrated how the Axiom Profiler supports the manual analysis of quantifier instantiation problems. For the common and severe problem of matching loops, our tool is also able to produce such explanations *automatically*, reducing the necessary debugging effort significantly.

Consider the example from Fig. 1, after fixing the first of the two matching loops as explained in the previous section. Recall that our *manual analysis* revealed that the second matching loop consists of repeated instantiations of quantifier Q_{srt}, which are sustained via equalities obtained from the quantifier Q_{nxt}. Applying our *automated analysis* produces the following explanation: (1) It identifies a potential matching loop involving the quantifiers Q_{nxt} and Q_{srt}. (2) It synthesises a template term lookup(h, next(slot(a,T_1))) whose presence, for any term T_1, sets off the matching loop. (3) It explains step by step: (a) how such a term triggers the quantifier Q_{nxt} (recall that we fixed the pattern to {next(slot(ar,i))}) to produce the equality next(slot(a,T_1))=slot(a,T_1+Int()), (b) how this equality is used to rewrite the template term to lookup(h, slot(a,T_1+Int()), (c) that the resulting term causes an instantiation of quantifier Q_{srt} to produce the term lookup(h, next(slot(a,T_1+Int()))), and (d) how this term sets off the next iteration by using T_1+Int() for T_1. Our algorithm to produce such explanations consists of four main steps, which we explain in the remainder of this section.

Step 1: Selecting Paths. Our algorithm starts by selecting a path through the instantiation graph that represents a likely matching loop. The user can influence this choice by selecting a node that must be on the path and by selecting a sub-graph that must contain the path. The algorithm then chooses a path heuristically, favouring long paths and paths with many instantiations per quantifier (more precisely, per matched pattern). Since it is common that paths contain several instantiations before actually entering a matching loop, our algorithm prunes path prefixes if their quantifiers do not occur frequently in the rest of the path.

Step 2: Identifying Repeating Sequences. Matching loops cause repeated sequences of quantifier instantiations. We abstract the instantiations on a path to a *string* (instantiations of the same quantifier and pattern get the same character), and efficiently find the substring (subsequence of instantiations) repeating *most often* using suffix trees [23]; in our example, this subsequence is Q_{nxt}, Q_{srt}.

Step 3: Generalising Repetitions. Each repetition of the subsequence identified in the previous step potentially represents an iteration of a matching loop. To produce a generalised explanation for the entire loop, we first produce explanations of each individual repetition and then generalise those explanations.

The automatic explanation of the individual repetitions works as summarised in steps 5a and 5c of our debugging recipe, and uses the same functionality that we used for the manual analysis in the previous section. In our example, the analysis reveals that the first repetition of the sequence is triggered by the term `lookup(h,slot(a,i))`, which comes from the assertion in line 13. This term triggers an instantiation of the quantifier Q_{srt}, which in turn triggers the quantifier Q_{nxt} to produce the equality `next(slot(a,i))=next(slot(a,i+1))`. Rewriting the term `lookup(h,next(slot(a,i)))` from the quantifier Q_{srt} with this equality produces `lookup(h,slot(a,i+1))`. Performing this analysis on the second repetition shows that it is triggered by exactly this term and, after the analogous sequence of steps, produces `lookup(h,slot(a,i+2))`, and so on.

The explanations for the individual repetitions of the sequence will differ in the exact terms they blame and equalities they use. However, since each repetition triggers the same patterns of the same quantifiers, these terms and equalities have term structure in common. We extract this common structure by performing anti-unification [19], that is, by replacing each position in which subterms *disagree* with fresh symbolic variables. In our example, anti-unification of the blamed terms for the first instantiation of each repetition produces `lookup(h,slot(a,`T_1`))`, that is, the disagreeing terms `i`, `i+1`, etc. have been replaced by the fresh symbolic variable T_1. Similarly, the used equalities are anti-unified to `next(slot(a,`T_2`))=next(slot(a,`T_3`+Int()))`.

Introducing a fresh symbolic variable in *each* such position loses information for terms originally occurring multiple times. For instance, in our example, anti-unifying the blamed terms and the used equalities introduces three symbolic variables T_1, T_2, T_3 even though the disagreeing terms are equal in each repetition of the sequence. This equality is vital for the explanation of the matching loop.

In simple examples such as this one, we need only keep the first introduced symbolic variable T; in general there may be different choices which can mutually express each other via function applications (e.g. $T = f(T')$ and $T' = g(T)$, for which *either* symbolic variable would be sufficient). We handle the general problem of selecting which symbolic variables to keep by building a directed graph to represent this expressibility relation between symbolic variables. We have developed an algorithm to efficiently select *some* subset of the symbolic variables with no redundant elements based on this graph; we then rewrite all generalised terms and equalities using only these variables. In our example, the graph reflects $T_1 \rightleftarrows T_2 \rightleftarrows T_3$ and, thus, we are able to rewrite the generalised equality to use only T_1 resulting in `next(slot(a,`T_1`))=next(slot(a,`T_1`+Int()))`.

Step 4: Characterising Matching Loops. Once we have generalised templates of the blamed terms and equalities, we use these to express the terms used to begin the *next* iteration of the repeating pattern; if this is a term with *additional* structure, we classify the overall path explained as a matching loop. In our example, we see that where T_1 was used, T_1`+Int()` is used in the next iteration, from which we conclude that this is indeed a matching loop. We add the information about these terms used to start the *next* iteration of the loop to our finalised explanations (*cf.* (d) in the explanation starting this section).

7   Implementation and Evaluation

Our work is implemented as a stand-alone application. We also submitted (accepted) patches to Z3 to obtain the full logging information that our tool requires; we now record equalities used for matching patterns, and justifications for *how* these equalities were derived from the solver's E-graph. These logging mechanisms are enabled via the additional `trace=true proof=true` logging options. Other SMT solvers could produce the same information (information on terms, equalities and matches), and reuse our work.

Example	Tool	#quants	#instantiations	#loops	longest	= used
compiler	Why3	1,473	195,961	1	12	
kmp	Why3	35	1,376	1	18	
blocking_semantics5	Why3	86	210,291	2	10	
fibonacci	Why3	234	32,647	2	19	
induction	Why3	2	197	1	20	
sf	Why3	5	2,020	2	16	
sumrange	Why3	10	1,837	2	19	
vstte10_queens	Why3	16	194	1	18	
unionfind	Viper	98	285,311	1	100	✓
linked_list_qp_append	Viper	196	17,470	1	96	
testHistoryLemmasPVL	Viper	4	271	2	100	✓
testHistoryThreadsLemmasPVL	Viper	4	270	2	100	✓
tree_delete_min	Viper	19	6,709	1	96	✓
list_insert	Viper	24	287,559	1	94	✓
list_insert_heuristics	Viper	23	181,392	1	94	✓
tree_delete_min_heuristics	Viper	19	29,747	1	96	✓
tree_delete_min_no_assert	Viper	19	120,776	1	98	✓
ComputationsLoop	Dafny	16	518	1	33	
ComputationsLoop2	Dafny	20	519	1	33	
NoTypeArgs	Dafny	59	40,110	1	98	✓
Lucas-down	Dafny	86	3,412	1	99	
Lucas-up	Dafny	129	46,877	1	91	

Fig. 4. An overview of the matching loops found in examples flagged by the automated analysis. "#quants" indicated the no. of quantifiers present (we only count those instantiated at least once). "longest" indicates the length of the longest path; "= used" indicates whether equality explanations occur in the generalised path explanation for this matching loop. Examples exhibiting similar matching loops are grouped together.

In order to demonstrate that the Axiom Profiler can be used to identify and help explain matching loops in real world problems, we ran experiments on a total of 34,159 SMT files, corresponding to the full test suites of a selection of verification tools which use Z3 as a backend: F* [22] (6,281 files), Why3 [10] (26,258 files), Viper (887 files) [18], Nagini [9] (266 files) and Dafny [13] (467 files)). Using a command-line interface for our tool, we analysed each of these files in an attempt to find matching loops. We note that since these are expert-written, polished (and, presumably performant) test suite examples, one might expect most, if not all such issues to have been eliminated.

For each file, the tool analysed the 40 longest paths in the instantiation graph, searching for matching loops using the analysis of Sect. 6. In order to eliminate most false positives (since paths were found with no user introspection, and repeating patterns do not always indicate matching loops), we searched for paths with at least *10* repetitions of some quantifier instantiation sequence. We found 51 such files, and inspected each by hand for matching loops, using the techniques of Sects. 4 and 6 to identify whether matching loops are present (false positives also occurred: for example, in tools which model lookups in program heaps using axioms, there are often long chains of instantiations of the same axiom but for different versions of the heap). For all investigated examples, our tool analyses these paths in a second or two: this manual classification is very efficient.

Figure 4 summarises the matching loops we discovered. We found 28 previously-unknown matching loops: 13 from Why3, 10 from Viper and 5 from Dafny; we didn't find any matching loops in the F* or Nagini suites (which could be due to highly-tuned or restrictive triggers). The matching loops we detected were of many varieties. In Why3, 10 stemmed from modelling recursively-defined concepts (e.g. $\forall$x: Int even(x). even(x) $\implies$ even(x + 2)). We also found more complex matching loops in Why3's axiomatization of lists and arrays. For example, an array axiom $\forall$x, y. {mk_ref(x,y)}. sort(ref(x),mk_ref(x,y)) yields a term matching a second axiom, yielding contents(ref(T_1), mk_ref(ref(T_1), mk_ref(T_1, T_2))). The outer mk_ref term is new; we can instantiate the first axiom again. Why3 leaves the selection of most patterns to the SMT-solver, and uses a timeout (along with alternative solvers); this explains the potential for matching loops.

Viper provides two verifiers; we extracted and ran SMT queries for both. We found 4 causes of matching loops; some manifested in multiple files. These include direct matching loops and more complex cases: e.g. in the testHistoryLemmasPVL example, an associativity axiom allows repeatedly generating new term structure, which feeds a parallel matching loop concerning a recursive function definition.

For Dafny, we also found some simple and some complex cases. One axiom $\forall$a, b, c {app(a, app(b, c))}. app(a, app(b, c)) = app(app(a, b), c) expressing associativity of a concatenation operator[3], in combination with a case-split assumption made by Z3 that one term a' instantiated for a is equal to Nil, and the known property Nil=app(Nil,Nil), allows rewriting the right-hand-side term learned from each instantiation with a new app application on which the same axiom can be matched. A similar problem is described by Moskal [16].

In all cases (including those which, when inspected manually turned out to be false positives), following our debugging recipe and applying the Axiom Profiler's features allowed us to quickly isolate and explain the matching loops present. We have communicated our findings to the respective tool authors, who all confirmed that these matching loops were previously-unknown and that they plan to investigate them further (potentially using the Axiom Profiler itself).

---

[3] The actual function name is concat; we abbreviate for readability.

8   Related Work

Since its origin in the Simplify prover [7], E-matching has been adapted and improved in implementations for a variety of SMT solvers [1, 2, 4, 11, 17]. Since E-matching-based instantiation gives weak guarantees for *satisfiable* problems (typically returning *unknown* as an outcome), for problem domains where satisfiability (and a corresponding model) is the desired outcome, alternative instantiation techniques have been proposed [12, 20, 21]. For specific domains, these are often preferable, but for problems in which many external concepts need to be modelled with quantifiers, such as deductive program verification, E-matching remains the only general solution. While our work focuses on E-matching support, it would be interesting future work to investigate to what extent we could also provide useful information about other quantifier instantiation strategies.

As discussed in the Introduction, we build upon the *VCC Axiom Profiler* [16] tool, which defined first versions of the logging in Z3 (without equality information), the raw data display (retained in our middle panel) and a basic display of information per quantifier, without explanations of equalities used to justify matches. The contributions of this paper make it practical to quickly navigate and understand even complicated SMT runs, in ways impossible with the previous tool. Nonetheless, this prior tool was a very helpful basis for our implementation.

The serious challenges of pattern selection have warranted papers both on expert strategies [14, 16], and for formalising the logical meaning of quantifiers equipped with patterns [8]. Various SMT solvers select patterns for quantifiers automatically (if omitted by the user). To reduce the uncertainty introduced in this way, many program verification tools select their own patterns when encoding to SMT (e.g., VCC [3], Viper [18], Dafny [13]). Leino and Pit-Claudel [15] present a technique for selecting patterns in Dafny while avoiding direct matching loops; the matching loops we found in Dafny tests arose in spite of this functionality.

9   Conclusions

In this paper, we presented a comprehensive solution for the analysis of quantifier instantiations in SMT solvers. Our newly-developed Axiom Profiler enables a user to effectively explore and understand the quantifier instantiations performed by an SMT run, their connections and potentially-problematic patterns which arise (e.g. due to matching loops). Our instantiation graph, customisable visualisation of information and automatic explanations for matching loops make investigating even complex SMT queries practical in reasonable time. Furthermore, we were able to script these analyses to uncover matching loops in a variety of test suites for existing tools; it would be interesting to analyse further tools in this way.

As future work, we plan to investigate tighter integration with tools that build on SMT solvers, e.g. to represent terms at a higher level of abstraction. We also plan to investigate whether theory-reasoning steps in the SMT solver can be made less opaque to our tool, especially with respect to justifying equalities. Automating explanations for matching loops with repeating structures more complex than single paths would be a challenging extension of our techniques.

Acknowledgements. We thank Frederik Rothenberger for his substantial work on visualisation features. We are grateful to Marco Eilers, Jean-Christophe Filliâtre, Rustan Leino, Nikhil Swamy for providing their test suites and advice on their verification tools. We thank Nikolaj Bjørner for his assistance with Z3, and Michał Moskal for generous advice and feedback on earlier versions of the tool. Finally, we are very grateful to Marco Eilers, Malte Schwerhoff and Arshavir Ter-Gabrielyan, for providing extensive feedback on our tool and paper drafts.

References

1. Bansal, K., Reynolds, A., King, T., Barrett, C., Wies, T.: Deciding local theory extensions via E-matching. In: Kroening, D., Păsăreanu, C.S. (eds.) CAV 2015, Part II. LNCS, vol. 9207, pp. 87–105. Springer, Cham (2015). https://doi.org/10.1007/978-3-319-21668-3_6

2. Barrett, C., et al.: CVC4. In: Gopalakrishnan, G., Qadeer, S. (eds.) CAV 2011. LNCS, vol. 6806, pp. 171–177. Springer, Heidelberg (2011). https://doi.org/10.1007/978-3-642-22110-1_14

3. Cohen, E., et al.: VCC: a practical system for verifying concurrent C. In: Berghofer, S., Nipkow, T., Urban, C., Wenzel, M. (eds.) TPHOLs 2009. LNCS, vol. 5674, pp. 23–42. Springer, Heidelberg (2009). https://doi.org/10.1007/978-3-642-03359-9_2

4. de Moura, L., Bjørner, N.: Efficient E-matching for SMT solvers. In: Pfenning, F. (ed.) CADE 2007. LNCS (LNAI), vol. 4603, pp. 183–198. Springer, Heidelberg (2007). https://doi.org/10.1007/978-3-540-73595-3_13

5. de Moura, L., Bjørner, N.: Z3 - a tutorial. Technical report, Microsoft Research (2010)

6. de Moura, L., Bjørner, N.: Z3: an efficient SMT solver. In: Ramakrishnan, C.R., Rehof, J. (eds.) TACAS 2008. LNCS, vol. 4963, pp. 337–340. Springer, Heidelberg (2008). https://doi.org/10.1007/978-3-540-78800-3_24

7. Detlefs, D., Nelson, G., Saxe, J.B.: Simplify: a theorem prover for program checking. J. ACM **52**(3), 365–473 (2005)

8. Dross, C., Conchon, S., Kanig, J., Paskevich, A.: Reasoning with triggers. In: Fontaine, P., Goel, A. (eds.) Satisfiability Modulo Theories (SMT). EPiC Series in Computing, vol. 20, pp. 22–31. EasyChair (2012)

9. Eilers, M., Müller, P.: Nagini: a static verifier for Python. In: Chockler, H., Weissenbacher, G. (eds.) CAV 2018. LNCS, vol. 10981, pp. 596–603. Springer, Cham (2018). https://doi.org/10.1007/978-3-319-96145-3_33

10. Filliâtre, J.-C., Paskevich, A.: Why3 — where programs meet provers. In: Felleisen, M., Gardner, P. (eds.) ESOP 2013. LNCS, vol. 7792, pp. 125–128. Springer, Heidelberg (2013). https://doi.org/10.1007/978-3-642-37036-6_8

11. Ge, Y., Barrett, C., Tinelli, C.: Solving quantified verification conditions using satisfiability modulo theories. In: Pfenning, F. (ed.) CADE 2007. LNCS (LNAI), vol. 4603, pp. 167–182. Springer, Heidelberg (2007). https://doi.org/10.1007/978-3-540-73595-3_12

12. Ge, Y., de Moura, L.: Complete instantiation for quantified formulas in satisfiabiliby modulo theories. In: Bouajjani, A., Maler, O. (eds.) CAV 2009. LNCS, vol. 5643, pp. 306–320. Springer, Heidelberg (2009). https://doi.org/10.1007/978-3-642-02658-4_25
13. Leino, K.R.M.: Dafny: an automatic program verifier for functional correctness. In: Clarke, E.M., Voronkov, A. (eds.) LPAR 2010. LNCS (LNAI), vol. 6355, pp. 348–370. Springer, Heidelberg (2010). https://doi.org/10.1007/978-3-642-17511-4_20
14. Leino, K.R.M., Monahan, R.: Reasoning about comprehensions with first-order SMT solvers. In: Proceedings of the 2009 ACM Symposium on Applied Computing, SAC 2009, pp. 615–622. ACM, New York (2009)
15. Leino, K.R.M., Pit-Claudel, C.: Trigger selection strategies to stabilize program verifiers. In: Chaudhuri, S., Farzan, A. (eds.) CAV 2016, Part I. LNCS, vol. 9779, pp. 361–381. Springer, Cham (2016). https://doi.org/10.1007/978-3-319-41528-4_20
16. Moskal, M.: Programming with triggers. In: SMT. ACM International Conference Proceeding Series, vol. 375, pp. 20–29. ACM (2009)
17. Moskal, M., Lopuszański, J., Kiniry, J.R.: E-matching for fun and profit. Electron. Notes Theor. Comput. Sci. **198**(2), 19–35 (2008)
18. Müller, P., Schwerhoff, M., Summers, A.J.: Viper: a verification infrastructure for permission-based reasoning. In: Jobstmann, B., Leino, K.R.M. (eds.) VMCAI 2016. LNCS, vol. 9583, pp. 41–62. Springer, Heidelberg (2016). https://doi.org/10.1007/978-3-662-49122-5_2
19. Plotkin, G.D.: A note on inductive generalization. In: Meltzer, B., Michie, D. (eds.) Machine Intelligence, pp. 153–163. Edinburgh University Press, Edinburgh (1970)
20. Reynolds, A., Tinelli, C., de Moura, L.: Finding conflicting instances of quantified formulas in SMT. In: Proceedings of the 14th Conference on Formal Methods in Computer-Aided Design, FMCAD 2014, pp. 31:195–31:202. FMCAD Inc., Austin (2014)
21. Reynolds, A., Tinelli, C., Goel, A., Krstić, S., Deters, M., Barrett, C.: Quantifier instantiation techniques for finite model finding in SMT. In: Bonacina, M.P. (ed.) CADE 2013. LNCS (LNAI), vol. 7898, pp. 377–391. Springer, Heidelberg (2013). https://doi.org/10.1007/978-3-642-38574-2_26
22. Swamy, N., Chen, J., Fournet, C., Strub, P.-Y., Bhargavan, K., Yang, J.: Secure distributed programming with value-dependent types. In: Proceedings of the 16th ACM SIGPLAN International Conference on Functional Programming, ICFP 2011, pp. 266–278. ACM, New York (2011)
23. Weiner, P.: Linear pattern matching algorithms. In: Switching and Automata Theory (SWAT), pp. 1–11. IEEE (1973)

9

Incremental Analysis of Evolving Alloy Models

Wenxi Wang[1][✉], Kaiyuan Wang[2][✉], Milos Gligoric[1][✉],
and Sarfraz Khurshid[1][✉]

[1] The University of Texas at Austin, Austin, USA
{wenxiw,gligoric,khurshid}@utexas.edu
[2] Google Inc., Sunnyvale, USA
kaiyuanw@google.com

Abstract. Alloy is a well-known tool-set for building and analyzing software designs and models. Alloy's key strengths are its intuitive notation based on relational logic, and its powerful analysis engine backed by propositional satisfiability (SAT) solvers to help users find subtle design flaws. However, scaling the analysis to the designs of real-world systems remains an important technical challenge. This paper introduces a new approach, iAlloy, for more efficient analysis of Alloy models. Our key insight is that users often make small and frequent changes and repeatedly run the analyzer when developing Alloy models, and the development cost can be reduced with the incremental analysis over these changes. iAlloy is based on two techniques – a static technique based on a lightweight *impact* analysis and a dynamic technique based on solution *re-use* – which in many cases helps avoid potential costly SAT solving. Experimental results show that iAlloy significantly outperforms Alloy analyzer in the analysis of evolving Alloy models with more than 50% reduction in SAT solver calls on average, and up to 7x speedup.

1 Introduction

Building software models and analyzing them play an important role in the development of more reliable systems. However, as the complexity of the modeled systems increases, both the cost of creating the models and the complexity of analyzing these models become high [24].

Our focus in this paper is to reduce the cost of analyzing models written in Alloy [5] – a relational, first-order logic with transitive closure. The Alloy analyzer provides automatic analysis of Alloy models. To analyze the model, the user writes Alloy *paragraphs* (e.g., signatures, predicates, functions, facts and assertions), and the analyzer executes the *commands* that define constraint solving problems. The analyzer translates the commands and related Alloy paragraphs into propositional satisfiability (SAT) formulas and then solves them using off-the-shelf SAT solvers. We focus on successive runs of the analyzer as the model undergoes development and modifications. The key insight is that during model development and validation phases, the user typically makes many changes that are relatively small, which enables the incremental analysis to reduce the subsequent analysis cost [1].

We introduce a novel technique called iAlloy that incrementally computes the analysis results. iAlloy introduces a two-fold optimization for Alloy analyzer. Firstly, iAlloy comes with a *static* technique that computes the *impact* of a change on commands based on a lightweight dependency analysis, and *selects* for execution a subset of commands that may be impacted. We call this technique *regression command selection* (RCS), since it shares the spirit of regression test selection for imperative code [4] and adapts it to declarative models in Alloy. Secondly, iAlloy comes with a *dynamic* technique that uses memoization to enable *solution reuse* (SR) by efficiently checking if an existing solution already works for a command that must be executed. SR uses a partial-order based on sets of parameters in predicate paragraphs to enable effective re-use of solutions across different commands.

To evaluate iAlloy we conduct experiments using two sets of Alloy models that have multiple versions. One set, termed *mutant version set*, uses simulated evolving Alloy models where different versions are created using the MuAlloy [21, 27] tool for generating *mutants* with small syntactic modifications of the given base Alloy models. This set includes 24 base Alloy models and 5 mutant versions for each base model. The other set, termed *real version set*, uses base Alloy models that had real faults and were repaired using the ARepair [25, 26] tool for fixing faulty Alloy models. For each faulty base model, its evolution is the corresponding fixed model. This set includes 36 base Alloy models and 2 versions for each model.

The experimental results show that iAlloy is effective at reducing the overall analysis cost for both sets of subject models. Overall, iAlloy provides more than 50% command execution reduction on average, and up to 7x speed up. In addition, SR performs surprisingly well in the real version set with 58.3% reduction of the selected commands, which indicates that our approach is promising for incrementally analyzing real-world evolving Alloy models.

This paper makes the following contributions:

- **Approach.** We introduce a novel approach, iAlloy, based on static analysis (regression command selection) and dynamic analysis (solution re-use) for incrementally analyzing evolving Alloy models, and embody the approach as a prototype tool on top of the Alloy analyzer.
- **Evaluation.** We conduct an extensive experimental evaluation of our approach using two sets of subject Alloy models, one based on syntactic mutation changes and the other based on fault fixing changes. The results show that iAlloy performs well on both sets.
- **Dataset.** We publicly release our subject Alloy models and their versions at the following URL: https://github.com/wenxiwang/iAlloy-dataset. Given the lack of common availability of Alloy models with evolution history, we believe that our dataset will be particularly useful for other researchers who want to evaluate their incremental analysis techniques for Alloy.

While our focus in this paper is the Alloy modeling language and tool-set, we believe our technique can generalize to optimize analysis for models in other declarative languages, e.g., Z [17] and OCL [2].

2   Background

In this section, we first introduce Alloy [5] based on an example which we use through the paper. Then, we describe MuAlloy [21, 27] – a mutation testing framework for Alloy, which we apply to create different versions of an Alloy model to simulate model evolutions. Finally, we briefly describe regression test selection (RTS) for imperative code. Although our regression command selection (RCS) applies to declarative code, the two methods share similar ideas.

2.1   Alloy

Alloy [5] is a declarative language for lightweight modeling and software analysis. The language is based on first-order logic with transitive closure. Alloy comes with an analyzer which is able to perform a bounded exhaustive analysis. The input of the Alloy analyzer is an Alloy model that describes the system properties. The analyzer translates the model into conjunctive normal form (CNF) and invokes an off-the-shelf SAT solver to search for solutions, i.e., boolean instances. The boolean instances are then mapped back to Alloy level instances and displayed to the end user.

Figure 1 shows the Dijkstra Alloy model which illustrates how mutexes are grabbed and released by processes, and how Dijkstra's mutex ordering constraint can prevent deadlocks. This model comes with the standard Alloy distribution (version 4.2). An Alloy model consists of a set of *relations* (e.g., signatures, fields and variables) and constraints (e.g., predicates, facts and assertions) which we call *paragraphs*. A signature (`sig`) defines a set of atoms, and is the main data type specified in Alloy. The running example defines 3 signatures (lines 3–6), namely `Process`, `Mutex` and `State`.

Facts (`fact`) are formulas that take no arguments and define constraints that must be satisfied by every instance that exists. The formulas can be further structured using predicates (`pred`) and functions (`fun`) which are parameterized formulas that can be invoked. Users can use Alloy's built-in `run` command to invoke a predicate and the Alloy analyzer either returns an instance if the predicate is satisfiable or reports that the predicate is unsatisfiable. The `IsStalled` predicate (lines 12–14) is invoked by the `GrabMutex` predicate (line 16) and the `run` command (line 53). The parameters of the `IsStalled` predicate are `s` and `p` with signature types `State` and `Process`, respectively. An assertion (`assert`) is also a boolean formula that can be invoked by the built-in `check` command to check if any counter example can refute the asserted formula. Assertions does not take any parameter. The `DijkstraPreventsDeadlocks` assertion (lines 45–47) is invoked by the `check` command (line 60) with a scope of up to 6 atoms for each signature.

2.2   MuAlloy

MuAlloy [21, 27] automatically generates mutants and filters out mutants that are semantically equivalent to the original base model. Table 1 shows the mutation operators supported in MuAlloy. *MOR* mutates signature multiplicity,

```
1.  open util/ordering [State] as so
2.  open util/ordering [Mutex] as mo
3.  sig Process {}
4.  sig Mutex {}
5.  sig State { holds, waits: Process -> Mutex }
6.  pred Initial [s: State] {
7.    no (s.holds + s.waits)
8.  }
9.  pred IsFree [s: State, m: Mutex] {
10.   no m.~(s.holds) // no process holds this mutex
11. }
12. pred IsStalled [s: State, p: Process] {
13.   some p.(s.waits)
14. }
15. pred GrabMutex [s: State, p: Process, m: Mutex, s': State] {
16.   !s.IsStalled[p] // a process can only act if it is not waiting for a mutex
17.   m !in p.(s.holds) // can only grab a mutex that is not yet hold
18.   all m': p.(s.holds) | mo/lt[m',m] // mutexes must be grabbed in order
19.   s.IsFree[m] => {
20.     p.(s'.holds) = p.(s.holds) + m // if the mutex is free, the process now holds it
21.     no p.(s'.waits) // the process is not stalled any more
22.   } else {
23.     p.(s'.holds) = p.(s.holds) // if the mutex is not free, the process still hold the same mutexes.
24.     p.(s'.waits) = m // and wait on the new mutex.
25.   }
26.   all otherProc: Process - p | { // other processes maintain the same state
27.     otherProc.(s'.holds) = otherProc.(s.holds)
28.     otherProc.(s'.waits) = otherProc.(s.waits)
29.   }
30. }
31. pred ReleaseMutex [s: State, p: Process, m: Mutex, s': State] {
32.   !s.IsStalled[p]
33.   ...
34. }
35. pred GrabOrRelease  {
36.   Initial[so/first] &&
37.   (all pre: State - so/last | let post =  so/next[pre] |   // for every pre and post state
38.   (post.holds = pre.holds && post.waits = pre.waits) ||  // either nothing happens
39.   (some p: Process, m: Mutex | pre.GrabMutex [p, m, post]) ||  // or a process grabs a mutex
40.   (some p: Process, m: Mutex | pre.ReleaseMutex [p, m, post]))  // or releases a mutex
41. }
42. pred Deadlock  {
43.   ...
44. }
45. assert DijkstraPreventsDeadlocks {
46.   GrabOrRelease => ! Deadlock
47. }
48. pred ShowDijkstra  {
49.  GrabOrRelease && Deadlock
50.   some waits
51. }
52. run Initial for 10
53. run IsStalled for 10
54. run IsFree for 10
55. run GrabMutex for 30
56. run ReleaseMutex for 35
57. run GrabOrRelease for 16
58. run Deadlock for 50 expect 1
59. run ShowDijkstra for 5 expect 1
60. check DijkstraPreventsDeadlocks for 6 expect 0
```

Fig. 1. Dijkstra Alloy model from standard Alloy distribution (version 4.2); the line written in red was absent from the faulty version

e.g., `lone sig` to `one sig`. *QOR* mutates quantifiers, e.g., `all` to `some`. *UOR*, *BOR* and *LOR* define operator replacement for unary, binary and formula list operators, respectively. For example, *UOR* mutates `a.*b` to `a.^b`; *BOR* mutates `a=>b` to `a<=>b`; and *LOR* mutates `a&&b` to `a||b`. *UOI* inserts an unary operator before expressions, e.g., `a.b` to `a.~b`. *UOD* deletes an unary operator, e.g., `a.*~b` to `a.*b`.

Table 1. Mutation Operators Supported in MuAlloy

Mutation Operator	Description
MOR	Multiplicity Operator Replacement
QOR	Quantifier Operator Replacement
UOR	Unary Operator Replacement
BOR	Binary Operator Replacement
LOR	Formula List Operator Replacement
UOI	Unary Operator Insertion
UOD	Unary Operator Deletion
LOD	Logical Operand Deletion
PBD	Paragraph Body Deletion
BOE	Binary Operand Exchange
IEOE	Imply-Else Operand Exchange

LOD deletes an operand of a logical operator, e.g., a| |b to b. *PBD* deletes the body of an Alloy paragraph. *BOE* exchanges operands for a binary operator, e.g., a=>b to b=>a. *IEOE* exchanges the operands of `imply-else` operation, e.g., a => b else c to a => c else b.

2.3   Regression Test Selection for Imperative Code

Regression test selection (RTS) techniques select a subset of test cases from an initial test suite. The subset of tests checks if the affected sources of a project continue to work correctly. RTS is *safe* if it guarantees that the subset of selected tests includes all tests whose behavior may be affected by the changes [4,32]. RTS is *precise* if tests that are not affected are also not selected. Typical RTS techniques has three phases: the *analysis phase* selects tests to run, the *execution phase* runs the selected tests, and the *collection phase* collects information from the current version for future analysis. RTS techniques can perform at different granularities. For example, FaultTracer [35] analyzes dependencies at the method level while Ekstazi [3] does it at the file level, and both tools target projects written in Java.

During the analysis phase, RTS tools commonly compute a checksum, i.e., a unique identifier, of each code entity (e.g., method or file) on which a test depends. If the checksum changes, we view its source code as changed, in which case the test is selected and executed; otherwise it is not selected. The execution phase is tightly integrated with the analysis phase and simply executes selected tests. During the collection phase, RTS either dynamically monitors the test execution [3] or statically analyzes the test [7] to collect accessed/used entities, which are saved for the analysis phase in the next run.

3   Motivating Example

This section describes how iAlloy works using two versions of the Dijkstra Alloy model. Line 18 (highlighted in red) in Fig. 1 was absent in a faulty version of the model which we denote as Version 1. The model in Fig. 1 is the correct version which we denote as Version 2.

First, we apply iAlloy to Version 1. iAlloy invokes commands `Initial` (line 52), `IsStalled` (line 53), `IsFree` (line 54) and `GrabMutex` (line 55) with the SAT solver. Before invoking command `ReleaseMutex` (line 56), iAlloy finds that the solution obtained from invoking `GrabMutex` can be reused as the solution of `ReleaseMutex`. Therefore, command `ReleaseMutex` is solved without invoking SAT. iAlloy continues to invoke the rest of the commands and finds that command `Deadlock` (line 58) can reuse the solution of `IsStalled`, and command `DijkstraPreventsDeadlocks` can reuse the solution of `ShowDijkstra`. Next, we apply iAlloy again to Version 2. iAlloy performs dependency analysis between Version 1 and Version 2, and only selects the commands that are affected by the change (Line 18 in Fig. 1), namely commands `GrabMutex`, `GrabOrRelease`, `ShowDijkstra` and `DijkstraPreventsDeadlocks`. iAlloy tries to reuse the solutions of previous runs when invoking the four selected commands and `GrabMutex` reuses the solution of command `GrabMutex` in Version 1.

Traditionally, Alloy analyzer needs to execute 18 commands with expensive SAT solving, which takes total of 103.01 seconds. In comparison, iAlloy only invokes 9 commands where 5 commands are saved by regression command selection and 4 commands are saved by solution reuse. In total, iAlloy takes 84.14 seconds. Overall, iAlloy achieves 1.22x speed-up with 18.87 seconds time saving. Section 5 evaluates more subjects and shows that iAlloy achieves 1.59x speed-up on average and reduces unnecessary command invocations by more than 50%.

4   Techniques

In an evolving Alloy model scenario, we propose a two-step incremental analysis to reduce the time overhead of command execution. The first step is regression command selection (RCS) based on static dependency analysis (Sect. 4.1). The second step is solution reuse (SR) using fast instance evaluation (Sect. 4.2). Note that RCS handles paragraph-level dependency analysis, while SR covers more sophisticated expression-level dependency analysis.

Algorithm 1 shows the general algorithm of our incremental analysis. For each version (m_v) in a sequence of model evolutions $(ModelVersionSeq)$, iAlloy first applies RCS $(RCmdSelection)$ to select the commands $(SelectCmdList)$ that are affected since the last version. Then, for each command in $SelectCmdList$, iAlloy further checks whether the solutions of previous commands can be reused in the new commands $(CheckReuse)$. Note that the solutions of commands in the same version can also be reused. However, if the signatures change in the current version, then SR is not applicable and all commands are executed. If none of the old solutions can be reused for the current command c, then iAlloy invokes the SAT solver $(Execute)$ to find a new solution which may be used for the next run.

Algorithm 1. General Algorithm for Incremental Alloy Model Solving

---

Input: model version sequence $ModelVersionSeq$
Output: solution for each command

1: **for** $m_v \in ModelVersionSeq$ **do**
2:　　$SelectCmdList$ = RCmdSelection(m_v);
3:　　**for** $c \in SelectCmdList$ **do**
4:　　　　**if** Changed($c.Dependency.SigList$) **then**
5:　　　　　　Execute(c, $SolutionSet$);
6:　　　　**else if** !CheckReuse(c, $SolutionSet$) **then**
7:　　　　　　Execute(c, $SolutionSet$);
8:　　　　**end if**
9:　　**end for**
10: **end for**

Algorithm 2. Algorithm for Regression Command Selection

Input: one model version m_v
Output: selected command list

1: **procedure** RCMDSELECTION(Model m_v)
2:　　List<Cmd> $SelectCmdList$;
3:　　Map<Cmd, Nodes> $Cmd2DpdParagraphs$ = DpdAnalysis($m_v.AllCmd$);
4:　　**for** $c \in m_v.AllCmd$ **do**
5:　　　$DpdParagraphs$ = $Cmd2DpdParagraphs$.get(c);
6:　　　**if** Exist($c.Dependency$) **then**　　　　　　　　　　▷ old dependency
7:　　　　$newDependency$ = CheckSum($DpdParagraphs$);
8:　　　　**if** Changed($c.Dependency$, $newDependency$) **then**
9:　　　　　Update(c, $newDependency$);
10:　　　　　$SelectCmdList$.add(c);　▷ update dependency and select commands
11:　　　　**end if**
12:　　　**else**
13:　　　　$dependency$ = CheckSum($DpdParagraphs$)
14:　　　　Update(c, $dependency$);
15:　　　　$SelectCmdList$.add(c);　　　▷ update dependency and select commands
16:　　　**end if**
17:　　**end for**
18:　　**return** $SelectCmdList$;
19: **end procedure**

4.1　Regression Command Selection (RCS)

Algorithm 2 presents the algorithm for RCS. iAlloy first gets the dependent paragraphs of each command ($Cmd2DpdParagraphs$) based on the dependency analysis ($DpdAnalysis$). For each command c in model version m_v, iAlloy generates a unique identifier, as described in Sect. 2.3, for each dependent paragraph ($CheckSum$). If the checksum of any dependent paragraph changes, iAlloy selects the corresponding command as the command execution candidate ($SelectCmdList$) and updates the dependency with new checksum.

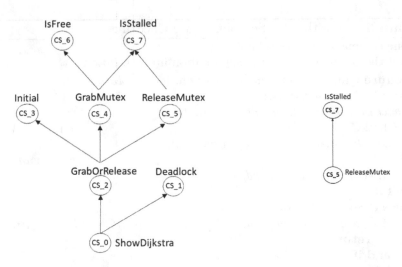

Fig. 2. Dependency graph for ShowDijkstra (left) and ReleaseMutex (right) command in the Dijkstra model

The dependency information of each command is the key for RCS. The dependency analysis for Alloy models can be either at the paragraph level or at the expression level. For safety reasons as we mentioned in Sect. 2.3, we do dependency analysis on the paragraph level in RCS. And we address further fine-grained expression level analysis in SR to achieve a better precision. To filter out the changes in comments and spaces, we traverse the AST of each paragraph and output the canonicalized string of the paragraph. The canonicalized string is hashed into a checksum which represents the unique version of the paragraph.

We take the Dijkstra Alloy model in Fig. 1 as an example. The dependency graph of command ShowDijkstra is shown in Fig. 2 (left), including transitively dependent Alloy paragraphs and their corresponding checksums CS_i. Since the checksum CS_4 of predicate GrabMutex is changed (line 18 in Fig. 1) and GrabMutex is in the dependency graph of command ShowDijkstra, command ShowDijkstra is selected. In comparison, the dependency graph of command ReleaseMutex is shown in Fig. 2 (right). Since the checksums of both IsStalled and ReleaseMutex do not change, command ReleaseMutex is not selected.

4.2 Solution Reuse (SR)

Algorithm 3 illustrates how iAlloy checks if a solution can be reused by the current command. The input to Algorithm 3 is each selected command (c) from RCS and a solution set containing all the previous solutions (*SolutionSet*). If the solution s from *SolutionSet* includes valuations of parameters of the Alloy paragraph (represented as *CheckList* which includes implicit Alloy facts) invoked by c (Sect. 4.2.1), and *CheckList* is satisfiable under s (Sect. 4.2.2), then s can be reused as the Alloy instance if c is invoked and c need not be invoked with expensive SAT solving (return true). Otherwise, SAT solving is involved to generate a

---

Algorithm 3. Algorithm for Solution Reuse Checking

Input: one command and the solution set
Output: if the command can reuse any solution in the solution set
 1: **procedure** CHECKREUSE(Cmd c, Set<Solution> $SolutionSet$)
 2:     List<Nodes> $CheckList$;
 3:     $CheckList$.add($c.Dependency.FactList$);
 4:     **if** CheckCmd(c) **then**   ▷ c is *check* command
 5:         $CheckList$.add($c.Dependency.Assert$);
 6:     **else**   ▷ c is *run* command
 7:         $CheckList$.add($c.Dependency.Pred$);
 8:     **end if**
 9:     **for** $s \in SolutionSet$ **do**
10:         **if** $c.param \subseteq s.cmd.param$ && $s.sol$.evaluator($CheckList$) = true **then**
11:             **return** true;
12:         **end if**
13:     **end for**
14:     **return** false;
15: **end procedure**

---

new solution (if there is any) which is stored for subsequent runs (Algorithm 4, Sect. 4.2.3).

Note that SR not only filters out the semantically equivalent regression changes, but also covers the sophisticated expression-level dependency analysis. For example, suppose the only change in an Alloy model is a boolean expression changed from A to A || B where || stands for disjunction and B is another boolean expression, the old solution of the corresponding command is still valid and can be reused. Besides, SR allows solutions from other commands to be reused for the current command, which further reduces SAT solving overhead.

4.2.1 Solution Reuse Condition

As described in Sect. 2, each command invokes either a predicate or an assert. Each predicate has multiple parameter types which we denote as *parameter set* for simplicity in the rest of the paper. The parameter set of any assertion is an empty set ($\varnothing$). As shown in the following equation, we define the parameter set of a command c (c.param) as the parameter set of the directly invoked predicate (ParamSet(c.pred)) or assertion ($\varnothing$).

$$c.param = \begin{cases} ParamSet(c.pred), & c \text{ is run command} \\ \varnothing, & c \text{ is check command} \end{cases}$$

A command that invokes an Alloy paragraph with parameters implicitly checks if there exists a set of valuations of the corresponding parameters that satisfies the paragraph. We observe that command c_2 can reuse the solution s_1 obtained by invoking c_1 if the parameter set of c_2 is a subset of that of c_1, namely $c_2.param \subseteq c_1.param$. The solution reuse complies to a partial order based on

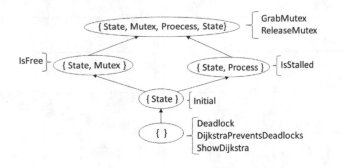

Fig. 3. Parameter relations of commands in the Dijkstra model

---

Algorithm 4. Algorithm for Command Execution

Input: one command and the solution set
Output: save the solution if it is SAT or print out UNSAT

1: **procedure** CMDEXECUTE(Cmd c, Set<Solution> $SolutionSet$)
2:     A4Solution sol = Alloy.solve(c);
3:     **if** sol.IsSat() **then**   ▷ if the solution is SAT;
4:         Solution s;
5:         $s.sol = sol$;   ▷ store the instance and corresponding command;
6:         $s.cmd = c$;
7:         $SolutionSet$.add(s);
8:     **else**
9:         print UNSAT
10:    **end if**
11: **end procedure**

---

the subset relation of command parameters. On the other hand, solution s_1 cannot be reused by c_2 if $c_2.param \subsetneq c_1.param$, in which case we do not know all the valuations of c_2's parameters.

Figure 3 shows how solution reuse is conducted based on the subset relations of command parameter set in the Dijkstra model. For instance, since the parameter set {} ($\varnothing$) is the subset of all parameter sets above it, the corresponding commands Deadlock, DijkstraPreventsDeadlocks and ShowDijkstra with parameter set {} can reuse all solutions of commands whose parameter sets are the super set of {}, namely Initial, IsFree, IsStalled, GrabMutex and ReleaseMutex. Since any parameter set is a subset of itself, a solution $s1$ of command c_1 can be reused by the command c_2 which has the same parameter set as c_1.

4.2.2 Solution Reuse Evaluation

Once a solution s can be reused for command c, we need to further check if s is actually the solution of c that satisfies the corresponding constraints. As described in Sect. 2, the constraints of a command come from all facts and the transitively invoked predicate/assertion. To reuse s in the old version, s must be

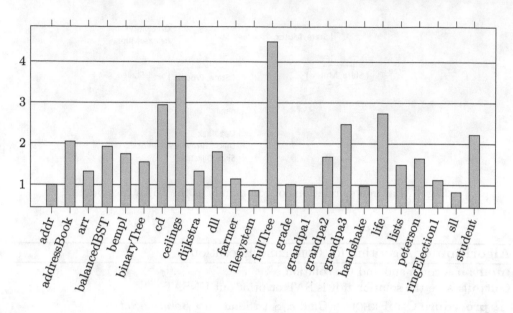

Fig. 4. Speedup results on Mutant Version Set

satisfiable for c in the new version. If c is unsatisfiable under the valuations of s, it does not imply that c is unsatisfiable in the solution space and thus c must be invoked with SAT solving. The satisfiability of command c is determined by the Alloy built-in evaluator under the valuation of s.

4.2.3 Command Execution

If none of the solutions can be reused by command c, iAlloy executes the command as described in Algorithm 4. If a solution sol is found (`Sol.IsSat()`), the solution sol together with the command c is saved for subsequent runs. To avoid saving too many solutions as the model evolves (which may slow down the SR and reduce the overall gain), we only keep the most recent solution for each command. In future work, we plan to evaluate how long a solution should be kept.

5   Experimental Evaluation

In this paper, we answer the following research questions to evaluate iAlloy:

- RQ1: How does iAlloy perform compared to traditional Alloy Analyzer (which we treat as the baseline)?
- RQ2: How much reduction of the commands executed does Regression Command Selection and Solution Reuse contribute in the two subject sets?
- RQ3: What is the time overhead of Regression Command Selection, Solution Reuse and command execution in iAlloy, respectively?

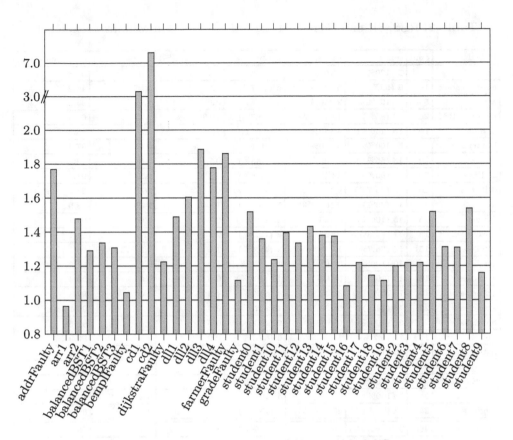

Fig. 5. Speedup results on Real Version Model Set

5.1 Experimental Setup

Subjects: There are two subject sets in the experiment. The first set of subjects is the simulated evolving Alloy model version sets, which we call Mutant Version Set. In this set, we take 24 Alloy models from the standard Alloy distribution (version 4.2) and use them as the first version. For each model in version 1, we use MuAlloy [27] to generate several mutants and randomly select one as version 2. This process continues until we get the fifth version. Thus, each subject in the Mutant Version Set includes five versions. The second subject set is called Real Version Set. Each subject in this set consists of two model versions: the real faulty model (version 1) from the ARepair [26] distribution and the correct model after the fix (version 2). There are 36 subjects in this set.

Baseline: The baseline in this experiment is the traditional Alloy Analyzer, which executes each command for each version.

Platform: We conduct all our experiments on Ubuntu Linux 16.04, an Intel Core-i7 6700 CPU (3.40 GHz) and 16 GB RAM. The version of Alloy we did experiments on is version 4.2.

Table 2. RCS, SR and Command Execution Results in Mutant Version Set

Model	cmd	select	reuse	execute	T_select (%)	T_reuse (%)	T_execute (%)
addr	5	5 (100%)	0 (0%)	5 (100%)	4.2	0.0	95.8
addressBook	10	9 (90%)	3 (33.3%)	6 (66.7%)	0.3	53.5	46.2
arr	5	5 (100%)	2 (40%)	3 (60%)	3.6	1.9	94.5
balancedBST	20	16 (80%)	13 (81.3%)	3 (18.7%)	12.3	23.7	64.0
bempl	10	10 (100%)	4 (40%)	6 (60%)	1.4	1.8	96.8
binaryTree	5	5 (100%)	3 (60%)	2 (40%)	1.7	0.9	97.4
cd	20	13 (65%)	9 (69.2%)	4 (30.8%)	0.7	0.8	98.5
ceilings	30	18 (60%)	13 (72.2%)	5 (27.8%)	2.9	5.3	91.7
dijkstra	30	23 (76.7%)	9 (39.1%)	14 (60.9%)	0.6	36.3	63.2
dll	20	14 (70%)	9 (64.3%)	5 (35.7%)	11.4	14.8	73.9
farmer	15	15 (100%)	3 (20%)	12 (80%)	0.3	1.6	98.1
filesystem	15	11 (73.3%)	3 (27.3%)	8 (72.7%)	27.9	17.4	54.7
fullTree	15	13 (86.7%)	11 (84.6%)	2 (15.4%)	1.6	2.3	96.1
grade	10	10 (100%)	0 (0%)	10 (100%)	1.2	0.9	97.9
grandpa1	15	15 (100%)	0 (0%)	15 (100%)	0.6	0.0	99.4
grandpa2	10	7 (70%)	3 (42.9%)	4 (57.1%)	1.2	1.0	97.8
grandpa3	25	16 (64%)	6 (37.5%)	10 (62.5%)	0.3	0.5	99.2
handshake	20	20 (100%)	0 (0%)	20 (100%)	0.5	0.0	99.5
life	15	7 (46.7%)	1 (14.3%)	6 (85.7%)	0.9	2.2	96.9
lists	20	20 (100%)	9 (45%)	11 (55%)	0.2	0.4	99.4
peterson	85	69 (81.2%)	41 (59.4%)	28 (40.6%)	0.8	7.8	91.5
ringElection1	30	30 (100%)	7 (23.3%)	23 (76.7%)	0.4	1.7	97.9
sll	5	5 (100%)	0 (0%)	5 (100%)	29.9	6.2	63.9
student	25	23 (92%)	20 (87.0%)	3 (13.0%)	9.2	21.5	69.3
Overall	460	379 (82.4%)	169 (44.6%)	210 (55.4%)	4.7	8.4	86.8

5.2   RQ1: Speed-up Effectiveness

Figures 4 and 5 show the speedup of iAlloy compared to the baseline on Mutant Version Set and Real Version Set, respectively. The x-axis denotes the subject names and the y-axis denotes the speed up. In Mutant Version Set, iAlloy achieves speed-up for 19 subjects (75% of the subject set), with up to 4.5x speed-up and 1.79x on average. The reason iAlloy did not speed up on the remaining 5 subjects is that either the change is in the signatures or many commands are unsatisfiable under the previous solutions, where the analysis time overhead in iAlloy (RCS and SR) is larger than the savings. In Real Version Set, we observe that iAlloy achieves a speedup of up to 7.66x and 1.59x on average over all subjects except one (97% of the subject set). iAlloy does not save any time on arr1 because there exists a single command in the subject and the command is unsatisfiable (in which case neither RCS nor SR can save any command executions).

5.3   RQ2: Command Selection and Solution Reuse Effectiveness

Columns 2–5 in Tables 2 and 3 show the total number of commands in each subject (cmd), the number of the selected commands and their percentage compared to the total number of commands (select), the number of solution reuse

Table 3. RCS, SR and Command Execution Results in Real Version Set

Model	cmd	select	reuse	execute	T_select (%)	T_reuse (%)	T_execute (%)
addr	2	2 (100%)	1 (50%)	1 (50%)	24.9	4.7	70.4
arr1	2	2 (100%)	0 (0%)	2 (100%)	7.4	0.0	92.6
arr2	2	2 (100%)	1 (50%)	1 (50%)	7.2	1.4	91.4
bBST1	8	8 (100%)	6 (75%)	2 (25%)	13.4	15.2	71.4
bBST2	8	8 (100%)	6 (75%)	2 (25%)	14.0	15.0	70.9
bBST3	8	8 (100%)	6 (75%)	2 (25%)	13.5	14.9	71.5
bempl	4	4 (100%)	0 (0%)	4 (100%)	1.8	0.4	97.8
cd1	8	7 (87.5%)	5 (71.4%)	2 (28.6%)	1.1	0.9	97.9
cd2	8	7 (87.5%)	6 (85.7%)	1 (14.3%)	3.5	3.0	93.5
dijk	12	10 (83.3%)	5 (50%)	5 (50%)	0.7	23.2	76.2
dll1	8	8 (100%)	6 (75%)	2 (25%)	13.2	16.0	70.8
dll2	8	8 (100%)	6 (75%)	2 (25%)	12.7	17.0	70.3
dll3	8	8 (100%)	7 (87.5%)	1 (12.5%)	16.3	22.3	61.3
dll4	8	8 (100%)	7 (87.5%)	1 (12.5%)	17.6	22.3	60.1
farmer	7	7 (100%)	2 (28.6%)	5 (71.4%)	0.7	2.5	96.8
grade	4	4 (100%)	1 (25%)	3 (75%)	3.6	1.7	94.8
stu0	10	10 (100%)	7 (70%)	3 (30%)	8.1	11.0	80.9
stu1	10	10 (100%)	6 (60%)	4 (40%)	5.8	8.3	85.9
stu10	10	10 (100%)	5 (50%)	5 (50%)	6.7	10.1	83.2
stu11	10	10 (100%)	7 (70%)	3 (30%)	7.6	10.4	81.9
stu12	10	10 (100%)	7 (70%)	3 (30%)	7.6	9.2	83.2
stu13	10	10 (100%)	7 (70%)	3 (30%)	6.4	9.5	84.1
stu14	10	10 (100%)	6 (60%)	4 (40%)	6.6	8.7	84.8
stu15	10	10 (100%)	6 (60%)	4 (40%)	6.9	6.7	86.4
stu16	10	10 (100%)	4 (40%)	6 (60%)	9.4	13.3	77.4
stu17	10	10 (100%)	5 (50%)	5 (50%)	6.7	8.0	85.3
stu18	10	10 (100%)	4 (40%)	6 (60%)	7.7	10.5	81.8
stu19	10	10 (100%)	4 (40%)	6 (60%)	6.1	9.8	84.1
stu2	10	10 (100%)	4 (40%)	6 (60%)	6.2	8.6	85.2
stu3	11	11 (100%)	5 (45.5%)	6 (54.5%)	5.3	8.9	85.8
stu4	10	10 (100%)	4 (40%)	6 (60%)	7.1	9.6	83.3
stu5	10	10 (100%)	7 (70%)	3 (30%)	8.1	8.2	83.7
stu6	10	10 (100%)	6 (60%)	4 (40%)	7.0	9.1	84.0
stu7	10	10 (100%)	6 (60%)	4 (40%)	6.6	8.9	84.5
stu8	10	10 (100%)	7 (70%)	3 (30%)	6.7	7.4	85.9
stu9	10	10 (100%)	4 (40%)	6 (60%)	7.1	11.0	81.9
Overall	306	302 (98.7%)	176 (58.3%)	126 (41.7%)	8.1	9.7	82.2

and their percentage in selected commands (reuse), and the number of actually executed commands and their percentage in selected commands (execute), for the Mutant and Real Version Set respectively. We can see that, both RCS and SR help reduce command execution in both subject sets, but to different extent. A smaller portion of commands are selected in Mutant Set (82.4%) than in Real Set (98.7%). This is due to the fact that there are more changes between versions in Real Set than in Mutant Set. However, smaller portion (41.7% vs. 55.4%) of the selected commands are executed and a larger portion (58.3% vs. 44.6%) of selected commands successfully reuse solutions in Real Set, comparing with Mutant Set. Besides, there are 54.3% command execution reduction $(\frac{cmd - execute}{cmd})$ in Mutant Set and 58.8% in Real Set. The result shows that iAlloy is promising in reducing the command executions in analyzing real world Alloy models as they evolve.

5.4   RQ3: Time Consumption

Columns 6–8 in Tables 2 and 3 present the percentage of time consumption in RCS (T_select), SR (T_reuse), and command execution (T_execute) in the Mutant Version Set and Real Version Set, respectively. We can see that in both subject sets, execution takes most of the time while RCS and SR are lightweight.

6   Related Work

A lot of work has been done to improve [20, 22, 24] and extend [10–13, 16, 19, 25, 28–31, 33] Alloy. We discuss work that is closely related to iAlloy.

Incremental Analysis for Alloy. Li et al. [9] first proposed the incremental analysis idea for their so-called consecutive Alloy models which are similar to the evolving models. They exploit incremental SAT solving to solve only the *delta* which is the set of boolean formulas describing the changed part between two model versions. Solving only the delta would result in a much improved SAT solving time than solving the new model version from scratch. Titanium [1] is an incremental analysis tool for evolving Alloy models. It uses all the solutions of the previous model version to potentially calculate tighter bounds for certain relational variables in the new model version. By tightening the bounds, Titanium reduces the search space, enabling SAT solver to find the new solutions at a fraction of the original solving time. These two approaches are the most relevant to our work that both focus on improving solving efficiency in the translated formulas. Whereas our incremental approach is to avoid the SAT solving phase completely, which is fundamentally different from existing approaches. In addition, Titanium has to find all the solutions in order to tighten the bounds, which would be inefficient when only certain number of solutions are needed.

Regression Symbolic Execution. Similar to the SAT solving applications such as Alloy analyzer, symbolic execution tools also face the scalability problems, in which case a lot of work has been done to improve the performance [6, 14, 23, 34]. The most closely related to our work is regression symbolic execution [14, 15, 34]. Similar to our RCS, symbolic execution on the new version is guided through the changed part with the previous versions. In addition, there is also work on verification techniques that reuses or caches the results [8, 18].

7   Conclusion and Future Work

In this paper, we proposed a novel incremental analysis technique with regression command selection and solution reuse. We implemented our technique in a tool called iAlloy. The experimental results show that iAlloy can speed up 90% of our subjects. Furthermore, it performs surprisingly well in models of the real faulty versions with up to 7.66 times speed up and above 50% command execution reduction. This indicates that iAlloy is promising in reducing time overhead of analyzing real-world Alloy models. In the future, we plan to extend iAlloy to support changes that involve Alloy signatures and perform a more fine-grained analysis to improve command selection.

Acknowledgments. We thank the anonymous reviewers for their valuable comments. This research was partially supported by the US National Science Foundation under Grants Nos. CCF-1566363, CCF-1652517, CCF-1704790 and CCF-1718903.

References

1. Bagheri, H., Malek, S.: Titanium: efficient analysis of evolving alloy specifications. In: International Symposium on Foundations of Software Engineering, pp. 27–38 (2016)
2. Rational Software Corporation: Object constraint language specification. Version 1.1 (1997)
3. Gligoric, M., Eloussi, L., Marinov, D.: Practical regression test selection with dynamic file dependencies. In: International Symposium on Software Testing and Analysis, pp. 211–222 (2015)
4. Graves, T.L., Harrold, M.J., Kim, J.-M., Porter, A., Rothermel, G.: An empirical study of regression test selection techniques. Trans. Softw. Eng. Methodol. **10**(2), 184–208 (2001)
5. Jackson, D.: Alloy: a lightweight object modelling notation. Trans. Softw. Eng. Methodol. **11**(2), 256–290 (2002)
6. Jia, X., Ghezzi, C., Ying, S.: Enhancing reuse of constraint solutions to improve symbolic execution. In: International Symposium on Software Testing and Analysis, pp. 177–187 (2015)
7. Legunsen, O., Shi, A., Marinov, D.: STARTS: STAtic regression test selection. In: Automated Software Engineering, pp. 949–954 (2017)
8. Leino, K.R.M., Wüstholz, V.: Fine-grained caching of verification results. In: Kroening, D., Păsăreanu, C.S. (eds.) CAV 2015. LNCS, Part I, vol. 9206, pp. 380–397. Springer, Cham (2015). https://doi.org/10.1007/978-3-319-21690-4_22
9. Li, X., Shannon, D., Walker, J., Khurshid, S., Marinov, D.: Analyzing the uses of a software modeling tool. Electron. Notes Theoret. Comput. Sci. **164**(2), 3–18 (2006)
10. Montaghami, V., Rayside, D.: Extending alloy with partial instances. In: Derrick, J., et al. (eds.) ABZ 2012. LNCS, vol. 7316, pp. 122–135. Springer, Heidelberg (2012). https://doi.org/10.1007/978-3-642-30885-7_9
11. Montaghami V., Rayside D.: Staged evaluation of partial instances in a relational model finder. In: Ait Ameur Y., Schewe KD. (eds) Abstract State Machines, Alloy, B, TLA, VDM, and Z. ABZ 2014. LNCS, vol. 8477, pp. 318–323. Springer, Heidelberg (2014). https://doi.org/10.1007/978-3-662-43652-3_32

12. Nelson, T., Saghafi, S., Dougherty, D.J., Fisler, K., Krishnamurthi, S.: Aluminum: principled scenario exploration through minimality. In: International Conference on Software Engineering, pp. 232–241 (2013)
13. Nijjar, J., Bultan, T.: Bounded verification of ruby on rails data models. In: International Symposium on Software Testing and Analysis, pp. 67–77 (2011)
14. Person, S., Yang, G., Rungta, N., Khurshid, S.: Directed incremental symbolic execution. SIGPLAN Not. **46**(6), 504–515 (2011)
15. Ramos, D.A., Engler, D.R.: Practical, low-effort equivalence verification of real code. In: Gopalakrishnan, G., Qadeer, S. (eds.) CAV 2011. LNCS, vol. 6806, pp. 669–685. Springer, Heidelberg (2011). https://doi.org/10.1007/978-3-642-22110-1_55
16. Regis, G., et al.: DynAlloy analyzer: a tool for the specification and analysis of alloy models with dynamic behaviour. In: Foundations of Software Engineering, pp. 969–973 (2017)
17. Spivey, J.M.: The Z Notation: A Reference Manual. Prentice-Hall Inc., Upper Saddle River (1989)
18. Strichman, O., Godlin, B.: Regression verification - a practical way to verify programs. In: Meyer, B., Woodcock, J. (eds.) VSTTE 2005. LNCS, vol. 4171, pp. 496–501. Springer, Heidelberg (2008). https://doi.org/10.1007/978-3-540-69149-5_54
19. Sullivan, A., Wang, K., Khurshid, S.: AUnit: a test automation tool for alloy. In: International Conference on Software Testing, Verification, and Validation, pp. 398–403 (2018)
20. Sullivan, A., Wang, K., Khurshid, S., Marinov, D.: Evaluating state modeling techniques in alloy. In: Software Quality Analysis, Monitoring, Improvement, and Applications (2017)
21. Sullivan, A., Wang, K., Zaeem, R.N., Khurshid, S.: Automated test generation and mutation testing for alloy. In: International Conference on Software Testing, Verification, and Validation, pp. 264–275 (2017)
22. Torlak, E., Jackson, D.: Kodkod: a relational model finder. In: Grumberg, O., Huth, M. (eds.) TACAS 2007. LNCS, vol. 4424, pp. 632–647. Springer, Heidelberg (2007). https://doi.org/10.1007/978-3-540-71209-1_49
23. Visser, W., Geldenhuys, J., Dwyer, M.B.: Green: reducing, reusing and recycling constraints in program analysis. In: International Symposium on the Foundations of Software Engineering, pp. 58:1–58:11 (2012)
24. Wang, J., Bagheri, H., Cohen, M.B.: An evolutionary approach for analyzing Alloy specifications. In: International Conference on Automated Software Engineering, pp. 820–825 (2018)
25. Wang, K., Sullivan, A., Khurshid, S.: ARepair: a repair framework for alloy. In: International Conference on Software Engineering, pp. 577–588 (2018)
26. Wang, K., Sullivan, A., Khurshid, S.: Automated model repair for alloy. In: Automated Software Engineering, pp. 577–588 (2018)
27. Wang, K, Sullivan, A., Khurshid, S.: MuAlloy: a mutation testing framework for alloy. In: International Conference on Software Engineering, pp. 29–32 (2018)
28. Wang, K., Sullivan, A., Koukoutos, M., Marinov, D., Khurshid, S.: Systematic generation of non-equivalent expressions for relational algebra. In: Butler, M., Raschke, A., Hoang, T.S., Reichl, K. (eds.) ABZ 2018. LNCS, vol. 10817, pp. 105–120. Springer, Cham (2018). https://doi.org/10.1007/978-3-319-91271-4_8
29. Wang, K., Sullivan, A., Marinov, D., Khurshid, S.: ASketch: a sketching framework for alloy. In: Symposium on the Foundations of Software Engineering, pp. 916–919 (2018)

30. Wang, K., Sullivan, A., Marinov, D., Khurshid, S.: Fault localization for declarative models in alloy. eprint arXiv:1807.08707 (2018)
31. Wang, K., Sullivan, A., Marinov, D., Khurshid, S.: Solver-based sketching of alloy models using test valuations. In: Butler, M., Raschke, A., Hoang, T.S., Reichl, K. (eds.) ABZ 2018. LNCS, vol. 10817, pp. 121–136. Springer, Cham (2018). https:// doi.org/10.1007/978-3-319-91271-4_9
32. Wang, K., Zhu, C., Celik, A., Kim, J., Batory, D., Gligoric, M.: Towards refactoring-aware regression test selection. In: IEEE/ACM 40th International Conference on Software Engineering (ICSE), pp. 233–244 (2018)
33. Wang, W., Wang, K., Zhang, M., Khurshid, S.: Learning to optimize the alloy analyzer. In: International Conference on Software Testing, Verification and Validation (2019, to appear)
34. Yang, G., Păsăreanu, C.S., Khurshid, S.: Memoized symbolic execution. In: International Symposium on Software Testing and Analysis, pp. 144–154 (2012)
35. Zhang, L., Kim, M., Khurshid, S.: Localizing failure-inducing program edits based on spectrum information. In: International Conference on Software Maintenance and Evolution, pp. 23–32 (2011)

10

Building Better Bit-Blasting for Floating-Point Problems

Martin Brain[1(✉)], Florian Schanda[2(✉)], and Youcheng Sun[1]

[1] Oxford University, Oxford, UK
{martin.brain,youcheng.sun}@cs.ox.ac.uk
[2] Zenuity GmbH, Unterschleißheim, Germany
florian.schanda@zenuity.com

Abstract. An effective approach to handling the theory of floating-point is to reduce it to the theory of bit-vectors. Implementing the required encodings is complex, error prone and requires a deep understanding of floating-point hardware. This paper presents SymFPU, a library of encodings that can be included in solvers. It also includes a verification argument for its correctness, and experimental results showing that its use in CVC4 out-performs all previous tools. As well as a significantly improved performance and correctness, it is hoped this will give a simple route to add support for the theory of floating-point.

Keywords: IEEE-754 · Floating-point ·
Satisfiability modulo theories · SMT

1 Introduction

From the embedded controllers of cars, aircraft and other "cyber-physical" systems, via JavaScript to the latest graphics, computer vision and machine learning accelerator hardware, floating-point computation is everywhere in modern computing. To reason about contemporary software, we must be able to efficiently reason about floating-point. To derive proofs, counter-examples, test cases or attack vectors we need bit-accurate results.

The vast majority of systems use IEEE-754 [1] floating-point implementations, or slight restrictions or relaxations. This makes unexpected behaviour rare; floating-point numbers behave enough like real numbers that programmers largely do not (need to) think about the difference. This gives a challenge for software verification: finding the rarely considered edge-cases that may result in incorrect, unsafe or insecure behaviour.

Of the many verification tools that can address these challenges, almost all use SMT solvers to find solutions to sets of constraints, or show they are infeasible. So there is a pressing need for SMT solvers to be able to reason about floating-point variables. An extension to the ubiquitous SMT-LIB standard to support floating-point [13] gives a common interface, reducing the wider problem to a question of efficient implementation within SMT solvers.

Most solvers designed for verification support the theory of bit-vectors. As floating-point operations can be implemented with circuits, the "bit-blasting" approach of reducing the floating-point theory to bit-vectors is popular. This method is conceptually simple, makes use of advances in bit-vector theory solvers and allows mixed floating-point/bit-vector problems to be solved efficiently.

Implementing the theory of floating-point should be as simple as adding the relevant circuit designs to the bit-blaster. However, encodings of floating-point operations in terms of bit-vectors, similarly to implementation of floating-point units in hardware, are notoriously complex and detailed. Getting a high degree of assurance in their correctness requires a solid understanding of floating-point operations and significant development effort.

Then there are questions of performance. Floating-point units designed for hardware are generally optimised for low latency, high throughput or low power consumption. Likewise software implementations of floating-point operations tend to focus on latency and features such as arbitrary precision. However, there is nothing to suggest that a design that produces a 'good' circuit will also produce a 'good' encoding or vice-versa.

To address these challenges this paper presents the following contributions:

- A comprehensive overview of the literature on automated reasoning for floating-point operations (Section 2).
- An exploration of the design space for floating-point to bit-vector encodings (Section 3) and the choices made when developing the SymFPU; a library of encodings that can be integrated into SMT solvers that support the theory of bit-vectors (Section 4).
- A verification case for the correctness of the SymFPU encodings and various other SMT solvers (Section 5).
- An experimental evaluation five times larger than previous works gives a comprehensive evaluation of existing tools and shows that the SymFPU encodings, even used in a naïve way significantly out-perform all other approaches (Section 6). These experiments subsume the evaluations performed in many previous works, giving a robust replication of their results.

2   The Challenges of Floating-Point Reasoning

Floating-point number systems are based on computing with a fixed number of *significant digits*. Only the significant digits are stored (the *significand*), along with their distance from the decimal point (the *exponent*) as the power of a fixed base. The following are examples of decimals numbers with three significant digits and their floating-point representations.

Arithmetic is performed as normal, but the result may have more than the specified number of digits and need to be rounded to a representable value. This gives the first major challenge for reasoning about floating-point numbers: rounding after each operation means that addition and multiplication are no longer associative, nor are they distributive.

Existence of identities, additive inverses[1] and symmetry are preserved except for special cases (see below) and in some cases addition even gains an absorptive property ($a+b = a$ for some non-zero b). However, the resulting structure is not a well studied algebra and does not support many symbolic reasoning algorithms.

Rounding ensures the significand fits in a fixed number of bits, but it does not deal with exponent overflow or underflow. Detecting, and graceful and efficient handling of these edge-cases was a significant challenge for older floating-point systems. To address these challenges, IEEE-754 defines floating-point numbers representing $\pm\infty$ and ± 0[2] and a class of fixed-point numbers known as *denormal* or *subnormal* numbers.

To avoid intrusive branching and testing code in computational hot-spots, all operations have to be defined for these values. This gives troubling questions such as "What is $\infty + -\infty$?" or "Is $0/0$ equal to $1/0$, $-1/0$, or neither?". The standard resolves these with a fifth class of number, not-a-number (NaN).

The proliferation of classes of number is the second source of challenges for automated reasoning. An operation as simple as an addition can result in a 125-way case split if each class of input number and rounding mode is considered individually. Automated reasoning systems for floating-point numbers need an efficient way of controlling the number of side conditions and edge cases.

As well as the two major challenges intrinsic to IEEE-754 floating-point, there are also challenges in how programmers use floating-point numbers. In many systems, floating-point values are used to represent some "real world" quantity – light or volume levels, velocity, distance, etc. Only a small fraction of the range of floating-point numbers are then meaningful. For example, a 64-bit floating-point number can represent the range $[1 * 10^{-324}, 1 * 10^{308}]$ which dwarfs the range of likely speeds (in m/s) of any vehicle[3] $[1 * 10^{-15}, 3 * 10^{8}]$. Apart from languages like Ada [35] or SPARK [3] that have per-type ranges, the required information on what are meaningful ranges is rarely present in – or can be inferred from – the program alone. This makes it hard to create "reasonable" preconditions or avoid returning laughably infeasible verification failures.

Despite the challenges, there are many use-cases for floating-point reasoning: testing the feasibility of execution paths, preventing the generation of ∞ and NaN, locating absorptive additions and catastrophic cancellation, finding language-level undefined behaviour (such as the much-cited Ariane 5 Flight 501 incident), showing run-time exception freedom, checking hardware and FPGA

---

[1] But not multiplicative ones for subtle reasons.

[2] Two distinct zeros are supported so that underflow from above and below can be distinguished, helping handle some branch cuts such as tan.

[3] Based on the optimistic use of the classical electron radius and the speed of light.

designs (such as the equally well cited Intel FDIV bug) and proving functional correctness against both float-valued and real-valued specifications.

2.1 Techniques

Current fully automatic[4] floating-point reasoning tools can be roughly grouped into four categories: bit-blasting, interval techniques, black-box optimisation approaches and axiomatic schemes.

Bit-Blasting. CBMC [17] was one of the first tools to convert from bit-vector formulae to Boolean SAT problems (so called "bit-blasting"). It benefited from the contemporaneous rapid improvement in SAT solver technology and lead to the DPLL(T) [29] style of SMT solver. Later versions of CBMC also converted floating-point constraints directly into Boolean problems [15]. These conversions were based on the circuits given in [44] and served as inspiration for a similar approach in MathSAT [16] and independent development of similar techniques in Z3 [24] and SONOLAR [39]. SoftFloat [34] has been used to simulate floating-point support for integer only tools [48] but is far from a satisfactory approach as the algorithms used for efficient software implementation of floating-point are significantly different from those used for hardware [45] and efficient encodings.

The principle disadvantage of bit-blasting is that the bit-vector formulae generated can be very large and complex. To mitigate this problem, there have been several approaches [15,56,57] to approximating the bit-vector formulae. This remains an under-explored and promising area.

Interval Techniques. One of the relational properties preserved by IEEE-754 is a weak form of monotonicity, e.g.: $0 < s \wedge a < b \Rightarrow a + s \leqslant b + s$. These properties allow efficient and tight interval bounds to be computed for common operations. This is used by the numerical methods communities and forms the basis for three independent lineages of automated reasoning tools.

Based on the formal framework of abstract interpretation, a number of techniques that partition abstract domains to compute an exact result[5] have been proposed. These include the ACDL framework [26] that generalises the CDCL algorithm used in current SAT solvers. Although this is applicable to a variety of domains, the use of intervals is widespread as an efficient and "precise enough" foundation. CDFPL [27] applied these techniques to programs and [11] implemented them within MathSAT. Absolute [47] uses a different partitioning scheme without learning, but again uses intervals.

---

[4] Machine assisted proof, such as interactive theorem provers are outside the scope of the current discussion. There has been substantial work in Isabelle, HOL, HOL Light, ACL2, PVS, Coq and Meta-Tarski on floating-point.

[5] This approach is operationally much closer to automated reasoning than classical abstract interpreters such as Fluctuat [31], Astrée [8], Polyspace [54], and CodePeer [2], as well as more modern tools such as Rosa [22] and Daisy [36] which compute over-approximate bounds or verification results.

From the automated reasoning community similar approaches have been developed. Originally implemented in the nlsat tool [37], mcSAT [25] can be seen as an instantiation of the ACDL framework using a constant abstraction and tying the generalisation step to a particular approach to variable elimination. Application of this technique to floating-point would likely either use intervals or a conversion to bit-vectors [58]. iSAT3 [51] implements an interval partitioning and learning system, which could be seen as another instance of ACDL. Independently, dReal [30] and raSAT [55] have both developed interval partitioning techniques which would be directly applicable to floating-point systems.

A third strand of convergent evolution in the development of interval based techniques comes from the constraint programming community. FPCS [43] uses intervals with sophisticated back-propagation rules [4] and smart partitioning heuristics [59]. Colibri [42] takes a slightly different approach, using a more expressive constraint representation of difference bounded matrices[6]. This favours more powerful inference over a faster search.

These approaches all have compact representations of spaces of possibilities and fast propagation which allow them to efficiently tackle "large but easy" problems. However they tend to struggle as the relations between expressions become more complex, requiring some kind or relational reasoning such as the learning in MathSAT, or the relational abstractions of Colibri. As these advantages and disadvantages fit well with those of bit-blasting, hybrid systems are not uncommon. Both MathSAT and Z3 perform simple interval reasoning during pre-processing and iSAT3 has experimented with using CBMC and SMT solvers for problems that seem to be UNSAT [46,52].

Optimisation Approaches. It is possible to evaluate many formulae quickly in hardware, particularly those derived from software verification tasks. Combined with a finite search space for floating-point variables, this makes local-search and other "black-box" techniques an attractive proposition. XSat [28] was the first tool to directly make use of this approach (although Ariadne [5] could be seen as a partial precursor), making use of an external optimisation solver. goSAT [38] improved on this by compiling the formulae to an executable form. A similar approach using an external fuzz-testing tool is taken by JFS [40].

These approaches have considerable promise, particularly for SAT problems with relatively dense solution spaces. The obvious limitation is that these techniques are often unable to identify UNSAT problems.

Axiomatic. Although rounding destroys many of the obvious properties, the algebra of floating-point is not without non-trivial results. Gappa [23] was originally created as a support tool for interactive theorem provers, but can be seen a solver in its own right. It instantiates a series of theorems about floating-point numbers until a sufficient error bound is determined. Although its saturation process is naïve, it is fast and effective, especially when directed by a more conventional SMT solver [20]. Why3 [9] uses an axiomatisation of floating-point

---

[6] In the abstract interpretation view this could be seen as a relational abstraction.

numbers based on reals when producing verification conditions for provers that only support real arithmetic. Combining these approaches Alt-Ergo [19] ties the instantiation of relevant theorems to its quantifier and non-linear real theory solvers. Finally, KLEE-FP [18] can be seen as a solver in the axiomatic tradition but using rewriting rather than theorem instantiation.

3 Floating-Point Circuits

Floating-point circuits have been the traditional choice for bit-blasting encoding. The 'classical' design[7] for floating-point units is a four stage pipeline [45]: unpacking, operation, rounding, and packing.

Unpacking. IEEE-754 gives an encoding for all five kinds of number. To separate the encoding logic from the operation logic, it is common to *unpack*; converting arguments from the IEEE-754 format to a larger, redundant format used within the floating-point unit (FPU). The unpacking units and intermediate format are normally the same for all operations within an FPU. A universal feature is splitting the number into three smaller bit-vectors: the sign, exponent and significand. Internal formats may also include some of the following features:

- Flags to record if the number is an infinity, NaN, zero or subnormal.
- The leading 1 for normal numbers (the so-called *hidden-bit*) may be added. Thus the significand may be regarded as a fix-point number in the range $[0, 1)$ or $[1, 2)$. Some designs go further allowing the significand range to be larger, allowing lazy normalisation.
- The exponent may be biased or unbiased[8].
- Subnormal numbers may be normalised (requiring an extended exponent), flagged, transferred to a different unit or even trapped to software.

Operate. Operations, such as addition or multiplication are performed on unpacked numbers, significantly simplifying the logic required. The result will be another unpacked number, often with an extended significand (two or three extra bits for addition, up to twice the number of bits for multiplication) and extended exponent (typically another one or two bits). For example, using this approach multiplication is relatively straight forward:

1. Multiply the two significands, giving a fixed-point number with twice the precision, in the range $[1, 4)$.

---

[7] Modern high-performance processors often only implement a fused mulitply-add (FMA) unit that computes $round(x * y + z)$ and then use a mix of table look-ups and Newton-Raphson style iteration to implement divide, square-root, etc.

[8] Although the exponent is interpreted as a signed number, it is encoded, in IEEE-754 format using a biased representation, so that the $000 \ldots 00$ bit-vector represents the smallest negative number rather than 0 and $111 \ldots 11$ represents the largest positive rather than the -1 in 2's complement encodings. This makes the ordering of bit-vectors and IEEE-754 floating-point numbers compatible.

2. Add the exponents ($2^{e_1} * 2^{e_2} = 2^{e_1+e_2}$) and subtract the bias if they are stored in a biased form.
3. Potentially renormalise the exponent into the range $[1, 2)$ (right shift the significand one place and increment the exponent).
4. Use the classification flags to handle special cases (∞, NaN, etc.).

Addition is more involved as the two significands must be aligned before they can be added or subtracted. In most cases, the location of the leading 1 in the resulting significand is roughly known, meaning that the renormalisation is simple (for example $s_1 \in [1, 2), s_2 \in [1, 2) \Rightarrow s_1 + s_2 \in [2, 4)$). However in the case of catastrophic cancellation the location of the leading 1 is non-obvious. Although this case is rare, it has a disproportionate effect on the design of floating-point adders: it is necessary to locate the leading 1 to see how many bits have been cancelled to determine what changes are needed for the exponent.

Round. Given the exact result in extended precision, the next step is to round to the nearest representable number in the target output format. Traditionally, the rounder would have been a common component of the FPU, shared between the functional units and would be independent of the operations. The operation of the rounder is relatively simple but the order of operations is very significant:

1. Split the significand into the representable bits, the first bit after (the *guard bit*) and the OR of the remaining bits (the *sticky bit*).
2. The guard bit and sticky bit determine whether the number is less than half way to the previous representable number, exact half way, or over half way. Depending on the rounding mode the significand may be incremented (i.e. rounded up).
3. The exponent is checked to see if it is too large (*overflow*) or too small (*underflow*) for the target format, and the output is set to infinity/the largest float or 0/the smallest float depending on the rounding mode.

To work out which bits to convert to the guard and sticky bits, *it is critical to know the position of the leading 1*, and if the number is subnormal or not.

Pack. The final step is to convert the result back into the packed IEEE-754 format. This is the converse of the unpacking stage, with flags for the type of number being used to set special values. Note that this can result in the carefully calculated and rounded result being ignored in favour of outputting the fixed bit-pattern for ∞ or NaN.

4 SymFPU

SymFPU is a C++ library of bit-vector encodings of floating-point operations. It is available at https://github.com/martin-cs/symfpu. The types used to represent signed and unsigned bit-vectors, Booleans, rounding-modes and floating-point formats are templated so that multiple "back-ends" can be implemented. This allows SymFPU to be used as an executable multi-precision library and to generate symbolic encodings of the operations. As well as the default executable back-end, integrations into CVC4 [6] and CBMC [17] have been developed. These typically require 300–500 effective lines of code, the majority of which is routine interfacing.

Packing Removal. By choosing an unpacked format that is bijective with the packed format, the following property holds: $pack \circ unpack = id = unpack \circ pack$. The encodings in CBMC do not have this property as the packing phase is used to mask out the significand and exponent when special values are generated. The property allows a key optimisation: the final unpack stage of an operation and the pack of the next can be eliminated. Hence values can be kept in unpacked form and whole chains of operations can be performed without packing. Although this is not necessarily a large saving on its own, it allows the use of unpacked formats which would be too expensive if every operation was packed.

Unpacked Format. Key to SymFPU's performance is the unpacked format. Flags are used for ∞, NaN and zero. This means that special cases can be handled at the end of the operation, bypassing the need to reason about the actual computation if one of the flags is set. Special cases share the same 'default' significand and exponent, so assignment to the flags will propagate values through the rest of the circuit.

The exponent is a signed bit-vector without bias, moving a subtract from the multiplier into the packing and unpacking (avoided as described above) and allowing decision procedures for signed bit-vectors to be used [32].

The significand is represented with the leading one and subnormal numbers are normalised. This adds considerable cost to the packing and unpacking but means that the leading one can be tracked at design time, avoiding the expensive normalisation phase before rounding that CBMC's encodings have. A normalisation phase is needed in the adder for catastrophic cancellation and the subnormal case of rounding is more expensive but critically both of these cases are rare (see below). Z3's encodings use a more complex system of lazy normalisation. This works well when operations include packing but is harder to use once packing has been removed. Integrating this approach is a challenge for future work.

Additional Bit-Vector Operations. SymFPU uses a number of non-standard bit-vector operations including add-with-carry (for including the renormalisation bit into exponents during multiply), conditional increment, decrement and left-shift (used for normalisation), max and min, count leading zeros, order encode (output has input number of bits), right sticky shift, and normalise. Work on creating optimal encodings [12] of these operations is on-going.

Invariants. As the significand in the unpacked format always has a leading one, it is possible to give strong invariants on the location of leading ones during the algorithms. Other invariants are general properties of IEEE-754 floating-point, for example the exponent of an effective addition is always $max(e_a, e_b)$ or $max(e_a, e_b) + 1$ regardless of rounding. Where possible, bit-vectors operations are used so that no overflows or underflows occur – a frustrating source of bugs in the CBMC encodings. Invariants in SymFPU can be checked with executable back-ends and used as auxiliary constraints in symbolic ones.

Probability Annotations. There are many sub-cases within operations which are unlikely or rare, for example rounding the subnormal result of a multiplication, catastrophic cancellation, or late detection of significand overflow during rounding. These are often more expensive to handle than the common cases. SymFPU contains probability annotations that mark likely and unlikely cases so that these can be handled separately.

5 Correctness

Developing a floating-point implementation, literal and symbolic, is a notoriously detailed and error prone task. For SymFPU we developed a substantial verification process which is summarised in Figure 1. Our verification case is based on system-level testing of SymFPU in CVC4, and double/triple diversity of checks, developers, references and implementations:

1. We use five test suites, four developed specifically for this project. These were developed independently by three different developers using different methodologies and different "ground truth" references. Where hardware was a reference, several different chips from different vendors were used.
2. The results of three different solvers (CVC4 with SymFPU, MathSAT, and Z3) are compared and each test is only regarded as passed when any discrepancy, between solvers or with the reference results, has been resolved. Each solver has its own, independently developed encodings and there is diversity in the algorithms used.

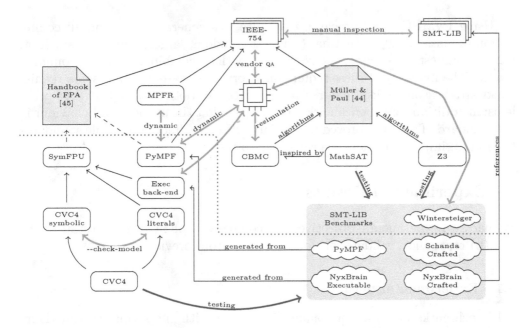

Fig. 1. The verification case for SymFPU. The contributions of this paper are below the dotted line. Thicker arrows are verification activities, and black arrows the usage of various documents and libraries.

As described above, SymFPU contains a significant number of dynamically-checked invariants. CVC4 also checks the models generated for satisfiable formulae, checking the symbolic back-end against the literal one. The experiments described in Section 6 also acted as system-level tests. This approach uncovered numerous bugs in the SymFPU encodings, the solvers and even our reference libraries. However, as it is a testing based verification argument, it cannot be considered to be complete. [41] used a similar technique successfully in a more limited setting without the emphasis on ground truth.

5.1 PyMPF

Testing-based verification is at best as good as the reference results for the tests – a high-quality test oracle is vital. Various solvers have their own multi-precision libraries, using these would not achieve the required diversity. MPFR [33] was considered but it does not support all of the operations in SMT-LIB, and has an awkward approach to subnormals.

To act as an oracle, we developed PyMPF [49], a Python multi-precision library focused on correctness through simplicity rather than performance. Unlike other multi-precision floating-point libraries it represents numbers as rationals rather than significand and exponent, and explicitly rounds to the nearest representable rational after each operation using a simple binary search. Where possible, all calculations are dynamically checked against a compiled C version of the operation and MPFR, giving triple diversity.

Using PyMPF as an oracle, a test suite was generated covering all combination of classes: ± 0, subnormal (smallest, random, largest), normal (smallest, random, largest, 1, $\frac{1}{2}$), $\pm\infty$, and NaN along with all combination of five rounding modes. The majority of these require only forwards reasoning, but some require backwards reasoning. Benchmarks are generated for both SAT and UNSAT problems; in addition some benchmarks correctly exploit the unspecified behaviour in the standard. This suite proved particularly effective, finding multiple soundness bugs in all implementations we were able to test.

6   Experimental Results

We had two experimental objectives: (a) compare SymFPU with the state of the art, (b) reproduce, validate, or update results from previous papers.

6.1   Experimental Setup

All benchmarks are available online [50], along with the scripts to run them. Experiments were conducted in the TACAS artefact evaluation virtual machine, hosted on an Intel i7-7820HQ laptop with 32 GiB RAM running Debian Stretch. All experiments were conducted with a one minute timeout[9] and 2500 MiB memory limit, set with a custom tool (rather than ulimit) that allowed us to reliably distinguish between tool crashes, timeouts, or memory use limits.

Solver responses were split into six classes: solved ("sat" or "unsat" response), unknown ("unknown" response), timeout, oom (out-of-memory), unsound ("sat" or "unsat" response contradicting the :status annotation), and error (anything else, including "unsupported" messages, parse errors or other tool output).

Although one minute is a relatively short limit, it best matches the typical industrial use-cases with SPARK; and trial runs with larger time-outs suggest that the additional time does not substantially change the qualitative nature of the results.

6.2   Benchmarks

We have tried to avoid arbitrary choices in benchmark selection as we want to demonstrate that SymFPU's encodings are a good general-purpose solution. As such we compare with some solvers in their specialised domain. Benchmarks are in logics QF_FP or QF_FPBV except for: Heizmann benchmarks include quantifiers and arrays; SPARK benchmarks (including Industrial_1) include arrays, datatypes, quantifiers, uninterpreted functions, integer and reals, and bitvectors. SAT, UNSAT or unknown here refers to the :status annotations in the benchmarks, not to our results.

---

[9] Except for the Wintersteiger suite where we used a 1 s timeout to deal with Alt-Ergo's behaviour.

Schanda 200 problems (34.0% SAT, 63.0% UNSAT, 3.0% unknown). Hand-written benchmarks accumulated over the years working on SPARK, user-supplied axioms, industrial code and problems, and reviewing papers and the SMT-LIB theory [13,14].

PyMPF 72,925 problems (52.3% SAT, 47.7% UNSAT). A snapshot of benchmarks generated using PyMPF [49] as described above.

NyxBrain 52,500 problems (99.5% SAT, 0.5% UNSAT). Hand-written edge-cases, and generated problems based on bugs in existing implementations.

Wintersteiger 39,994 problems (50.0% SAT, 50.0% UNSAT). Randomly generated benchmarks that cover many aspects of the floating-point theory.

Griggio 214 problems (all unknown). Benchmark set deliberately designed to highlight the limitations of bit-blasting and the advantages of interval techniques. They were the most useful in reproducing other paper's results.

Heizmann 207 problems (1.0% SAT, 99.0% unknown). Taken from the Ultimate Automizer model checker.

Industrial_1 388 problems (all UNSAT). Extracted from a large industrial Ada 2005 code base. We used the SPARK 2014 tools to produce (identifier obfuscated) verification conditions.

Industrial_1 QF 388 problems (all unknown). As above, but with quantifiers and data-types removed.

SPARK FP 2950 problems (5.3% UNSAT, 94.7% unknown). The floating-point subset of the verification conditions from the SPARK test suite[10], generated using a patched[11] SPARK tool to map the square root function of the Ada Standard library to `fp.sqrt`.

SPARK FP QF 2950 problems (all unknown). As above, but with all quantifiers and data-types removed.

CBMC 54 problems (7.4% UNSAT, 92.6% unknown). Non-trivial benchmarks from SV-COMP's floating-point collection [7], fp-bench [21] benchmarks that contained checkable post-conditions, the benchmarks used by [5], and the sample programs from [59]. The benchmarks are provided in SMT-LIB and the original C program for comparing to CBMC's floating-point solver.

Not all SMT solvers support all features of SMT-LIB, hence we provide alternative encodings in some cases. In particular Alt-Ergo does not parse moden SMT-LIB at all; so Griggio and Wintersteiger have been translated with the `fp-smt2-to-why3`[12] tool from [19] and the SPARK FP benchmarks have been generated by SPARK directly for Alt-Ergo, where possible (since Alt-Ergo does not support the `ite` contruct, there is a translation step inside Why3 that attempts to remove it, but it sometimes runs out of memory).

---

[10] Github: AdaCore/spark2014, directory testsuite/gnatprove/tests.

[11] Github: florianschanda/spark_2014 and florianschanda/why3.

[12] https://gitlab.com/OCamlPro-Iguernlala/Three-Tier-FPA-Benchs/tree/master/ translators/fp-smt2-to-why3.

6.3 Solvers

We have benchmarked the following solvers in the following configurations on the benchmarks described above: CVC4 [6] (with SymFPU)[13], Z3 (4.8.1) [24], Z3 Smallfloats (3a3abf82) [57], MathSAT (5.5.2) [16], MathSAT (5.5.2) using ACDCL [11], SONOLAR (2014-12-04) [39], Colibri (r1981) [42], Alt-Ergo (2.2.0) [19], and goSAT (4e475233) [38].

We have also attempted to benchmark XSat [28], but we were unable to reliably use the tools as distributed at the required scale ($\approx$ 200k benchmarks). However, we understand that goSAT is an evolution of the ideas implemented in XSat, and its results should be representative.

We would have liked to benchmark iSAT3 [51], Coral [53] and Gappa [23], but they do not provide SMT-LIB front-ends and there are no automatic translators we are aware of to their native input language. Binaries for FPCS [43] and Alt-Ergo/Gappa [20] were not available.

6.4 Results

Overall. Table 1 shows the overall summary of how many benchmarks any given solver was able to solve (correct SAT or UNSAT answer). CVC4 using the SymFPU encodings solves the most problems in all but two categories. In the case of the "Griggio" suite this is not surprising, given it's purpose. A detailed breakdown of that benchmark suite can be found in Table 2.

Griggio Suite. Table 2 shows the detailed results for the Griggio suite. Since the benchmark suite was designed to be difficult for bit-blasting solvers, it is not surprising that MathSAT (ACDCL) and Colibri do very well here, as they are not bit-blasting solvers. Though it is claimed in [19] that "Bit-blasting based techniques perform better on Griggio benchmarks", this is evidently not the case.

Heizmann Suite. Table 3 shows the detailed results for the benchmarks from the Ultimate Automizer project. These benchmarks were particularly useful to include as they are industrial in nature and are generated independent of all solver developers and the authors of this paper. The errors mainly relate to quantifiers (MathSAT, Colibri, SONOLAR), conversions (MathSAT-ACDCL), sorts (Colibri), and arrays (SONOLAR).

CBMC Suite. Table 4 shows a comparison between CBMC and SMT Solvers when attempting to solve the same problem. The original benchmark in C is given to CBMC, and SMT Solvers attempt to either solve a hand-encoding of the same problem or the encoding of the problem generated by CBMC.

---

[13] https://github.com/martin-cs/cvc4/tree/floating-point-symfpu.

Table 1. Percentage of solved benchmarks. Solver names abbreviated: AE (Alt-Ergo), Col (Colibri), MS (MathSAT), MS-A (MathSAT ACDCL), SON (SONOLAR), Z3-SF (Z3 SmallFloats), VBS (Virtual Best Solver). A ✓ indicates that all problems are solved, a blank entry indicates that the solver did not solve any problem for the given benchmark suite. In this table and all subsequent tables a * indicates that at least one benchmark was expressed in a solver-specific dialect, and the best result for each benchmark is typeset in bold.

Benchmark	AE	Col	CVC4	goSAT	MS	MS-A	SON	Z3	Z3-SF	VBS
CBMC		**66.7**	55.6	9.3	50.0	**66.7**	38.9	42.6	46.3	83.3*
Schanda		82.5	**85.5**	1.0	68.0*	28.0*		84.0	82.0	96.0*
Griggio	0.9*	61.7	61.2	41.1	59.3	**69.2**	67.8	33.2	46.3	89.3
Heizmann		14.0	**74.9**		58.5	27.5	2.9	51.7	42.0	91.8
Industrial 1			**91.2**					65.2	62.9	91.8
Industrial 1 (QF)		93.0	**98.2**		97.2	88.1		85.8	83.2	99.7
NyxBrain		99.8	**99.9**	34.2	95.4	95.0	99.2	99.9	99.9	>99.9
PyMPF		92.2	**99.7**	0.3	39.4	35.9		99.3	98.4	99.8
SPARK FP	68.6*		**85.6**					82.0	73.6	90.2*
SPARK FP (QF)		94.0	**95.8**		83.3	78.9		90.3	90.3	99.7
Wintersteiger	49.9*	✓	✓	13.9	85.8	85.8		✓	✓	✓*

Table 2. Results for benchmark 'Griggio' 214 problems (all unknown), ordered by % solved. Total time includes timeouts. A ✓ in "Unsound" indicates 0 unsound results.

Solver	Solved	Unknown	Timeout	Oom	Error	Unsound	Total time (m:s)
MathSAT (ACDCL)	**69.2%**	0	66	**0**	✓	✓	1:11:03
SONOLAR	67.8%	0	59	10	✓	✓	1:19:35
Colibri	61.7%	0	73	2	7	✓	1:22:13
CVC4	61.2%	0	77	6	✓	✓	1:40:47
MathSAT	59.3%	0	85	2	✓	✓	1:53:26
Z3 (SmallFloat)	46.3%	0	99	16	✓	✓	2:13:28
goSAT	41.1%	120	**6**	**0**	✓	✓	**8:28**
Z3	33.2%	0	124	19	✓	✓	2:34:16
Alt-Ergo FPA	0.9%*	2	210	**0**	✓	✓	3:32:40
Virtual best	89.3%	17	6	0	✓	✓	12:53

6.5 Replication

As part of our evaluation we have attempted to reproduce, validate or update results from previous papers. We have encountered issues with unclear solver configurations and versions and arbitrary benchmark selections.

The Z3 approximation paper [57] uses the Griggio test suite with a 20 minute timeout. It reported that there is little difference between Z3 and Z3-SmallFloats, and MathSAT outperformed both. Our results in Table 2 confirm this.

The MathSAT ACDCL [11] paper also looks at the Griggio test suite with a 20 minute timeout, our results in Table 2 are roughly ordered as theirs and can be considered to confirm these results.

Although the total number of SAT/UNSAT varied based on algorithm selection (i.e. the tool was clearly unsound) in [38], goSAT has been fixed and the results are broadly reproducible. We discovered some platform dependent behaviour (different SAT/UNSAT answers) between AMD and Intel processors. This can likely be fixed with appropriate compilation flags.

Table 3. Results for benchmark 'Heizmann' 207 problems (1.0% SAT, 99.0% unknown), ordered by % solved. Total time includes timeouts.

Solver	Solved	Unknown	Timeout	Oom	Error	Unsound	Total time (m:s)
CVC4	**74.9%**	48	**0**	**0**	4	✓	0:39.20
MathSAT	58.5%	**0**	**0**	**0**	86	✓	0:35.48
Z3	51.7%	**0**	91	9	✓	✓	2:03:36
Z3 (SmallFloat)	42.0%	**0**	111	9	✓	✓	2:13:13
MathSAT (ACDCL)	27.5%	**0**	**0**	**0**	150	✓	0:25.33
Colibri	14.0%	**0**	**0**	**0**	178	✓	0:30.34
SONOLAR	2.9%	**0**	**0**	**0**	201	✓	**0:7.92**
Virtual best	91.8%	17	0	0	✓	✓	5:36

Table 4. Results for benchmark 'CBMC' 54 problems (7.4% UNSAT, 92.6% unknown), ordered by number of unsound answers and then by % solved. Total time includes timeouts.

Solver	Solved	Unknown	Timeout	Oom	Error	Unsound	Total time (m:s)
Colibri	**66.7%**	**0**	14	**0**	4	✓	16:04
CBMC	61.1%*	**0**	17	4	✓	✓	19:25
CBMC −refine	61.1%*	**0**	21	**0**	✓	✓	23:30
CVC4	55.6%	**0**	17	7	✓	✓	23:41
MathSAT	50.0%	**0**	22	5	✓	✓	26:34
Z3 (SmallFloat)	46.3%	**0**	22	7	✓	✓	27:32
Z3	42.6%	**0**	22	9	✓	✓	29:29
SONOLAR	38.9%	**0**	**0**	**0**	33	✓	0:19.20
goSAT	9.3%	**0**	**0**	**0**	49	✓	**0:0.55**
MathSAT (ACDCL)	**66.7%**	**0**	9	**0**	7	2	9:51
Virtual best	83.3%*	0	9	0	✓	✓	9:55

We were unable to reproduce the results of the XSat [28] paper, as we could not get the tools to work reliably. In particular the docker instance cannot be used in our testing infrastructure as the constant-time overhead of running docker ruins performance, and eventually the docker daemon crashes.

We were only able to reproduce small parts from the Alt-Ergo FPA [19] paper. The biggest problem is benchmark selection and generation, which was not repeatable from scratch. Two particular measurements are worth commenting on: while they have roughly equal solved rate for SPARK VCs for Alt-Ergo and Z3 (40% and 36% respectively), as can be seen in Table 1 we get (68% and 86%) - although as noted we could not fully replicate their benchmark selection. However even more surprising are their results for the Griggio suite where they report a mere 4% for MathSAT-ACDCL which does not match our results of 69% as seen in Table 2.

7 Conclusion

By careful consideration of the challenges of floating-point reasoning (Section 2) and the fundamentals of circuit design (Section 3) we have designed a library of encodings that reduce the cost of developing a correct and efficient floating-point solver to a few hundred lines of interface code (Section 4). Integration into CVC4 gives a solver that substantially out-performs all previous systems (Section 6) despite using the most direct and naïve approach[14]. The verification process used to develop SymFPU ensures a high-level of quality, as well as locating tens of thousands of incorrect answers from hundreds of bugs across all existing solvers.

At a deeper level our experimental work raises some troubling questions about how developments in solver technology are practically evaluated. It shows that the quality of implementation (even between mature systems) can make a larger difference to performance than the difference between techniques [10]. Likewise the difficulty we had in replicating the trends seen in previous experimental work underscores the need for diverse and substantial benchmark sets.

References

1. IEEE standard for floating-point arithmetic. IEEE Std 754-2008, pp. 1–70, August 2008. https://doi.org/10.1109/IEEESTD.2008.4610935
2. AdaCore: CodePeer. https://www.adacore.com/codepeer
3. Altran, AdaCore: SPARK 2014. https://adacore.com/sparkpro
4. Bagnara, R., Carlier, M., Gori, R., Gotlieb, A.: Filtering floating-point constraints by maximum ULP (2013). https://arxiv.org/abs/1308.3847v1
5. Barr, E.T., Vo, T., Le, V., Su, Z.: Automatic detection of floating-point exceptions. In: Proceedings of the 40th Annual ACM SIGPLAN-SIGACT Symposium on Principles of Programming Languages, POPL 2013, pp. 549–560. ACM, New York (2013). https://doi.org/10.1145/2429069.2429133

---

[14] SymFPU (as it is used in CVC4) is an eager bit-blasting approach. These were first published in 2006, predating all approaches except some interval techniques.

6. Barrett, C., et al.: CVC4. In: Gopalakrishnan, G., Qadeer, S. (eds.) CAV 2011. LNCS, vol. 6806, pp. 171–177. Springer, Heidelberg (2011). https://doi.org/10.1007/978-3-642-22110-1_14

7. Beyer, D.: SV-COMP. https://github.com/sosy-lab/sv-benchmarks

8. Blanchet, B., et al.: A static analyzer for large safety-critical software. In: Proceedings of the ACM SIGPLAN 2003 Conference on Programming Language Design and Implementation, PLDI 2003, pp. 196–207. ACM, New York (2003). https://doi.org/10.1145/781131.781153

9. Bobot, F., Filliâtre, J.C., Marché, C., Paskevich, A.: Why3: shepherd your herd of provers. In: Boogie 2011: First International Workshop on Intermediate Verification Languages, pp. 53–64. Wroclaw, Poland (2011). https://hal.inria.fr/hal-00790310

10. Brain, M., De Vos, M.: The significance of memory costs in answer set solver implementation. J. Logic Comput. **19**(4), 615–641 (2008). https://doi.org/10.1093/logcom/exn038

11. Brain, M., D'Silva, V., Griggio, A., Haller, L., Kroening, D.: Deciding floating-point logic with abstract conflict driven clause learning. Formal Methods Syst. Des. **45**(2), 213–245 (2014). https://doi.org/10.1007/s10703-013-0203-7

12. Brain, M., Hadarean, L., Kroening, D., Martins, R.: Automatic generation of propagation complete SAT encodings. In: Jobstmann, B., Leino, K.R.M. (eds.) VMCAI 2016. LNCS, vol. 9583, pp. 536–556. Springer, Heidelberg (2016). https://doi.org/10.1007/978-3-662-49122-5_26

13. Brain, M., Tinelli, C.: SMT-LIB floating-point theory, April 2015. http://smtlib.cs.uiowa.edu/theories-FloatingPoint.shtml

14. Brain, M., Tinelli, C., Rümmer, P., Wahl, T.: An automatable formal semantics for IEEE-754, June 2015. http://smtlib.cs.uiowa.edu/papers/BTRW15.pdf

15. Brillout, A., Kroening, D., Wahl, T.: Mixed abstractions for floating-point arithmetic. In: FMCAD, pp. 69–76. IEEE (2009). https://doi.org/10.1109/FMCAD.2009.5351141

16. Cimatti, A., Griggio, A., Schaafsma, B.J., Sebastiani, R.: The MathSAT5 SMT solver. In: Piterman, N., Smolka, S.A. (eds.) TACAS 2013. LNCS, vol. 7795, pp. 93–107. Springer, Heidelberg (2013). https://doi.org/10.1007/978-3-642-36742-7_7

17. Clarke, E., Kroening, D., Lerda, F.: A tool for checking ANSI-C programs. In: Jensen, K., Podelski, A. (eds.) TACAS 2004. LNCS, vol. 2988, pp. 168–176. Springer, Heidelberg (2004). https://doi.org/10.1007/978-3-540-24730-2_15

18. Collingbourne, P., Cadar, C., Kelly, P.H.: Symbolic crosschecking of floating-point and SIMD code. In: Proceedings of the Sixth Conference on Computer Systems, EuroSys 2011, pp. 315–328. ACM, New York (2011). https://doi.org/10.1145/1966445.1966475

19. Conchon, S., Iguernlala, M., Ji, K., Melquiond, G., Fumex, C.: A three-tier strategy for reasoning about floating-point numbers in SMT. In: Majumdar, R., Kunčak, V. (eds.) CAV 2017. LNCS, vol. 10427, pp. 419–435. Springer, Cham (2017). https://doi.org/10.1007/978-3-319-63390-9_22

20. Conchon, S., Melquiond, G., Roux, C., Iguernelala, M.: Built-in treatment of an axiomatic floating-point theory for SMT solvers. In: Fontaine, P., Goel, A. (eds.) 10th International Workshop on Satisfiability Modulo Theories, pp. 12–21. Manchester, United Kingdom, June 2012. https://hal.inria.fr/hal-01785166

21. Damouche, N., Martel, M., Panchekha, P., Qiu, C., Sanchez-Stern, A., Tatlock, Z.: Toward a standard benchmark format and suite for floating-point analysis. In: Bogomolov, S., Martel, M., Prabhakar, P. (eds.) NSV 2016. LNCS, vol. 10152, pp. 63–77. Springer, Cham (2017). https://doi.org/10.1007/978-3-319-54292-8_6

22. Darulova, E., Kuncak, V.: Sound compilation of reals. In: Proceedings of the 41st ACM SIGPLAN-SIGACT Symposium on Principles of Programming Languages, POPL 2014, pp. 235–248. ACM, New York (2014). https://doi.org/10.1145/2535838.2535874

23. Daumas, M., Melquiond, G.: Certification of bounds on expressions involving rounded operators. ACM Trans. Math. Softw. **37**(1), 2:1–2:20 (2010). https://doi.org/10.1145/1644001.1644003

24. de Moura, L., Bjørner, N.: Z3: an efficient SMT solver. In: Ramakrishnan, C.R., Rehof, J. (eds.) TACAS 2008. LNCS, vol. 4963, pp. 337–340. Springer, Heidelberg (2008). https://doi.org/10.1007/978-3-540-78800-3_24

25. de Moura, L., Jovanović, D.: A model-constructing satisfiability calculus. In: Giacobazzi, R., Berdine, J., Mastroeni, I. (eds.) VMCAI 2013. LNCS, vol. 7737, pp. 1–12. Springer, Heidelberg (2013). https://doi.org/10.1007/978-3-642-35873-9_1

26. D'Silva, V., Haller, L., Kroening, D.: Abstract conflict driven learning. In: Proceedings of the 40th Annual ACM SIGPLAN-SIGACT Symposium on Principles of Programming Languages, POPL 2013, pp. 143–154. ACM, New York (2013). https://doi.org/10.1145/2429069.2429087

27. D'Silva, V., Haller, L., Kroening, D., Tautschnig, M.: Numeric bounds analysis with conflict-driven learning. In: Flanagan, C., König, B. (eds.) TACAS 2012. LNCS, vol. 7214, pp. 48–63. Springer, Heidelberg (2012). https://doi.org/10.1007/978-3-642-28756-5_5

28. Fu, Z., Su, Z.: XSat: a fast floating-point satisfiability solver. In: Chaudhuri, S., Farzan, A. (eds.) CAV 2016. LNCS, vol. 9780, pp. 187–209. Springer, Cham (2016). https://doi.org/10.1007/978-3-319-41540-6_11

29. Ganzinger, H., Hagen, G., Nieuwenhuis, R., Oliveras, A., Tinelli, C.: DPLL(T): fast decision procedures. In: Alur, R., Peled, D.A. (eds.) CAV 2004. LNCS, vol. 3114, pp. 175–188. Springer, Heidelberg (2004). https://doi.org/10.1007/978-3-540-27813-9_14

30. Gao, S., Kong, S., Clarke, E.M.: dReal: an SMT solver for nonlinear theories over the reals. In: Bonacina, M.P. (ed.) CADE 2013. LNCS (LNAI), vol. 7898, pp. 208–214. Springer, Heidelberg (2013). https://doi.org/10.1007/978-3-642-38574-2_14

31. Goubault, E., Putot, S.: Static analysis of numerical algorithms. In: Yi, K. (ed.) SAS 2006. LNCS, vol. 4134, pp. 18–34. Springer, Heidelberg (2006). https://doi.org/10.1007/11823230_3

32. Hadarean, L., Bansal, K., Jovanović, D., Barrett, C., Tinelli, C.: A tale of two solvers: eager and lazy approaches to bit-vectors. In: Biere, A., Bloem, R. (eds.) CAV 2014. LNCS, vol. 8559, pp. 680–695. Springer, Cham (2014). https://doi.org/10.1007/978-3-319-08867-9_45

33. Hanrot, G., Zimmermann, P., Lefèvre, V., Pèlissier, P., Thèveny, P., et al.: The GNU MPFR Library. http://www.mpfr.org

34. Hauser, J.R.: SoftFloat. http://www.jhauser.us/arithmetic/SoftFloat.html

35. ISO/IEC JTC 1/SC 22/WG 9 Ada Rapporteur Group: Ada reference manual. ISO/IEC 8652:2012/Cor.1:2016 (2016). http://www.ada-auth.org/standards/rm12_w_tc1/html/RM-TOC.html

36. Izycheva, A., Darulova, E.: On sound relative error bounds for floating-point arithmetic. In: Proceedings of the 17th Conference on Formal Methods in Computer-Aided Design, FMCAD 2017, pp. 15–22. FMCAD Inc, Austin, TX (2017). http://dl.acm.org/citation.cfm?id=3168451.3168462

37. Jovanović, D., de Moura, L.: Solving non-linear arithmetic. In: Gramlich, B., Miller, D., Sattler, U. (eds.) IJCAR 2012. LNCS (LNAI), vol. 7364, pp. 339–354. Springer, Heidelberg (2012). https://doi.org/10.1007/978-3-642-31365-3_27

38. Khadra, M.A.B., Stoffel, D., Kunz, W.: goSAT: floating-point satisfiability as global optimization. In: Formal Methods in Computer Aided Design, FMCAD 2017, pp. 11–14. IEEE (2017). https://doi.org/10.23919/FMCAD.2017.8102235
39. Lapschies, F.: SONOLAR the solver for non-linear arithmetic (2014). http://www.informatik.uni-bremen.de/agbs/florian/sonolar
40. Liew, D.: JFS: JIT fuzzing solver. https://github.com/delcypher/jfs
41. Liew, D., Schemmel, D., Cadar, C., Donaldson, A.F., Zähl, R., Wehrle, K.: Floating-point symbolic execution: a case study in n-version programming, pp. 601–612. IEEE, October 2017. https://doi.org/10.1109/ASE.2017.8115670
42. Marre, B., Bobot, F., Chihani, Z.: Real behavior of floating point numbers. In: SMT Workshop (2017). http://smt-workshop.cs.uiowa.edu/2017/papers/SMT2017_paper_21.pdf
43. Michel, C., Rueher, M., Lebbah, Y.: Solving constraints over floating-point numbers. In: Walsh, T. (ed.) CP 2001. LNCS, vol. 2239, pp. 524–538. Springer, Heidelberg (2001). https://doi.org/10.1007/3-540-45578-7_36
44. Mueller, S.M., Paul, W.J.: Computer Architecture: Complexity and Correctness. Springer, Heidelberg (2000). https://doi.org/10.1007/978-3-662-04267-0
45. Muller, J.M., et al.: Handbook of Floating-Point Arithmetic. Birkhäuser (2009). https://doi.org/10.1007/978-0-8176-4705-6
46. Neubauer, F., et al.: Accurate dead code detection in embedded C code by arithmetic constraint solving. In: Ábrahám, E., Davenport, J.H., Fontaine, P. (eds.) Proceedings of the 1st Workshop on Satisfiability Checking and Symbolic Computation. CEUR, vol. 1804, pp. 32–38, September 2016. http://ceur-ws.org/Vol-1804/paper-07.pdf
47. Pelleau, M., Miné, A., Truchet, C., Benhamou, F.: A constraint solver based on abstract domains. In: Giacobazzi, R., Berdine, J., Mastroeni, I. (eds.) VMCAI 2013. LNCS, vol. 7737, pp. 434–454. Springer, Heidelberg (2013). https://doi.org/10.1007/978-3-642-35873-9_26
48. Romano, A.: Practical floating-point tests with integer code. In: McMillan, K.L., Rival, X. (eds.) VMCAI 2014. LNCS, vol. 8318, pp. 337–356. Springer, Heidelberg (2014). https://doi.org/10.1007/978-3-642-54013-4_19
49. Schanda, F.: Python arbitrary-precision floating-point library (2017). https://www.github.com/florianschanda/pympf
50. Schanda, F., Brain, M., Wintersteiger, C., Griggio, A., et al.: SMT-LIB floating-point benchmarks, June 2017. https://github.com/florianschanda/smtlib_schanda
51. Scheibler, K., Kupferschmid, S., Becker, B.: Recent improvements in the SMT solver iSAT. In: Haubelt, C., Timmermann, D. (eds.) Methoden und Beschreibungssprachen zur Modellierung und Verifikation von Schaltungen und Systemen (MBMV), Warnemünde, Germany, pp. 231–241, 12–14 March 2013. Institut für Angewandte Mikroelektronik und Datentechnik, Fakultät für Informatik und Elektrotechnik, Universität Rostock (2013), http://www.avacs.org/fileadmin/Publikationen/Open/scheibler.mbmv2013.pdf
52. Scheibler, K., et al.: Accurate ICP-based floating-point reasoning. In: Proceedings of the 16th Conference on Formal Methods in Computer-Aided Design FMCAD 2016, pp. 177–184. FMCAD Inc, Austin, TX (2016). http://dl.acm.org/citation.cfm?id=3077629.3077660
53. Souza, M., Borges, M., d'Amorim, M., Păsăreanu, C.S.: CORAL: solving complex constraints for symbolic PathFinder. In: Bobaru, M., Havelund, K., Holzmann, G.J., Joshi, R. (eds.) NFM 2011. LNCS, vol. 6617, pp. 359–374. Springer, Heidelberg (2011). https://doi.org/10.1007/978-3-642-20398-5_26

54. The MathWorks Inc: Polyspace. https://www.mathworks.com/polyspace
55. Tung, V.X., Van Khanh, T., Ogawa, M.: raSAT: an SMT solver for polynomial constraints. Formal Methods Syst. Des. **51**(3), 462–499 (2017). https://doi.org/10.1007/s10703-017-0284-9
56. Zeljic, A., Backeman, P., Wintersteiger, C.M., Rümmer, P.: Exploring approximations for floating-point arithmetic using UppSAT. In: Automated Reasoning - 9th International Joint Conference, IJCAR 2018, Held as Part of the Federated Logic Conference, FloC 2018, Oxford, UK, 14–17 July 2018, Proceedings, pp. 246–262 (2018). https://doi.org/10.1007/978-3-319-94205-6_17
57. Zeljić, A., Wintersteiger, C.M., Rümmer, P.: Approximations for model construction. In: Demri, S., Kapur, D., Weidenbach, C. (eds.) IJCAR 2014. LNCS (LNAI), vol. 8562, pp. 344–359. Springer, Cham (2014). https://doi.org/10.1007/978-3-319-08587-6_26
58. Zeljić, A., Wintersteiger, C.M., Rümmer, P.: Deciding bit-vector formulas with mcSAT. In: Creignou, N., Le Berre, D. (eds.) SAT 2016. LNCS, vol. 9710, pp. 249–266. Springer, Cham (2016). https://doi.org/10.1007/978-3-319-40970-2_16
59. Zitoun, H., Michel, C., Rueher, M., Michel, L.: Search strategies for floating point constraint systems. In: Beck, J.C. (ed.) CP 2017. LNCS, vol. 10416, pp. 707–722. Springer, Cham (2017). https://doi.org/10.1007/978-3-319-66158-2_45

11

Decomposing Farkas Interpolants

Martin Blicha[1,2]([✉]) [ID], Antti E. J. Hyvärinen[1] [ID], Jan Kofroň[2] [ID],
and Natasha Sharygina[1] [ID]

[1] Università della Svizzera italiana (USI), Lugano, Switzerland
{martin.blicha,antti.hyvaerinen,natasha.sharygina}@usi.ch
[2] Faculty of Mathematics and Physics, Charles University, Prague, Czech Republic
{martin.blicha,jan.kofron}@d3s.mff.cuni.cz

Abstract. Modern verification commonly models software with Boolean logic and a system of linear inequalities over reals and over-approximates the reachable states of the model with Craig interpolation to obtain, for example, candidates for inductive invariants. Interpolants for the linear system can be efficiently constructed from a Simplex refutation by applying the Farkas' lemma. However, Farkas interpolants do not always suit the verification task and in the worst case they may even be the cause of divergence of the verification algorithm. This work introduces the decomposed interpolants, a fundamental extension of the Farkas interpolants obtained by identifying and separating independent components from the interpolant structure using methods from linear algebra. We integrate our approach to the model checker Sally and show experimentally that a portfolio of decomposed interpolants results in immediate convergence on instances where state-of-the-art approaches diverge. Being based on the efficient Simplex method, the approach is very competitive also outside these diverging cases.

Keywords: Model checking · Satisfiability modulo theory ·
Linear arithmetic · Craig interpolation

1 Introduction

A central task in model checking systems with respect to safety properties [27] consists of proving facts and attempting to generalize the obtained proofs. The generalizations serve as a basis for inductive invariants needed for guiding the search for a correctness proof in approaches such as IC3 [8] and k-induction [39], both known to scale to the verification of highly complex systems.

Finding good proofs and generalizing them is hard. A widely used approach, Satisfiability Modulo Theories (SMT) [7,13], models a system with propositional logic and a range of first-order logics. Solvers for SMT combine a resolution-based variant of the DPLL-algorithm [11,12,40] for propositional logic with decision procedures for first-order logics. A vast range of first-order logics is maintained as part of the SMT-LIB Initiative [6]. What is common to these logics is that their solving requires typically only a handful of algorithms. Arguably, the two most important algorithms are a congruence closure algorithm for deciding quantifier-free equality logic with uninterpreted functions [31], and a Simplex-based procedure for linear arithmetic over real or rational numbers [16].

Generalizing proofs to inductive invariants is commonly done by Craig interpolation [10]. Here, the model is split into two parts, say, A and B, resulting in an *interpolation problem* (A, B). The proof of unsatisfiability for $A \wedge B$ is used to extract an *interpolant I*, a formula that is defined over the common symbols of A and B, is implied by A, and is unsatisfiable with B. Several interpolants can be computed for a given interpolation problem, and not all of them are useful for proving safety. Typically, this is a phenomenon used to construct a *portfolio* [20] of interpolation algorithms that is then applied in the hopes of aiding to find the safety proof.

The approaches to interpolation based on Farkas' lemma construct an LRA interpolant by summing all inequalities appearing in A into a single inequality. We call the resulting interpolant the *Farkas interpolant*. While a single inequality is desirable in some cases, it prevents IC3-style algorithms from converging in other ones [36]. We present how methods from linear algebra can be applied on a Farkas interpolant to obtain *decomposed interpolants* that do not consist of a single inequality and guarantee the convergence of the model-checking algorithm for some of the cases where Farkas interpolants do not converge. A major advantage of decomposed interpolants is that they can be computed using Simplex-based decision procedures as a black box, allowing us to make use of the highly tuned implementations present in many state-of-the-art SMT solvers.

Intuitively, while computing the decomposed interpolants we do not directly sum the inequalities in A, but, instead, we split the sum into sub-sums. The result is an interpolant that is a conjunction of often more than one component of the Farkas interpolant. This allows us not only to solve the convergence problem observed in model checking examples, but also to gain more control over the strength of LRA interpolants. In summary, the main contributions of this paper are

1. a new Farkas-lemma-based interpolation algorithm for LRA that is able to deal with convergence problems in model-checking benchmarks while still relying on a highly efficient Simplex-based decision procedure,
2. establishing properties regarding logical strength of interpolants produced by our interpolation algorithm with respect to the original Farkas interpolants,
3. implementation of our new interpolation algorithm in OPENSMT, our SMT solver, and integration of our approach with the model checker SALLY
4. experiments showing that the new approach is efficient in model checking, in particular in showing systems unsafe.

While the underlying intuition is simple, we quote here Jean D'Alembert (1717–1783) in saying that *Algebra is generous; she often gives more than is asked of her*: Our detailed analysis in Sects. 4 and 5 shows that the structure of the problem is surprisingly rich. Our experiments in Sect. 6 verify that the phenomena are practically relevant. Overall a portfolio constructed from our interpolation algorithm is significantly better than a portfolio based purely on Farkas interpolants. We furthermore show for individual instances that the effect is consistent instead of arising from random effects.

Related Work. The work on interpolation in LRA dates back to [32]. A compact set of rules for deriving LRA interpolants from the proof of unsatisfiability in an inference system was presented in [29]. The interpolants in these works were the Farkas interpolants. Current methods usually compute Farkas interpolants from explanations of unsatisfiability extracted directly from the Simplex-based decision procedure inside the SMT solver [16]. Recently in [3], we presented a way of computing an infinite family of interpolants between a primal and a dual interpolant with variable strength. However, those interpolants are still restricted to single inequalities.

The work most closely related to ours is [36] where the authors independently recognized the weakness of interpolation based on Farkas coefficients. They introduce a new interpolation procedure that gives guarantees of convergence of a special sequence of interpolation problems often occurring in model checking problems. However, this interpolation algorithm is based on a different decision procedure, called conflict resolution [26], which, based on the results reported in [36], is not as efficient as the Simplex-based decision procedure. In contrast, we show how the original approach based on the Simplex-based decision procedure and Farkas coefficients can be modified to produce interpolants not restricted to the single-inequality form, while additionally obtaining strength guarantees with respect to the original Farkas interpolants.

Other work on LRA interpolants include e.g. [1, 35, 37]. Both [1] and [37] focus on producing simple overall interpolants by attempting to reuse (partial) interpolants from pure LRA conflicts. Our focus is not on the overall interpolant, but on a single LRA conflict. However, in the context of interpolants from proofs produced by SMT solvers, our approach also has a potential for re-using components of interpolants for LRA conflicts across the whole proof. Beside algorithms for interpolants for LRA conflicts, there exist a large body of work on propositional interpolation [2, 14, 19, 23].

The structure of the paper is as follows. In Sect. 2 we provide a concrete example model-checking problem where our approach guarantees immediate convergence but Farkas interpolation diverges. In Sect. 3 we define the notation used in the paper, and in Sects. 4 and 5 detail our main theoretical contribution. We provide experimental results in Sect. 6, and finally conclude in Sect. 7.

2   Motivation

Consider the transition system $S = (I, T, Err)$, where I and Err are, respectively, predicates that capture the initial and error states, and T is the transition function. The symbols x, y are real variables, and x', y' are their next-state versions.[1]

$$S = \begin{cases} I \equiv (x = 0) \wedge (y = 0), \\ T \equiv (x' = x + y) \wedge (y' = y + 1), \\ Err \equiv (x < 0) \end{cases} \tag{1}$$

---

[1] This example was first brought to our attention by Prof. Arie Gurfinkel. A similar example appears in [36].

The system is one variant from a family of similar transition systems that are known to not converge in straightforward implementations of IC3-based algorithms using LRA interpolation. For example, both SPACER [25] (using interpolation algorithm of Z3 [30]) and SALLY [24] (using interpolation algorithm of MathSAT [9]) fail to compute a safe inductive invariant for this transition system. However, SALLY with our interpolation algorithm succeeds in computing the safe inductive invariant.[2] Closer examination of SALLY and SPACER reveals that the tools in their default configurations produce a divergent series of candidate invariants of the form $0 \leq kx + y$ for $k = 1, 2, 3, \ldots$. The reason for producing such a series is that both tools rely on Farkas interpolants that always consist of a single inequality. Instead of generalizing the Farkas interpolants, an approach advocated in this work, interpolation based on a different decision procedure was proposed for SALLY in [36], whereas SEAHORN [18] with SPACER as its underlying reasoning engine solves this issue with abstract interpretation.

In this work we show how to modify the interpolation algorithm to produce in the general case a *conjunction* of multiple inequalities, leading, in this case, to the discovery of an inductive safe invariant $x \geq 0 \land y \geq 0$. To avoid here a lengthy discussion on internals of IC3 but nevertheless provide a concrete example of the power of decomposed interpolants, we apply decomposed interpolants in a simple, interpolation-based procedure for computing inductive invariants for transition systems. This approach is a simplified version of k-induction (see, e.g., [28]). When applied to the system in Eq. (1), we show that computing the Farkas interpolant fails and decomposed interpolant succeeds in producing a safe inductive invariant. A safe, inductive invariant for (I, T, Err) is a predicate R that satisfies (1) $I(X) \rightarrow R(X)$, (2) $R(X) \land T(X, X') \rightarrow R(X)$, and (3) $R(X) \land Err(X) \rightarrow \bot$. We may opportunistically try to synthesise R by interpolating over the interpolation problem $(I(X), T(X, X') \land Err(X'))$. Using the system S of Eq. (1), we obtain $(x \geq 0 \land y \geq 0, x' = x + y \land y' = y + 1 \land x' < 0)$. A Farkas interpolant, the sum of the components from the A-part, is $x + y \geq 0$, which is neither safe nor inductive for S. However, the *decomposed interpolant* $x \geq 0 \land y \geq 0$ is an inductive invariant.

3   Preliminaries

We work in the domain of *Satisfiability Modulo Theories* (SMT) [7,13], where satisfiability of formulas is determined with respect to some background theory. In particular, we are concerned with the *lazy* approach to SMT, that combines SAT solver dealing with the propositional structure of a formula and *theory* solver for checking consistency of a conjunction of theory literals. The proof of unsatisfiability in this approach is basically a propositional proof that incorporates *theory lemmas* learnt by the theory solver and propagated to the SAT solver.

---

[2] Current implementation of SPACER does not support conjunctions of inequalities as interpolants, and therefore we are at the moment unable to try our approach on SPACER.

The proof-based interpolation algorithm then combines any propositional-proof-based interpolation algorithm with *theory interpolator*. Theory interpolator provides an interpolant for each theory conflict—an unsatisfiable conjunction of theory literals.

Linear Arithmetic and Linear Algebra. We use the letters x, y, z to denote variables and c, k to denote constants. Vector of n variables is denoted by $\mathbf{x} = (x_1, \ldots, x_n)^\mathsf{T}$ where n is usually known from context. $\mathbf{x}[i]$ denotes the element of $\mathbf{x}$ at position i, i.e. $\mathbf{x}[i] = x_i$. The vector of all zeroes is denoted as $\mathbf{0}$ and $\mathbf{e_i}$ denotes the unit vector with $\mathbf{e_i}[i] = 1$ and $\mathbf{e_i}[j] = 0$ for $j \neq i$. For two vectors $\mathbf{x} = (x_1, \ldots, x_n)^\mathsf{T}$ and $\mathbf{y} = (y_1, \ldots, y_n)^\mathsf{T}$ we say that $\mathbf{x} \leq \mathbf{y}$ iff $x_i \leq y_i$ for each $i \in \{1, \ldots, n\}$. $\mathbb{Q}$ denotes the set of rational numbers, $\mathbb{Q}^n$ the n-dimensional vector space of rational numbers and $\mathbb{Q}^{m \times n}$ the set of rational matrices with m rows and n columns. A transpose of matrix M is denoted as M^T. A kernel (also nullspace) of a matrix M is the vector space $ker(M) = \{\mathbf{x} \mid M\mathbf{x} = \mathbf{0}\}$.

We adopt the notation of matrix product for linear arithmetic. For a linear term $l = c_1 x_1 + \cdots + c_n x_n$, we write $\mathbf{c}^\mathsf{T}\mathbf{x}$ to denote l. Without loss of generality we assume that all linear inequalities are of the form $\mathbf{c}^\mathsf{T}\mathbf{x} \bowtie c$ with $\bowtie \in \{\leq, <\}$. By linear system over variables $\mathbf{x}$ we mean a finite set of linear inequalities $S = \{C_i \mid i = 1, \ldots, m\}$, where each C_i is a linear inequality over $\mathbf{x}$. Note that from the logical perspective, each C_i is an atom in the language of the theory of linear arithmetic, thus system S can be expressed as a formula $\bigwedge_{i=1}^{m} C_i$ and we use these representations interchangeably. A linear system is satisfiable if there exists an evaluation of variables that satisfies all inequalities; otherwise, it is unsatisfiable. This is the same as the (un)satisfiability of the formula representing the system.

We extend the matrix notation also to the whole linear system. For the sake of simplicity we use $\leq$ instead of $\bowtie$, even if the system contains a mix of strict and non-strict inequalities. The only important difference is that a (weighted) sum of a linear system (as defined below) results in a strict inequality, instead of a non-strict one, when at least one strict inequality is present in the sum with a non-zero coefficient. The theory, proofs and algorithm remain valid also in the presence of strict inequalities. We write $C\mathbf{x} \leq \mathbf{c}$ to denote the linear system S where C denotes the matrix of all coefficients of the system, $\mathbf{x}$ are the variables and $\mathbf{c}$ is the vector of the right sides of the inequalities. With the matrix notation, we can easily express the sum of (multiples) of inequalities. Given a system of inequalities $C\mathbf{x} \leq \mathbf{c}$ and a vector of "weights" (multiples) of the inequalities $\mathbf{k} \geq \mathbf{0}$, the inequality that is the (weighted) sum of the system can be expressed as $\mathbf{k}^\mathsf{T} C\mathbf{x} \leq \mathbf{k}^\mathsf{T}\mathbf{c}$.

Craig Interpolation. Given two formulas $A(\mathbf{x}, \mathbf{y})$ and $B(\mathbf{y}, \mathbf{z})$ such that $A \wedge B$ is unsatisfiable, a *Craig interpolant* [10] is a formula $I(\mathbf{y})$ such that $A \implies I$ and $I \implies \neg B$.

The pair of formulas (A, B) is also referred to as an *interpolation problem*. In linear arithmetic, the interpolation problem is a linear system S partitioned into two parts: A and B.

One way to compute a solution to an interpolation problem in linear arithmetic, used in many modern SMT solvers, is based on Farkas' lemma [17,38]. Farkas' lemma states that for an unsatisfiable system of linear inequalities $S \equiv C\mathbf{x} \leq \mathbf{c}$ there exist *Farkas* coefficients $\mathbf{k} \geq \mathbf{0}$ such that $\mathbf{k}^\mathsf{T} C\mathbf{x} \leq \mathbf{k}^\mathsf{T}\mathbf{c} \equiv 0 \leq -1$. In other words, the weighted sum of the system given by the Farkas coefficients is a contradictory inequality. If a strict inequality is part of the sum, the result might also be $0 < 0$.

The idea behind the interpolation algorithm based on Farkas coefficients is simple. Intuitively, given the partition of the linear system into A and B, we compute only the weighted sum of A. It is not hard to see that this sum is an interpolant. It follows from A because a weighted sum of a linear system with non-negative weights is always implied by the system. It is inconsistent with B because its sum with the weighted sum of B (using Farkas coefficients) is a contradictory inequality by Farkas lemma. Finally, it cannot contain any A-local variables, because in the weighted sum of the whole system all variables are eliminated, A-local variables are not present in B, so they must be eliminated already in the weighted sum of A.

More formally, for an unsatisfiable linear system $S \equiv C\mathbf{x} \leq \mathbf{c}$ over n variables, where $C \in \mathbb{Q}^{m \times n}, \mathbf{c} \in \mathbb{Q}^m$, and its partition to $A \equiv C_A\mathbf{x} \leq \mathbf{c_A}$ and $B \equiv C_B\mathbf{x} \leq \mathbf{c_B}$, where $C_A \in \mathbb{Q}^{k \times n}$, $C_B \in \mathbb{Q}^{l \times n}$, $\mathbf{c_A} \in \mathbb{Q}^k$, $\mathbf{c_B} \in \mathbb{Q}^l$ and $k + l = m$, there exist Farkas coefficients $\mathbf{k}^\mathsf{T} = (\mathbf{k_A^\mathsf{T}} \ \mathbf{k_B^\mathsf{T}})$ such that

$$(\mathbf{k_A^\mathsf{T}} \ \mathbf{k_B^\mathsf{T}}) \begin{pmatrix} C_A \\ C_B \end{pmatrix} = 0, (\mathbf{k_A^\mathsf{T}} \ \mathbf{k_B^\mathsf{T}}) \begin{pmatrix} \mathbf{c_A} \\ \mathbf{c_B} \end{pmatrix} = -1,$$

and the *Farkas interpolant* for (A, B) is the inequality

$$I^f \equiv \mathbf{k_A^\mathsf{T}} C_A\mathbf{x} \leq \mathbf{k_A^\mathsf{T}}\mathbf{c_A} \tag{2}$$

4 Decomposed Interpolants

In this section, we present our new approach to computing interpolants in linear arithmetic based on Farkas coefficients. The definition of Farkas interpolant of Eq. (2) corresponds to the weighted sum of A-part of the unsatisfiable linear system. This sum can be decomposed into j sums by decomposing the vector $\mathbf{k_A}$ into j vectors

$$\mathbf{k_A} = \sum_{i=1}^{j} \mathbf{k_{A,i}} \tag{3}$$

such that $\mathbf{0} \leq \mathbf{k_{A,i}} \leq \mathbf{k_A}$ for all i, thus obtaining j inequalities

$$I_i \equiv \mathbf{k_{A,i}^\mathsf{T}} C_A\mathbf{x} \leq \mathbf{k_{A,i}^\mathsf{T}}\mathbf{c_A} \tag{4}$$

If $\mathbf{k_{A,i}}$ are such that the left-hand side of the inequalities I_i contains only shared variables, the decomposition has an interesting application in interpolation, as illustrated below.

Definition 1 (decomposed interpolants). *Given an interpolation instance* (A, B)*, if there exists a sum of the form Eq. (3) such that the left side of Eq. (4) contains only shared variables for all* $1 \leq i \leq j$*, then the set of inequalities* $S = \{I_1, \ldots, I_j\}$ *is a* decomposition. *In that case the formula* $\bigwedge_{i=1}^{j} I_i$ *is a* decomposed interpolant *(DI) of size* j *for* (A, B).

The decomposed interpolants are proper interpolants, as stated in the following theorem.

Theorem 1. *Let* (A, B) *be an interpolation problem in linear arithmetic. If* $S = \{I_1, \ldots, I_k\}$ *is a decomposition, then* $I^{DI} = I_1 \wedge \ldots \wedge I_k$ *is an interpolant for* (A, B).

Proof. Let $I^{DI} = I_1 \wedge \ldots \wedge I_k$. First, $A \implies I^{DI}$ holds since for all I_i, $A \implies I_i$. This is immediate from the fact that A is a system of linear inequalities $C_A \mathbf{x} \leq \mathbf{c_A}$, $I_i \equiv \mathbf{k_{A,i}^T} C_A \mathbf{x} \leq \mathbf{k_{A,i}^T} \mathbf{c_A}$ and $0 \leq \mathbf{k_{A,i}}$. Second, $I^{DI} \wedge B \implies \bot$ since I^{DI} implies Farkas interpolant I^f. This holds because $\mathbf{k_A} = \sum_i \mathbf{k_{A,i}}$ and $0 \leq \mathbf{k_{A,i}}$. Third, I^{DI} contains only shared variables by the definition of decomposition (Definition 1). Therefore, I^{DI} is an interpolant. $\square$

Each interpolation instance has a *DI* of size one, a *trivial* decomposition, corresponding to the Farkas interpolant of Eq. (2). However, interpolation problems in general can admit bigger decompositions. In the following we give a concrete example of an instance with decomposition of size two.

Example 1. Let (A, B) be an interpolation problem in linear arithmetic with $A = (x_1 + x_2 \leq 0) \wedge (x_1 + x_3 \leq 0) \wedge (-x_1 \leq 0)$ and $B = (-x_2 - x_3 \leq -1)$. The linear systems corresponding to A and B are

$$C_A = \begin{pmatrix} 1 & 1 & 0 \\ 1 & 0 & 1 \\ -1 & 0 & 0 \end{pmatrix}, \quad \mathbf{c_A} = \begin{pmatrix} 0 \\ 0 \\ 0 \end{pmatrix}, \quad \text{and} \quad C_B = \begin{pmatrix} 0 & -1 & -1 \end{pmatrix}, \quad \mathbf{c_B} = \begin{pmatrix} -1 \end{pmatrix}.$$

Farkas coefficients are

$$\mathbf{k_A^T} = \begin{pmatrix} 1 & 1 & 2 \end{pmatrix} \text{ and } \mathbf{k_B^T} = \begin{pmatrix} 1 \end{pmatrix},$$

while Farkas interpolant for (A, B) is the inequality $I^f \equiv x_2 + x_3 \leq 0$. However, if we decompose $\mathbf{k_A}$ into

$$\mathbf{k_{A,1}^T} = \begin{pmatrix} 1 & 0 & 1 \end{pmatrix} \text{ and } \mathbf{k_{A,2}^T} = \begin{pmatrix} 0 & 1 & 1 \end{pmatrix},$$

we obtain the decomposition $\{x_2 \leq 0, x_3 \leq 0\}$ corresponding to the decomposed interpolant $I^{DI} \equiv x_2 \leq 0 \wedge x_3 \leq 0$ of size two.

4.1 Strength-Based Ordering of Decompositions

Decomposition of Farkas coefficients for a single interpolation problem is in general not unique. However, we can provide some structure to the space of possible interpolants by ordering interpolants with respect to their logical strength. To achieve this, we define the *coarseness* of a decomposition based on its ability to partition the terms of the interpolant into finer sums, and then prove that coarseness provides us with a way of measuring the interpolant strength.

Definition 2. *Let D_1, D_2 denote two decompositions of the same interpolation problem of size m, n, respectively, where $n < m$. Let $(\mathbf{q_1}, \ldots, \mathbf{q_m})$ denote the decomposition of Farkas coefficients corresponding to D_1 and let $(\mathbf{r_1}, \ldots, \mathbf{r_n})$ denote the decomposition of Farkas coefficients corresponding to D_2. We say that decomposition D_1 is finer than D_2 (or equivalently D_2 is coarser than D_1) and denote this as $D_1 \prec D_2$ when there exists a partition $P = \{p_1, \ldots, p_n\}$ of the set $\{\mathbf{q_1}, \ldots, \mathbf{q_m}\}$ such that for each i with $1 \le i \le n$, $\mathbf{r_i} = \sum_{\mathbf{q} \in p_i} \mathbf{q}$.*

Interpolants of decompositions ordered by their coarseness can be ordered by logical strength, as stated by the following lemma:

Lemma 1. *Assume D_1, D_2 are two decompositions of the same interpolation problem such that $D_1 \prec D_2$. Let I^{D_1}, I^{D_2} be the decomposed interpolants corresponding to D_1, D_2. Then I^{D_1} implies I^{D_2}.*

Proof. Informally, the implication follows from the fact that each linear inequality of I^{D_2} is a sum of some inequalities in I^{D_1}.

Formally, let I_i denote the i-th inequality in I^{D_2}. Then $I_i \equiv \mathbf{r_i}^\mathsf{T} C_A \mathbf{x} \le \mathbf{r_i}^\mathsf{T} \mathbf{c_A}$. Since $D_1 \prec D_2$, there is a set $\{I_{i_1}, \ldots, I_{i_j}\} \subseteq D_1$ such that for each k with $1 \le k \le j$, $I_{i_k} \equiv \mathbf{q_{i_k}}^\mathsf{T} C_A \mathbf{x} \le \mathbf{q_{i_k}}^\mathsf{T} \mathbf{c_A}$ and $\mathbf{r_i} = \sum_{k=1}^{j} \mathbf{q_{i_k}}$.

Since $\mathbf{q_{i_k}} \ge \mathbf{0}$, it holds that $I_{i_1} \wedge \cdots \wedge I_{i_j} \implies I_i$. This means that I^{D_1} implies every conjunct of I^{D_2}. $\square$

Note that the trivial, single-element decomposition corresponding to Farkas interpolant is the greatest element of this decomposition ordering. Also, for any decomposition of size more than one, replacing any number of elements by their sum yields a coarser decomposition. A possible reason to use a coarser decomposition may be that summing up some of the elements of a decomposition may result in eliminating a shared variable from the decomposition.

4.2 Strength of the Dual Interpolants

Let *Itp* denote an interpolation procedure and let $Itp(A, B)$ stand for the interpolant computed by *Itp* for an interpolation problem (A, B). Then by Itp' we denote the *dual* interpolation procedure, which works as follows: $Itp'(A, B) = \neg Itp(B, A)$. The duality theorem for interpolation states that Itp' is correct interpolation procedure. This can be shown by verifying that the three interpolation conditions hold for $Itp'(A, B)$, given they hold for $Itp(B, A)$.

Let us denote the interpolation procedure based on Farkas' lemma as Itp_F and the interpolation procedure computing decomposed interpolants as Itp_{DI}. The relation between Itp_F and its dual Itp'_F has been established in [3], namely that $Itp_F(A, B) \implies Itp'_F(A, B)$. We have shown in Lemma 1 that decomposed interpolant always implies Farkas interpolant computed from the same Farkas coefficients. This means that $Itp_{DI}(A, B) \implies Itp_F(A, B)$.

We can use this result to establish similar result for the dual interpolation procedures. Since $Itp_{DI}(B, A) \implies Itp_F(B, A)$, it follows that $\neg Itp_F(B, A) \implies \neg Itp_{DI}(B, A)$ and consequently $Itp'_F(A, B) \implies Itp'_{DI}(A, B)$.

Putting all the results on logical strength together, we obtain

$$Itp_{DI}(A, B) \implies Itp_F(A, B) \implies Itp'_F(A, B) \implies Itp'_{DI}(A, B).$$

Note that while both Itp_F and Itp'_F produce interpolants which are a single inequality and interpolants produced by Itp_{DI} are *conjunctions* of inequalities, interpolants produced by Itp'_{DI} are *disjunctions* of inequalities.

In the following section, we describe the details of the Itp_{DI} interpolation procedure.

5 Finding Decompositions

In this section we present our approach for finding decompositions for linear arithmetic interpolation problems given their Farkas coefficients.

We focus on the task of finding decomposition of $k_A^\mathsf{T} C_A x$. Recall that $C_A \in \mathbb{Q}^{l \times n}$ and x is a vector of variables of length n. Without loss of generality assume that there are no B-local variables since columns of C_A corresponding to B-local variables would contain all zeroes by definition in any case.

Furthermore, without loss of generality, assume the variables in the inequalities of A are ordered such that all A-local variables are before the shared ones. Then let us write

$$C_A = \begin{pmatrix} L & S \end{pmatrix}, \quad x^\mathsf{T} = \begin{pmatrix} x_L^\mathsf{T} & x_S^\mathsf{T} \end{pmatrix} \tag{5}$$

with x_L the vector of A-local variables of size p, x_S the vector of shared variables of size q, $n = p + q$, $L \in \mathbb{Q}^{l \times p}$ and $S \in \mathbb{Q}^{l \times q}$. We know that $k_A^\mathsf{T} L = 0$ and the goal is to find $k_{A,i}$ such that $\sum_i k_{A,i} = k_A$ and for each i $0 \le k_{A,i} \le k_A$ and $k_{A,i}^\mathsf{T} L = 0$.

In the following we will consider two cases for computing the decompositions. We first study a common special case where the system A contains rows with no local variables, and give a linear-time algorithm for computing the decompositions. We then move to the general case where the rows of A contain local variables, and provide a decomposition algorithm based on computing a vector basis for a null space of a matrix obtained from A.

5.1 Trivial Elements

First, consider a situation where there is a linear inequality with no local variables. This means there is a row j in C_A (denoted as C_{Aj}) such that all entries in columns corresponding to local variables are 0, i.e., $L_j = \mathbf{0}^\mathsf{T}$. Then $\{I_1, I_2\}$ for $\mathbf{k_{A,1}} = \mathbf{k_A}[j] \times \mathbf{e_j}$ and $\mathbf{k_{A,2}} = \mathbf{k_A} - \mathbf{k_{A,1}}$ is a decomposition. Intuitively, any linear inequality that contains only shared variables can form a stand-alone element of a decomposition. When looking for finest decomposition, we do this iteratively for all inequalities with no local variables. In the next part we show how to look for a non-trivial decomposition when dealing with local variables.

5.2 Decomposing in the Presence of Local Variables

For this section, assume that L has no zero rows (we have shown above how to deal with such rows). We are going to search for a non-trivial decomposition starting with the following observation:

Observation. $\mathbf{k_A^\mathsf{T}} L = 0$. Equivalently, there are no A-local variables in the Farkas interpolant. It follows that $L^\mathsf{T} \mathbf{k_A} = 0$ and $\mathbf{k_A}$ is in the *kernel* of L^T.

Let us denote by $\mathbb{K} = ker(L^\mathsf{T})$ the kernel of L^T.

Theorem 2. *Let* $\mathbf{v_1}, \ldots, \mathbf{v_n}$ *be* n *vectors from* $\mathbb{K}$ *such that* $\exists \alpha_1, \ldots, \alpha_n$ *with* $\alpha_i \mathbf{v_i} \geq \mathbf{0}$ *for all* i *and* $\mathbf{k_A} = \sum_{i=1}^{n} \alpha_i \mathbf{v_i}$. *Then* $\{\mathbf{w_1}, \ldots, \mathbf{w_n}\}$ *for* $\mathbf{w_i} = \alpha_i \mathbf{v_i}$ *is a decomposition of* $\mathbf{k_A}$ *and* $\{I_1, \ldots, I_n\}$ *for* $I_i \equiv \mathbf{w_i} C_A \mathbf{x} \leq \mathbf{c_A}$ *is a decomposition.*

Proof. The theorem follows from the definition of decomposition (Definition 1). From the assumptions of the theorem we immediately obtain $\mathbf{k_A} = \sum_{i=1}^{n} \mathbf{w_i}$ and $\mathbf{w_i} \geq \mathbf{0}$. Moreover, $\mathbf{w_i} \in \mathbb{K}$, since $\mathbf{v_i} \in \mathbb{K}$ and $\mathbf{w_i} = \alpha_i \mathbf{v_i}$. As a consequence, $L^\mathsf{T} \mathbf{w_i} = 0$ and it follows that there are no A-local variables in $\mathbf{w_i}^\mathsf{T} C_A \mathbf{x}$. $\square$

Note that if the vectors are not linearly independent then the decomposition contains redundant elements. For example, if $w_3 = w_1 + w_2$ then $I_1 \wedge I_2 \implies I_3$ and I_3 is a redundant conjunct in the corresponding decomposed interpolant.

Good candidates that satisfy most of the assumptions of Theorem 2 (and avoid redundancies) are bases of the vector space $\mathbb{K}$. If $B = \{\mathbf{b_1}, \ldots, \mathbf{b_n}\}$ is a basis of $\mathbb{K}$ such that $\mathbf{k_A} = \sum_{i=1}^{n} \alpha_i \mathbf{b_i}$ with $\alpha_i \mathbf{b_i} \geq \mathbf{0}$ for all i, then $\{\alpha_1 \mathbf{b_1}, \ldots, \alpha_n \mathbf{b_n}\}$ is a decomposition. Moreover, the decomposition generated by a basis cannot be refined (in the sense of the decomposition order $\prec$) without introducing redundancies. This follows from the fact that replacing one generator in a basis by more that one vector necessarily introduces linear dependency between the generators of the vector space. Thus, the decomposed interpolant from a basis has *maximal* logical strength. The search for a decomposition of Farkas coefficients $\mathbf{k_A}$ by computing a basis of the kernel of the matrix of A-local variables L is described in Algorithm 1.

Function `Nullity` returns the dimension of the kernel. This can be efficiently computed for example using *Rank-Nullity Theorem* by computing Row Echelon Form of M by Gaussian elimination. Only if nullity is at least 2, we can hope to find any non-trivial decomposition. Function `KernelBasis` returns a basis of the kernel of a given matrix while function `Coordinates` returns the coordinates of the given vector with respect to the given basis. An algorithm to compute a basis of the kernel of a matrix can be found in any good introductory book on Linear

---

input : matrix M, vector $\mathbf{v}$ such that $\mathbf{v} \in ker(M)$ and $\mathbf{v} > \mathbf{0}$
output: $(\mathbf{w_1}, \ldots, \mathbf{w_m})$, a decomposition of $\mathbf{v}$, such that $\mathbf{w_i} \in ker(M), \mathbf{w_i} \geq \mathbf{0}$
    and $\sum \mathbf{w_i} = \mathbf{v}$
1 $n \leftarrow \texttt{Nullity}(M)$
2 **if** $n \leq 1$ **then return** $(\mathbf{v})$
3 $(\mathbf{b_1}, \ldots, \mathbf{b_n}) \leftarrow \texttt{KernelBasis}(M)$
4 $(\alpha_1, \ldots, \alpha_n) \leftarrow \texttt{Coordinates}(\mathbf{v}, (\mathbf{b_1}, \ldots, \mathbf{b_n}))$
5 $(\mathbf{w_1}, \ldots, \mathbf{w_n}) \leftarrow (\alpha_1 \mathbf{b_1}, \ldots, \alpha_n \mathbf{b_n})$
6 **if** $\mathbf{w_i} \geq \mathbf{0}$ *for each* i **then return** $(\mathbf{w_1}, \ldots, \mathbf{w_n})$
7 **else return** $(\mathbf{v})$

Algorithm 1. Algorithm for decomposition of Farkas coefficients

Algebra, see e.g. [5]. If any component of the linear combination is negative, the combination cannot be used and we fall back to the trivial decomposition leading to the original Farkas interpolant. As a basis of a vector space is not unique, the implementation of KernelBasis may return an unsuitable basis even if a suitable one exists. This happened even in simple cases, so we implemented a strategy to replace unsuitable elements by a suitable sum of elements, if possible. Our preliminary results using this strategy are promising.

6   Experiments

We have implemented our algorithm in our SMT solver OPENSMT [21], which had already provided a variety of interpolation algorithms for propositional logic [22,33], theory of uninterpreted functions [4] and theory of linear real arithmetic [3]. We implemented both primal and dual versions of decomposed interpolation algorithm, which return the finest decomposition they can find.

We evaluated the effect of decomposed interpolants in a model-checking scenario using the model checker SALLY relying on OPENSMT for interpolation.[3] The PDKIND engine of SALLY was used, relying on YICES [15] for satisfiability queries and OPENSMT for interpolation queries. We experimented with four LRA interpolation algorithms: the original interpolation algorithms based on Farkas' lemma, Itp_F and Itp'_F, and the interpolation algorithm computing decomposed interpolants, Itp_{DI} and Itp'_{DI}. In each case, we used McMillan's interpolation rules [28] for the Boolean part. For comparison, we ran also a version of SALLY using MATHSAT in its default settings as an interpolation engine instead of OPENSMT. Since OPENSMT does not support the combination of incrementality and interpolation, MATHSAT was also used in non-incremental mode in this setting. The results are summarised in Figs. 1 and 2, and Table 1. The result of a portfolio is the virtual best of the results of individual algorithms

---

[3] Detailed description of the set-up and specifications of the experiments, together with all the results, can be found at http://verify.inf.usi.ch/content/decomposed-interpolants.

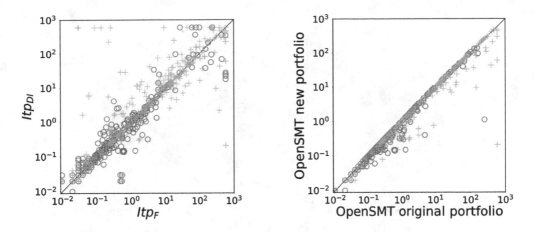

Fig. 1. Evaluation of the decomposed interpolants in model checking scenario. On the left, comparison of performance of SALLY using OPENSMT with different interpolation procedures, Itp_F and Itp_{DI}. On the right, the benefit of adding Itp_{DI} and Itp'_{DI} to the portfolio of interpolation procedures.

in the portfolio. The original portfolio of OPENSMT consists of Itp_F and Itp'_F, while in the new portfolio Itp_{DI} and Itp'_{DI} are added.

We used the same benchmarks as in [36]. They consist of several problem sets related to fault-tolerant algorithms (**om, ttesynchro, ttastartup, unifapprox, azadmanesh, approxagree, hacms, misc**), benchmarks from software model checking (**cav12, ctigar**), benchmark suite of KIND model checker (**lustre**), simple concurrent programs (**conc**), and problems modeling a lock-free hash table (**lfht**). Each benchmark is a transition system with formulas characterizing initial states, a transition relation and a property that should hold. SALLY can finish with two possible answers (or run out of resources without an answer): *valid* means the property holds and an invariant implying the property has been found; *invalid* means the property does not hold and a counterexample leading to a state where the property does not hold has been found. In the plots, we denote the answers as + and ○, respectively. The benchmarks were run on Linux machines with Intel E5-2650 v3 processor (2.3 GHz) with 64 GB of memory. Each benchmark was restricted to 600 s of running time and to 4 GB of memory.

Figure 1 illustrates the benefit of adding Itp_{DI} and Itp'_{DI} to the portfolio of OPENSMT interpolation algorithms. The direct comparison of Itp_F and Itp_{DI} clearly shows that in many cases the use of decomposed interpolants outperforms the original procedure, sometimes by an order of magnitude. The comparison of the old and the new portfolio shows that the importance of decomposition is still significant even after taking the capabilities of dual versions into account.

Figure 2 shows the benefit of the new portfolio by comparing the model checker performance to one using a different SMT solver. As far as we know, MATHSAT also computes interpolants from the proof of unsatisfiability and uses interpolation algorithm based on Farkas' lemma for LRA conflicts. Comparing to OPENSMT's Itp_F, we see that the version of SALLY using MATHSAT is superior, most probably

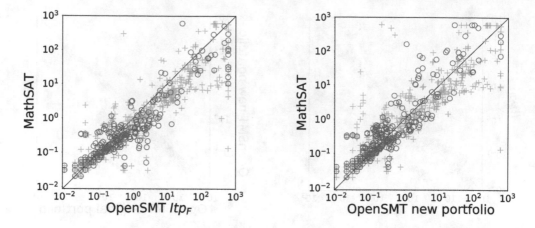

Fig. 2. Comparison of performance for the use of the interpolation procedure of MATH-SAT and OPENSMT—original Itp_F and the whole portfolio, respectively.

due to the differences in the implementation of the SMT solver. However, using the portfolio of interpolation procedures available in OPENSMT bridges the gap and allows SALLY to solve more benchmarks as can be seen in Table 1. This also shows a potential improvement for MATHSAT if it would offer the same portfolio of interpolation procedures as OPENSMT does.

Table 1 demonstrates the gain in the performance of the model checker from adding Itp_{DI} and Itp'_{DI} to the interpolation portfolio. The results are summarised *by category* with the name of the category and its number of benchmarks in the first column. The two columns per interpolation engine show the number of benchmarks successfully solved (validated/invalidated) within the limits and the total running time for *solved* benchmarks. Not only does the model checker with the extended portfolio solve *more* instances, but it also does so in *less* time.

Table 2 answers the question how often the new interpolation procedure manages to decompose Farkas coefficients, thus returning a different interpolant than the original procedure would. The statistics differ for Itp_{DI} and Itp'_{DI} due to the special nature of the interpolation problems in this model checking algorithm, as B-part *always* contains *only* shared symbols. Theoretically, this means Itp'_{DI} cannot discover any non-trivial elements of decomposition as there are no B-local variables. On the other hand, the decomposition to trivial elements is always possible, as all B-inequalities contain only shared variables. In our implementation, however, we consider the locality of a variable not from the global point of the whole interpolation problem, but from the local point of the current theory conflict. Consequently, even if a variable is shared in the whole problem, it can be local for the current theory conflict and the interpolant is not decomposed even if, from a global point, it could have been.

For Itp_{DI}, the first column reports the number of benchmarks with at least a *single* decomposition (any; with at least one trivial element; with at least one non-trivial element). The second column ("#non-triv. LRA itps") reports the total number of interpolation problems for theory conflict, not counting those without

Table 1. Performance of SALLY with old and new OPENSMT interpolation capabilities. Comparison with MATHSAT with its default interpolation included.

Problem set	OPENSMT portfolio Itp_F, Itp'_F		OPENSMT portfolio Itp_F, Itp'_F, Itp_{DI}, Itp'_{DI}		MATHSAT	
	solved (V/I)	Σ time(s)	solved (V/I)	Σ time(s)	solved (V/I)	Σ time(s)
approxagree (9)	9 (8/1)	101	9 (8/1)	72	9 (8/1)	173
azadmanesh (20)	16 (13/3)	74	16 (13/3)	69	19 (16/3)	102
cav12 (99)	63 (46/17)	3,427	63 (46/17)	2,960	64 (47/17)	796
conc (6)	3 (3/0)	48	4 (4/0)	347	3 (3/0)	38
ctigar (110)	70 (51/19)	1,812	72 (53/19)	1,493	75 (55/20)	1,803
hacms (5)	1 (1/0)	147	1 (1/0)	84	1 (1/0)	55
lfht (27)	17 (17/0)	502	17 (17/0)	502	16 (16/0)	518
lustre (790)	757 (423/334)	5,122	759 (425/334)	4,903	752 (420/332)	5,610
misc (10)	7 (6/1)	80	7 (6/1)	80	7 (6/1)	36
om (9)	9 (7/2)	7	9 (7/2)	7	9 (7/2)	6
ttastartup (3)	1 (1/0)	2	1 (1/0)	2	1 (1/0)	13
ttesynchro (6)	6 (3/3)	11	6 (3/3)	10	6 (3/3)	6
unifapprox (11)	10 (7/3)	21	10 (7/3)	20	11 (8/3)	125
	969 (586/383)	11,354	974 (591/383)	10,549	973 (591/382)	9,281

even theoretical possibility for decomposition. These include the problems where all inequalities were from one part of the problem (resulting in trivial interpolants, either ⊤ or ⊥) and the problems with a single inequality in the A-part (trivially yielding an interpolant equal to that inequality). The last column reports the number of successfully decomposed interpolants (with at least one trivial element; with at least one non-trivial element). Note that it can happen that a successful decomposition contains both trivial and non-trivial elements. For Itp'_{DI}, statistics regarding decompositions with non-trivial elements are left out as these decompositions were extremely rare. We see that at least one decomposition was possible in only roughly half of all the benchmarks. This explains why there are many points on the diagonal in Fig. 1. On the other hand, it shows that the test for the *possibility* of decomposition is very cheap and does not present a significant overhead. Another conclusion we can draw is that when the structure of the benchmark allows decomposition, the decomposition can often be discovered in many theory conflicts that appear during the solving.

During the evaluation we noticed that a small change in the solver sometimes had a huge effect on the performance of the model checker for a particular benchmark. It made previously unsolved instance easily solvable (or the other way around). To confirm that on some benchmarks Itp_{DI} is really better than Itp_F, we ran the model checker 100 times on chosen benchmarks, each time with a different random seed for the interpolating solver. For the benchmark **dillig03.c.mcmt** from category **ctigar** the model checker using Itp_F did *not* converge (in all runs) while Itp_{DI} ensured convergence in 0.2 s (in all runs). Itp_F also did not solve **fib_bench_safe_v1.mcmt** from category **conc**

Table 2. Interpolation statistics – pwd stands for "Number of problems with at least one decomposition". The numbers in parentheses denote "Decompositions with trivial and with non-trivial elements" (trivial/non-trivial).

Problem set	Itp_{DI}			Itp'_{DI}		
	pwd	#non-triv. LRA itps	#decomp. itps	pwd	#non-triv. LRA itps	#decomp. itps
approxagree (9)	1 (1/0)	7	7 (7/0)	1	18	18
azadmanesh (20)	4 (0/4)	4,831	266 (0/266)	4	4,353	4,353
cav12 (99)	31 (25/15)	1,368,187	7,399 (1,690/5,738)	45	204,036	57,127
conc (6)	3 (3/3)	424,145	215,376 (1,256/214,120)	3	13	13
ctigar (110)	73 (56/70)	2,982,559	826,621 (29,378/797,871)	77	152,613	152,612
hacms (5)	5 (5/5)	363,265	15,282 (532/14,750)	5	58,416	58,416
lfht (27)	13 (12/13)	838,094	12,785 (169/12,616)	14	111,060	111,060
lustre (790)	356 (356/192)	2,571,091	1,851,213 (855,958/1,054,516)	500	1,833,310	1,833,310
misc (10)	5 (4/5)	195,819	62,865 (8,700/55,042)	6	35,131	35,108
om (9)	4 (4/3)	1,150	236 (206/30)	3	168	168
ttastartup (3)	2 (2/2)	69,699	924 (16/908)	3	11,528	11,528
ttesynchro (6)	4 (4/0)	64	38 (38/0)	5	310	310
unifapprox (11)	0 (0/0)	0	0 (0/0)	2	25	25

and **large_const_c.mcmt** from category **ctigar**, while Itp_{DI} solved them in 42 runs on average in 377 s, and in 80 runs on average in 97 s, respectively. Finally, the benchmark **DRAGON_13.mcmt** from **lustre** was solved by Itp_F in 5 runs on average in 539 s, while it was solved by Itp_{DI} in 23 runs on average in 441 s.

7   Conclusion

In this paper, we have presented a new interpolation algorithm for linear real arithmetic that generalizes the interpolation algorithm based on Farkas' lemma used in modern SMT solvers. We showed that the algorithm is able to compute interpolants in the form of a *conjunction* of inequalities that are logically stronger than the single inequality returned by the original approach. This is useful in the IC3-style model-checking algorithms where Farkas interpolants have been shown to be a source of incompleteness. In our experiments, we have demonstrated that the opportunity to decompose Farkas interpolants occurs frequently in practice and that the decomposition often leads to (i) shortening of solving time and, in some cases, to (ii) solving a problem not solvable by the previous approach.

As the next steps, we plan to investigate how to automatically determine what kind of interpolant would be more useful for the current interpolation query in IC3-style model-checking algorithms. We also plan to investigate other uses of interpolation in model checking where stronger (or weaker) interpolants are desirable [34].

Acknowledgements. We would like to thank Dejan Jovanović for providing the benchmarks and for the help with integrating OPENSMT into SALLY. This work was supported by the Czech Science Foundation project 17-12465S and by the Swiss National Science Foundation (SNSF) grant 200020_166288.

References

1. Albarghouthi, A., McMillan, K.L.: Beautiful Interpolants. In: Sharygina, N., Veith, H. (eds.) CAV 2013. LNCS, vol. 8044, pp. 313–329. Springer, Heidelberg (2013). https://doi.org/10.1007/978-3-642-39799-8_22

2. Alt, L., Fedyukovich, G., Hyvärinen, A.E.J., Sharygina, N.: A proof-sensitive approach for small propositional interpolants. In: Gurfinkel, A., Seshia, S.A. (eds.) VSTTE 2015. LNCS, vol. 9593, pp. 1–18. Springer, Cham (2016). https://doi.org/10.1007/978-3-319-29613-5_1

3. Alt, L., Hyvärinen, A.E.J., Sharygina, N.: LRA interpolants from no man's land. In: Strichman, O., Tzoref-Brill, R. (eds.) HVC 2017. LNCS, vol. 10629, pp. 195–210. Springer, Cham (2017). https://doi.org/10.1007/978-3-319-70389-3_13

4. Alt, L., Hyvärinen, A.E.J., Asadi, S., Sharygina, N.: Duality-based interpolation for quantifier-free equalities and uninterpreted functions. In: Stewart, D., Weissenbacher, G. (eds.) FMCAD 2017, pp. 39–46. IEEE (2017)

5. Andrilli, S., Hecker, D.: Elementary Linear Algebra, 5th edn. Academic Press, Cambridge (2016). https://doi.org/10.1016/C2013-0-19116-7

6. Barrett, C., de Moura, L., Ranise, S., Stump, A., Tinelli, C.: The SMT-LIB initiative and the rise of SMT. In: Barner, S., Harris, I., Kroening, D., Raz, O. (eds.) HVC 2010. LNCS, vol. 6504, p. 3. Springer, Heidelberg (2011). https://doi.org/10.1007/978-3-642-19583-9_2

7. Barrett, C., Sebastiani, R., Seshia, S., Tinelli, C.: Satisfiability modulo theories. Frontiers in Artificial Intelligence and Applications, 1 edn., vol. 185, pp. 825–885 (2009)

8. Bradley, A.R.: SAT-based model checking without unrolling. In: Jhala, R., Schmidt, D. (eds.) VMCAI 2011. LNCS, vol. 6538, pp. 70–87. Springer, Heidelberg (2011). https://doi.org/10.1007/978-3-642-18275-4_7

9. Cimatti, A., Griggio, A., Schaafsma, B.J., Sebastiani, R.: The MathSAT5 SMT solver. In: Piterman, N., Smolka, S.A. (eds.) TACAS 2013. LNCS, vol. 7795, pp. 93–107. Springer, Heidelberg (2013). https://doi.org/10.1007/978-3-642-36742-7_7

10. Craig, W.: Three uses of the Herbrand-Gentzen theorem in relating model theory and proof theory. J. Symbolic Logic **22**(3), 269–285 (1957)

11. Davis, M., Logemann, G., Loveland, D.W.: A machine program for theorem-proving. Commun. ACM **5**(7), 394–397 (1962)

12. Davis, M., Putnam, H.: A computing procedure for quantification theory. J. ACM **7**(3), 201–215 (1960)

13. Detlefs, D., Nelson, G., Saxe, J.B.: Simplify: a theorem prover for program checking. J. ACM **52**(3), 365–473 (2005)

14. D'Silva, V., Kroening, D., Purandare, M., Weissenbacher, G.: Interpolant strength. In: Barthe, G., Hermenegildo, M. (eds.) VMCAI 2010. LNCS, vol. 5944, pp. 129–145. Springer, Heidelberg (2010). https://doi.org/10.1007/978-3-642-11319-2_12

15. Dutertre, B.: Yices 2.2. In: Biere, A., Bloem, R. (eds.) CAV 2014. LNCS, vol. 8559, pp. 737–744. Springer, Cham (2014). https://doi.org/10.1007/978-3-319-08867-9_49

16. Dutertre, B., de Moura, L.: A fast linear-arithmetic solver for DPLL(T). In: Ball, T., Jones, R.B. (eds.) CAV 2006. LNCS, vol. 4144, pp. 81–94. Springer, Heidelberg (2006). https://doi.org/10.1007/11817963_11

17. Farkas, G.: A Fourier-féle mechanikai elv alkalmazásai (Hungarian) (On the applications of the mechanical principle of Fourier) (1894)

18. Gurfinkel, A., Kahsai, T., Komuravelli, A., Navas, J.A.: The SeaHorn verification framework. In: Kroening, D., Păsăreanu, C.S. (eds.) CAV 2015. LNCS, vol. 9206, pp. 343–361. Springer, Cham (2015). https://doi.org/10.1007/978-3-319-21690-4_20

19. Gurfinkel, A., Rollini, S.F., Sharygina, N.: Interpolation properties and SAT-based model checking. In: Van Hung, D., Ogawa, M. (eds.) ATVA 2013. LNCS, vol. 8172, pp. 255–271. Springer, Cham (2013). https://doi.org/10.1007/978-3-319-02444-8_19

20. Huberman, B.A., Lukose, R.M., Hogg, T.: An economics approach to hard computational problems. Science **275**(5296), 51–54 (1997)

21. Hyvärinen, A.E.J., Marescotti, M., Alt, L., Sharygina, N.: OpenSMT2: An SMT solver for multi-core and cloud computing. In: Creignou, N., Le Berre, D. (eds.) SAT 2016. LNCS, vol. 9710, pp. 547–553. Springer, Cham (2016). https://doi.org/10.1007/978-3-319-40970-2_35

22. Jančík, P., Alt, L., Fedyukovich, G., Hyvärinen, A.E.J., Kofroň, J., Sharygina, N.: PVAIR: Partial Variable Assignment InterpolatoR. In: Stevens, P., Wąsowski, A. (eds.) FASE 2016. LNCS, vol. 9633, pp. 419–434. Springer, Heidelberg (2016). https://doi.org/10.1007/978-3-662-49665-7_25

23. Jančík, P., Kofroň, J., Rollini, S.F., Sharygina, N.: On interpolants and variable assignments. In: FMCAD 2014, pp. 123–130. IEEE (2014)

24. Jovanović, D., Dutertre, B.: Property-directed k-induction. In: FMCAD 2016, pp. 85–92. IEEE (2016)

25. Komuravelli, A., Gurfinkel, A., Chaki, S.: SMT-based model checking for recursive programs. In: Biere, A., Bloem, R. (eds.) CAV 2014. LNCS, vol. 8559, pp. 17–34. Springer, Cham (2014). https://doi.org/10.1007/978-3-319-08867-9_2

26. Korovin, K., Tsiskaridze, N., Voronkov, A.: Conflict resolution. In: Gent, I.P. (ed.) CP 2009. LNCS, vol. 5732, pp. 509–523. Springer, Heidelberg (2009). https://doi.org/10.1007/978-3-642-04244-7_41

27. Manna, Z., Pnueli, A.: Temporal Verification of Reactive Systems: Safety. Springer, Heidelberg (1995). https://doi.org/10.1007/978-1-4612-4222-2

28. McMillan, K.L.: Interpolation and SAT-based model checking. In: Hunt, W.A., Somenzi, F. (eds.) CAV 2003. LNCS, vol. 2725, pp. 1–13. Springer, Heidelberg (2003). https://doi.org/10.1007/978-3-540-45069-6_1

29. McMillan, K.L.: An interpolating theorem prover. Theoret. Comput. Sci. **345**(1), 101–121 (2005)

30. de Moura, L., Bjørner, N.: Z3: An efficient SMT solver. In: Ramakrishnan, C.R., Rehof, J. (eds.) TACAS 2008. LNCS, vol. 4963, pp. 337–340. Springer, Heidelberg (2008). https://doi.org/10.1007/978-3-540-78800-3_24

31. Nieuwenhuis, R., Oliveras, A.: Proof-producing congruence closure. In: Giesl, J. (ed.) RTA 2005. LNCS, vol. 3467, pp. 453–468. Springer, Heidelberg (2005). https://doi.org/10.1007/978-3-540-32033-3_33

32. Pudlák, P.: Lower bounds for resolution and cutting plane proofs and monotone computations. J. Symbolic Logic **62**(3), 981–998 (1997)

33. Rollini, S.F., Alt, L., Fedyukovich, G., Hyvärinen, A.E.J., Sharygina, N.: PeRIPLO: a framework for producing effective interpolants in SAT-based software verification. In: McMillan, K., Middeldorp, A., Voronkov, A. (eds.) LPAR 2013. LNCS, vol. 8312, pp. 683–693. Springer, Heidelberg (2013). https://doi.org/10.1007/978-3-642-45221-5_45

34. Rollini, S.F., Sery, O., Sharygina, N.: Leveraging interpolant strength in model checking. In: Madhusudan, P., Seshia, S.A. (eds.) CAV 2012. LNCS, vol. 7358, pp. 193–209. Springer, Heidelberg (2012). https://doi.org/10.1007/978-3-642-31424-7_18

35. Rybalchenko, A., Sofronie-Stokkermans, V.: Constraint solving for interpolation. In: Cook, B., Podelski, A. (eds.) VMCAI 2007. LNCS, vol. 4349, pp. 346–362. Springer, Heidelberg (2007). https://doi.org/10.1007/978-3-540-69738-1_25

36. Schindler, T., Jovanović, D.: Selfless interpolation for infinite-state model checking. In: Dillig, I., Palsberg, J. (eds.) VMCAI 2018. LNCS, vol. 10747, pp. 495–515. Springer, Cham (2018). https://doi.org/10.1007/978-3-319-73721-8_23

37. Scholl, C., Pigorsch, F., Disch, S., Althaus, E.: Simple interpolants for linear arithmetic. In: DATE 2014, pp. 1–6. IEEE (2014)

38. Schrijver, A.: Theory of Linear and Integer Programming. Wiley, New York (1998)

39. Sheeran, M., Singh, S., Stålmarck, G.: Checking safety properties using induction and a SAT-solver. In: Hunt, W.A., Johnson, S.D. (eds.) FMCAD 2000. LNCS, vol. 1954, pp. 127–144. Springer, Heidelberg (2000). https://doi.org/10.1007/3-540-40922-X_8

40. Silva, J.P.M., Sakallah, K.A.: GRASP: A search algorithm for propositional satisfiability. IEEE Trans. Comput. 48(5), 506–521 (1999)

12

On the Empirical Time Complexity of Scale-Free 3-SAT at the Phase Transition

Thomas Bläsius[1]([✉]), Tobias Friedrich[1], and Andrew M. Sutton[2]

[1] Hasso Plattner Institute, Potsdam, Germany
thomas.blaesius@hpi.de
[2] University of Minnesota Duluth, Duluth, MN, USA

Abstract. The hardness of formulas at the solubility phase transition of random propositional satisfiability (SAT) has been intensely studied for decades both empirically and theoretically. Solvers based on stochastic local search (SLS) appear to scale very well at the critical threshold, while complete backtracking solvers exhibit exponential scaling. On industrial SAT instances, this phenomenon is inverted: backtracking solvers can tackle large industrial problems, where SLS-based solvers appear to stall. Industrial instances exhibit sharply different structure than uniform random instances. Among many other properties, they are often *heterogeneous* in the sense that some variables appear in many while others appear in only few clauses.

We conjecture that the *heterogeneity* of SAT formulas alone already contributes to the trade-off in performance between SLS solvers and complete backtracking solvers. We empirically determine how the run time of SLS vs. backtracking solvers depends on the heterogeneity of the input, which is controlled by drawing variables according to a scale-free distribution. Our experiments reveal that the efficiency of complete solvers at the phase transition is strongly related to the heterogeneity of the degree distribution. We report results that suggest the depth of satisfying assignments in complete search trees is influenced by the level of heterogeneity as measured by a power-law exponent. We also find that incomplete SLS solvers, which scale well on uniform instances, are not affected by heterogeneity. The main contribution of this paper utilizes the scale-free random 3-SAT model to isolate heterogeneity as an important factor in the scaling discrepancy between complete and SLS solvers at the uniform phase transition found in previous works.

1 Introduction

The worst-case time complexity of propositional satisfiability (SAT) entails that no known algorithm can solve it in polynomial time [12]. Nevertheless, many large industrial SAT instances can be solved efficiently in practice by modern solvers. So far, this discrepancy is not well-understood.

Studying random SAT instances provides a way to explain this discrepancy between theory and practice as it replaces the worst case with the average case.

A large amount of both theoretical and experimental research effort focuses almost exclusively on the *uniform random* distribution. Uniform random SAT instances are generated by choosing, for each clause, the variables included in this clause uniformly at random among all variables. Uniform random formulas are easy to construct, and are comparatively more accessible to probabilistic analysis due to their uniformity and the stochastic independence of choices. The analysis of this model can provide valuable insights into the SAT problem in general and has led to the development of tools that are useful also in other areas. However, considering the average-case complexity of solving uniform random formulas cannot explain why SAT solvers work well in practice: in the interesting case that the clause-variable ratio is close to the satisfiability threshold (i.e., the formulas are not trivially satisfiable or trivially unsatisfiable), SAT solvers that perform well on industrial instances struggle to solve the randomly generated formulas fast and algorithms tuned for random formulas perform poorly on industrial instances [14, 27, 33].

The comparative efficiency of existing solvers on real-world SAT instances is somewhat surprising given not only worst-case complexity theoretic results, but also the apparent hardness of uniform random formulas sampled from the critically-constrained regime [8, 31]. Katsirelos and Simon [26] comment that even though the ingredients for building a good SAT solver are mostly known, we still currently cannot explain their strong performance on real-world problems.

This picture is further complicated by the fact that solvers based on stochastic local search (SLS) appear to scale *polynomially* in the critically constrained region of uniform random SAT, whereas complete backtracking solvers scale *exponentially* on these formulas [32]. We are interested in identifying structural aspects of formulas that do not occur in uniform random instances, but can somehow be exploited by solvers.

Industrial SAT instances are complex, and possess many structural characteristics. Among these are *modularity* [4], *heterogeneity* [2], *self-similarity* [1], and *locality* [22]. Modularity measures how well the formula (when modeled as a graph representing the inclusion relation between variables and clauses) can be separated into communities with many internal and few external connections. It is generally assumed that the high modularity of industrial instances is one of the main reasons for the good performance of SAT solvers. Though it is possible to develop models that generate formulas with high modularity [21, 35], there is, however, no established model with this property. Enforcing high modularity can lead to complicated stochastic dependencies, making analysis difficult.

Heterogeneity measures the imbalance in distribution of variables over the clauses of the formula. A highly heterogeneous formula contains only few variables that appear in many clauses and many variables appearing in few clauses. Many industrial instances, particularly from formal verification, exhibit a high heterogeneity. Ansótegui, Bonet, and Levy [3] proposed a number of non-uniform models that produce heterogeneous instances. One such model they introduced was the *scale-free* model. Often, the degree distribution (the *degree* of a variable is the number of clauses containing it as a literal) roughly follows a *power-law* [2], i.e., the number of variables of degree d is proportional to $d^{-\beta}$.

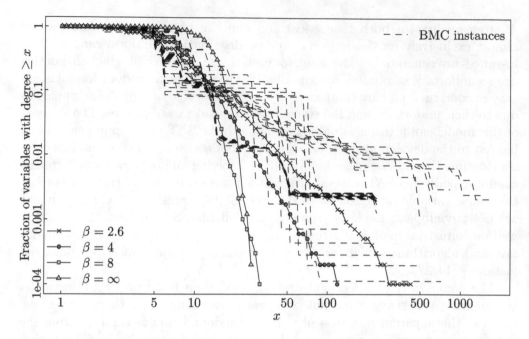

Fig. 1. Empirical cumulative degree distributions on power-law formulas for different β, $n = 10000$, and hardware model checking instances from SAT 2017 competition. Power-law distributions appear as a line on a log-log plot with slope determined by β. As β increases, we observe the power-law distributions converging to uniform ($\beta = \infty$).

Here β is the *power-law exponent*. Figure 1 illustrates a number of empirical cumulative degree distributions for both industrial and synthetic power-law formulas. The industrial formulas come from the SAT-encoded deep bound hardware model checking instance benchmarks submitted to the 2017 SAT competition [7] that had measured empirical power law exponents below 5.

A degree distribution that follows a power law is only a sufficient condition for heterogeneity. Nevertheless, we argue that the scale-free model allows for fine-tuned parametric control over the extent of heterogeneity in the form of the power-law exponent β (see Proposition 1).

No single one of the above properties (e.g., heterogeneity, modularity, locality, etc.) can completely characterize the scaling effects observed on industrial instances vs. uniform random instances. However, a first step toward explaining the performance of SAT solvers in different environments is to isolate these features and determine what kinds of structural properties do influence the run time of different solvers. Our goal in this paper is to empirically determine the impact of heterogeneity (as produced by a scale-free degree distribution) on the run time of SLS-based vs. complete backtracking solvers.[1]

Though it seems natural that a more realistic model is better suited to explain the run times observed in practice, it is unclear whether the heterogeneity is

---

[1] A solver is *complete* if it always finds a solution or a proof that no solution exists. In contrast, SLS-based solvers only terminate if they find a solution.

actually even a relevant factor. It might as well be that other mentioned properties, such as modularity, or self-similarity lead to good run times independent of
the degree distribution. The experiments Ansótegui et al. [3] performed on their
different models indicate that the heterogeneity in fact helps solvers that also
perform well on industrial instances. However, these experiments did not address
the phenomenon observed by Mu and Hoos [32] where SLS solvers outperform
complete solvers. Our goal is to demonstrate that heterogeneity of the degree
distribution has a strong positive impact on the scaling of complete solvers, but
not on SLS-based solvers.

To study this impact, we perform large-scale experiments on scale-free random 3-SAT instances with varying power-law exponents β. We note that small
power-law exponents lead to heterogeneous degree distributions while increasing β makes the instances more and more homogeneous; see Fig. 1. In fact, for
$\beta \to \infty$, scale-free random 3-SAT converges to the uniform random 3-SAT model.
Thus, it can be seen as a generalization of the uniform model with a parameter
β that directly adjusts the heterogeneity.

Our experiments clearly show a distinct crossover in performance with respect
to a set of complete backtracking (CDCL- and DPLL-based) SAT solvers and
a set of SLS-based solvers as we interpolate between highly heterogeneous
instances and uniform random instances. Moreover, the performance of SLS-
based solvers remain relatively unaffected by the degree distribution. These
results might partially explain the effect observed on uniform random instances
by Mu and Hoos [32]. In this case, complete backtracking solvers scale poorly
on random instances with a homogeneous degree distribution, while SLS-based
solvers perform best.

2 Scale-Free Formulas and Heterogeneity

A random 3-SAT formula Φ on n Boolean variables $x_1, \ldots, x_n$ and m clauses is a
conjunction of m clauses $\Phi := C_1 \wedge C_2 \wedge \cdots \wedge \cdots \wedge C_m$ where $C_i := (\ell_{i,1} \vee \ell_{i,2} \vee \ell_{i,3})$
is a disjunction of exactly three literals. A literal is a possibly negated variable. A
formula Φ is satisfiable if there is exists variable assignment for which Φ evaluates
to true.

The canonical distribution for random 3-SAT formulas is the *uniform distribution*, which is the uniform measure taken over all formulas with n variables
and m clauses. The uniform 3-SAT distribution is sampled by selecting uniformly
m 3-sets of variables and negating each variable with probability $1/2$ to form
the clauses of the formula. The *scale-free* random 3-SAT distribution is similar,
except the degree distribution of the variables is not homogeneous.

In the scale-free model introduced by Ansótegui, Bonet and Levy [3], a formula is constructed by sampling each clause independently at random. In contrast to the classical uniform random model, however, the variable probabilities
$p_i := \Pr(X = x_i)$ to choose a variable x_i are non-uniform. In particular, a
scale-free formula is generated by using a *power-law* distribution for the variable
distribution. To this end, we assign each variable x_i a *weight* w_i and sample it
with probability $p_i := \Pr(X = x_i) = \frac{w_i}{\sum_j w_j}$. To achieve a power-law distribution,

we use the following concrete sequence of weights.

$$w_i := \frac{\beta - 2}{\beta - 1} \left(\frac{n}{i}\right)^{\frac{1}{\beta-1}} \tag{1}$$

for $i = 1, 2 \ldots, n$, which is a canonical choice for power-law weights, cf. [9]. This sequence guarantees $\sum_j w_j \to n$ for $n \to \infty$ and therefore

$$p_i \to \frac{1}{n} \frac{\beta - 2}{\beta - 1} \left(\frac{n}{i}\right)^{\frac{1}{\beta-1}}. \tag{2}$$

To draw Φ, we generate each clause C_i as follows. (1) Sample three variables independently at random according to the distribution p_i. Repeat until no variables coincide. (2) Negate each of the three variables independently at random with probability $1/2$.

Note that Ansótegui et al. [3] use α instead of β as the power-law exponent and define $\beta := 1/(\alpha - 1)$. We instead follow the notational convention of Chung and Lu, cf. [9].

As already noted in the introduction, the power-law exponent β can be seen as a measure of how heterogeneous the resulting formulas are. This can be formalized as follows.

Proposition 1. *For a fixed number of variables, scale-free random 3-SAT converges to uniform random 3-SAT as $\beta \to \infty$.*

Proof. First observe that, for any fixed n and $\beta \to \infty$, the weights w_i as defined in Eq. (1) converge to 1. When generating a scale-free random 3-SAT instance, variables are chosen to be included in a clause with probability proportional to w_i. Thus, for $\beta \to \infty$, each variable is chosen with the same probability $1/n$ as it is the case for uniform random 3-SAT.   □

We note that the model converges rather quickly: The difference between the weights is maximized for w_1 and w_n (with w_1 being the largest and w_n being the smallest). By choosing $\beta = c \log n$, the maximum weight difference $w_1 - w_n$ converges to the small constant $e^{1/c} - 1$ for growing n. Thus, when choosing $\beta \in \omega(\log n)$ (i.e., β grows asymptotically faster than $\log n$), this difference actually goes to 0 for $n \to \infty$, leading to the uniform model. This quick convergence can also be observed in Fig. 1 where the difference between $\beta = 8$ and the uniform case ($\beta = \infty$) is rather small.

2.1   The Solubility Phase Transition

The *constraint density* of a distribution of formulas on n variables and m clauses is measured as the ratio of clauses to variables m/n. A *phase transition* in a random satisfiability model is the phenomenon of a sharp transition as a function of constraint density between formulas that are almost surely satisfiable and formulas that are almost surely not satisfiable. The location of such a transition is called the *critical density* or *threshold*.

Threshold phenomena in the uniform random model have been studied for decades. The *satisfiability threshold conjecture* maintains that if Φ is a formula drawn uniformly at random from the set of all k-CNF formulas with n variables and m clauses, there exists a real number r_k such that

$$\lim_{n \to \infty} \Pr\{\Phi \text{ is satisfiable}\} = \begin{cases} 1 & m/n < r_k; \\ 0 & m/n > r_k. \end{cases}$$

This transition is sharp [18] in the sense that the probability of satisfiability as a function of constraint density m/n approaches a unit step function as $n \to \infty$. For $k = 2$, the location of the transition is known exactly to be $r_2 = 1$ [10]. For $k \geq 3$, bounds asymptotic in k [11] and exact results for large constant k [16] are now known.

The phenomenon of a sharp solubility transition is also interesting from the perspective of computational complexity and algorithm engineering, since it appears to coincide with a regime of formulas that are particularly difficult to solve by complete SAT solvers [31].

In the scale-free model, the location of the critical threshold $r_k(\beta)$ is a function of power-law exponent β. In the case of $k = 2$, it was proved that the critical density is bounded as $r_2(\beta) \leq \frac{(\beta-1)(\beta-3)}{(\beta-2)^2}$ [19]. Recently, Levy [28] proved this bound for $k = 2$ is tight. Similar to the uniform model, the critical density $r_k(\beta)$ for $k > 2$ seems to be more elusive.

2.2 Characterizing the Scale-Free Phase Transition

Ansótegui et al. [3] empirically located the phase transition of the scale-free 3-SAT model and noted that the critical density for very low β was small, and the threshold approaches the critical point of the uniform model at ≈ 4.26 as $\beta \to \infty$.[2] They report the critical threshold values as a function of β by testing 200 formulas at each value of β in the set $\{2, 7/3, 3, 5, \infty\}$.

Nevertheless, a number of details about the nature of the scale-free phase transition is still lacking from this picture. First, the sharpness of the phase transition as β evolves is not immediately clear. Furthermore, even though most previous work assumes the hardest instances are located at the phase transition region [3, Section 4], it is not obvious what the shape and extent of an easy-hard-easy transition (if it even exists) would be for scale-free formulas, nor is it known how the effect is influenced by β. Finally, previous works have so far not addressed the curious phenomenon of SLS solvers and complete solvers that seem to scale so differently on uniform random and industrial problems. We tackle this issue in the next section.

To better characterize the phase transition in the scale-free model, we generated formulas as follows. For any particular n and β, taking a sequence of 300 equidistant values $\alpha_i \in [2, 5]$ for $i \in \{1, \ldots, 300\}$, we sample 100 formulas from

---

[2] We are translating the term they refer to as β to the term we refer to as β, as mentioned above.

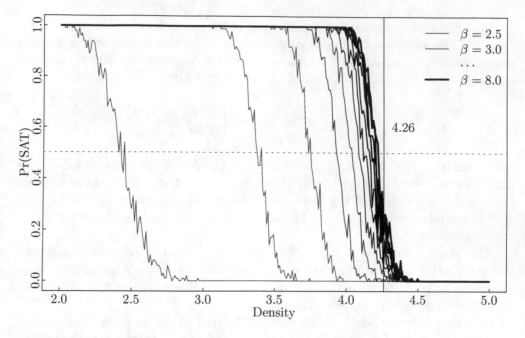

Fig. 2. Proportion of satisfiable formulas ($n = 500$) as a function of constraint density m/n for various power-law exponents β. Threshold approaches the critical density of the uniform random 3-SAT model: $r_3 \approx 4.26$.

the scale-free distribution with n variables, power-law exponent β, and density α_i (i.e., $m = \alpha_i n$). In other words, each value of n and β corresponds to 30000 formulas at various densities.

To estimate the location of the critical threshold, we decide the satisfiability of each formula with the DPLL-based solver march_hi [25]. We then find the density α_i yielding half the formulas satisfiable. This is the approach for locating the threshold in the uniform model [13]. However, in the case of the random scale-free model, the threshold depends on β.

Using this approach, we generated sets of formulas at the phase transition varying both n and β. For each $n \in \{500, 600, 700\}$, we generated formulas with $\beta \in \{2.5, 2.6, \ldots, 5.0\}$. We find the run times of the complete solvers exhibit a strong positive correlation with β. This is consistent with complete solvers performing poorly on uniform random ($\beta = \infty$) problems of even modest sizes, but it unfortunately restricts us to more modest formula sizes. To determine the effect of very large power-law exponents, we also generated formulas for $n = 500$, $\beta \in \{5, 6, 7, 8\}$.

The sharpness of the transition appears to evolve with β. Figure 2 reports the proportion of satisfiable formulas as a function of constraint density with $n = 500$. As $\beta \to \infty$, the solubility transition shifts toward the supposed critical density of the uniform random 3-SAT model, i.e., $r_3 \approx 4.26$. This is consistent with previous work on this model, but we also can see from this that the transition becomes steeper with increasing β, despite the fact that n is held constant.

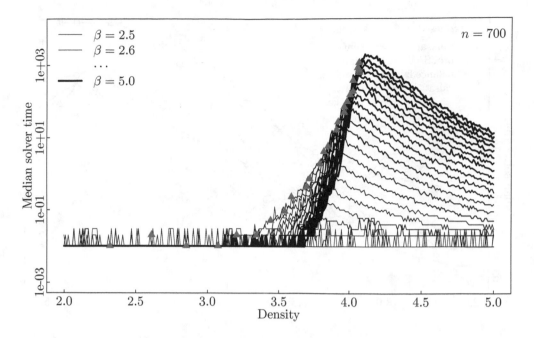

Fig. 3. Median solver times for march_hi on formulas of size $n = 700$ as β evolves toward the uniform distribution. Red triangles (▲) mark the exact density at which empirical threshold was determined. (Color figure online)

On the uniform random model, the hardest formulas for complete backtracking solvers lie at the solubility phase transition because they produce deeper search trees [31]. We also observe this so-called easy-hard-easy pattern for the scale free model in the trends for median time for march_hi to solve formulas of size $n = 700$ in Fig. 3. Moreover, the power-law exponent β is strongly correlated with the height of the hardness peak and we conjecture that the complexity of the resulting search tree is strongly coupled to the heterogeneity of the degree distribution. The empirically determined critical point, indicated in the figure with a red triangle (▲) tightly corresponds with the hardness peaks.

3 Scaling Across Solver Types

Our main goal is to understand the influence of the heterogeneity of the degree distribution at the phase transition on SLS-based solvers and complete backtracking solvers. The original paper by Mu and Hoos [32] investigated three DPLL-based SAT solvers: kcnfs [15], march_hi [25], and march_br [24]; and three SLS-based solvers: WalkSAT/SKC [34], BalancedZ [29], and ProbSAT [5]. They found the three DPLL-based solvers scaled exponentially at the uniform critical threshold and the SLS-based solvers did not. To investigate the role of heterogeneity in this context, we used the same solvers as the original Mu and Hoos paper.

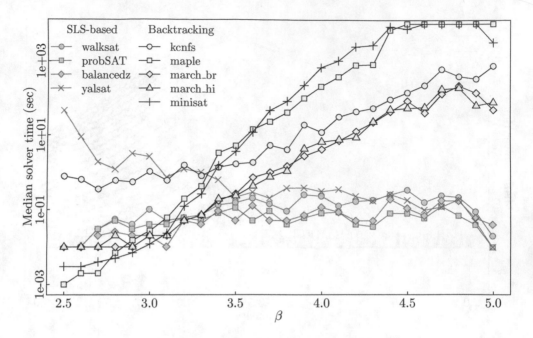

Fig. 4. Median solver time at the phase transition for all solvers on formulas with $n = 700$. Top of plot corresponds to one hour cutoff.

In addition to the DPLL solvers, we tested MiniSAT [17], and the MiniSAT-based CDCL solver MapleCOMSPS [30]. These choices are motivated by a number of reasons. First, MiniSAT has performed well in industrial categories in previous SAT competitions, as has MapleCOMSPS on the Applications Benchmark at the SAT 2016 competition and the Main Track and No Limit Track at the SAT 2017 competition. Second, we want to know if architectural decisions such as branching heuristic, look-ahead, backtracking strategy, or clause learning has any effect. We also supplemented the SLS-based solvers with YalSAT [6], which won first place in the Random Track of the SAT 2017 competition.

SLS-based solvers are *incomplete* in the sense that they can only decide satisfiability. Studies that involve such solvers need to be constrained to satisfiable formulas [20,32,36]. We use the standard rejection sampling approach to filtering for satisfiable formulas. For each n and β value, we filtered out the unsatisfiable formulas at the phase transition located as described above. For each of these formulas, we ran each of the above SLS-based and complete solvers to compare the required CPU time until a solution was determined. We imposed a solver cutoff time of one hour. In Fig. 4, we chart the median solution time on formulas of size $n = 700$ at the phase transition as a function of power law exponent β. For low β (highly heterogeneous) formulas, the complete solvers outpace the SLS-based solvers (though solution time for both is fast). We observe a crossover point around $\beta = 3.5$ where the required time for complete solvers begins to dominate the median time for the SLS techniques.

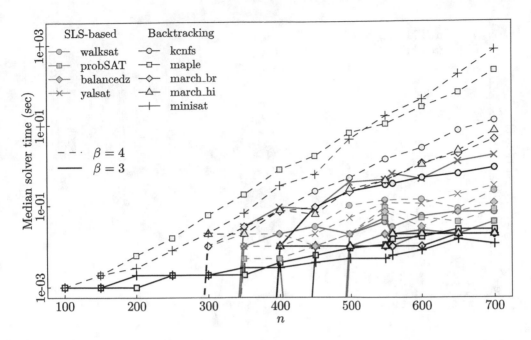

Fig. 5. Median solver time at the phase transition for all solvers on formulas with $\beta = 3$ (—) and $\beta = 4$ (- -).

Figure 4 reveals that the CDCL-based solvers MiniSAT and MapleCOM-SPS had worse performance degradation with decreasing heterogeneity than the DPLL-based solvers. Moreover, YalSAT seems to perform worse on highly heterogeneous formulas. This is interesting behavior, as YalSAT implements variants of ProbSAT with a Luby restart strategy and is conjectured to be identical to ProbSAT on uniform random instances [6]. Our results confirm that YalSAT and ProbSAT are indistinguishable as β increases, but we have evidence that the restart schedule might somehow affect performance on heterogeneous formulas.

To better quantify the influence of scaling with n, we consider the median solver time as a function of n for two representative values of β (3 and 4) in Fig. 5. To obtain a clearer picture, we repeated the formula generation process for smaller formulas ($n = 100, 200, \dots$). The exponential scaling in complete solvers with large β (dashed lines) is easy to observe in this plot. On smaller β (solid lines), the complete solvers scale more efficiently.

To take variance into account, we compare solver performance in Fig. 6.[3] Here we have removed the CDCL-based solvers and YalSAT for clarity. This is therefore the solver set originally investigated by Mu and Hoos [32]. We again can identify a distinct crossover point at $\beta = 3.5$. Figure 7 repeats the results for $n = 500$. For this size of formula, the small β regime is extremely easy, and the results are somewhat obscured. However, these formulas are small enough that

---

[3] In all box blots, the boxes show the interquartile range, the bold line is the median, and the whiskers extend to $3/2 \cdot$ IQR below (respectively, above) the 25th (respectively, the 75th) percentile. All points beyond this are outliers.

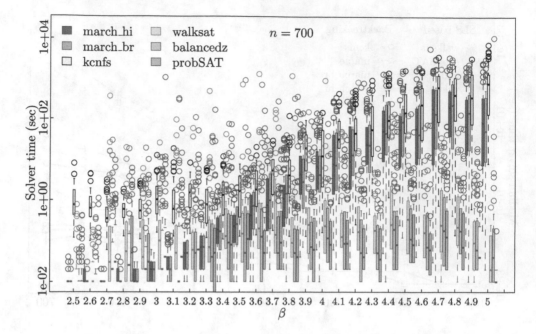

Fig. 6. CPU time to solve formulas at the scale-free phase transition with $n = 700$.

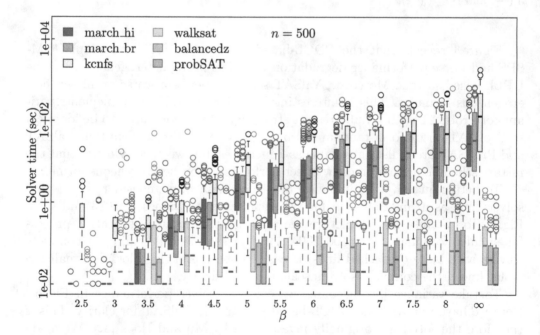

Fig. 7. CPU time to solve formulas at the scale-free phase transition with $n = 500$. Rightmost group ($\beta = \infty$) denotes satisfiable uniform random formulas with $n = 500$ and $m = 2131$.

we are able to consistently solve high β formulas, and we report the results up to $\beta = 8$. The rightmost group of the figure represents filtered uniform random formulas with $n = 500$ and $m = 2131$. To estimate the correct critical density for the uniform formulas, we used the parametric model from [32, Eq. (3)].

4   Effect of Heterogeneity on Search Trees

The discrepancy in solver efficiency across different levels of heterogeneity observed in the preceding section suggests that the degree distribution strongly affects the decisions of a wide range of solvers in a systematic way. We hypothesize that, for fixed n and m, heterogeneous 3-SAT formulas have more satisfying assignments on average, and these assignments tend to be more quickly reachable, because partial assignments tend to produce more implied literals.

Even for small formulas, it is infeasible to enumerate all satisfying assignments. Propositional model counting offers a technique in the form of an exhaustive extension to DPLL in which the branchpoint after a satisfying assignment is followed [23]. When a branch corresponding to a partial assignment of t fixed variables is marked as satisfiable at depth d, it is already possible to conclude that there are 2^{n-t} solutions at depth at least d. Using this technique, we can count the satisfying assignments to formulas generated by the scale-free model to measure the influence of heterogeneity on the solution count. The left panel of Fig. 8 reports the number of satisfying assignments found in satisfiable scale-free formulas generated at each β value.

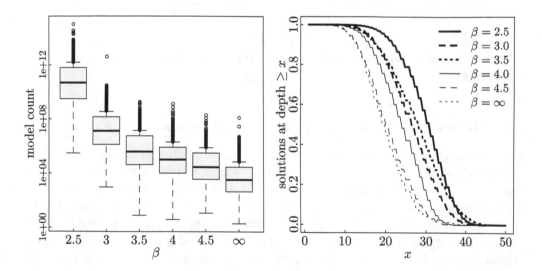

Fig. 8. Left: count of satisfying assignments on satisfiable scale-free formulas at each power-law exponent at the phase transition. For each $\beta \in \{2.5, 3.0, \dots, 4.5, \infty\}$, we filter from 1000 generated random formulas at the phase transition with $n = 100$. Right: empirical degree distributions reporting the proportion of solutions at depth equal or greater than x aggregated over all formulas at each β value.

To obtain a more detailed picture, we plot the empirical cumulative distribution functions of solution depth on the right panel of Fig. 8. The curves represent the proportion $P(x)$ of solutions at a depth equal or greater than x.

As mentioned above, shallower solutions arise from the abundance of implied literals. We find that highly heterogeneous formulas tend to have many more constraint propagations leading to either satisfying assignments or contradictions. We recorded this data and display it in Fig. 9.

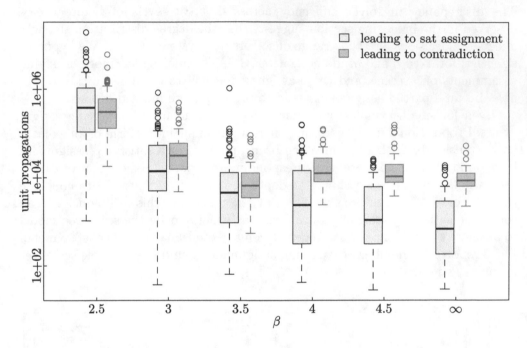

Fig. 9. Number of constraint propagations leading to a satisfying assignment or contradiction as a function of β.

4.1 Relaxed Bounded Model Checking Instances

Our aim has been to isolate heterogeneity as an impacting factor in the relative performance discrepancy between SLS solvers and complete solvers. Nevertheless, we also conjecture that the behavior of complete solvers on synthetic scale-free formulas is comparable to their behavior on certain industrial instances with power-law degree distributions. To investigate this, we compare the complexity of the remaining formula after selecting a branching literal during runs of march_hi, which was the highest performing backtracking solver for our data. Each solid line in Fig. 10 displays the average remaining formula complexity measured as clauses not yet satisfied as a percentage of original formula size. These run average are taken over all satisfiable powerlaw formulas of $n = 500$ for different values of β. Note that some early averages exceed 100%, which likely occurs because march_hi also adds binary resolvents during the solving process. Moreover, the complexity may increase during the run, as complete solvers utilize backtracking.

We compare this with the well-known BMC DIMACS benchmark set from CMU[4]. Our motivation for this choice was to utilize a widely available set of bounded model checking formulas of reasonable size. To provide a fair comparison to the filtered scale-free formulas, we "relaxed" each BMC formula by iteratively removing a single clause at random until the first time it was satisfiable. This preserves the statistical characteristics of the degree distribution while producing a satisfiable formula.

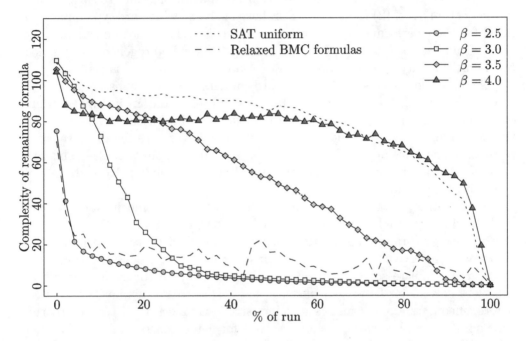

Fig. 10. Average complexity of the remaining formula depending on the percentage of already made branching decisions in a run. Reported are runs of march_hi on scale-free formulas of varying β, and satisfiable real-world model checking formulas: uniform (⋯), industrial (- -), and synthetic (—).

The profile of the industrial bounded model checking formulas closely matches the solver behavior on the heterogeneous scale-free formulas, whereas the solver behavior on the uniform suite corresponds to the behavior on more homogeneous formulas. We conjecture that the power-law degree distribution in the bounded model checking formulas (cf. Fig. 1) affect the search tree in similar ways.

5   Conclusions

We have investigated a parameterized distribution over propositional formulas that allows us to carefully control the heterogeneity (via the power-law exponent) to interpolate smoothly between highly heterogeneous random formulas

---

[4] http://fmv.jku.at/bmc/.

and nearly-uniform random formulas. This allows us to observe the exact influence of this kind of heterogeneity on hardness for two different solver classes. Our empirical analysis uncovers an interesting crossover effect in the performance of SLS-based vs. complete backtracking solvers, depending on the heterogeneity.

We summarize our main findings as follows. (1) Complete solvers tuned for industrial instances perform significantly better on heterogeneous formulas than uniform formulas. This is likely due to the fact that the search space of highly heterogeneous formulas have more solutions, and solutions tend to be shallower in the decision tree. (2) Incomplete SLS-based solvers, which are typically recognized for their performance on uniform random k-SAT, do not benefit much (if at all) from heterogeneity. (3) Random instances (even heterogeneous ones) close to the satisfiability threshold are harder to solve than many industrial instances.

The first two insights are a step towards understanding the disaccording runtime behaviors of different solvers on industrial and random instances. Moreover, these findings suggest that the behavior of SLS-based solvers are relatively heterogeneity-invariant, whereas complete solvers are far more sensitive to the homogeneous degree distributions of uniform random formulas. This may explain, at least in part, the exponential scaling of complete solvers at the uniform phase transition observed by Mu and Hoos [32].

On the other hand, the third insight shows that heterogeneity alone cannot explain why industrial instances can be solved so fast in practice. On the upside, this means that random scale-free formulas chosen close to the satisfiability threshold can serve as hard benchmark instances. It would be interesting to see whether incomplete solvers can be tuned to catch up to (or even outperform) complete solvers on heterogeneous instances. Due to the similarities between heterogeneous random formulas and industrial instances with respect to runtime behavior, we believe that tuning solvers for heterogeneous random formulas can actually lead to techniques that also help solving industrial instances faster.

The behavior of solvers on uniform random formulas is well-studied. However, there is no obvious reason to believe that solver performance near the scale-free phase transition is identical to performance near the uniform phase transition. Our work suggests that there is some kind of structure in formulas with heavy-tailed degree distributions that is being exploited by complete solvers. It is important to stress that a scale-free degree distribution alone is not enough to characterize the complex structure of real problems. Our results provide context by isolating heterogeneity (as realized by the power-law exponent) as an important feature impacting the performance of state-of-the-art CDCL- and DPLL-based SAT solvers. Other non-uniform models exist, and a future avenue of work is to investigate such models, especially the Popularity-Similarity model recently introduced by Giráldez-Cru and Levy [22], which can generate formulas with both a scale-free degree distribution and high modularity.

References

1. Ansótegui, C., Bonet, M.L., Giráldez-Cru, J., Levy, J.: The fractal dimension of SAT formulas. In: Demri, S., Kapur, D., Weidenbach, C. (eds.) IJCAR 2014. LNCS (LNAI), vol. 8562, pp. 107–121. Springer, Cham (2014). https://doi.org/10.1007/978-3-319-08587-6_8

2. Ansótegui, C., Bonet, M.L., Levy, J.: On the structure of industrial SAT instances. In: Gent, I.P. (ed.) CP 2009. LNCS, vol. 5732, pp. 127–141. Springer, Heidelberg (2009). https://doi.org/10.1007/978-3-642-04244-7_13

3. Ansótegui, C., Bonet, M.L., Levy, J.: Towards industrial-like random SAT instances. In: Proceedings of the Twenty-First International Joint Conference on Artificial Intelligence (IJCAI), pp. 387–392 (2009)

4. Ansótegui, C., Giráldez-Cru, J., Levy, J.: The community structure of SAT formulas. In: Cimatti, A., Sebastiani, R. (eds.) SAT 2012. LNCS, vol. 7317, pp. 410–423. Springer, Heidelberg (2012). https://doi.org/10.1007/978-3-642-31612-8_31

5. Balint, A., Schöning, U.: probSAT and pprobSAT. In: Proceedings of the 2014 SAT Competition, p. 63 (2014)

6. Biere, A.: CaDiCaL, Lingeling, Plingeling, Treengeling and YalSAT. In: Proceedings of SAT Competition 2017, pp. 14–15 (2017)

7. Biere, A.: Deep bound hardware model checking instances, quadratic propagations benchmarks and reencoded factorization problems submitted to the SAT competition 2017. In: Proceedings of SAT Competition 2017, pp. 40–41 (2017)

8. Cheeseman, P., Kanefsky, B., Taylor, W.M.: Where the really hard problems are. In: Proceedings of the Twelfth International Joint Conference on Artificial Intelligence (IJCAI), pp. 331–340 (1991)

9. Chung, F., Lu, L.: The average distances in random graphs with given expected degrees. PNAS **99**(25), 15879–15882 (2002)

10. Chvátal, V., Reed, B.: Mick gets some (the odds are on his side). In: Proceedings of the Thirty-Third IEEE Annual Symposium on Foundations of Computer Science (FOCS), pp. 620–627, October 1992

11. Coja-Oghlan, A.: The asymptotic k-SAT threshold. In: Proceedings of the Forty-Sixth Annual Symposium on Theory of Computing (STOC), pp. 804–813 (2014)

12. Cook, S.A.: The complexity of theorem-proving procedures. In: Proceedings of the Third Annual Symposium on Theory of Computing (STOC), pp. 151–158 (1971)

13. Crawford, J.M., Auton, L.D.: Experimental results on the crossover point in random 3-SAT. Artif. Intell. **81**(1–2), 31–57 (1996)

14. Crawford, J.M., Baker, A.B.: Experimental results on the application of satisfiability algorithms to scheduling problems. In: Proceedings of the Twelftfh AAAI Conference on Artificial Intelligence, pp. 1092–1097 (1994)

15. Dequen, G., Dubois, O.: *kcnfs*: an efficient solver for random k-SAT formulae. In: Giunchiglia, E., Tacchella, A. (eds.) SAT 2003. LNCS, vol. 2919, pp. 486–501. Springer, Heidelberg (2004). https://doi.org/10.1007/978-3-540-24605-3_36

16. Ding, J., Sly, A., Sun, N.: Proof of the satisfiability conjecture for large k. In: Proceedings of the Forty-Seventh Annual Symposium on Theory of Computing (STOC), pp. 59–68 (2015)

17. Eén, N., Sörensson, N.: An extensible SAT-solver. In: Giunchiglia, E., Tacchella, A. (eds.) SAT 2003. LNCS, vol. 2919, pp. 502–518. Springer, Heidelberg (2004). https://doi.org/10.1007/978-3-540-24605-3_37

18. Friedgut, E.: Sharp thresholds of graph properties, and the k-SAT problem. J. Am. Math. Soc. **12**(4), 1017–1054 (1999)

19. Friedrich, T., Krohmer, A., Rothenberger, R., Sutton, A.M.: Phase transitions for scale-free SAT formulas. In: Proceedings of the Twenty-First AAAI Conference on Artificial Intelligence, pp. 3893–3899 (2017)

20. Gent, I.P., Walsh, T.: Towards an understanding of hill-climbing procedures for SAT. In: Proceedings of the Eleventh AAAI Conference on Artificial Intelligence, pp. 28–33 (1993)

21. Giráldez-Cru, J., Levy, J.: A modularity-based random SAT instances generator. In: Proceedings of the Twenty-Fourth International Joint Conference on Artificial Intelligence (IJCAI), pp. 1952–1958 (2015)

22. Giráldez-Cru, J., Levy, J.: Locality in random SAT instances. In: Proceedings of the Twenty-Sixth International Joint Conference on Artificial Intelligence (IJCAI), pp. 638–644 (2017)

23. Gomes, C.P., Sabharwal, A., Selman, B.: Model counting. In: Biere, A., Heule, M., van Maaren, H., Walsh, T. (eds.) Handbook of Satisfiability. Frontiers in Artificial Intelligence and Applications, vol. 185, pp. 633–654. IOS Press, Amsterdam (2009)

24. Heule, M.J.H.: march_br. In: Proceedings of SAT Competition 2013 (2013)

25. Heule, M., van Maaren, H.: march_hi. In: Proceedings of the 2009 SAT Competition, pp. 27–28 (2009)

26. Katsirelos, G., Simon, L.: Eigenvector centrality in industrial SAT instances. In: Milano, M. (ed.) CP 2012. LNCS, pp. 348–356. Springer, Heidelberg (2012). https://doi.org/10.1007/978-3-642-33558-7_27

27. Konolige, K.: Easy to be hard: difficult problems for greedy algorithms. In: Proceedings of the Fourth International Conference on Principles of Knowledge Representation and Reasoning (KR), pp. 374–378 (1994)

28. Levy, J.: Percolation and phase transition in SAT. ArXiv e-prints, July 2017. arXiv:1708.06805

29. Li, C., Huang, C., Xu, R.: Balance between intensification and diversification: a unity of opposites. In: Proceedings of SAT Competition 2014, pp. 10–11 (2014)

30. Liang, J.H., Oh, C., Ganesh, V., Czarnecki, K., Poupar, P.: MapleCOMSPS, MapleCOMSPS_lrb, MapleCOMSPS_CHB. In: Proceedings of the 2016 SAT Competition, pp. 52–53 (2016)

31. Mitchell, D.G., Selman, B., Levesque, H.J.: Hard and easy distributions of SAT problems. In: Proceedings of the Tenth AAAI Conference on Artificial Intelligence, pp. 459–465 (1992)

32. Mu, Z., Hoos, H.H.: On the empirical time complexity of random 3-SAT at the phase transition. In: Proceedings of the Twenty-Fourth International Joint Conference on Artificial Intelligence (IJCAI), pp. 367–373 (2015)

33. Rish, I., Dechter, R.: Resolution versus search: two strategies for SAT. J. Autom. Reasoning **24**(1–2), 225–275 (2000)

34. Selman, B., Kautz, H.A., Cohen, B.: Noise strategies for improving local search. In: Proceedings of the Twelfth AAAI Conference on Artificial Intelligence, pp. 337–343 (1994)

35. Slater, A.: Modelling more realistic SAT problems. In: McKay, B., Slaney, J. (eds.) AI 2002. LNCS (LNAI), vol. 2557, pp. 591–602. Springer, Heidelberg (2002). https://doi.org/10.1007/3-540-36187-1_52

36. Yokoo, M.: Why adding more constraints makes a problem easier for hill-climbing algorithms: analyzing landscapes of CSPs. In: Smolka, G. (ed.) CP 1997. LNCS, vol. 1330, pp. 356–370. Springer, Heidelberg (1997). https://doi.org/10.1007/BFb0017451

13

Reachability Analysis for Termination and Confluence of Rewriting

Christian Sternagel[1]($\boxtimes$)(iD) and Akihisa Yamada[2]($\boxtimes$)(iD)

[1] University of Innsbruck, Innsbruck, Austria
christian.sternagel@uibk.ac.at
[2] National Institute of Informatics, Tokyo, Japan
akihisayamada@nii.ac.jp

Abstract. In term rewriting, reachability analysis is concerned with the problem of deciding whether or not one term is reachable from another by rewriting. Reachability analysis has several applications in termination and confluence analysis of rewrite systems. We give a unified view on reachability analysis for rewriting with and without conditions by means of what we call reachability constraints. Moreover, we provide several techniques that fit into this general framework and can be efficiently implemented. Our experiments show that these techniques increase the power of existing termination and confluence tools.

Keywords: Reachability analysis · Termination · Confluence · Conditional term rewriting · Infeasibility

1 Introduction

Reachability analysis for term rewriting [6] is concerned with the problem of, given a rewrite system $\mathcal{R}$, a source term s and a target term t, deciding whether the source reduces to the target by rewriting, which is usually written $s \to_\mathcal{R}^* t$. A useful generalization of this problem is the (un)satisfiability of the following reachability problem: given terms s and t containing variables, decide whether there is a substitution σ such that $s\sigma \to_\mathcal{R}^* t\sigma$ or not. This problem, also called (in)feasibility by Lucas and Guitiérrez [11], has various applications in termination and confluence analysis for plain and conditional rewriting.

This can be understood as a form of safety analysis, as illustrated below.

Example 1. Let $\mathcal{R}$ be a term rewrite system consisting of the following rules for division (where s stands for "successor"):

$$x - 0 \to x \qquad \mathsf{s}(x) - \mathsf{s}(y) \to x - y \qquad 0 \div \mathsf{s}(y) \to 0$$
$$\mathsf{s}(x) \div \mathsf{s}(y) \to \mathsf{s}((x - y) \div \mathsf{s}(y)) \qquad x \div 0 \to \mathsf{err}(\texttt{"division by zero"})$$

The question "Can division yield an error?" is naturally formulated as the satisfiability of reachability from $x \div y$ to $\mathsf{err}(z)$. Unsurprisingly, the solution

$$\sigma = [y \mapsto 0, z \mapsto \texttt{"division by zero"}]$$

shows that it is actually possible to obtain an error.

In termination analysis we are typically interested in unsatisfiability of reachability and can thereby rule out certain recursive calls as potential source of nontermination. For confluence analysis of conditional term rewriting, infeasibility is crucial: some other techniques do not apply before critical pairs are shown infeasible, and removal of infeasible rules simplifies proofs.

In this work we provide a formal framework that allows us to uniformly speak about (un)satisfiability of reachability for plain and conditional rewriting, and give several techniques that are useful in practice.

More specifically, our contributions are as follows:

- We introduce the syntax and semantics of *reachability constraints* (Sect. 3) and formulate their satisfiability problem. We recast several concrete techniques for reachability analysis in the resulting framework.
- We present a new, simple, and efficient technique for reachability analysis based on what we call the *symbol transition graph* of a rewrite system (Sect. 4.1) and extend it to conditional rewriting (Sect. 5.2).
- Additionally, we generalize the prevalent existing technique for term rewriting to what we call *look-ahead reachability* (Sect. 4.2) and extend it to the conditional case (Sect. 5.3).
- Then, we present a new result for conditional rewriting that is useful for proving conditional rules infeasible (Sect. 5.1).
- Finally, we evaluate the impact of our work on existing automated tools NaTT [16] and ConCon [13] (Sect. 6).

2 Preliminaries

In the remainder, we assume some familiarity with term rewriting. Nevertheless, we recall required concepts and notations below. For further details on term rewriting, we refer to standard textbooks [3, 14].

Throughout the paper $\mathcal{F}$ denotes a set of function symbols with associated arities, and $\mathcal{V}$ a countably infinite set of variables (so that fresh variables can always be picked) such that $\mathcal{F} \cap \mathcal{V} = \varnothing$. A *term* is either a variable $x \in \mathcal{V}$ or of the form $f(t_1, \ldots, t_n)$, where n is the arity of $f \in \mathcal{F}$ and the arguments $t_1, \ldots, t_n$ are terms. The set of all terms over $\mathcal{F}$ and $\mathcal{V}$ is denoted by $\mathcal{T}(\mathcal{F}, \mathcal{V})$. The set of variables occurring in a term t is denoted by $\mathsf{Var}(t)$. The *root symbol* of a term $t = f(t_1, \ldots, t_n)$ is f and denoted by $\mathsf{root}(t)$. When we want to indicate that a term is not a variable, we sometimes write $f(\ldots)$, where "..." denotes an arbitrary list of terms.

A *substitution* is a mapping $\sigma : \mathcal{V} \to \mathcal{T}(\mathcal{F}, \mathcal{V})$. Given a term t, $t\sigma$ denotes the term obtained by replacing every occurrence of variable x in t by $\sigma(x)$. The *domain* of a substitution σ is $\mathsf{Dom}(\sigma) := \{x \in \mathcal{V} \mid x\sigma \neq x\}$, and σ is *idempotent* if $\mathsf{Var}(x\sigma) \cap \mathsf{Dom}(\sigma) = \varnothing$ for every $x \in \mathcal{V}$. A *renaming* is a bijection $\alpha : \mathcal{V} \to \mathcal{V}$.

Two terms s and t are *unifiable* if $s\sigma = t\sigma$ for some substitution σ, which is called a *unifier* of s and t.

A *context* is a term with exactly one occurrence of the special symbol $\Box$. We write $C[t]$ for the term resulting from replacing $\Box$ in context C by term t.

A *rewrite rule* is a pair of terms, written $l \to r$, such that the *variable conditions* $l \notin \mathcal{V}$ and $\mathsf{Var}(l) \supseteq \mathsf{Var}(r)$ hold. By a *variant* of a rewrite rule we mean a rule that is obtained by consistently renaming variables in the original rule to fresh ones. A *term rewrite system (TRS)* is a set $\mathcal{R}$ of rewrite rules. A function symbol $f \in \mathcal{F}$ is *defined* in $\mathcal{R}$ if $f(...) \to r \in \mathcal{R}$, and the set of defined symbols in $\mathcal{R}$ is $\mathcal{D}_\mathcal{R} := \{f \mid f(...) \to r \in \mathcal{R}\}$. We call $f \in \mathcal{F} \setminus \mathcal{D}_\mathcal{R}$ a *constructor*.

There is an $\mathcal{R}$-*rewrite step* from s to t, written $s \to_\mathcal{R} t$, iff there exist a context C, a substitution σ, and a rule $l \to r \in \mathcal{R}$ such that $s = C[l\sigma]$ and $t = C[r\sigma]$. We write $s \xrightarrow{\epsilon}_\mathcal{R} t$ if $C = \Box$ (called a *root step*), and $s \xrightarrow{>\epsilon}_\mathcal{R} t$ (called a *non-root step*), otherwise. We say a term s_0 is $\mathcal{R}$-*terminating* if it starts no infinite rewrite sequence $s_0 \to_\mathcal{R} s_1 \to_\mathcal{R} s_2 \to_\mathcal{R} \cdots$, and say $\mathcal{R}$ is *terminating* if every term is $\mathcal{R}$-terminating.

For a relation $\rightarrowtail\ \subseteq A \times A$, we denote its transitive closure by $\rightarrowtail^+$ and reflexive transitive closure by $\rightarrowtail^*$. We say that $a_1, \ldots, a_n \in A$ are *joinable* (*meetable*) at $b \in A$ with respect to $\rightarrowtail$ if $a_i \rightarrowtail^* b$ ($b \rightarrowtail^* a_i$) for every $i \in \{1, \ldots, n\}$.

3   Reachability Constraint Satisfaction

In this section we introduce the syntax and semantics of reachability constraints, a framework that allows us to unify several concrete techniques for reachability analysis on an abstract level. Reachability constraints are first-order formulas[1] with a single binary predicate symbol whose intended interpretation is reachability by rewriting with respect to a given rewrite system.

Definition 1 (Reachability Constraints). *Reachability constraints are given by the following grammar (where $s, t \in \mathcal{T}(\mathcal{F}, \mathcal{V})$ and $x \in \mathcal{V}$)*

$$\phi, \psi, \cdots ::= \top \mid \bot \mid s \twoheadrightarrow t \mid \phi \vee \psi \mid \phi \wedge \psi \mid \neg\phi \mid \forall x.\, \phi \mid \exists x.\, \phi$$

To save some space, we use conventional notation like $\bigwedge_{i \in I} \phi_i$ and $\exists x_1, \ldots, x_n.\, \phi$.

As mentioned above, the semantics of reachability constraints is defined with respect to a given rewrite system. In the following we define satisfiability of constraints with respect to a TRS. (This definition will be extended to conditional rewrite systems in Sect. 5).

Definition 2 (Satisfiability). *We define[2] inductively when a substitution σ satisfies a reachability constraint ϕ modulo a TRS $\mathcal{R}$, written $\sigma \models_\mathcal{R} \phi$, as follows:*

---

[1] While in general we allow an arbitrary first-order logical structure for formulas, for the purpose of this paper, negation and universal quantification are not required.

[2] It is also possible to give a model-theoretic account for these notions. However, the required preliminaries are outside the scope of this paper.

- $\sigma \models_{\mathcal{R}} \top$;
- $\sigma \models_{\mathcal{R}} s \twoheadrightarrow t$ if $s\sigma \to_{\mathcal{R}}^* t\sigma$;
- $\sigma \models_{\mathcal{R}} \phi \vee \psi$ if $\sigma \models_{\mathcal{R}} \phi$ or $\sigma \models_{\mathcal{R}} \psi$;
- $\sigma \models_{\mathcal{R}} \phi \wedge \psi$ if $\sigma \models_{\mathcal{R}} \phi$ and $\sigma \models_{\mathcal{R}} \psi$;
- $\sigma \models_{\mathcal{R}} \neg\phi$ if $\sigma \models_{\mathcal{R}} \phi$ does not hold;
- $\sigma \models_{\mathcal{R}} \forall x.\, \phi$ if $\sigma' \models_{\mathcal{R}} \phi$ for every σ' that coincides with σ on $\mathcal{V} \setminus \{x\}$.
- $\sigma \models_{\mathcal{R}} \exists x.\, \phi$ if $\sigma' \models_{\mathcal{R}} \phi$ for some σ' that coincides with σ on $\mathcal{V} \setminus \{x\}$.

We say ϕ and ψ are equivalent modulo $\mathcal{R}$, written $\phi \equiv_{\mathcal{R}} \psi$, when $\sigma \models_{\mathcal{R}} \phi$ iff $\sigma \models_{\mathcal{R}} \psi$ for all σ. We say ϕ and ψ are (logically) equivalent, written $\phi \equiv \psi$, if they are equivalent modulo any $\mathcal{R}$. We say ϕ is satisfiable modulo $\mathcal{R}$, written $\mathsf{SAT}_{\mathcal{R}}(\phi)$, if there is a substitution σ that satisfies ϕ modulo $\mathcal{R}$, and call σ a solution of ϕ with respect to $\mathcal{R}$.

Checking for satisfiability of reachability constraints is for example useful for proving termination of term rewrite systems via the *dependency pair method* [2], or more specifically in *dependency graph* analysis. For the dependency pair method, we assume a fresh *marked* symbol $f^\sharp$ for every $f \in \mathcal{D}_{\mathcal{R}}$, and write $s^\sharp$ to denote the term $f^\sharp(s_1, \ldots, s_n)$ for $s = f(s_1, \ldots, s_n)$. The set of *dependency pairs* of a TRS $\mathcal{R}$ is $\mathsf{DP}(\mathcal{R}) := \{ l^\sharp \to r^\sharp \mid l \to C[r] \in \mathcal{R},\ r \notin \mathcal{V},\ \mathsf{root}(r) \in \mathcal{D}_{\mathcal{R}} \}$. The standard definition of the dependency graph of a TRS [2] can be recast using reachability constraints as follows:

Definition 3 (Dependency Graph). *Given a TRS $\mathcal{R}$, its* dependency graph *$\mathsf{DG}(\mathcal{R})$ is the directed graph over $\mathsf{DP}(\mathcal{R})$ where there is an edge from $l^\sharp \to s^\sharp$ to $t^\sharp \to r^\sharp$ iff $\mathsf{SAT}_{\mathcal{R}}(s^\sharp \twoheadrightarrow t^\sharp \alpha)$, where α is a renaming of variables such that $\mathsf{Var}(t^\sharp \alpha) \cap \mathsf{Var}(s^\sharp) = \varnothing$.*

The nodes of the dependency graph correspond to the possible recursive calls in a program (represented by a TRS), while its edges encode the information which recursive calls can directly follow each other in arbitrary program executions. This is the reason why dependency graphs are useful for investigating the termination behavior of TRSs, as captured by the following result.

Theorem 1 ([10]). *A TRS $\mathcal{R}$ is terminating iff for every strongly connected component $\mathcal{C}$ of an over approximation of $\mathsf{DG}(\mathcal{R})$, there is no infinite chain $s_0 \xrightarrow{\epsilon}_{\mathcal{C}} t_0 \to_{\mathcal{R}}^* s_1 \xrightarrow{\epsilon}_{\mathcal{C}} t_1 \to_{\mathcal{R}}^* \cdots$ where every t_i is $\mathcal{R}$-terminating.*

Example 2. Consider the TRS $\mathcal{R}$ of Toyama [15] consisting of the single rule $\mathsf{f}(0, 1, x) \to \mathsf{f}(x, x, x)$. Its dependency graph $\mathsf{DG}(\mathcal{R})$ consists of the single node:

$$\mathsf{f}^\sharp(0, 1, x) \to \mathsf{f}^\sharp(x, x, x) \tag{1}$$

To show $\mathcal{R}$ terminates it suffices to show that $\mathsf{DG}(\mathcal{R})$ has no edge from (1) back to (1), that is, the unsatisfiability of the constraint (with a fresh variable x')

$$\mathsf{f}^\sharp(x, x, x) \twoheadrightarrow \mathsf{f}^\sharp(0, 1, x') \tag{2}$$

The most popular method today for checking reachability during dependency graph analysis is unifiability between the target and an approximation of the topmost part of the source (its "cap") that does not change under rewriting, which is computed by the $\mathsf{tcap}_\mathcal{R}$ function [9].

Definition 4 (tcap). *Let $\mathcal{R}$ be a TRS. We recursively define $\mathsf{tcap}_\mathcal{R}(t)$ for a given term t as follows: $\mathsf{tcap}_\mathcal{R}(x)$ is a fresh variable if $x \in \mathcal{V}$; $\mathsf{tcap}_\mathcal{R}(f(t_1,\ldots,t_n))$ is a fresh variable if $u = f(\mathsf{tcap}_\mathcal{R}(t_1),\ldots,\mathsf{tcap}_\mathcal{R}(t_n))$ unifies with some left-hand side of the rules in $\mathcal{R}$; otherwise, it is u.*

The standard way of checking for nonreachability that is implemented in most tools is captured by of the following proposition.

Proposition 1. *If $\mathsf{tcap}_\mathcal{R}(s)$ and t are not unifiable, then $s \twoheadrightarrow t \equiv_\mathcal{R} \bot$.*

Example 3. Proposition 1 cannot prove the unsatisfiability of (2) of Example 2, since the term cap of the source $\mathsf{tcap}_\mathcal{R}(\mathsf{f}^\sharp(x,x,x)) = \mathsf{f}^\sharp(z,z',z'')$, where z, z', z'' are fresh variables, is unifiable with the target $\mathsf{f}^\sharp(0,1,x')$.

4 Reachability in Term Rewriting

In this section we introduce some techniques for analyzing (un)satisfiability of reachability constraints. The first one described below formulates an obvious observation: no root rewrite step is applicable when starting from a term whose root is a constructor.

Definition 5 (Non-Root Reachability). *For terms $s = f(\ldots)$ and $t = g(\ldots)$, we define the* non-root *reachability constraint $s \xrightarrow{>\epsilon} t$ as follows:*

- $s \xrightarrow{>\epsilon} t = \bot$ *if $f \neq g$, and*
- $f(s_1,\ldots,s_n) \xrightarrow{>\epsilon} f(t_1,\ldots,t_n) = s_1 \twoheadrightarrow t_1 \wedge \ldots \wedge s_n \twoheadrightarrow t_n.$

The intention of non-root reachability constraints is to encode zero or more steps of non-root rewriting, in the following sense.

Lemma 1. *For $s,t \notin \mathcal{V}$, $s\sigma \xrightarrow{>\epsilon}{}^*_\mathcal{R} t\sigma$ iff $\sigma \models_\mathcal{R} s \xrightarrow{>\epsilon} t$.*

Proof. The claim vacuously follows if $\mathsf{root}(s) \neq \mathsf{root}(t)$. So let $s = f(s_1,\ldots,s_n)$ and $t = f(t_1,\ldots,t_n)$. We have $f(s_1,\ldots,s_n)\sigma \xrightarrow{>\epsilon}{}^*_\mathcal{R} f(t_1,\ldots,t_n)\sigma$ iff $s_1\sigma \to^*_\mathcal{R} t_1\sigma,\ldots,s_n\sigma \to^*_\mathcal{R} t_n\sigma$ iff $\sigma \models_\mathcal{R} s_1 \twoheadrightarrow t_1 \wedge \ldots \wedge s_n \twoheadrightarrow t_n$. $\qquad\square$

Combined with the observation that no root step is applicable to a term whose root symbol is a constructor, we obtain the following reformulation of a folklore result that reduces reachability to direct subterms.

Proposition 2. *If $s = f(\ldots)$ with $f \notin \mathcal{D}_\mathcal{R}$ and $t \notin \mathcal{V}$, then $s \twoheadrightarrow t \equiv_\mathcal{R} s \xrightarrow{>\epsilon} t$.*

Proposition 2 is directly applicable in the analysis of dependency graphs.

Example 4. Consider again the constraint $\mathsf{f}^\sharp(x,x,x) \twoheadrightarrow \mathsf{f}^\sharp(0,1,x')$ from Example 2. Since $\mathsf{f}^\sharp$ is not defined in $\mathcal{R}$, Proposition 2 reduces this constraint to $\mathsf{f}^\sharp(x,x,x) \xrightarrow{>\epsilon} \mathsf{f}^\sharp(0,1,x')$, that is,

$$x \twoheadrightarrow 0 \wedge x \twoheadrightarrow 1 \wedge x \twoheadrightarrow x' \tag{3}$$

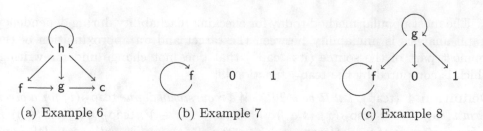

(a) Example 6   (b) Example 7   (c) Example 8

Fig. 1. Example symbol transition graphs.

4.1 Symbol Transition Graphs

Here we introduce a new, simple and efficient way of overapproximating reacha-bility by tracking the relation of root symbols of terms according to a given set of rewrite rules. We first illustrate the intuition by an example.

Example 5. Consider a TRS $\mathcal{R}$ consisting of rules of the following form:

$$\mathsf{f}(\ldots) \to \mathsf{g}(\ldots) \qquad\qquad \mathsf{g}(\ldots) \to \mathsf{c}(\ldots) \qquad\qquad \mathsf{h}(\ldots) \to x$$

Moreover, suppose $s \to_{\mathcal{R}}^* t$. Then we can make the following observations:

- If $\mathsf{root}(s) = \mathsf{c}$, then $\mathsf{root}(t) = \mathsf{c}$ since non-root steps preserve the root symbol and no root steps are applicable to terms of the form $\mathsf{c}(\ldots)$.
- If $\mathsf{root}(s) = \mathsf{g}$, then $\mathsf{root}(t) \in \{\mathsf{g},\mathsf{c}\}$ since non-root steps preserve the root symbol and the only possible root step is $\mathsf{g}(\ldots) \to \mathsf{c}(\ldots)$.
- If $\mathsf{root}(s) = \mathsf{f}$, then $\mathsf{root}(t) \in \{\mathsf{f},\mathsf{g},\mathsf{c}\}$ by the same reasoning.
- If $\mathsf{root}(s) = \mathsf{h}$, then t can be any term and $\mathsf{root}(t)$ can be arbitrary.

This informal argument is captured by the following definition.

Definition 6 (Symbol Transition Graphs). *The symbol transition graph* $\mathsf{SG}(\mathcal{R})$ *of a TRS* $\mathcal{R}$ *over signature* $\mathcal{F}$ *is the graph* $\langle \mathcal{F}, \rightarrowtail_{\mathcal{R}} \rangle$, *where* $f \rightarrowtail_{\mathcal{R}} g$ *iff* $\mathcal{R}$ *contains a rule of form* $f(\ldots) \to g(\ldots)$ *or* $f(\ldots) \to x$ *with* $x \in \mathcal{V}$.

The following result tells us that for non-variable terms the symbol transition graph captures the relation between the root symbols of root rewrite steps.

Lemma 2. *If* $s \xrightarrow{\epsilon}_{\mathcal{R}} t$ *then* $t \in \mathcal{V}$ *or* $\mathsf{root}(s) \rightarrowtail_{\mathcal{R}} \mathsf{root}(t)$.

Proof. By assumption there exist $l \to r \in \mathcal{R}$ and σ such that $s = l\sigma$ and $r\sigma = t$. If $r \in \mathcal{V}$ then either $t \in \mathcal{V}$ or $\mathsf{root}(s) = \mathsf{root}(l) \rightarrowtail_{\mathcal{R}} \mathsf{root}(t)$. Otherwise, $\mathsf{root}(s) = \mathsf{root}(l) \rightarrowtail_{\mathcal{R}} \mathsf{root}(r) = \mathsf{root}(t)$. $\qquad\square$

Since every rewrite sequence is composed of subsequences that take place entirely below the root (and hence do not change the root symbol) separated by root steps, we can extend the previous result to rewrite sequences.

Lemma 3. *If* $s = f(\ldots) \to_{\mathcal{R}}^* g(\ldots) = t$ *then* $f \rightarrowtail_{\mathcal{R}}^* g$.

Proof. We prove the claim for arbitrary s and f by induction on the derivation length of $s \to_{\mathcal{R}}^* t$. The base case is trivial, so consider $s \to_{\mathcal{R}} s' \to_{\mathcal{R}}^n t\sigma$. Since $t \notin \mathcal{V}$, we have $f' \in \mathcal{F}$ with $s' = f'(...)$. Thus the induction hypothesis yields $f' \rightarrowtail_{\mathcal{R}}^* g$. If $s \xrightarrow{\epsilon}_{\mathcal{R}} s'$ then by Lemma 2 we conclude $f \rightarrowtail_{\mathcal{R}} f' \rightarrowtail_{\mathcal{R}}^* g$, and otherwise $f = f' \rightarrowtail_{\mathcal{R}}^* g$. $\qquad\square$

It is now straightforward to derive the following from Lemma 3.

Corollary 1. *If $f \rightarrowtail_{\mathcal{R}}^* g$ does not hold, then $f(...) \twoheadrightarrow g(...) \equiv_{\mathcal{R}} \bot$.*

Example 6. The symbol transition graph for Example 5 is depicted in Fig. 1(a). By Corollary 1 we can conclude, for instance, $g(...) \twoheadrightarrow f(...)$ is unsatisfiable.

Corollary 1 is useful for checking (un)satisfiability of $s \twoheadrightarrow t$, only if neither s nor t is a variable. However, the symbol transition graph is also useful for unsatisfiability in the case when s and t may be variables.

Proposition 3. *If $\mathsf{SAT}_{\mathcal{R}}(x \twoheadrightarrow t_1 \wedge \ldots \wedge x \twoheadrightarrow t_n)$ for $t_1 = g_1(...), \ldots, t_n = g_n(...)$, then $g_1, \ldots, g_n$ are meetable with respect to $\rightarrowtail_{\mathcal{R}}$.*

Proof. By assumption there is a substitution σ such that $x\sigma \to_{\mathcal{R}}^* t_1\sigma, \ldots, x\sigma \to_{\mathcal{R}}^* t_n\sigma$. Clearly $x\sigma \in \mathcal{V}$ is not possible. Thus, suppose $x\sigma = f(...)$ for some f. Finally, from Lemma 3, we have $f \rightarrowtail_{\mathcal{R}}^* g_1, \ldots, f \rightarrowtail_{\mathcal{R}}^* g_n$ and thereby conclude that $g_1, \ldots, g_n$ are meetable at f. $\qquad\square$

The dual of Proposition 3 is proved in a similar way, but with some special care to ensure $x\sigma \in \mathcal{V}$.

Proposition 4. *If $\mathsf{SAT}_{\mathcal{R}}(s_1 \twoheadrightarrow x \wedge \ldots \wedge s_n \twoheadrightarrow x)$ for $s_1 = f_1(...), \ldots, s_n = f_n(...)$, then $f_1, \ldots, f_n$ are joinable with respect to $\rightarrowtail_{\mathcal{R}}$.*

Example 7 (Continuation of Example 4). Due to Proposition 3, proving (3) unsatisfiable reduces to proving that 0 and 1 are not meetable with respect to $\rightarrowtail_{\mathcal{R}}$. This is obvious from the symbol transition graph depicted in Fig. 1(b). Hence, we conclude the termination of $\mathcal{R}$.

Example 8. Consider the following extension of $\mathcal{R}$ from Example 2.

$$\mathsf{f}(0, 1, x) \to \mathsf{f}(x, x, x) \qquad \mathsf{g}(x, y) \to x \qquad \mathsf{g}(x, y) \to y$$

The resulting system is not terminating [15]. The corresponding symbol transition graph is depicted in Fig. 1(c), where 0 and 1 are meetable, as expected.

4.2   Look-Ahead Reachability

Here we propose another method for overapproximating reachability, which eventually subsumes the tcap-unifiability method when target terms are linear. Note that this condition is satisfied in the dependency graph approximation of left-linear TRSs. Our method is based on the observation that any rewrite sequence either contains at least one root step, or takes place entirely below the root. This observation can be captured using our reachability constraints.

Definition 7 (Root Narrowing Constraints). *Let $l \to r$ be a rewrite rule with $\mathrm{Var}(l) = \{x_1, \ldots, x_n\}$. Then for terms s and t not containing $x_1, \ldots, x_n$, the* root narrowing constraint *from s to t via $l \to r$ is defined by*

$$s \rightsquigarrow_{l \to r} t := \exists x_1, \ldots, x_n.\, s \xrightarrow{\geq \epsilon} l \wedge r \twoheadrightarrow t$$

We write $s \rightsquigarrow_{\mathcal{R}} t$ for $\bigvee_{l \to r \in \mathcal{R}'} s \rightsquigarrow_{l \to r} t$, where $\mathcal{R}'$ is a variant of $\mathcal{R}$ in which variables occurring in s or t are renamed to fresh ones.

In the definition above, the intuition is that if there are any root steps inside a rewrite sequence then we can pick the first one, which is only preceded by non-root steps. The following theorem justifies this intuition.

Theorem 2. *If $s, t \notin \mathcal{V}$, then $s \twoheadrightarrow t \equiv_{\mathcal{R}} s \xrightarrow{\geq \epsilon} t \vee s \rightsquigarrow_{\mathcal{R}} t$.*

Proof. Let $s = f(s_1, \ldots, s_n)$ and σ be a substitution. We show $\sigma \models_{\mathcal{R}} s \twoheadrightarrow t$ iff $\sigma \models_{\mathcal{R}} s \xrightarrow{\geq \epsilon} t \vee s \rightsquigarrow_{\mathcal{R}} t$. For the "if" direction suppose the latter. If $\sigma \models_{\mathcal{R}} s \xrightarrow{\geq \epsilon} t$, then t is of form $f(t_1, \ldots, t_n)$ and $s_i \sigma \to_{\mathcal{R}}^* t_i \sigma$ for every $i \in \{1, \ldots, n\}$, and thus $s\sigma \to_{\mathcal{R}}^* t\sigma$. If $\sigma \models_{\mathcal{R}} s \rightsquigarrow_{\mathcal{R}} t$, then we have a renamed variant $l \to r$ of a rule in $\mathcal{R}$ such that $\sigma \models_{\mathcal{R}} s \rightsquigarrow_{l \to r} t$. This indicates that there exists a substitution σ' that coincides with σ on $\mathcal{V} \setminus \mathrm{Var}(l)$, and satisfies

- $\sigma' \models_{\mathcal{R}} s \xrightarrow{\geq \epsilon} l$, that is, $l = f(l_1, \ldots, l_n)$ and $s_i \sigma' \to_{\mathcal{R}}^* l_i \sigma'$;
- $\sigma' \models_{\mathcal{R}} r \twoheadrightarrow t$, that is, $r\sigma' \to_{\mathcal{R}}^* t\sigma'$.

In combination, we have $s\sigma = s\sigma' \xrightarrow{\geq \epsilon}_{\mathcal{R}}^* l\sigma' \xrightarrow{\epsilon}_{\mathcal{R}} r\sigma' \to_{\mathcal{R}}^* t\sigma' = t\sigma$.

Now consider the "only if" direction. Suppose that σ is an idempotent substitution such that $s\sigma \to_{\mathcal{R}}^* t\sigma$. We may assume idempotence, since from any solution σ' of $s \twoheadrightarrow t$, we obtain idempotent solution σ by renaming variables in $\mathrm{Var}(s) \cup \mathrm{Var}(t)$ to fresh ones. We proceed by the following case analysis:

- *No root step is involved:* $s\sigma \xrightarrow{\geq \epsilon}_{\mathcal{R}}^* t\sigma$. Then Lemma 1 implies $\sigma \models_{\mathcal{R}} s \xrightarrow{\geq \epsilon} t$.
- *At least one root step is involved:* there is a rule $l \to r \in \mathcal{R}$ and a substitution θ such that $s\sigma \xrightarrow{\geq \epsilon}_{\mathcal{R}}^* l\theta$ and $r\theta \to_{\mathcal{R}}^* t\sigma$. Since variables in $l\theta$ must occur in $s\sigma$ (due to our assumptions on rewrite rules), we have $l\theta = l\theta\sigma$ since σ is idempotent. Thus from Lemma 1 we have $\sigma \models_{\mathcal{R}} s \xrightarrow{\geq \epsilon} l\theta$. Further, variables in $r\theta$ must occur in $l\theta$ and thus in $s\theta$, we also have $r\theta\sigma = r\theta \to_{\mathcal{R}}^* t\sigma$, and hence $\sigma \models_{\mathcal{R}} r\theta \twoheadrightarrow t$. This concludes $\sigma \models_{\mathcal{R}} s \rightsquigarrow_{l \to r} t$. $\square$

Proposition 2 is a corollary of Theorem 2 together with the following easy lemma, stating that if the root symbol of the source term is not a defined symbol, then no root step can occur.

Lemma 4. *If $c \notin \mathcal{D}_{\mathcal{R}}$ then $c(\ldots) \rightsquigarrow_{\mathcal{R}} t \equiv \bot$.*

Example 9. Consider the TRS $\mathcal{R}$ consisting of the following rules:

$$0 > x \to \mathsf{false} \qquad \mathsf{s}(x) > 0 \to \mathsf{true} \qquad \mathsf{s}(x) > \mathsf{s}(y) \to x > y$$

Applying Theorem 2 once reduces the reachability constraint $0 > z \twoheadrightarrow \mathsf{true}$ to the disjunction of

1. $0 > z \xrightarrow{>\epsilon} \mathsf{true}$,
2. $\exists x.\ 0 > z \xrightarrow{>\epsilon} 0 > x\ \wedge\ \mathsf{false} \twoheadrightarrow \mathsf{true}$
3. $\exists x.\ 0 > z \xrightarrow{>\epsilon} \mathsf{s}(x) > 0\ \wedge\ \mathsf{true} \twoheadrightarrow \mathsf{true}$
4. $\exists x, y.\ 0 > z \xrightarrow{>\epsilon} \mathsf{s}(x) > \mathsf{s}(y)\ \wedge\ x > y \twoheadrightarrow \mathsf{true}$

Disjuncts 1, 3, and 4 expand to $\bot$ by definition of $\xrightarrow{>\epsilon}$. For disjunct 2, applying Theorem 2 or Proposition 2 to $\mathsf{false} \twoheadrightarrow \mathsf{true}$ yields $\bot$.

Note that Theorem 2 can be applied arbitrarily often. Thus, to avoid nontermination in an implementation, we need to control how often it is applied. For this purpose we introduce the following definition.

Definition 8 (k-**Fold Look-Ahead**). *We define the k-fold look-ahead transformation with respect to a TRS $\mathcal{R}$ as follows:*

$$\mathsf{L}^k_{\mathcal{R}}(s \twoheadrightarrow t) := \begin{cases} \mathsf{L}^k_{\mathcal{R}}(s \xrightarrow{>\epsilon} t) \vee s \rightsquigarrow^k_{\mathcal{R}} t & \text{if } k \geq 1 \text{ and } s, t \notin \mathcal{V} \\ s \twoheadrightarrow t & \text{otherwise} \end{cases}$$

which is homomorphically extended to reachability constraints. Here, $\rightsquigarrow^k_{\mathcal{R}}$ is defined as in Definition 7, but k controls the number of root steps to be expanded:

$$s \rightsquigarrow^k_{l \to r} t := \exists x_1, \ldots, x_n.\ \mathsf{L}^k_{\mathcal{R}}(s \xrightarrow{>\epsilon} l) \wedge \mathsf{L}^{k-1}_{\mathcal{R}}(r \twoheadrightarrow t)$$

It easily follows from Theorem 2 and induction on k that the k-fold look-ahead preserves the semantics of reachability constraints.

Corollary 2. $\mathsf{L}^k_{\mathcal{R}}(\phi) \equiv_{\mathcal{R}} \phi$.

The following results indicate that, whenever $\mathsf{tcap}_{\mathcal{R}}$-unifiability (Proposition 1) proves $s \twoheadrightarrow t$ unsatisfiable for linear t, $\mathsf{L}^1_{\mathcal{R}}$ can also conclude it.

Lemma 5. *Let $s = f(s_1, \ldots, s_n)$ and $t \notin \mathcal{V}$ be a linear term, and suppose that $f(\mathsf{tcap}_{\mathcal{R}}(s_1), \ldots, \mathsf{tcap}_{\mathcal{R}}(s_n))$ does not unify with t or any left-hand side in $\mathcal{R}$. Then $\mathsf{L}^1_{\mathcal{R}}(s \twoheadrightarrow t) \equiv \bot$.*

Proof. By structural induction on s. First, we show $\mathsf{L}^1_{\mathcal{R}}(s \xrightarrow{>\epsilon} t) \equiv \bot$. This is trivial if $\mathsf{root}(t) \neq f$. So let $t = f(t_1, \ldots, t_n)$. By assumption there is an $i \in \{1, \ldots, n\}$ such that $\mathsf{tcap}_{\mathcal{R}}(s_i)$ does not unify with t_i. Hence $\mathsf{tcap}_{\mathcal{R}}(s_i)$ cannot be a fresh variable, and thus s_i is of the form $g(u_1, \ldots, u_m)$ and $\mathsf{tcap}_{\mathcal{R}}(s_i) = g(\mathsf{tcap}_{\mathcal{R}}(u_1), \ldots, \mathsf{tcap}_{\mathcal{R}}(u_m))$ is not unifiable with any left-hand side in $\mathcal{R}$. Therefore, the induction hypothesis applies to s_i, yielding $\mathsf{L}^1_{\mathcal{R}}(s_i \twoheadrightarrow t_i) \equiv \bot$. This concludes $\mathsf{L}^1_{\mathcal{R}}(s \xrightarrow{>\epsilon} t) = \mathsf{L}^1_{\mathcal{R}}(s_1 \twoheadrightarrow t_1) \wedge \ldots \wedge \mathsf{L}^1_{\mathcal{R}}(s_n \twoheadrightarrow t_n) \equiv \bot$.

Second, we show $\mathsf{L}^1_{\mathcal{R}}(s \rightsquigarrow^1_{\mathcal{R}} t) \equiv \bot$. To this end, we show for an arbitrary variant $l \to r$ of a rule in $\mathcal{R}$ that $\mathsf{L}^1_{\mathcal{R}}(s \xrightarrow{>\epsilon} l) \equiv \bot$. This is clear if $\mathsf{root}(l) \neq f$. So let $l = f(l_1, \ldots, l_n)$. By assumption there is an $i \in \{1, \ldots, n\}$ such that $\mathsf{tcap}_{\mathcal{R}}(s_i)$ and l_i are not unifiable. By a similar reasoning as above the induction hypothesis applies to s_i and yields $\mathsf{L}^1_{\mathcal{R}}(s_i \twoheadrightarrow l_i) \equiv \bot$. This concludes $\mathsf{L}^1_{\mathcal{R}}(s \xrightarrow{>\epsilon} l) \equiv \bot$. $\square$

Corollary 3. *If $\mathsf{tcap}_{\mathcal{R}}(s)$ and t are not unifiable, then $\mathsf{L}^1_{\mathcal{R}}(s \twoheadrightarrow t) \equiv \bot$.*

5   Conditional Rewriting

Conditional rewriting is a flavor of rewriting where rules are guarded by conditions. On the one hand, this gives us a boost in expressiveness in the sense that it is often possible to directly express equations with preconditions and that it is easier to directly express programming constructs like the where-clauses of Haskell. On the other hand, the analysis of conditional rewrite systems is typically more involved than for plain rewriting.

In this section we first recall the basics of conditional term rewriting. Then, we motivate the importance of reachability analysis for the conditional case. Finally, we extend the techniques of Sect. 4 to conditional rewrite systems.

Preliminaries. A *conditional rewrite rule* $l \rightarrow r \Leftarrow \phi$ consists of two terms $l \notin \mathcal{V}$ and r (the left-hand side and right-hand side, respectively) and a list ϕ of pairs of terms (its *conditions*). A *conditional term rewrite system* (CTRS for short) is a set of conditional rewrite rules. Depending on the interpretation of conditions, conditional rewriting can be separated into several classes. For the purposes of this paper we are interested in *oriented* CTRSs, where conditions are interpreted as reachability constraints with respect to conditional rewriting. Hence, from now on we identify conditions $\langle s_1, t_1 \rangle, \ldots, \langle s_n, t_n \rangle$ with the reachability constraint $s_1 \twoheadrightarrow t_1 \wedge \ldots \wedge s_n \twoheadrightarrow t_n$, and the empty list with $\top$ (omitting "$\Leftarrow \top$" from rules).

The rewrite relation of a CTRS is layered into *levels*: given a CTRS $\mathcal{R}$ and level $i \in \mathbb{N}$, the corresponding (unconditional) TRS $\mathcal{R}_i$ is defined recursively:

$$\mathcal{R}_0 := \varnothing$$
$$\mathcal{R}_{i+1} := \{ l\sigma \rightarrow r\sigma \mid l \rightarrow r \Leftarrow \phi \in \mathcal{R}, \ \sigma \models_{\mathcal{R}_i} \phi \}$$

Then the *(conditional) rewrite relation at level i*, written $\rightarrow_{\mathcal{R},i}$ (or $\rightarrow_i$ whenever $\mathcal{R}$ is clear from the context), is the plain rewrite relation $\rightarrow_{\mathcal{R}_i}$ induced by the TRS $\mathcal{R}_i$. Finally, the *induced (conditional) rewrite relation* of a CTRS $\mathcal{R}$ is defined by $\rightarrow_{\mathcal{R}} := \bigcup \{ \rightarrow_i \mid i \geq 0 \}$. At this point Definition 2 is extended to the conditional case in a straightforward manner.

Definition 9 (Level Satisfiability). *Let $\mathcal{R}$ be a CTRS and ϕ a reachability constraint. We say that a substitution σ satisfies ϕ modulo $\mathcal{R}$ at level i, whenever $\sigma \models_{\mathcal{R},i} \phi$. If we are not interested in a specific satisfying substitution we say that ϕ is satisfiable modulo $\mathcal{R}$ at level i and write $\mathsf{SAT}_{\mathcal{R},i}(\phi)$ (or just $\mathsf{SAT}_i(\phi)$ whenever $\mathcal{R}$ is clear from the context).*

5.1   Infeasibility

The main area of interest for reachability analysis in the conditional case is checking for *infeasibility*. While a formal definition of this concept follows below, for the moment, think of it as unsatisfiability of conditions. The two predominant applications of infeasibility are: (1) if the conditions of a rule are unsatisfiable, the rule can never be applied and thus safely be removed without changing the induced rewrite relation; (2) if the conditions of a conditional critical pair (which arises from confluence analysis of CTRSs) are unsatisfiable, then it poses no problem to confluence and can safely be ignored.

Definition 10 (Infeasibility). *We say that a conditional rewrite rule $l \to r \Leftarrow \phi$ is* applicable at level i *with respect to a CTRS $\mathcal{R}$ iff* $\mathsf{SAT}_{\mathcal{R},i-1}(\phi)$. *A set $\mathcal{S}$ of rules is* infeasible *with respect to $\mathcal{R}$ when no rule in $\mathcal{S}$ is applicable at any level.*

The next theorem allows us to remove some rules from a CTRS while checking for infeasibility of rules.

Theorem 3. *A set $\mathcal{S}$ of rules is infeasible with respect to a CTRS $\mathcal{R}$ iff it is infeasible with respect to $\mathcal{R} \setminus \mathcal{S}$.*

Proof. The 'only if' direction is trivial. Thus we concentrate on the 'if' direction. To this end, assume that $\mathcal{S}$ is infeasible with respect to $\mathcal{R} \setminus \mathcal{S}$, but not infeasible with respect to $\mathcal{R}$. That is, at least one rule in $\mathcal{S}$ is applicable at some level with respect to $\mathcal{R}$. Let m be the minimum level such that there is a rule $l \to r \Leftarrow \phi \in \mathcal{S}$ that is applicable at level m with respect to $\mathcal{R}$. Now if $m = 0$ then $l \to r \Leftarrow \phi$ is applicable at level 0 and thus $\mathsf{SAT}_{\mathcal{R},0}(\phi)$, which trivially implies $\mathsf{SAT}_{\mathcal{R}\setminus\mathcal{S},0}(\phi)$, contradicting the assumption that all rules in $\mathcal{S}$ are infeasible with respect to $\mathcal{R} \setminus \mathcal{S}$. Otherwise, $m = k+1$ for some $k \geq 0$ and since $l \to r \Leftarrow \phi$ is applicable at level m we have $\mathsf{SAT}_{\mathcal{R},k}(\phi)$. Moreover, the rewrite relations $\to_{\mathcal{R},k}$ and $\to_{\mathcal{R}\setminus\mathcal{S},k}$ coincide (since all rules in $\mathcal{S}$ are infeasible at levels smaller than m by our choice of m). Thus we also have $\mathsf{SAT}_{\mathcal{R}\setminus\mathcal{S},k}(\phi)$, again contradicting the assumption that all rules in $\mathcal{S}$ are infeasible with respect to $\mathcal{R} \setminus \mathcal{S}$. □

The following example from *the confluence problems data base* (Cops)[3] shows that Theorem 3 is beneficial for showing infeasibility of conditional rewrite rules.

Example 10 (Cops 794). Consider the CTRS $\mathcal{R}$ consisting of the two rules:

$$a \to c \Leftarrow f(a) \twoheadrightarrow f(b) \qquad\qquad f(b) \to b$$

The tcap-method does not manage to conclude infeasibility of the first rule, since $\mathsf{tcap}_{\mathcal{R}}(f(a)) = x$ for some fresh variable x and thus unifies with $f(b)$. The reason for this result was that for computing $\mathsf{tcap}_{\mathcal{R}}$ we had to recursively (in a bottom-up fashion) try to unify arguments of functions with left-hand sides of rules, which succeeded for the left-hand side of the first rule and the argument a of $f(a)$, thereby obtaining $f(x)$ which, in turn, unifies with the left-hand side of the second rule. But by Theorem 3 we do not need to consider the first rule for computing the term cap and thus obtain $\mathsf{tcap}_{\{f(b)\to b\}}(f(a)) = f(a)$ which does not unify with $f(b)$ and thereby shows that the first rule is infeasible.

---

[3] http://cops.uibk.ac.at/?q=ctrs+oriented.

Fig. 2. Inductive and plain symbol transition graph of Example 11.

5.2   Symbol Transition Graphs in the Presence of Conditions

In the presence of conditions in rules we replace Definition 6 by the following inductive definition:

Definition 11 (Inductive Symbol Transition Graphs). *The symbol transition graph* $\mathsf{SG}(\mathcal{R})$ *of a CTRS* $\mathcal{R}$ *over a signature* $\mathcal{F}$ *is the graph* $\langle \mathcal{F}, \rightarrowtail_{\mathcal{R}} \rangle$ *where* $\rightarrowtail_{\mathcal{R}}$ *is defined inductively by the following two inference rules:*

$$\frac{f(...) \to x \Leftarrow \phi \in \mathcal{R} \quad \forall \langle s, t \rangle \in \phi.\, s \in \mathcal{V} \vee t \in \mathcal{V} \vee \mathsf{root}(s) \rightarrowtail^*_{\mathcal{R}} \mathsf{root}(t)}{f \rightarrowtail_{\mathcal{R}} g} \; g \in \mathcal{F}$$

$$\frac{f(...) \to g(...) \Leftarrow \phi \in \mathcal{R} \quad \forall \langle s, t \rangle \in \phi.\, s \in \mathcal{V} \vee t \in \mathcal{V} \vee \mathsf{root}(s) \rightarrowtail^*_{\mathcal{R}} \mathsf{root}(t)}{f \rightarrowtail_{\mathcal{R}} g}$$

The example below shows the difference between the symbol transition graph for TRSs (which can be applied as a crude overapproximation also to CTRSs by dropping all conditions) and the inductive symbol transition graph for CTRSs.

Example 11 (Cops 293). Consider the CTRS consisting of the three rules:

$$\mathsf{a} \to \mathsf{b} \qquad\qquad \mathsf{a} \to \mathsf{c} \qquad\qquad \mathsf{b} \to \mathsf{c} \Leftarrow \mathsf{b} \rightarrowtail \mathsf{c}$$

The corresponding inductive symbol transition graph is depicted in Fig. 2(a) and implies unsatisfiability of $\mathsf{b} \rightarrowtail \mathsf{c}$. Note that this conclusion cannot be drawn from the plain symbol transition graph of the TRS obtained by dropping the condition of the third rule, shown in Fig. 2(b).

The inductive symbol transition graph gives us a sufficient criterion for concluding nonreachability with respect to a given CTRS, as shown in the following.

Lemma 6. *If* $f(...) \to^*_{\mathcal{R}} g(...)$ *then* $f \rightarrowtail^*_{\mathcal{R}} g$.

Proof. Let $s = f(...)$ and $u = g(...)$ and assume that s rewrites to u at level i, that is, $s \to^*_i u$. We prove the statement by induction on the level i. If $i = 0$ then we are done, since $\to_0$ is empty and therefore $f(...) = s = u = g(...)$, which trivially implies $f \rightarrowtail^*_{\mathcal{R}} g$. Otherwise, $i = j + 1$ and we obtain the induction hypothesis (IH) that $s \to^*_j t$ implies $\mathsf{root}(s) \rightarrowtail^*_{\mathcal{R}} \mathsf{root}(t)$ for arbitrary non-variable terms s and t. We proceed to show that $s \to^*_i u$ implies $f \rightarrowtail^*_{\mathcal{R}} g$ by an inner induction on the length of this derivation. If the derivation is empty, then $f(...) = s =$

$u = g(...)$ and therefore trivially $f \rightarrowtail_{\mathcal{R}}^* g$. Otherwise, the derivation is of the shape $s \rightarrow_i^* t \rightarrow_i u$ for some non-variable term $t = h(...)$ and we obtain the inner induction hypothesis that $f \rightarrowtail_{\mathcal{R}}^* h$. It remains to show $h \rightarrowtail_{\mathcal{R}}^* g$ in order to conclude the proof. To this end, consider the step $t = C[l\sigma] \rightarrow_i C[r\sigma] = u$ for some context C, substitution σ, and rule $l \rightarrow r \Leftarrow \phi \in \mathcal{R}$ such that $\sigma \models_j \phi$. Now, by IH, we obtain that $s' \in \mathcal{V}$ or $t' \in \mathcal{V}$ or $\mathsf{root}(s') \rightarrowtail_{\mathcal{R}}^* \mathsf{root}(t')$ for all $\langle s', t' \rangle \in \phi$. Thus, by Definition 11, we obtain that $\mathsf{root}(l\sigma) \rightarrowtail_{\mathcal{R}} \mathsf{root}(r\sigma)$. We conclude by a case analysis on the structure of the context C. If C is empty, that is $C = \square$, then $h = \mathsf{root}(l\sigma) \rightarrowtail_{\mathcal{R}}^* \mathsf{root}(r\sigma) = g$ and we are done. Otherwise, $h = \mathsf{root}(t) = \mathsf{root}(u) = g$ and therefore trivially $h \rightarrowtail_{\mathcal{R}}^* g$. $\square$

Corollary 4. *If $f \rightarrowtail_{\mathcal{R}}^* g$ does not hold, then $f(...) \rightarrow g(...) \equiv_{\mathcal{R}} \perp$.*

5.3 Look-Ahead Reachability in the Presence of Conditions

In the following definition we extend our look-ahead technique from plain rewriting to conditional rewriting.

Definition 12 (Conditional Root Narrowing Constraints). *Let $l \rightarrow r \Leftarrow \phi$ be a conditional rewrite rule with $\mathsf{Var}(l) = \{x_1, \ldots, x_n\}$. Then for terms s and t not containing $x_1, \ldots, x_n$, the conditional root narrowing constraint from s to t via $l \rightarrow r \Leftarrow \phi$ is defined by*

$$s \rightsquigarrow_{l \rightarrow r \Leftarrow \phi} t := \exists x_1, \ldots, x_n. \, s \xrightarrow{> \epsilon} l \wedge r \rightarrow t \wedge \phi$$

We write $s \rightsquigarrow_{\mathcal{R}} t$ for $\bigvee_{l \rightarrow r \Leftarrow \phi \in \mathcal{R}'} s \rightsquigarrow_{l \rightarrow r \Leftarrow \phi} t$, where $\mathcal{R}'$ is a variant of $\mathcal{R}$ in which variables occurring in s or t are renamed to fresh ones.

And we obtain a result similar to Theorem 2.

Lemma 7. *If $s, t \notin \mathcal{V}$, then $s \rightarrow t \equiv_{\mathcal{R}} s \xrightarrow{> \epsilon} t \vee s \rightsquigarrow_{\mathcal{R}} t$.*

Example 12 (Cops 793). Consider the CTRS $\mathcal{R}$ consisting of the two rules:

$$\mathsf{a} \rightarrow \mathsf{a} \Leftarrow \mathsf{f}(\mathsf{a}) \twoheadrightarrow \mathsf{a} \qquad \mathsf{f}(x) \rightarrow \mathsf{a} \Leftarrow x \twoheadrightarrow \mathsf{b}$$

To show infeasibility of the first rule we can safely remove it from $\mathcal{R}$ by Theorem 3, resulting in the modified CTRS $\mathcal{R}'$. Then we have to check $\mathsf{SAT}_{\mathcal{R}'}(\mathsf{f}(\mathsf{a}) \twoheadrightarrow \mathsf{a})$ which is made easier by the following chain of equivalences:

$$
\begin{aligned}
\mathsf{f}(\mathsf{a}) \twoheadrightarrow \mathsf{a} &\equiv_{\mathcal{R}'} \mathsf{f}(\mathsf{a}) \xrightarrow{> \epsilon} \mathsf{a} \vee \mathsf{f}(\mathsf{a}) \rightsquigarrow_{\mathsf{f}(x) \rightarrow \mathsf{a} \Leftarrow x \twoheadrightarrow \mathsf{b}} \mathsf{a} && \text{(by Lemma 7)} \\
&\equiv_{\mathcal{R}'} \mathsf{f}(\mathsf{a}) \rightsquigarrow_{\mathsf{f}(x) \rightarrow \mathsf{a} \Leftarrow x \twoheadrightarrow \mathsf{b}} \mathsf{a} && \text{(by Definition 5)} \\
&\equiv_{\mathcal{R}'} \exists x. \mathsf{f}(\mathsf{a}) \xrightarrow{> \epsilon} \mathsf{f}(x) \wedge \mathsf{a} \rightarrow \mathsf{a} \wedge x \twoheadrightarrow \mathsf{b} && \text{(by Definition 12)} \\
&\equiv_{\mathcal{R}'} \exists x. \mathsf{a} \rightarrow x \wedge \mathsf{a} \rightarrow \mathsf{a} \wedge x \twoheadrightarrow \mathsf{b} && \text{(by Definition 5)}
\end{aligned}
$$

Since satisfiability of the final constraint above implies $\mathsf{SAT}_{\mathcal{R}'}(\mathsf{a} \twoheadrightarrow \mathsf{b})$ and we also have $\mathsf{a} \not\rightarrowtail_{\mathcal{R}}^* \mathsf{b}$, we can conclude unsatisfiability of the original constraint by Corollary 4 and hence that the first rule of $\mathcal{R}$ is infeasible.

Table 1. Experimental results for dependency graph analysis (TRSs).

		Look-ahead				
		$L_{\mathcal{R}}^{0}$	$L_{\mathcal{R}}^{1}$	$L_{\mathcal{R}}^{2}$	$L_{\mathcal{R}}^{3}$	$L_{\mathcal{R}}^{8}$
None	UNSAT	0	104 050	105 574	105 875	105 993
	time (s)	33.96	38.98	38.13	39.15	116.52
Corollary 1	UNSAT	307 207	328 216	328 430	328 499	328 636
	time (s)	38.50	42.71	42.72	43.00	66.82

6 Assessment

We implemented our techniques in the TRS termination prover NaTT [16][4] version 1.8 for dependency graph analysis, and the CTRS confluence prover Con-Con [13][5] version 1.7 for infeasibility analysis. In both cases we only need a complete satisfiability checker, or equivalently, a sound unsatisfiability checker. Hence, to conclude unsatisfiability of given reachability constraints, we apply Corollary 2 with appropriate k together with a complete approximation of constraints. One such approximation is the symbol transition graph (Corollary 1). In the following we describe the experimental results on TRS termination and CTRS confluence. Further details of our experiments can be found at http://cl-informatik.uibk.ac.at/experiments/reachability/.

TRS Termination. For plain rewriting, we take all the 1498 TRSs from the TRS standard category of the *termination problem data base* version 10.6,[6] the benchmark used in the annual *Termination Competition* [8], and over-approximate their dependency graphs. This results in 1 133 963 reachability constraints, which we call "edges" here. Many of these edges are actually satisfiable, but we do not know the exact number (the problem is undecidable in general).

For checking unsatisfiability of edges, we combine Corollary 2 for various values of k (0, 1, 2, 3, and 8), and either Corollary 1 or 'None'. Here 'None' concludes unsatisfiability only for constraints that are logically equivalent to $\bot$. In Table 1 we give the number of edges that could be shown unsatisfiable. Here, the 'UNSAT' row indicates the number of detected unsatisfiable edges and the 'time' row indicates the total runtime in seconds. (We ran our experiments on an Amazon EC2 instance model c5.xlarge: 4 virtual 3.0 GHz Intel Xeon Platinum CPUs on 8 GB of memory).

The starting point is $L_{\mathcal{R}}^{1}$ + None, which corresponds to the tcap technique, the method that was already implemented in NaTT before. The benefit of symbol transition graphs turns out to be quite significant, while the overhead in runtime seems acceptable. Moreover, increasing k of the look-ahead reasonably improves the power of unsatisfiability checks, both with and without the symbol transition

---

[4] https://www.trs.css.i.nagoya-u.ac.jp/NaTT/.

[5] http://cl-informatik.uibk.ac.at/software/concon/.

[6] http://www.termination-portal.org/wiki/TPDB.

graph technique. In terms of the overall termination proving power, NaTT using only tcap solves 1039 out of the 1498 termination problems, while using $L_{\mathcal{R}}^8$ and Corollary 1, it proves termination of 18 additional problems.

CTRS Confluence. For conditional rewriting, we take the 148 oriented CTRSs of Cops,[7] a benchmark of confluence problems used in the annual *Confluence Competition* [1]. Compared to version 1.5 of ConCon (the winner of the CTRS category in the last competition in 2018) our new version (1.7) can solve five more systems (that is a gain of roughly 3%) by incorporating a combination of Theorem 3, inductive symbol transition graphs (Corollary 4), and k-fold look-ahead (Lemma 7), where for the latter we fixed $k = 1$ since we additionally have to control the level of conditional rewriting.

7 Related Work

Reachability is a classical topic in term rewriting; cf. Genet [7] for a survey. Some modern techniques include the tree-automata-completion approach [5,6] and a Knuth-Bendix completion-like approach [4]. Compared to these lines of work, first of all our interest is not directly in reachability problems but their (un)satisfiability. Middeldorp [12] proposed tree-automata techniques to approximate dependency graphs and made a theoretical comparison to an early term-cap-unifiability method [2], a predecessor of the tcap-based method. It is indeed possible (after some approximations of input TRSs) to encode our satisfiability problems into reachability problems between regular tree languages. However, our main motivation is to efficiently test reachability when analyzing other properties like termination and confluence. In that setting, constructing tree automata often leads to excessive overhead.

Our work is inspired by the work of Lucas and Gutiérrez [11]. Their *feasibility sequences* serve the same purpose as our reachability constraints, but are limited to atoms and conjunctions. Our formulation, allowing other constructions of logic formulas, is essential for introducing look-ahead reachability.

8 Conclusion

We introduced reachability constraints and their satisfiability problem. Such problems appear in termination and confluence analysis of plain and conditional rewriting. Moreover, we proposed two efficient techniques to prove (un)satisfiability of reachability constraints, first for plain and then for conditional rewriting. Finally, we implemented these techniques in the termination prover NaTT and the confluence prover ConCon, and experimentally verified their significance.

---

[7] http://cops.uibk.ac.at/?q=oriented+ctrs.

Acknowledgments. We thank Aart Middeldorp and the anonymous reviewers for their insightful comments. This work is supported by the Austrian Science Fund (FWF) project P27502 and ERATO HASUO Metamathematics for Systems Design Project (No. JPMJER1603), JST.

References

1. Aoto, T., Hirokawa, N., Nagele, J., Nishida, N., Zankl, H.: Confluence competition 2015. In: Felty, A.P., Middeldorp, A. (eds.) CADE 2015. LNCS (LNAI), vol. 9195, pp. 101–104. Springer, Cham (2015). https://doi.org/10.1007/978-3-319-21401-6_5
2. Arts, T., Giesl, J.: Termination of term rewriting using dependency pairs. Theor. Compt. Sci. **236**(1–2), 133–178 (2000). https://doi.org/10.1016/S0304-3975(99)00207-8
3. Baader, F., Nipkow, T.: Term Rewriting and All That. Cambridge University Press, Cambridge (1998)
4. Burel, G., Dowek, G., Jiang, Y.: A completion method to decide reachability in rewrite systems. In: Lutz, C., Ranise, S. (eds.) FroCoS 2015. LNCS (LNAI), vol. 9322, pp. 205–219. Springer, Cham (2015). https://doi.org/10.1007/978-3-319-24246-0_13
5. Felgenhauer, B., Thiemann, R.: Reachability, confluence, and termination analysis with state-compatible automata. Inf. Comput. **253**, 467–483 (2017). https://doi.org/10.1016/j.ic.2016.06.011
6. Feuillade, G., Genet, T., Viet Triem Tong, V.: Reachability analysis over term rewriting systems. J. Autom. Reason. **33**(341), 341–383 (2004). https://doi.org/10.1007/s10817-004-6246-0
7. Genet, T.: Reachability analysis of rewriting for software verification. Habilitation à diriger des recherches, Université de Rennes 1 (2009)
8. Giesl, J., Mesnard, F., Rubio, A., Thiemann, R., Waldmann, J.: Termination competition (termCOMP 2015). In: Felty, A.P., Middeldorp, A. (eds.) CADE 2015. LNCS (LNAI), vol. 9195, pp. 105–108. Springer, Cham (2015). https://doi.org/10.1007/978-3-319-21401-6_6
9. Giesl, J., Thiemann, R., Schneider-Kamp, P.: Proving and disproving termination of higher-order functions. In: Gramlich, B. (ed.) FroCoS 2005. LNCS (LNAI), vol. 3717, pp. 216–231. Springer, Heidelberg (2005). https://doi.org/10.1007/11559306_12
10. Hirokawa, N., Middeldorp, A.: Dependency pairs revisited. In: van Oostrom, V. (ed.) RTA 2004. LNCS, vol. 3091, pp. 249–268. Springer, Heidelberg (2004). https://doi.org/10.1007/978-3-540-25979-4_18
11. Lucas, S., Gutiérrez, R.: Use of logical models for proving infeasibility in term rewriting. Inf. Process. Lett. **136**, 90–95 (2018). https://doi.org/10.1016/j.ipl.2018.04.002
12. Middeldorp, A.: Approximating dependency graphs using tree automata techniques. In: Goré, R., Leitsch, A., Nipkow, T. (eds.) IJCAR 2001. LNCS, vol. 2083, pp. 593–610. Springer, Heidelberg (2001). https://doi.org/10.1007/3-540-45744-5_49
13. Sternagel, T., Middeldorp, A.: Conditional confluence (system description). In: Dowek, G. (ed.) RTA 2014. LNCS, vol. 8560, pp. 456–465. Springer, Cham (2014). https://doi.org/10.1007/978-3-319-08918-8_31

14. TeReSe: Term Rewriting Systems. Cambridge Tracts in Theoretical Computer Science, vol. 55. Cambridge University Press, Cambridge (2003)
15. Toyama, Y.: Counterexamples to termination for the direct sum of term rewriting systems. Inf. Process. Lett. **25**(3), 141–143 (1987). https://doi.org/10.1016/0020-0190(87)90122-0
16. Yamada, A., Kusakari, K., Sakabe, T.: Nagoya termination tool. In: Dowek, G. (ed.) RTA 2014. LNCS, vol. 8560, pp. 466–475. Springer, Cham (2014). https://doi.org/10.1007/978-3-319-08918-8_32

Permissions

The contributors of this book come from diverse backgrounds, making this book a truly international effort. This book will bring forth new frontiers with its revolutionizing research information and detailed analysis of the nascent developments around the world.

We would like to thank all the contributing authors for lending their expertise to make the book truly unique. They have played a crucial role in the development of this book. Without their invaluable contributions this book wouldn't have been possible. They have made vital efforts to compile up to date information on the varied aspects of this subject to make this book a valuable addition to the collection of many professionals and students.

This book was conceptualized with the vision of imparting up-to-date information and advanced data in this field. To ensure the same, a matchless editorial board was set up. Every individual on the board went through rigorous rounds of assessment to prove their worth. After which they invested a large part of their time researching and compiling the most relevant data for our readers.

The editorial board has been involved in producing this book since its inception. They have spent rigorous hours researching and exploring the diverse topics which have resulted in the successful publishing of this book. They have passed on their knowledge of decades through this book. To expedite this challenging task, the publisher supported the team at every step. A small team of assistant editors was also appointed to further simplify the editing procedure and attain best results for the readers.

Apart from the editorial board, the designing team has also invested a significant amount of their time in understanding the subject and creating the most relevant covers. They scrutinized every image to scout for the most suitable representation of the subject and create an appropriate cover for the book.

The publishing team has been an ardent support to the editorial, designing and production team. Their endless efforts to recruit the best for this project, has resulted in the accomplishment of this book. They are a veteran in the field of academics and their pool of knowledge is as vast as their experience in printing. Their expertise and guidance has proved useful at every step. Their uncompromising quality standards have made this book an exceptional effort. Their encouragement from time to time has been an inspiration for everyone.

The publisher and the editorial board hope that this book will prove to be a valuable piece of knowledge for researchers, students, practitioners and scholars across the globe.

List of Contributors

Ludovic Le Frioux
LRDE, EPITA, 94270 Le Kremlin-Bicêtre, France
Sorbonne Université, CNRS, LIP6, UMR 7606, 75005 Paris, France

Souheib Baarir
Sorbonne Université, CNRS, LIP6, UMR 7606, 75005 Paris, France
Université Paris Nanterre, 92000 Nanterre, France

Julien Sopena
Sorbonne Université, CNRS, LIP6, UMR 7606, 75005 Paris, France
Inria, DELYS Team, 75005 Paris, France

Fabrice Kordon
Sorbonne Université, CNRS, LIP6, UMR 7606, 75005 Paris, France

Martin Blicha
Università della Svizzera italiana (USI), Lugano, Switzerland
Faculty of Mathematics and Physics, Charles University, Prague, Czech Republic

Antti E. J. Hyvärinen and Natasha Sharygina
Università della Svizzera italiana (USI), Lugano, Switzerland

Marijn J. H. Heule
Department of Computer Science, The University of Texas, Austin, USA

Benjamin Kiesl
Institute of Logic and Computation, TU Wien, Vienna, Austria
CISPA Helmholtz Center for Information Security, Saarbrücken, Germany

Armin Biere
Institute for Formal Models and Verification, Johannes Kepler University, Linz, Austria

Muhammad Osama and Anton Wijs
Eindhoven University of Technology, 5600 MB Eindhoven, The Netherlands

Rahul Gupta, Shubham Sharma and Subhajit Roy
Indian Institute of Technology Kanpur, Kanpur, India

Kuldeep S. Meel
National University of Singapore, Singapore, Singapore

Thomas Bläsius and Tobias Friedrich
Hasso Plattner Institute, Potsdam, Germany

Andrew M. Sutton
University of Minnesota Duluth, Duluth, MN, USA

Martin Brain and Youcheng Sun
Oxford University, Oxford, UK

Florian Schanda
Zenuity GmbH, Unterschleißheim, Germany

Nils Becker, Peter Müller and Alexander J. Summers
Department of Computer Science, ETH Zurich, Zurich, Switzerland

Petar Vukmirović
Vrije Universiteit Amsterdam, Amsterdam, The Netherlands

Jasmin Christian Blanchette
Vrije Universiteit Amsterdam, Amsterdam, The Netherlands
Max-Planck-Institut für Informatik, Saarland Informatics Campus, Saarbrücken, Germany

Simon Cruanes
Aesthetic Integration, Austin, TX, USA

Jan Kofroň
Faculty of Mathematics and Physics, Charles
University, Prague, Czech Republic

**Pengfei Gao, Hongyi Xie, Jun Zhang and
Fu Song**
School of Information Science and Technology,
ShanghaiTech University, Shanghai, China

Taolue Chen
Department of Computer Science and
Information Systems, Birkbeck, University of
London, London, UK

**Wenxi Wang, Milos Gligoric and Sarfraz
Khurshid**
The University of Texas at Austin, Austin, USA

Stephan Schulz
DHBW Stuttgart, Stuttgart, Germany

Kaiyuan Wang
Google Inc., Sunnyvale, USA

Benjamin Bisping and Uwe Nestmann
Technische Universität Berlin, Berlin,
Germany

Christian Sternagel
University of Innsbruck, Innsbruck, Austria

Akihisa Yamada
National Institute of Informatics, Tokyo,
Japan

Index

Printed in the USA
CPSIA information can be obtained
at www.ICGtesting.com
JSHW060040240424
61720JS00005B/106

9 781647 284473